The State and the Grassroots

The State and the Grassroots

Immigrant Transnational Organizations in Four Continents

Edited by
Alejandro Portes and Patricia Fernández-Kelly

berghahn
NEW YORK · OXFORD
www.berghahnbooks.com

Published by

Berghahn Books

www.berghahnbooks.com

Library of Congress Cataloging-in-Publication Data

The state and the grassroots : immigrant transnational organizations in four
continents / edited by Alejandro Portes and Patricia Fernández-Kelly.
     pages cm
Includes bibliographical references.
ISBN 978-1-78238-734-3 (hardback) — ISBN 978-1-78533-440-5 (paperback) —
ISBN 978-1-78238-735-0 (ebook)
1. Immigrants—Societies, etc.—Case studies. 2. Immigrants—Cultural
assimilation—Case studies. 3. Emigration and immigration—Social aspects—
Case studies. 4. Transnationalism—Social aspects—Case studies. I. Portes,
Alejandro, 1944– editor of compilation. II. Fernández-Kelly, María Patricia, 1948–
editor of compilation.
JV6225.S73 2015
369′.3—dc23

2014039966

British Library Cataloguing in Publication Data

A catalogue record for this book is available from the British Library

ISBN 978-1-78238-734-3 hardback
ISBN 978-1-78533-440-5 paperback
ISBN 978-1-78238-735-0 ebook

Contents

Section II. Immigrant Organizations in Europe

Illustrations

Figures

Tables

Preface

The idea for the project that provides the basis for this book came out of two conversations, held respectively in Baltimore in 2007 and in Utrecht, the Netherlands, in 2010. During the first, the senior editor and the senior author of the chapter on Chinese organizations discussed the applicability of the methodology developed by the Comparative Immigrant Organizations Project (CIOP) to the case of Asian communities in the United States. The CIOP was a project launched by the Center for Migration and Development at Princeton University to study the effects of Latin American immigrant organizations on (a) the sociopolitical incorporation of these immigrants to American society and (b) the collective contributions of these organizations to local and national development in their countries of origin.

With support from the MacArthur Foundation of Chicago, the CIOP successfully completed a series of studies of Mexican, Colombian, and Dominican organizations in the United States. Results were published in a series of articles in specialized journals in the late 2000s (Portes, Escobar, and Walton Radford 2007; Portes, Escobar, and Arana 2008; 2009; Escobar 2010). The methodology of these studies consisted of compiling exhaustive inventories of formal and informal organizations created by immigrants from each selected country; interviewing leaders of the thirty to fifty largest in person; supplementing these interviews with others conducted via telephone or Internet with leaders of smaller organizations; and finally traveling to the sending country to conduct interviews with government officials with responsibility for their expatriates and with counterparts of organizations contacted in the United States. The objective of these country-of-origin trips and interviews was, first, to ascertain whether the transnational philanthropic and development projects claimed by the leaders of US-based organizations had actually taken place and, second, to establish the relative importance attributed by governments of home countries to their expatriate communities and the policies planned or implemented toward them.

The Baltimore conversation between Portes and Zhou was about the feasibility of replicating this methodology among Asian communities in the United States, in particular the Chinese. With support from the Princeton Center for Migration and Development (CMD), Zhou agreed to undertake this project in the major Chinese areas of concentration in the United States, followed by extensive periods of fieldwork in China. Results of this large study have been published in several venues (Portes and Zhou 2012; Zhou and Lee 2013) and constitute the basis for the chapter on Chinese transnational organizations in this volume.

The success of the Chinese study encouraged us to extend it to other large Asian communities in the United States, in particular the Indian and Vietnamese, as well as to another major Latin American group concentrated in South Florida, Nicaraguans. With additional support from the MacArthur Foundation, replications of the original study were commissioned to Rina Agarwala of Johns Hopkins University, Jennifer Huynh of Princeton, and Margarita Rodríguez of the University of Miami. Results of the respective studies are also presented in chapters dedicated to each of these nationalities in this book.

The second conversation, in Utrecht, took place after Portes presented results of the CIOP study in the Van Zuylen Lecture at Utrecht University. His hosts, professors Annelies Zoomers and Gery Nijenhuis in particular, noted how very little was known about immigrant organizations in the Netherlands despite the significant size of several national communities in the country. The idea came up of replicating the CIOP research design by a team based at Utrecht University. Shortly thereafter, a proposal to several Dutch financial sources to carry out the study was drafted.

The implementation of the Dutch initiative also led to a consideration of the possibility of extending the project to other European countries. For this purpose, Portes held conversations with Belgian, French, and Spanish social scientists specializing on immigration to their respective countries and invited them to join in the then-incipient network. In each case, European studies were supported by local sources, but sought to apply the tried-and-tested CIOP methodology. In the case of France, the study concentrated on the long-term experiences of Moroccans in that country; in the case of Belgium, the Netherlands, and Spain, the respective research teams assumed responsibility for contacting organizations created by several major immigrant nationalities in each country, including Moroccans, Colombians, Congolese, and others.

The newly created International Network for Research on Immigrant Organizations and Development was not an isolated initiative. Comparable studies of immigrant organizations in Europe were being conducted roughly at the same time as the CIOP project in the United States. In particular, Laura Morales and her colleagues carried out systematic surveys of immigrant organizations in Spain and other Western European countries (Morales and Ramiro 2011; Morales and Giugni 2010). The TRAMO project, directed by Ludger Pries of the University of Ruhr-Bochum, employed the same methodology in intensive studies of immigrant organizations in Germany, Poland, Spain, and the United Kingdom and developed a systematic typology of these organizations (Pries and Sezgin 2012; Pries 2008).

These valuable intra-European studies differed in three ways from those conducted by the CIOP and the new International Network for Research on Immigrant Organizations and Development. First, they focused, primarily or exclusively, on the domestic scene in various European countries and the role of immigrant organizations in fostering social and political incorporation into them. Less attention was paid to the role and political significance of these organizations in the social and economic development of sending countries. Second, these comparative studies did not include extensive fieldwork in the sending countries, with the purpose of assessing their potential developmental contributions. Third, they did not include a North American component and, hence, did not provide an empirical basis for systematic trans-Atlantic comparisons. While most useful in their own right, the Morales and colleagues and Pries studies must be viewed as alternative projects guided by a different theoretical framework and interests than those motivating the present book.

To bring the emerging International Network for Research on Immigrant Organizations and Development into reality, the CMD obtained funds from the Russell Sage Foundation to convene its members at Princeton University. The meeting took place in the spring of 2011, was attended by all scholars taking part in the network, and yielded a commitment to produce final reports on each country or immigrant group in one year's time. At this point, Patricia Fernández-Kelly joined the network as project commentator and reviewer.

The next meeting of this international network took place in May 2012 when final reports were presented and discussed. Edited versions of these reports constitute the basis of the following chapters. The last conference and the reports culminated in the CIOP project amply fulfilling its original goals: from a study limited to assessing the developmental effects of Latin American immigrant organizations in the United States, the project grew to encompass major Asian immigrant communities and then crossed the Atlantic to incorporate studies in four European countries.

Finally, three items are worth noting. First, the collection of studies presented in this book differs from other recent volumes on immigration and development by presenting original findings obtained with the same research design. In that sense, this is not the typical edited book bringing together disparate contributions. The amount of original information on immigrant transnational organizations and their developmental activities presented in the next pages—from Indian groups in the United States to Moroccans in France and Surinamese in the Netherlands—is, to our knowledge, unprecedented.

Second, in addition to descriptive data, these studies provide the basis to address authoritatively issues concerning the bearing of immigration on social and economic development in sending nations, as well as the incorporation of first and second generation immigrants into receiving societies. The introduction frames the collection, summarizing past debates on immigrant incorporation and on migration and development; the conclusion presents a synthesis, drawing on the project's empirical findings to locate various immigrant groups and their organizations in the conceptual space created by the intersection between different modes of incorporation and the passage of time.

Last, it is clear that the sample of eighteen different immigrant nationalities in five countries described in the following pages does not exhaust by any means the number of such groups or the diversity of their domestic and transnational projects. Much more needs to be done. In that sense, what has been accomplished by the CIOP and the International Network for Research on Immigrant Organizations and Development should provide a stimulus for additional studies in other countries and a suitable model for their implementation. We certainly hope that this is the case.

Alejandro Portes and Patricia Fernández-Kelly
Princeton, Summer 2014

References

Escobar, Cristina. 2010. "Exploring Transnational Civil Society: A Comparative Study of Colombian, Dominican and Mexican Immigrant Organizations in the United States." *Journal of Civil Society* 6, no. 3 (December): 205–35.

Morales, Laura, and Marco Giugni, eds. 2010. *Social Capital, Political Participation and Migration in Europe: Making Multicultural Democracy Work?* Basingstoke, UK: Palgrave Macmillan.

Morales, Laura, and Luis Ramiro. 2011. "Gaining Political Capital through Social Capital: Policy-Making Inclusion and Network Embeddedness of Migrants' Associations in Spain." *Mobilization* 16, no. 2: 147–64.

Portes, Alejandro, Cristina Escobar, and Renelinda Arana. 2008. "Bridging the Gap: Transnational and Ethnic Organizations in the Political Incorporation of Immigrants in the United States." *Ethnic and Racial Studies* 31 (September): 1056–90.

Portes, Alejandro, Cristina Escobar, and Alexandria Walton Radford. 2007. "Immigrant Transnational Organizations and Development: A Comparative Study." *International Migration Review* 41 (Spring): 242–81.

Portes, Alejandro, and Min Zhou. 2012. "Transnationalism and Development: Mexican and Chinese Immigrant Organizations in the United States." *Population and Development Review* 38, no. 2: 191–220.

Pries, Ludger. 2008. *Rethinking Transnationalism: The Meso-link of Organizations.* Abingdon, UK: Routledge.

Pries, Ludger, and Zayned Sezgin. 2012. *Cross Border Migrant Organization in Comparative Perspective.* Basingstoke, UK: Palgrave Macmillan.

Zhou, Min, and Rennie Lee. 2013. "Transnationalism and Community Building: Chinese Immigrant Organizations in the United States." *The ANNALS of the American Academy of Political and Social Science* 647: 22–49.

Introduction

Immigration, Transnationalism, and Development

The State of the Question

Alejandro Portes

The study of migration and development has focused traditionally on the forces driving persons from their home regions, the demographic and social consequences of their departure, and the subsequent effects of their remittances on local and national economies. The unit of analysis has normally been the individual migrant - identified by classical economics as the central decision maker in the process or the family, privileged by sociology and the "new economics" of migration - as the actual determinant of migration decisions. When aggregated, the decisions of individual actors and family units are said to have major effects on the social and economic prospects of sending regions and nations (Thomas 1973; Borjas 1990; Stark 1991; Massey et al. 1998). Similarly, the extensive debate over the incorporation of immigrants into the receiving societies has featured a range of arguments - from those that disparage the possibilities of successful integration among all or certain groups of foreigners - to alternatives that see such integration as almost inevitable (Huntington 2004b; Brimelow 1995; Zolberg 2006; Alba and Nee 1997, 2003; Morales and Giugni 2010).

Left out of the picture have been the organizational efforts of the migrants themselves and their possible bearing on sending areas, as well as on the incorporation in host societies. The individualistic focus has persisted both in critical accounts of the role of migration that regarded the

Notes for this chapter begin on page 21.

departure of migrants as another symptom of underdevelopment, and in optimistic ones that focused on the role of migrant remittances as an almost miraculous solution to local poverty and national underdevelopment (Diaz-Briquets and Weintraub 1991; Stark 1984; De Haas 2012). The possibility that purposefully - created organizations by expatriates could play a significant role was almost entirely neglected in the development literature. Similarly, conflicting accounts of sociopolitical incorporation into host societies focused overwhelmingly on the characteristics of individual migrants, neglecting their organizational life (Waldinger and Fitzgerald 2004). Only recently have empirical studies in several European countries focused on the role of migrant associations in social and political incorporation (Morales and Ramiro 2011; Pries and Sezgin 2012).

Alert sending country governments have begged to differ, engaging with migrant organizations in a multiplicity of development projects and even creating such organizations where none existed previously. Initially, these contacts were prompted by the discovery of the volume and aggregate significance of individual remittances and the interest of sending country officials in preserving these flows. Gradually, however, it dawned on them that the scope and importance - political and economic - of organized expatriate initiatives could go much farther than individual money transfers (Iskander, this volume; Zhou and Lee, this volume). For countries like Mexico, Colombia, Morocco, and China, to name but a few, their populations abroad became increasingly salient and important interlocutors, both as sources of monetary and technological transfers and as political actors capable of affecting the course of events in home communities and even entire regions (Escobar, this volume; Iskander, this volume; Goldring 2002; Saxenian 2002).

A parallel literature exploring determinants of citizenship acquisition and political participation among immigrant groups identified ethnic association as key mediators of these activities. Individual migrants seldom take part in politics on their own, and those with modest levels of education seldom begin alone the complex process of citizenship acquisition. Instead, ethnic associations of different kinds encourage and guide this process (Bloemraad 2006; Ramakrishnan and Espenshade 2001; Portes and Rumbaut 2006: chap. 5).

The history of the growth of immigrant organizations and their interactions with home communities, local authorities, and national governments is complex and varies greatly across particular communities and countries. So are the repercussions that these interactions can have on the prospects for sociopolitical incorporation and the development of sending nations. An early empirical study of transnational organizations created by Latin American immigrant communities in the United States concluded that differences among them were so great, despite a common language and culture, that results did not provide any basis for generalization to other nationalities or their home countries (Portes, Escobar, and Walton Radford, 2007).

This realization provided the impetus, however, to extend the successful methodology employed in that original study (described in the Preface) to large Asian nationalities in the United States and, subsequently, to immigrant groups in several European countries. Applying the same methodology, the resulting network extended it to a total of eighteen immigrant nationalities in five different nations. Although the original focus was on the impact of immigrant organizations on sending countries, the actual conduct of these studies also brought to the fore their central role in the integration process in the host societies.

The successive steps of this collaborative project are described in the Preface, which also cites parallel comparative studies in Europe. As a prelude to chapters presenting the empirical results of this project, I review next the theoretical controversies in the field of immigration and development, the role of the concept of "transnationalism" in opening a path for the resolution of such controversies, and its parallel relationship to the process of incorporation into social and political life in receiving countries. While it is true that a sample of eighteen immigrant nationalities in five countries may not be enough to generalize to the universe of all such organizations, it provides a basis for advancing tentative conclusions of cross-national applicability. A common research design, employed on both sides of the Atlantic, lends authority to these findings.

Theoretical Controversies

Migration and Development

The relationship between migration and development has been viewed from diametrically opposing lenses. Scholars from sending countries in the Global South have often taken a critical stance toward such flows, viewing them both as a symptom of underdevelopment and a cause of its perpetuation. Migration is accused of depopulating entire regions, turning sending families from producers into rentiers, and allowing governments to escape their responsibilities by relying on migrant remittances. The structural importance of migration is not related, according to this view, to its capacity to change things for the better, but to its role in perpetuating systems of inequality by providing a safety valve for their consequences. Entrenched elites have taken full advantage of this option. This view has long been voiced by analysts of migration and development in the advanced world (Reichert 1981; De Haas 2012), but it is best captured by a series of "declarations" signed by scholars from major migrant sending countries, including Mexico, Morocco, and the Philippines:

> The development model adopted in the immense majority of labour exporting American countries has not generated opportunities for growth nor economic or social development. On the contrary, it has meant the emergence of regressive dynamics: unemployment and job precarization; greater social inequalities; loss of qualified workers; productive disarticulation and stagnation; inflation and greater economic dependency. As a consequence, we experience a convergence between depopulation and the abandonment of productive activities in areas of high emigration. (Declaration of Cuernavaca 2006[1])

The parallel literature concerning professional-level labor flows was dubbed "brain drain." This view emphasizes how the superior economic and technological resources of rich countries penetrate weaker peripheral ones, altering their internal social order. The result is a process of "structural unbalancing" leading to several negative outcomes, including labor outflows. In the case of professional migration, the process includes several concatenated steps. Professional standards and training practices are disseminated from the core nations to the rest of the world and are readily copied by emerging countries aiming at "catching up" with the West. Young professionals trained according to these standards look for occupational opportunities that allow them to put their advanced skills to use and to develop them further. Unfortunately, such opportunities are scarce in the local economy, with the result that many experience relative deprivation. In the interim, high-tech firms and universities in the advanced world experiencing scarcities of domestic talent seek to supplement it by recruiting abroad. Naturally, the first place to look at is among the well-trained labor pools created by imported professional standards in less developed nations (Portes 1976; Portes and Celaya 2013; Zucker and Darby 2007).

The fit between the goals of young professionals experiencing relative deprivation in less developed countries and the demand for their skills abroad sets the stage for the "brain drain." In this fashion, poorer countries end up subsidizing the high-tech labor needs of richer ones (De Haas 2012). Structural imbalancing thus ensures that the effort of emerging nations to imitate advanced ones is compromised, at every step, by the superior fit between human talent trained according to modern standards and skilled labor demand in the countries from which these standards emanate in the first place. Figure 0.1 graphically summarizes the process.

Mid-income peripheral countries seeking to create professional talent import advanced educational training practices from abroad	Scientific innovations and advanced professional training are diffused abroad via government programs and private initiatives

↓ ↓

Students are socialized in professional practices and expectations congruent with those of the advanced world	Sustained growth through scientific / technological innovation and consumer demand for advanced services lead to labor shortages in skilled fields

↓ ↓

Local opportunities for advanced professional practice and career development are limited, leading to relative deprivation	Governments, corporations, and other institutions look abroad to supplement scarce domestic talent

↓ ↓

Professionals unable to access scarce opportunities at home look abroad for ways of redressing this imbalance	Search zeroes in on countries that have imported and implemented advanced forms of professional training

Professional labor migration begins

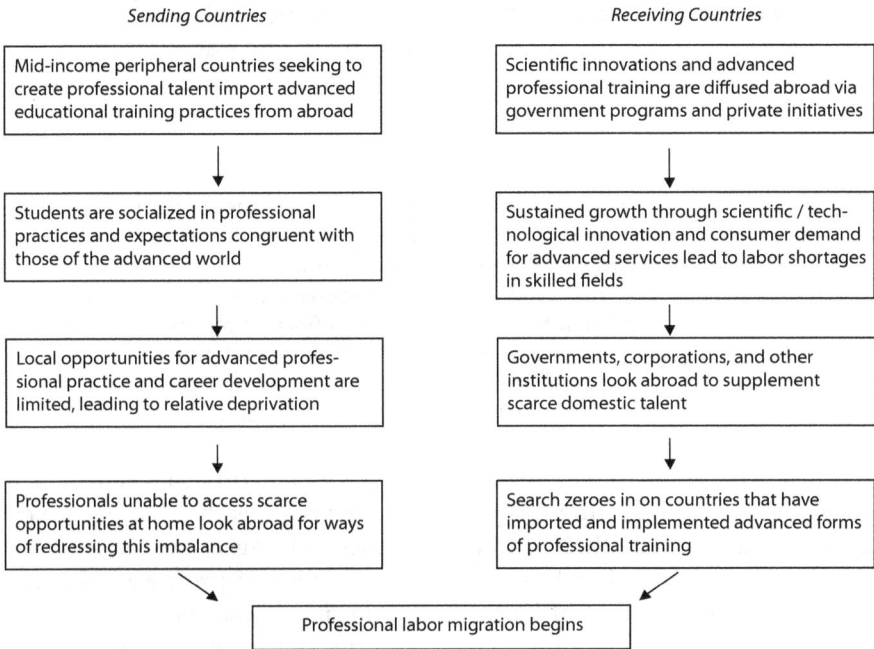

Figure 0.1. Determinants of the Brain Drain.
Source: Portes and Celaya (2013).

The opposite view to these negative conclusions is primarily associated with the "new economics" of migration. This school takes a positive stance toward the consequences of labor migration, emphasizing the multiplier effects of remittances and their capacity to overcome the negative consequences of imperfect or nonexistent market mechanisms at home (Stark 1984, 1991). The migrant worker functions in a sense as his family's social security and credit cards all rolled into one. For this school, the migrant's remittances always have positive effects in sending economies because they stimulate demand that is met by domestic production. Massey and colleagues (1987, 1998) have argued that every "migradollar" sent by Mexicans in the United States generated a $2.90 contribution to Mexico's gross national product (GNP) in the 1990s. Supporters of this view also stress the role of social networks in maintaining continuity of cross-border labor flows and the back-and-forth movement of people and resources between places of origin and destination (Stark 1991). The positive contributions of individual and collective remittances have been documented in a number of empirical studies (Landolt 2001; Marqués and Santos 2001; Agarwala, this volume; Rodríguez, this volume).

"New economics" scholars have criticized the pessimistic views associated with the "Declaration of Cuernavaca" perspective as too narrow and too focused on immediate consequences. As Massey and colleagues (1998: 262) put it:

> One important reason for the pessimism that characterizes most community studies is the lack of a good theoretical yardstick to measure the effects of migration on economic growth. Village studies universally confuse consumption with the non-productive use of remittances, ignoring the extensive and potentially large economic linkages that remittances create in local economies. They also tend to confound remittances use with the effect on remittances on family expenditures; and many studies employ a rather limited definition of "productive investments," restricting them to investments in equipment while ignoring productive spending on livestock, schooling, housing, and land.

At the level of professional migration, the positive approach is reflected in recent results highlighting the potential contributions that highly skilled migrants can make to their sending countries in terms of business investments and technological transfers. A community of professional expatriates has the potential of having a significant impact on the scientific and technological development of their home country. In this fashion, the original "brain drain" from sending countries can be transformed into a significant "brain gain" (Saxenian 1999; Portes and Celaya 2013; Zhou and Lee, this volume).

Reasons for professional expatriates to engage in these activities are straightforward: in addition to national loyalties and the weight of nostalgia, migrant professionals often have a sense of obligation to the institutions that educated them. When, on the basis of that education, they achieve wealth, security, and status abroad, it is only natural that they seek to repay the debt. Some do so through philanthropic activities; others through transferring information and technology; and still others through sponsoring the training of younger colleagues. Professionals who have become successful entrepreneurs abroad may go further and endow their alma maters or even found institutions of higher learning and research at home (Saxenian 2002; Vertovec 2004).

The recent research literature supports these conclusions. As the cases of China, India, and Israel show, the growth of sizable expatriate populations of scientists and engineers has not necessarily meant the hollowing out of these countries' scientific and research institutions, but energized them through a dense traffic of personal contacts and ideas. Saxenian (2006), who studied these cases in detail, attributes the growth of dynamic information technology poles in cities like Bangalore in India, Shanghai in China, and Tel Aviv in Israel to the entrepreneurial initiatives of their professionals abroad (see also Agarwala, this volume; Zhou and Lee, this volume).

How can these opposite conclusions and results be reconciled? An important difference between both positions is that while the negative school tends to emphasize the effects of permanent outflows for sending countries, the more optimistic perspective focuses on the diverse forms in which migrant communities relate back to their place of origin. Family remittances, like technological transfers and business investments, are all ways of creating a return flow of resources to the benefit of individuals and countries left behind. Put differently, while permanent out-migration may depopulate sending areas and weaken their production structures, various forms of cyclical outflows, marked by monetary and information transfers followed by the eventual return of migrants themselves, can have positive developmental effects. As studies of new technological centers created by migrant transfers show, these return activities induce development by infusing new economic and social dynamism in previously stagnant areas. At the level of less skilled labor migration, the contributions and eventual return of migrants may also mitigate the negative consequences highlighted by critics of migration.

The Advent of Transnationalism

The concept of transnationalism was coined to give theoretical form to the empirical observation that international migrants seldom leave behind their communities of origin, but engage instead in "multi-stranded" activities and linkages with them (Levitt and Glick Schiller 2004; Guarnizo, Portes, and Haller 2003; Basch, Glick Schiller, and Szanton Blanc 1994). Contrary to the postulates of earlier theories of immigration that envisioned a one-way flow out of misery and want, empirical studies portrayed a very different reality. Most immigrants maintain regular contacts with family and friends left behind, and a sizable minority engages in a routine traffic of back-and-forth interaction in the pursuit of economic, political, and cultural ends (Itzigsohn 2009; Landolt 2001; Basch, Glick Schiller, and Szanton Blanc 1994).

The significance of the transnational perspective is that it highlights the *circularity* of migration flows and the various forms that it can assume. Hence, it provides a conceptual framework where the positive evaluations of the migration-development linkage by authors of the "new economics" school and by analysts of advanced technology transfers can fit. While, in line with the negative view of migration for development, some authors have noted several deleterious consequences of transnational activities (Glick Schiller and Fouron 1999; De Haas 2012), the empirical consensus leans in the opposite direction. These activities have the potential to spur local, regional, and even national development insofar as they are oriented to promote the well-being of families and communities left behind (Landolt 2001; Itzigsohn et al. 1999; Zhou and Lee, this volume).

The empirical literature on the topic uncovered two additional important facts. First, developmentally relevant activities tend to be conducted by organizations, rather than individuals. Aside from family remittances and occasional gifts, most individual migrants are in no position to implement projects of real significance for their communities, much less countries of origin. Instead, they band together in a multiplicity of organizations, ranging from modest hometown associations to regional and national federations of these associations to professional and business groups (Iskander, this volume; Portes and Zhou 2012). Referred to as "globalization from below" (Guarnizo and Smith 1998), transnational organizations engage in a variety of economic, civic, and philanthropic activities in their home localities and regions, seeking to improve life conditions there. Professional and business associations can go further, transferring technological know-how and making capital investments of national relevance (Saxenian 2006; Agarwala, this volume).

Second, empirical studies have repeatedly found that it is the more educated and economically and legally secure immigrants who are most likely to lead and participate in transnational organizations (Guarnizo, Portes, and Haller 2003; Portes, Escobar, and Arana 2008; Pries, Halm, and Sezgin 2012). Thus, the circularity of migrant flows and transfers promoted by transnational organizations are not generally associated with short-term or temporal migration, but with better-established communities. In line with Skeldon's (2012) argument, it is long-term rather than short-term circulatory movements that provide the more reliable pathways to migrant developmental contributions. By the same token, such contributions can be implemented *even if migrants do not return permanently*. This is particularly the case among professionals and entrepreneurs living abroad (Saxenian 2006; Portes and Yiu 2013; Zhou and Lee, this volume).

To summarize the discussion so far, the negative position on the effects of migration in sending countries and regions is largely based on the assumption of its *permanence*. More recent studies have highlighted the positive developmental impact of circular flows, primarily long-term ones, that include not only the return of migrants themselves but also the economic and knowledge transfers that they can make. The concept of "transnationalism" gives theoretical form to this dynamic process. Although the focus of this literature has been on the transnational activities of individuals, it is evident that important philanthropic and developmental contributions generally require collective efforts. The organizations that implement these efforts are led and staffed by more educated and established members of immigrant communities, a pattern common to the United States and Western Europe. The chapters that follow present a wealth of original information describing the origins, character, and impact of immigrant organizations as they affect the development prospects of sending nations.

Assimilation and Transnationalism

A final theoretical controversy pertains to the effect that immigrant organizations in general and those operating transnationally in particular have on the social and political incorporation of immigrants into the receiving society. In the United States, advocates of prompt assimilation have expressed fears that such activities would slow down or even derail the process. Such fears have been eloquently articulated for the case of Latin American immigrants by prominent academics such as the late Harvard political scientist Samuel Huntington:

> In this new era, the single most immediate and most serious challenge to America's traditional identity comes from the immense and continuing immigration from Latin America, especially from Mexico, and the fertility rates of these immigrants. … The extent and nature of this immigration differ fundamentally from those of previous immigrations, and the assimilation successes of the past are unlikely to be duplicated with the contemporary flood of immigrants from Latin America. (Huntington 2004a: 31)

Findings from past research concerning participation in transnational organizations have a direct bearing on this point. As just seen, it is better established, educated, and legally secure immigrants that are more likely to participate in these activities (Guarnizo, Portes, and Haller 2003; Pries, Halm, and Sezgin 2012). But these are also the best candidates for citizenship acquisition and political integration, raising the likelihood that assimilation and transnationalism may not be at odds. Results from the first phase of the Comparative Immigrant Organizations Project (CIOP) reinforce this finding by showing that membership in transnational organizations is heavily skewed toward older and better educated immigrants, those with higher occupational status, and those with larger periods of residence in the country. Table 0.1 presents results of that study. Of particular interest is that significant majorities of members of these organizations have lived in the United States for ten years or more, had become US citizens, and spoke English fluently.

Table 0.1. Characteristics of Members of Transnational Organizations

Characteristic	Colombian	Dominican	Mexican	Total
Age				
30 years or less, %	12.1	11.1	24.8	15.2
40 years or more, %	53.2	53.8	33.6	48.3
Education				
Less than high school, %	7.4	29.7	28.7	20.9
College degree or more, %	52.3	50.5	27.0	45.7
Occupation				
Manual laborer, %	18.0	26.4	40.1	26.6
Professional/business owner, %	49.8	61.5	36.0	50.3
Knowledge of English				
Very little, %	11.9	18.7	5.0	12.4
Well or very well, %	64.2	49.7	60.9	58.5
Legal Status				
Does not have entry visa, %	6.3	3.5	27.9	10.7
US citizen, %	56.3	48.5	38.4	49.1
Length of US Residence				
Less than 5 years, %	10.1	5.8	10.4	8.7
10 years or more, %	68.9	66.8	69.5	69.3
N	31	30	29	90

Source: CIOP first survey, reported in Portes, Escobar, and Walton Radford (2007).

A subsequent survey, also conducted as part of this project, targeted directly the role of immigrant organizations in acculturation and political incorporation by asking organizational leaders directly about their views on political incorporation into the host society and for reports of their organizations' political activities in the United States. Table 0.2 presents the distribution of responses of leaders of Colombian, Dominican, and Mexican organizations to those questions.

Table 0.2. Leaders' Evaluations of Organizational Effects on Immigrant Political Incorporation

	Colombian %	Dominican %	Mexican %	Total % (N)
1. "This organization contributes to the successful integration of its members to American society."				
Agrees	77.08	85.19	89.92	86.64
Neutral/unsure	10.42	9.26	6.98	7.69
Disagrees	12.50	5.55	3.10	5.68
				100.00

2. "[Colombian/Dominican/Mexican] immigrants should acquire US citizenship as soon as possible."

Agrees	85.00	90.91	96.15	91.18
Neutral/unsure	10.00	9.09	3.85	7.35
Disagrees	5.00	0.00	0.00	1.47
				100.00

3. "Participation in this organization helps its members maintain ties with their home country."

Agrees	95.83	85.19	83.72	84.21
Neutral/unsure	4.17	5.56	9.30	7.69
Disagrees	0.00	9.25	6.98	8.10
				100.00

4. "Participation in this organization retards the acquisition of US citizenship."

Agrees	2.08	5.56	2.33	2.83
Neutral/unsure	18.75	7.40	19.38	16.60
Disagrees	79.17	87.04	78.29	80.57
				100.00

5. "This organization contributes to more active participation of [Colombian/Dominican/Mexican] immigrants in US politics."

Agrees	37.50	77.78	66.67	61.94
Neutral/unsure	18.75	5.56	17.83	15.38
Disagrees	43.75	16.66	15.50	22.67
				100.00

6. "It is possible to acquire US citizenship and continue being a good [Colombian/Dominican/Mexican]."

Agrees	93.75	96.30	89.92	90.28
Neutral/unsure	6.25	3.70	7.75	8.50
Disagrees	0.00	0.00	2.33	1.22
				100.00

7. "[Colombian/Dominican/Mexican] immigrants place their obligations toward their home country above their integration to American society."

Agrees	22.92	29.63	13.18	18.62
Neutral/unsure	14.58	27.78	16.28	20.24
Disagrees	62.50	42.59	70.54	61.14
				100.00

8. "It is possible for immigrants to integrate to American society and continue taking part in their home country politics."

Agrees	81.25	85.19	88.37	83.00
Neutral/unsure	6.25	14.81	5.43	10.93
Disagrees	12.50	0.00	6.20	6.07
				100.00
N	50	56	133	239

Source: CIOP second survey, reported in Portes, Escobar, and Arana (2008).

Leaders' evaluations were nearly unanimous in asserting that: (1) their organizations contributed to the successful incorporation of immigrants into American society; (2) they simultaneously helped immigrants maintain ties to their home countries; and (3) there was no contradiction between both aims. Most leaders could not understand that the goals of successful integration and home country loyalty would be opposites. Close to 90 percent believed that their organizations helped their members assimilate better to their new social surroundings and almost 100 percent endorsed the view that immigrants should acquire US citizenship "as soon as possible." Ninety percent asserted that it was entirely possible for an immigrant to become a good American citizen and, at the same time, continue to be loyal to his/her country of birth.

The activities the immigrant organizations engaged in consistently supported this stance. The same survey included three indicators to gauge objective participation in American politics: (1) the existence of organizational ties with American political authorities at the local, state, and federal levels; (2) whether the organizations had taken part in civic/political campaigns or related activities in the United States; and (3) the character and number of such activities. Tables 0.3 and 0.4 present these results.

The data show that three-fourths of immigrant organizations maintain regular ties with American political authorities and that two-thirds have engaged in some form of political activism in the United States. These include one or more of the following: (a) support candidates to elective office; (b) organize political debates; (c) provide civic and political infor-

Table 0.3. Political Ties and Civic/Political Activities of Immigrant Organizations in the United States

	Nationality			
	Colombian %	Dominican %	Mexican %	Total %
Organization maintains regular ties with US political authorities at the local, state, or federal levels.				
No	40.00	22.73	15.38	25.00
Yes	60.00	77.27	84.62	75.00
				100.00
Organization participates in civic/political activities in the United States.				
No	48.00	28.57	33.08	35.63
Yes	52.00	71.43	66.92	64.37
				100.00
N	50	56	133	239

Source: CIOP second survey, reported in Portes, Escobar, and Arana (2008).

Table 0.4. Count of Civic/Political Activities in the United States by Nationality of Organization

Nationality	None %	One %	Two %	Three %	Four or More %	Total %
Colombian	47.92	22.92	14.58	12.50	2.08	100.00
Dominican	29.63	9.26	22.2	14.82	24.07	100.00
Mexican	32.56	20.93	24.81	15.50	6.20	100.00
N^1	86	42	54	35	24	241

Source: CIOP second survey, reported in Portes, Escobar, and Arana (2008).

mation to members of the organization; (d) disseminate civic/political information to the immigrant community as a whole; (e) participate in various civic and political campaigns. Table 0.4 shows that most immigrant organizations engage in at least one of these activities.

Results of the successive phases of the CIOP study indicate that the conflict between transnational activism and incorporation into the American political system is largely illusory. In practice, both processes tend to occur simultaneously and reinforce each other, as when experiences and skills acquired in one realm are transferred into the other. Later studies, such as the TRAMO project in Europe, supported these findings by pointing toward a paced process of social and cultural incorporation in which newly arrived immigrants struggle to find an economic niche and secure a stable legal status in the host country. It is only in later years, when these initial hurdles have been overcome, that immigrants are able to secure citizenship, engage in local politics in their adopted communities, *and* join transnational organizations seeking to help the places that they came from (Pries and Sezgin 2012; Escobar, this volume).

The extension of the CIOP methodology to Asian immigrant groups in the United States provided additional comparative evidence. For the most part, these results are supportive of the conclusions reached on the basis of the original Latin American samples. Chinese, Indian, and Vietnamese organizations also partake of a dual role, simultaneously promoting development programs in the home countries and the integration of immigrants into American society. Hence, just as in the case of the migration and development debate, the weight of existing evidence leans in a positive direction. Just as the individual and collective contributions of migrants can have a significant bearing on the development of sending regions and nations, the passage of time leads steadily toward social and political incorporation into the host societies. Immigrant organizations play a central role in both processes.

Enter the State

As a form of "globalization from below," the grassroots activities of immigrants and their organizations could not but attract the attention of powerful institutions, in particular governments. First to be the object of this attention were remittances. As sending country governments realized the volume and economic importance of these transfers, they started taking steps to ensure their continuity and, if possible, their growth. International organizations, such as the World Bank, chimed in with schemes to channel migrant remittances from consumption to productive investments. Guarnizo (2003) notes the irony that the modest contributions of individual migrants to help their families survive at home become contabilized in the banking houses of world financial centers and even used as collateral for loans to sending country governments.

Immigrant organizations, including small hometown committees, then came to the attention of state officials. They did so for two reasons: First, as their civic and philanthropic projects became better known, sending country governments came to see them as potential partners, but also as forces in need of monitoring and control (Goldring 2002; Landolt 2001). Second, government officials wishing to engage with expatriate communities for various purposes realized that they could not do so individually, but only through the mediation of organizations. Consequently, leaders of such groups acquired growing importance as interlocutors of both sending and receiving states.

The entry of state agencies into the transnational field changed it profoundly. What had previously been a spontaneous collection of grassroots mobilizations and projects now became a negotiated space where expatriate organizations and government officials alternatively competed and cooperated, each seeking to extract maximum advantage from their engagement. Sending country governments came first as they became aware of the aggregate importance of migrant investments. Host country governments then jumped into the fray as they sought some sort of dialogue with their immigrant populations and as the notion of "co-development" took hold for controlling and possibly preventing future migrant flows (Morales and Giugni 2010; Cebolla Boado and López-Sala, this volume). As we shall see, the changing dynamics of this relationship evolved from a dialogue between self-initiated migrant organizations and state agencies to the gradual sponsorship and even creation of associations by their state interlocutors.

Sending States

The activities of sending states in relation to their expatriate communities and their intervention in the transnational field have taken the most varied forms. They have been guided by goals ranging from propitiating immigrant remittances and investments to politically controlling migrants and ensuring their political loyalty. A number of sending country governments originally regarded the migrants as little more than defectors from their own national projects; only later did they come to see them as important contributors to these same projects. Mexico and China, each in its own way, traversed that path (Iskander 2010; Delano 2011; Portes and Zhou 2012). The Moroccan monarchy endeavored for many years to politically control their large expatriate population and prevent their assimilation to European host nations. Only in recent years has it adopted a more conciliatory stance, establishing a dialogue with large migrant organizations and collaborating with them in selected developmental activities (Lacroix 2005; Lacroix and Dumont, this volume).

Some governments have engaged in extensive partnerships with migrant organizations in the implementation of development projects. In Mexico, this has taken the form of the well-known Three-for-One Program in which each migrant dollar invested in a development project in Mexico is matched by a dollar each from the federal and state governments, as well as the municipality benefiting from that project. Agencies have been created at the federal and state levels to promote Three-for-One initiatives, supervise their implementation, and prevent malfeasance (Iskander, this volume; Goldring 2002). In China, state agencies at all governmental levels (*qiao-ban*), as well as branches of the Communist Party (*qiao-lian*), have also engaged in these types of collaborative ventures. Organized migrant contributions have financed everything - from modest village water projects to university buildings (Zhou and Lee, this volume; Leung 2008). Given the nature of the Communist regime, it is not surprising that migrant initiatives have been tightly controlled and monitored. There are no civil society counterparts to Chinese transnational organizations abroad; only state and party agencies exist, although both have been very active in recent years.

In some sending states, governments have in recent decades initiated greater dialogue with individual members of the diaspora, but have been less active in engaging with diaspora *organizations*. For example, after decades of ignoring its diaspora, the Indian Government began to initiate new policies and institutions to strengthen its bonds with its diaspora in the mid-1980s (Agarwala this volume). To date, these efforts while new and significant in their effects, have focused on attracting individual overseas Indians' travel in and out of India, investments in property, and foreign exchange earnings. These efforts include specialized bank accounts, new visa status cards, as well as important symbolic gestures such as politicians' personal visits to meet with the US Diaspora and an inaugural conference in India to commemorate and network with overseas Indians.

In 2005, the Indian Government created a cabinet-level Ministry of Overseas Indian Affairs (MOIA) in 2005, to manage and coordinate the states' interactions with the diaspora. MOIA may be more involved in organization-level engagement in the future.

Other sending states are in no position to engage in this type of full-fledged collaborative venture (with individuals or organizations), either because of the feebleness of their resources or suspicion of the intentions of their expatriates. First-generation Vietnamese, for example, represent a case of "blocked transnationalism" because of their continuing opposition to the Hanoi regime and the refusal of the latter to allow independent migrant initiatives. The Vietnamese state has been much more proactive toward the US-born second generation, seeking to engage it in developmental projects and technology transfers in a manner similar to those implemented in China (Huynh and Yiu, this volume). Weaker states that also seek to promote the remittances and transnational development projects of their expatriates may seek to compensate for their lack of resources with symbolic gestures, such as the granting of dual citizenship and the right to vote in home country elections. This is the case of several Latin American nations, including Colombia, the Dominican Republic, and El Salvador (Escobar, this volume; Landolt 2001; Perez-Sainz and Andrade-Eekhoff 2003; Lungo and Kandel 1999).

Dual citizenship and the right to vote in home country elections are contested issues. On the positive side, they help preserve home loyalties and often encourage migrants to acquire the citizenship of the host country, since they incur no penalties in doing so (Bloemraad 2006; Escobar 2007). On the other hand, they violate the principle, enshrined in international law, that every person must have one nationality *and one only*. Critics in the host societies argue that dual citizenship places native citizens at a disadvantage and retards the process of political assimilation of immigrants, although, as seen previously, evidence of such slowdown is lacking. Sending country critics complain, in turn, that the expatriate vote can result in elections at the local and even at the national level being decided by people who do not live in the country and do not have to face the consequences of their choices (Freeman 1995; Hollifield 2004). For this reason, while the number of countries granting or accepting dual citizenship has grown, others have resisted doing so. Large Global South countries, such as India and China, have been, so far, the principal exceptions to the dual citizenship bandwagon.[2]

The different orientations and behavior of sending country governments toward their expatriates can be arranged in a typology, such as that presented in Figure 0.2. Countries included in each cell are representative of current trends, with the cautions that exceptions may exist at the sub-

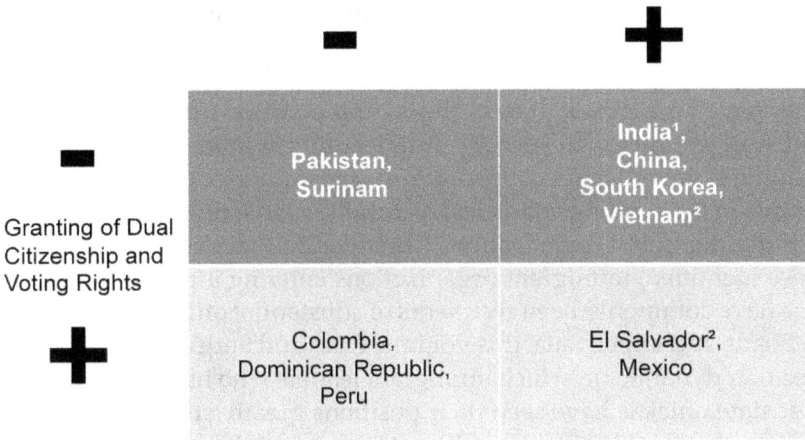

	—	+
— Granting of Dual Citizenship and Voting Rights	Pakistan, Surinam	India[1], China, South Korea, Vietnam[2]
+	Colombia, Dominican Republic, Peru	El Salvador[2], Mexico

[1] National government only; state government policies vary.
[2] Recent implementation of proactive policies toward expatriates or their offspring.

Figure 0.2. Sending Country Policies toward Immigrant Transnational Organizations: A Typology

national level (i.e., at the level of states, provinces, and home localities) and that there have been sudden reversals in the policies of governments toward their emigrants in the past that may recur in the future. Differences in the policies of sending states should not obscure the fact that their involvement in the transnational field highlights the developmental potential of immigrant communities and their organizational initiatives, as described previously.

Receiving States

Until recently, the research literature on immigrant transnationalism and transnational organizations focused overwhelmingly on the United States. As a consequence, discussion and analysis of the role of host states was generally absent, since the US government takes a laissez-faire attitude toward these activities and has seldom intervened, either to prevent or to support them. The situation is quite different in Western Europe, where governments have sought to actively engage with their foreign populations and to enact various policies aimed at accelerating their integration and at preventing future flows (Nijenhuis and Zoomers, this volume; Hollifield 2004; Morales and Ramiro 2011; De Haas 2012).

A good part of this effort has been guided by the concept of "co-development," meaning a joint effort by sending and receiving states to implement various development projects. In theory, such projects should improve the well-being of the population of sending countries and hence reduce future pressures toward out-migration. Although results of these policies have been mixed at best, the central point is that they have stimulated host countries to identify interlocutors within their immigrant communities in order to collaborate in the implementation of various programs in the sending countries. Naturally, such interlocutors have not been individuals, but organizations (Iskander 2010; Lacroix 2005).

Once identified, immigrant organizations entering into this kind of dialogue have commonly been recipients of substantial official support (Cebolla Boado and López-Sala, this volume; Pries and Sezgin 2012). This sets up peculiar dynamics in which immigrant leaders who have gained access to host state officials have seen their positions greatly strengthened: they have been able to rent offices and hire staff, present themselves as important intermediaries to their own coethnic communities, and even gain the ear of sending country authorities.

The deliberate sponsorship and even creation of transnational organizations by Western European states has received so far mixed reviews. On the one hand, this policy does strengthen certain organizational activities among immigrant communities and provides resources for the implementation of civic and philanthropic projects at home (Godin et al., this volume; Cebolla Boado and López-Sala, this volume). On the other hand, it sets up a sharp divide between organizational initiatives that succeed or fail in gaining the attention and support of government officials. In the worst-case scenario, these policies can evolve into a clientelistic situation where chosen organizations become progressively insulated and more interested in preserving their financial prerogatives than in implementing real development projects at home.

The end result may be the creation of a new bureaucratic layer of immigrant "officials" that have gained access to and interact with both sending and receiving state authorities, but whose representativeness and developmental effectiveness become increasingly questionable. Ironically, European governmental efforts to promote development in immigrants' home countries may fail, while grassroots efforts by immigrant organizations in the United States without any US state support may prove more effective. Whether co-development projects succeed or not depends on the monitoring capacities of government officials, the values and motivations of immigrant leaders themselves, and the characteristics of specific expatriate communities.

The inclusion of European cases in the expanded CIOP study thus raises a new dimension absent from the American scene. The activities of European states do not negate earlier conclusions concerning the developmental potential of transnational organizations, but they introduce a novel element that may strengthen that potential in some cases and derail it in others. The chapters in the second part of this book describe immigrant transnational organizations in various European countries and examine in greater detail these dynamics.

Conclusion: An Evolving and Contested Relationship

The debate between opponents of out-migration as a cause of depopulation and external dependency and supporters that emphasize its positive multiplier effects can be considered dated by now. While both processes take place, the debate is resolved by separating permanent from circular migration flows and, especially, by noting the long-term potential and actual contributions of transnational organizations and entrepreneurs. As shown in Figure 0.3, this distinction applies to low-skilled labor migration as well as to professional outflows.

The older debate on migration and development has been superseded, not only because of the proliferation of immigrant remittances and organized philanthropic activities, but also because the entry of governments into this field has endowed it with new energies, possibilities, and dangers. The transformation of immigrant grassroots initiatives into a series of activities channeled and sponsored by nation-states raises a series of interesting questions for the future. Among expatriate communities for whom the proactive stance of sending states is paramount—China and Mexico at the forefront—the question of how to balance the significant in-

	Permanent	**Circular**
Low-skilled	·· Depopulation of sending areas ·· Gradual decline in remittances as family members depart ·· Weakening of local productive structures	·· Investment of migrant savings in sending areas ·· Preservation of intact families. ·· Migrant remittances and savings as tools to overcome market imperfections
High-skilled	·· Loss of national talent ·· Waste of scarce local resources in training personnel for jobs abroad ·· Perpetuation of technological/scientific inequality with the advanced world	·· Regular transfers of knowledge ·· Migrant investments as triggers to creation of high-tech growth poles in home countries ·· Reduction of technological/scientific inequalities

* Effects in each cell are summaries of those described or hypothesized in the research literature. See also Portes (2009).

Figure 0.3. Types of Migration and Their Developmental Effects

crease in the developmental potential of immigrant transfers and philanthropy with their increasing regulation by state agencies becomes central.

Programs like the Three-for-One Program in Mexico or those sponsored by the *qiao-ban* and *qiao-lian* in China certainly multiply the developmental impact of transnational projects, but also restrict the scope of action of immigrant organizations. In particular, the capacity of these organizations, by virtue of their being based abroad, to promote democracy-enhancing movements at home can be compromised by their co-optation by state agencies. At worst, the result may be to reinforce the power of entrenched elites at home and to prevent democratic change, precisely the fears voiced by traditional opponents of out-migration (Delgado-Wise and Cypher 2007; De Haas 2012).

Similarly, for immigrant organizations sponsored or created by host country governments, the question is how the increase in economic resources brought about by this sponsorship balances out against the subordination of immigrant priorities to those of state agencies. In particular, the transformation of grassroots organizations into a new layer of quasi-official bureaucracy between sending and receiving countries looms as a threat to this form of sponsored transnationalism. In either case, what we are witnessing at present is a contest between popular actors who seek, through multiple initiatives, to by-pass the constraints imposed on them by dominant political and economic forces and the reaction of at least some of these forces in order to bring such initiatives under official guidance and control. The result of these encounters remains to be seen.

Thus, the resolution of older theoretical debates concerning the relationship of migration to socioeconomic development and of transnationalism to political incorporation in host countries has brought in its wake a new set of problematic issues in need of close attention. The specific experiences of immigrant nationalities and their home and host countries related in the following pages should greatly sharpen our understanding of the issues at play and extend our knowledge of these complex dynamics.

Alejandro Portes is Howard Harrison and Gabrielle Snyder Beck Professor of Sociology (Emeritus) at Princeton University and research professor at the University of Miami. His most recent publications are *Institutions Count: Their Role and Significance in Latin American Development* (with Lori D. Smith; University of California Press, 2012) and *Immigrant America: A Portrait*, 4th edition (with Rubén Rumbaut; University of California Press, 2014). His current research interests are on the comparative study of the immigrant second generation and the role of immigrant transnational organizations in socio-economic development.

Notes

1. Cited in Delgado-Wise and Marques Covarrubias (2007: no pp.)
2. India does grant its expatriates an Overseas Citizenship of India (OCI) identification. While this facilitates travel back and forth from the country, OCI holders have no political rights, being prevented from voting in Indian elections or holding public office (Naujoks 2013: 58). It should also be noted that a bill has been introduced to allow for dual citizenship in India, and although it has not yet been enacted, current discussions indicate that it will soon be passed into law.

References

Alba, Richard, and Victor Nee. 1997. "Rethinking Assimilation Theory for a New Era of Immigration." *International Migration Review* 31 (Winter): 826–74.

———. 2003. *Remaking the American Mainstream: Assimilation and Contemporary Immigration.* Cambridge, MA: Harvard University Press.

Basch, Linda G., Nina Glick Schiller, and Cristina Szanton Blanc. 1994. *Nations Unbound: Transnational Projects, Post-colonial Predicaments, and De-territorialized Nation-States.* Langhorne, PA: Gordon and Breach.

Bloemraad, Irene. 2006. *Becoming a Citizen.* Berkeley: University of California Press.

Borjas, George. 1990. *Friends or Strangers, the Impact of Immigrants on the U.S. Economy.* New York: Basic Books.

Brimelow, Peter. 1995. *Alien Nation, Common Sense about America's Immigration Disaster.* New York: Random House.

De Haas, Hein. 2012. "The Migration and Development Pendulum: A Critical View on Research and Policy." *International Migration* 50, no. 3: 8–25.

Delano, Alexandra. 2011. *Mexico and Its Diaspora in the United States: Policies of Emigration since 1848.* New York: Cambridge University Press.

Delgado-Wise, Raúl, and Humberto Márquez Covarrubias. 2007. *The Reshaping of Mexican Labor Exports under NAFTA: Paradoxes and Challenges.* Zacatecas, Mexico: University of Zacatecas, International Network of Migration and Development.

Delgado-Wise, Raúl, and James M. Cypher. 2007. "The Strategic Role of Mexican Labor under NAFTA: Critical Perspectives on Current Economic Integration." *The Annals of the American Academy of Political and Social Science* 610, no. 1: 119–42.

Diaz-Briquets, Sergio, and Sidney Weintraub. 1991. *Migration, Remittances, and Small Business Development: Mexico and Caribbean Basin Countries.* Boulder, CO: Westview Press.

Escobar, Cristina. 2007. "Migración y derechos ciudadanos: El caso mexicano." In *El país transnacional: Migración mexicana y cambio social a través de la frontera,* ed. Marina. Ariza and Alejandro. Portes, 231–74. Mexico City: INM and Porrua Editores.

Freeman, Gary P. 1995. "Modes of Immigration Politics in Liberal Democratic States." *International Migration Review* 29 (Winter): 881–902.

Glick-Schiller and George Fouron. 1999. "Terrains of Global Blood and Nation: Haitian Transnational Social Fields." *Ethnic and Racial Studies* 22 (March): 340–66.

Goldring, Luin. 2002. "The Mexican State and Transmigrant Organizations: Negotiating the Boundaries of Membership and Participation." *Latin American Research Review* 37: 55–99.

Guarnizo, Luis E. 2003. "The Economics of Transnational Living." *International Migration Review* 37, no. 3: 666–99.

Guarnizo, Luis E., Alejandro Portes, and William J. Haller. 2003. "Assimilation and Transnationalism: Determinants of Transnational Political Action among Contemporary Immigrants." *American Journal of Sociology* 108, no. 6: 1211–48.

Guarnizo, Luis E., and Michael P. Smith. 1998. "The Locations of Transnationalism." In *Transnationalism from Below,* ed. Michael Peter Smith and Luis Eduardo Guarnizo, 3–34. New Brunswick, NJ: Transaction Books.

Hollifield, James. 2004. "The Emerging Migration State." *International Migration Review* 38, no. 3: 885–912.

Huntington, Samuel. 2004a. "The Hispanic Challenge." *Foreign Policy* 141, no. 2: 30–45.

———. 2004b. *Who Are We?* New York: Simon and Schuster.

Iskander, Natasha Nefertiti. 2010. *Creative State: Forty Years of Migration and Development Policy in Morocco and Mexico.* Ithaca, NY: Cornell University Press.

Itzigsohn, Jose. 2009. *Encountering American Faultlines: Race, Class, and the Dominican Experience.* New York: Russell Sage Foundation.

Itzigsohn, Jose, Carlos Dore, Esther Fernandez, and Obed Vazquez. 1999. "Mapping Dominican Transnationalism: Narrow and Broad Transnational Practices." *Ethnic and Racial Studies* 22 (March): 316–39.

Lacroix, Thomas. 2005. *Les réseaux marocains du développement.* Paris: Presses de la Fondation Nationale de Sciences Politiques.

Landolt, Patricia. 2001. "Salvadoran Economic Transnationalism: Embedded Strategies for Household Maintenance, Immigrant Incorporation, and Entrepreneurial Expansion." *Global Networks* 1, no. 3: 217–42.

Leung, Maggi W. H. 2008. "Homeward Bound Investors: The Role of Overseas Chinese in China's Economic Development." In *Global Migration and Development,* ed. Ton Van Naerssen, Ernst. Spaan, and Annelies. Zoomers, 288–308. New York: Routledge.

Levitt, Peggy, and Nina Glick Schiller. 2004. "Conceptualizing Simultaneity: A Transnational Social Field Perspective on Society." *International Migration Review* 38, no. 3: 1002–39.

Lungo, Mario, and Susan Kandel. 1999. *Transformando El Salvador: Migración, Sociedad y Cultura.* San Salvador: Fundación Nacional para el Desarrollo.

Marqués, Maria M., and Rui Santos. 2001. "Ariadne's Thread: Cape Verdean Women in Transnational Webs." *Global Networks* 1: 283–306.

Massey, Douglas, Rafael Alarcon, Jorge Durand, and Humberto Gonzalez. 1990. *Return to Aztlan: The Social Process of International Migration from Western Mexico.* Berkeley: University of California Press.

Massey, Douglas S., Joaquin Arango, Graeme Hugo, Ali Kouaouci, and Adela Pellegrino. 1999. *Worlds in Motion: Understanding International Migration at the End of the Millennium.* Oxford: Oxford University Press.

Morales, Laura, and Marco Giugni. 2010. *Social Capital, Political Participation, and Migration in Europe: Making Multicultural Democracy Work?* Basingstoke, UK: Palgrave.

Morales, Laura, and Luis Ramiro. 2011. "Gaining Political Capital through Social Capital: Policy-Making Inclusion and Network Embeddedness of Migrants' Associations in Spain." *Mobilization* 16, no. 2: 147–64.

Naujoks, Daniel. 2013. *Migration, Citizenship and Development.* New Delhi: Oxford University Press.

Perez-Sainz, Juan Pablo, and Katharine Andrade-Eekhoff. 2003. *Communities in Globalization.* Lanham, MD: Rowman and Littlefield.

Portes, Alejandro. 1976. "Determinants of the Brain Drain." *International Migration Review* 10: 489–508.

Portes, Alejandro, and Adrienne Celaya. 2013. "Modernization for Emigration: Determinants and Consequences of the Brain Drain." *Daedalus* 142, no. 3: 170–84.

Portes, Alejandro, Cristina Escobar, and Renelinda Arana. 2008. "Bridging the Gap: Transnational and Ethnic Organizations in the Political Incorporation of Immigrants in the United States." *Ethnic and Racial Studies* 31 (September): 1056–90.

Portes, Alejandro, Cristina Escobar, and Alexandria Walton Radford. 2007. "Immigrant Transnational Organizations and Development: A Comparative Study." *International Migration Review* 41, no. 1: 242–81.

Portes, Alejandro, and Rubén G. Rumbaut. 2006. *Immigrant America: A Portrait.* 3rd ed. Berkeley: University of California Press.

Portes, Alejandro, and Jessica Yiu. 2013. "Entrepreneurship, Transnationalism, and Development." *Migration Studies* 1, no. 1: 75–95.

Portes, Alejandro, and Min Zhou. 2012. "Transnationalism and Development: Mexican and Chinese Immigrant Organizations in the United States." *Population and Development Review* 38, no. 2: 191–220.

Pries, Ludger, Dirk Halm, and Zeynep Sezgin. 2012. "CBMOs in Their Organizational and Institutional Environment: A Comparison of Countries and Cases." In *Cross Border Migrant Organizations in Comparative Perspective,* ed. L. Pries and Z. Sezgin. Basingstoke, UK: Palgrave Macmillan: 579–601.

Pries, Ludger, and Zeynep Sezgin. 2012. *Cross Border Migrant Organizations in Comparative Perspective.* Basingstoke, UK: Palgrave Macmillan.

Ramakrishnan, S. Karthick, and Thomas J. Espenshade. 2001. "Immigrant Incorporation and Political Participation in the United States." *International Migration Review* 35, no. 3: 870–909.

Reichert, Joshua S. 1981. "The Migrant Syndrome: Seasonal U.S. Wage Labor and Rural Development in Central Mexico." *Human Organization* 40 (Spring): 59–66.

Saxenian, Anna Lee. 1999. *Silicon Valley's New Immigrant Entrepreneurs.* San Francisco: Public Policy Institute of California.

———. 2002. *Local and Global Networks of Immigrant Professionals in Silicon Valley.* San Francisco: Public Policy Institute of California.

———. 2006. *The New Argonauts: Regional Advantage in a Global Economy.* Cambridge, MA: Harvard University Press.

Skeldon, Ronald. 2012. "Going Round in Circles: Migration, Poverty Alleviation and Marginality." *International Migration* 50, no. 3: 43–60.

Stark, Oded. 1984. "Migration Decision Making." In *Migration Decision Making: Multidisciplinary Approaches to Microlevel Studies in Developed and Developing Countries.* Ed. Gordon F. De Jong, and Robert W. Gardner. Pergamon: New York. 215–59.

———. 1991. *The Migration of Labour.* Oxford: Blackwell.

Thomas, Brinley. 1973. *Migration and Economic Growth: A Study of Great Britain and the Atlantic Economy.* Cambridge: Cambridge University Press.

Vertovec, Steven. 2004. "Migrant Transnationalism and Modes of Transformation." *International Migration Review* 38, no. 3: 970–1001.

Waldinger, Roger, and David Fitzgerald. 2004. "Transnationalism in Question." *American Journal of Sociology* 109, no. 5: 1177–95.

Zolberg, Aristide. 2006. *A Nation by Design.* New York: Russell Sage Foundation.

Zucker, Lynne G., and Michael R. Darby. 2007. "Star Scientists, Innovation, and Regional and National Immigration." No. W13547. National Bureau of Economic Research.

Immigrant Organizations in the United States

Chapter 1

Traversing Ancestral and New Homelands

Chinese Immigrant Transnational Organizations in the United States

Min Zhou and Rennie Lee

O ver the past three decades, immigrant transnational organizations in the United States have proliferated with accelerated international migration and the rise of new transportation and communication technologies that facilitate long-distance and cross-border ties. Their impact and influence have grown in tandem with immigrants' drive to make it in America—their new homeland—as well as with the need for remittances and investments in sending countries—their ancestral homelands. Numerous studies of immigrant groups found that remittances and migrant investments represent one of the major sources of foreign exchange of sending countries and were used as "collateral" for loans from international financial institutions (Basch, Glick Schiller, and Szanton Blanc 1994; Glick Schiller, Basch, and Szanton Blanc 1995; Portes, Guarnizo, and Landolt 1999). Past studies also found that transnational flows were not merely driven by individual behavior but by collective forces via organizations as well (Goldring 2002; Landolt 2000; Moya 2005; Piper 2009; Popkin 1999; Portes, Escobar, and Walton Radford 2007; Portes and Zhou 2012; Schrover and Vermeulen 2005; Waldinger, Popkin, and Aquiles Magana 2008).

But the density and strength of the economic, sociocultural, and political ties of immigrant groups vary across borders, as do the effects of im-

Notes for this chapter begin on page 54.

migrant transnational organizations on homeland development (Portes, Guarnizo, and Landolt 1999; Portes, Escobar, and Walton Radford 2007). Nevertheless, the sum total of the transnational movements and the subsequent contributions of immigrants to families and communities left behind acquire "structural" importance for both sending and receiving countries, as these flows affect both the pace and forms of incorporation of immigrants into the United States and the economic prospects of those they left behind.

There are obvious gaps in the existing literature, however. Prior research on immigrant transnationalism in the United States has given greater attention to immigrant groups from Latin America than those from Asia and has focused more on the individual than the organization as the unit of analysis. This chapter aims to fill the gap by focusing on the Chinese case. The focus on Chinese immigrant transnational organizations in the United States is important for three reasons. First, Americans of Chinese ancestry are one of the oldest immigrant groups in the United States, with a long-standing ethnic community and a high proportion of recent immigrants. Second, the People's Republic of China (PRC) is the largest immigrant sending country in the world. It is not an underdeveloped country in the conventional sense, but one with a rapidly expanding global economy, high rates of migration, and a large reserve of potential migrants.

Third, the United States and the PRC are the largest trade partners and economic competitors in the world. Thus, studies of immigrant transnationalism would simply be incomplete without considering Chinese Americans and their ancestral homeland. This chapter explores three main questions: (1) What are the types, scope, and nature of Chinese immigrant organizations in the United States? (2) How does the Chinese state influence its expatriates' organizational transnationalism? (3) How does organizational transnationalism matter for the individual, the ethnic community, and the ancestral homeland?

Immigrant Transnationalism

Transnationalism is an old phenomenon inherent to immigrant experiences. It is generally defined as "the processes by which immigrants forge and sustain multi-stranded social relations that link together their societies of origin and settlement" (Basch, Glick Schiller, and Szanton Blanc 1994: 6). As noted by Fernández-Kelly (this volume), what is new about contemporary transnationalism is the scale, diversity, density, and regularity of such movements and their socioeconomic consequences as a result of jet flights, long-distance telephone and fax services, the Internet, and, most importantly, the globalization of capital and labor. It is the intensity of exchanges, not just the occurrences of all trips, occasional contacts, or activities, that becomes a justifiable topic of investigation.

Transnational activity is associated with immigrant status (e.g., racial discrimination), human capital (e.g., education, skills, and citizenship status), and other key demographic characteristics (e.g., age, sex, and marital status) (Guarnizo, Portes, and Haller 2003; Portes, Guarnizo, and Haller 2002). However, highly educated immigrants have been found quitting their well-paying salaried jobs to engage in economic activities across borders because they can better utilize their skills, bilingual literacy, and social networks to reap material gains. Low-skilled immigrants also engage in transnational activities, but their practices are limited to sending remittances regularly to support families and kin, buying land or building houses for their own transnational lives, and establishing small businesses in their homelands. These are effective ways to convert the wages earned in the United States into material gains and social status recognition in their countries of origin (Diaz-Briquets and Weintraub 1991; Itzigsohn et al. 1999; Goldring 2002; Popkin 1999; Portes and Guarnizo 1991).

The level of homeland development also leads to different types of transnational activities depending on the immigrant group. For example, in sending countries where industrialization and development are in their early stages, informal trade and informal couriers predominate. For instance, Mexicans, Salvadorans, Colombians, and Dominicans travel back and forth to engage in informal activities, bypassing existing laws and state regulatory agencies in both sending and receiving countries (Portes and Guarnizo 1991). In contrast, in more developed sending countries, formal and large-scale transnational activities predominate. These include import/export agencies, transnational banking, and investment in knowledge-intensive and labor-intensive industries, as seen among Taiwanese and Koreans (Min 1986/87; Yoon 1995; Li 1997).

Regarding the effects of transnationalism, recent studies have focused on the well-being of families left behind or on homeland development (Glick Schiller and Fouron 1999; Guarnizo, Portes, and Haller 2003; Jones-Correa 1998; Østergaard-Nielsen 2001; Rouse 1989; Smith 2005). The most salient feature of transnationalism is monetary remittances for supporting migrant families left behind (Grasmuck and Pessar 1991; Mahler 1995; Chin, Yoon, and Smith 1996; Durand, Parrado, and Massey 1996; Gold 2001; Goldring 2002; Guarnizo, Sanchez, and Roach 1999; Itzigsohn et al. 1999; Landolt 2000; Levitt 2001; Portes, Guarnizo, and Haller 2002). Other forms of transnationalism include religious remittances (Levitt 2007), political remittances (transfer of egalitarian ideology and leadership styles), activism, migrant rights (Piper 2009), and social remittances (ideas, behaviors, identities, and social capital that flow from receiving- to sending-country communities) (Levitt 1998; Levitt and Lamba-Nieves 2011).

There are two oversights in the existing literature regarding homeland development. First, the emphasis is almost exclusively on individuals and families, overlooking the role of organizations (Portes and Zhou 2012). Portes and his associates have argued that transnational activities conducted on an individual basis are exceptional, and many activities are channeled through organizations (Guarnizo, Portes, and Haller 2003; Portes, Escobar, and Walton Radford 2007). This position was the rationale for the project of which this chapter is part. Second, there is greater emphasis on the role of individual agency than that of the sending state. Iskander (2010, this volume) noted the transformative effect of migrant remittances on sending-country economies but argued that such an effect depends on the interaction between migrants and various levels of sending-country government through ongoing processes of social learning and innovation.

Methodology

This chapter is based on a study from the Comparative Immigrant Organizations Project (CIOP), which combined a quantitative approach to document the number and size of immigrant organizations with a qualitative approach to focus on the views and activities of their leaders and their home country counterparts.[1] The CIOP research design required developing directories of all existing associations for each national origin group and categorizing them by type, with particular attention to the difference between those involved in programs focused solely on the domestic needs of immigrant communities and those involved in cross-national activities (Portes and Zhou 2012).

We used a mixed methods approach because data on immigrant organizations are scant, and national sampling frames are nonexistent for any representative sampling. Thus, our data were collected both in the United States and the PRC, including the compilation of an organizational inventory, a survey of organizational leaders, in-depth interviews, field observations, and focused group discussions. In the United States, we constructed an inventory of ethnic Chinese organizations through: (a) Chinese-language business directories in major US cities; (b) organizational newsletters and websites; (c) discussions with informants in the Chinese immigrant community; and (d) official listings in the Chinese consulates and government agencies in China. The US portion focused on three major metropolitan areas with the largest concentrations of Chinese immigrants and their organizations—Los Angeles, San Francisco, and New York. In 2010, more than half of the Chinese in the United States were concentrated in the states of California (37 percent) and New York (17 percent).

Chinese immigrants cluster in traditional Chinatowns, as well as in middle-class suburbs where they establish visible "ethnoburbs," middle-class suburbs dominated by immigrants of diverse origins. We compiled an inventory of 1,371 organizations, most registered as nonprofits in San Francisco, Los Angeles, and New York. Although this inventory is national, it focused on the three main cities.[2] Furthermore, the inventory list represents only a fraction of all Chinese organizations in the US, but captures the range of these organizations in size, type, and scope.

A survey of fifty-five organizations was conducted, using a close-ended questionnaire with a few open-ended questions. Leaders of these organizations were interviewed by telephone and in person.[3] The organizations selected for the survey, as well as for fieldwork, were not chosen at random, but as "emblematic" of the principal types detected in the national inventory. Many are long-standing, well-established, and have a history of completed projects in China. The size of these organizations allows them to make significant contributions and programmatic initiatives at the local level and, potentially, the national level.

Fieldwork included site visits to organizational meetings or activities. We also focused on the interactions between organizations and their members. Site visits to organizational activities included luncheons of alumni associations in San Francisco, Los Angeles, and New York; an annual convention of professional organizations held in Southern California; fund-raising luncheons and dinners by various organizations in Los Angeles's Chinatown and Monterey Park; traditional holiday celebrations in Los Angeles's Chinatown; welcoming banquets for Chinese officials visiting Los Angeles sponsored by various Chinese organizations; and the PRC National Day (1 October) party sponsored by the Chinese consulate general in Los Angeles.

In China, we collected data from fieldwork (sixty-two in-person interviews, focus group discussions, and numerous site visits) in Beijing, the capital, and two provinces, Guangdong and Fujian, China's most prominent home regions for overseas Chinese, or *qiao-xiang*.[4] Guangdong is the largest *qiao-xiang*; about 70 percent of all pre–World War II Chinese emigrants were from Guangdong, and nearly 80 percent of all pre–World War II Chinese migrants to North America were from the same province.[5] Twenty-five interviews were conducted in Guandong, including the cities of Guangzhou, Jiangmen, Sunde, and Zhongshan.[6]

Fujian is the second-largest *qiao-xiang*.[7] People from Fujian have a long history of emigration, but those who arrived in the United States in large

numbers arrived after the late 1980s. About nine million Chinese overseas find their roots in Fujian. Major sending places in Fujian for migrants
to the United States include Fuzhou (the provincial capital), Changle,
Fuqing, and Lianjian. Twenty-five interviews were conducted in Fujian.[8]
Beijing has emerged as a new *qiao-xiang* since the 1980s, as many highly
skilled Chinese immigrants had attended universities and worked in Beijing before migration. Twelve interviews were conducted there.[9]

Immigration and Organizational Development across Time and Space

Outside of Southeast Asia, the United States has the largest ethnic Chinese population in the world, estimated at 3.8 million in 2010. Much of the
growth in the Chinese American population has been due to contemporary
immigration. In 1965, the US Congress passed the Hart-Celler Act, which
allowed for family reunification and migration of the highly skilled. This
ushered in a new era of Chinese immigration, first from Taiwan and Hong
Kong and then from mainland China and other parts of the world. In 1978,
China began to implement its open-door policy and economic reform. It
normalized diplomatic relations with the United States in 1979, leading to
rapid urbanization and massive international migration with the United
States being most preferred destination for new Chinese immigrants. As
the upper panel of Table 1.1 shows, China has a population of 1.34 billion,
the second largest in the world. Its urban population increased from 26
percent in 1990 to 47 percent in 2010.[10]

   China's economy had experienced double-digit growth since the late
1980s, becoming the second-largest economy in the world with a gross
domestic product (GDP), at purchasing power parity (PPP), of $11.29 tril-
lion.[11] Overall, China has a high labor force participation rate and low unemployment. Such development leads to two trends: continually high rates
of emigration for those seeking better opportunities abroad and return migration for those attempting to capture economic opportunities in China.

   Due to high rates of contemporary Chinese immigration, Chinese Americans have become the largest immigrant group of Asian origin and the
second-largest contemporary immigrant group in the United States. The
ethnic Chinese population in the United States has grown exponentially,
from 435,062 in 1970 to 3.8 million in 2010. As of 2009, over 60 percent
of the ethnic population was foreign-born, and among them, 31 percent
arrived after 2000. As seen in the lower panel of Table 1.1, contemporary
Chinese immigrants are positively selected, with higher average educa-

Table 1.1. Select Characteristics of China and Chinese America

Ancestral Homeland: China[a]

Total population, 2012 (in millions)	1,343
Urban population, 2010 (%)	47
GDP per capita, 2011 ($)	8,400
Gini index of inequality, 2009[b]	0.48
Educational attainment, 2009[b]	
College graduate or more, age 25+ (%)	9.0
Secondary/technical school graduate (%)	14.0
Unemployment, 2010[b] (%)	4.1
Labor force participation, 2009[b] (%)	61.8
Capital city	Beijing

New Homeland: Chinese Americans in the United States[c]

Chinese American population, 2009	3,796,796
Foreign-born, 2009 (%)	60.7
As a proportion of Asian American population, 2009 (%)	22.7
Legal immigrants admitted to the US, 2000–9[d] (N)	741,951
Total legal immigration to the US, 2000–9[d] (%)	7.2
Rank in total legal immigration, 2009[d]	2
College graduates, 2009, age 25+ (%)	50.8
Professional specialty occupations, 2010, age 16+ (%)	52.8
Median household income, 2009 ($)	$69,037
Persons living poverty, 2009 (%)	12.2
Types of immigration[e]	Mostly legal, some unauthorized
Principal cities of immigrant destination[f]	New York (32%); Los Angeles (11%); San Francisco (10%)

Notes:

[a] See https://www.cia.gov/library/publications/the-world-factbook/fields/2172.html (accessed 2 May 2012).

[b] National Bureau of Statistics of China, China Statistical Yearbook, 2011.

[c] US Census Bureau, 2009 American Community Survey 1-Year Estimates.

[d] 2009 Yearbook of Immigration Statistics, table 2 (http://www.dhs.gov/xlibrary/assets/statistics/yearbook/2009/ois_yb_2009.pdf).

[e] Portes and Rumbaut (2006).

[f] Office of Immigration Statistics, 2008, Supplemental Table 2 (http://www.dhs.gov/files/statistics/publications/LPR08.shtm).

tion levels and socioeconomic characteristics than the general population in China. They are concentrated in traditional immigrant gateway cities and nearby ethnoburbs. Since the late 1970s, transnational linkages between China and Chinatowns or the newly emerged Chinese ethnoburbs have been renewed, strengthened, and developed by immigrants and their organizations.

Pre-1980 Organizational Developments

Historically, Chinese diasporic communities were supported by the ethnic economy and three "pillars" — Chinese education, the language media, and ethnic organizations (i.e., guilds, associations, and nongovernmental civic organizations) (Liu 1998). The ethnic Chinese community in the United States has followed a similar organizational pattern, with ethnic businesses serving as the base for ethnic organizations. In the era of Chinese exclusion prior to World War II, the ethnic Chinese community displayed several distinctive features: (1) a small merchant class that established a firm foothold at the outset of Chinatown's formation; (2) interpersonal relations that were based primarily on blood, kin, or place of origin; (3) ethnic businesses that were interconnected to ethnic institutions that guided and controlled interpersonal and interorganizational relations; and (4) the ethnic enclave, which operated on the basis of ethnic solidarity and social exclusion (Zhou and Kim 2001).

Traditional organizations that were based in Chinatowns comprised of three main types: family/clan associations based on kinship; district or hometown associations based on place of origin; and merchant guilds or tongs based on common interest and/or sworn brotherhood. All operated as mutual aid societies (Kuo 1977; Wong 1988; Zhou and Kim 2001). Family/clan associations encompassed not only close kin but also the entire clan, whose members were not related by blood but had the same surname or descent from common ancestors. There were single-surname clan associations, such as the Eng Family Benevolent Association, or multiple-surname clan associations, such as the Lung Kong Tin Yee Association (Lau, Kwan, Cheung, and Chiu). Family/clan associations were patriarchal and varied in size (Kuo 1977; Wong 1988).

Hometown associations (also known as *hui guan* or *tongxiang hui*) were organized around a common place of birth or origin. These associations were usually named after a village or a district (township, county, or a place encompassing several counties) in the homeland and members were recruited based on these specific places of origin (Zhou and Kim 2001). Members also spoke the same dialect. Examples are the Yeong Wo Benevolent Association, the NingYeung Hui Guan, and the Hainan Hui Guan.[12]

Merchant guilds and tongs (brotherhoods) were organized as merchant labor associations. These organizations were not based on blood, surname, ancestral descent, or village of origin. Tongs, in particular, used to operate as "secret societies." Tong members pledged allegiance to one another as "brothers in blood." Each tong had a military force, seen as necessary for self-defense (Chin 1996; Kwong 1987; Wong 1988). With intricate ties to family and hometown associations, tongs controlled the economic life of a large portion of old Chinatown and were involved in homeland politics as well.

Most of the above-mentioned traditional organizations were established in the late nineteenth century with chapters in major Chinatowns. At the early stage of organizational development, ethnic organizations were conflict-prone, and turf wars between organizations within Chinatown were common. The Chinese Consolidated Benevolent Association (CCBA) was established in the late nineteenth century as an overarching ethnic federation, acting as the only legitimate government of Chinatown to maintain social order. Known originally as the Six Companies in San Francisco's Chinatown, this overarching "inner government" unified existing family, hometown, and merchant associations under a unifying leadership, mediated internal conflicts, controlled the social behavior of its members, and represented the interests of the community.

The CCBA in New York was established in 1883 and was comprised of sixty member organizations representing a cross-section of the Chinese community in New York.[13] Los Angeles's CCBA was established in 1889 and was composed of twenty-seven family/clan, hometown, and merchant associations and other civic organizations.[14] To a large extent, Chinese exclusion created opportunities for organizations and gave rise to an ethnic infrastructure in which the enclave economy and ethnic organizations were interconnected and where the relations among coethnics—individuals and organizations—were interdependent (Zhou 2009). Even in the contemporary era, traditional organizations have continued to exert influence in the ethnic life of the Chinese community, but their authority and functions have been weakened for several reasons.

First, there are more opportunities for social mobility in the host society, allowing those with higher socioeconomic status to move out of urban enclaves. Second, new immigrants are no longer low-skilled sojourners from the same village that depend entirely on their family or district organizations; rather, they have migrated with their families and can access a wider variety of services. Third, new immigrants, especially the highly skilled, arrive from major metropolitan areas outside of traditional sending regions in China, creating tremendous diversity. Fourth, rapid urbanization in China has transformed the notion of "hometown" beyond village or township.

Post-1980 Organizational Developments

With accelerated emigration from mainland China, Chinese America has experienced drastic transformations since 1980. While traditional China-towns continue to receive new immigrants, new Chinatowns and Chinese ethnoburbs have developed to accommodate newcomers of diverse origins and socioeconomic backgrounds. New immigrants also disperse in predominantly white middle-class suburbs upon arrival or after a short time in the United States. Organizational development beyond old Chinatowns reflects these demographic trends. Table 1.2 is a summary of the organizational inventory that we compiled in Los Angeles, San Francisco, and New York. Organizational density is paralleled by the development of the Chinese enclave economy, which is partially reflected in the *2010 Chinese Consumer Yellow Pages,* a 3.5-inch thick and 2,790-page bilingual telephone directory of firms and organizations.

As Table 1.2 shows, traditional organizations, which are historically based in Chinatown, are the most numerous, making up nearly 40 percent of all organizations in our inventory. Modern organizations in our inventory list are roughly grouped into the following broad categories: civic, cultural, educational, music/arts, sports, health, social services, religious, political, economic or business, alumni, and professional organizations. There are several unique characteristics in modern Chinese organizations: First, they emerge on the basis of ethnicity, but most are not based in Chinatowns. Second, they function primarily to help rebuild social ties and share information. Third, they deemphasize the importance of place of origin, do not have organizationally owned properties, and have no physical imprints or addresses in the ethnic community. Among modern Chinese immigrant organizations, four types are particularly noteworthy—extended hometown associations, economic and business associations, alumni associations, and professional organizations—because they engage the homeland in different ways than traditional organizations.

Extended Hometown Associations

Modern-day hometown associations have a very different vision of the hometown, extending beyond traditional sending villages because of rapid industrialization and urbanization.[15] Newly established hometown associations are often named after a town (as in Guantou Association), a county (as in Lianjiang Association), a city (as in Changle Association), a region (as in Wuyi Association), a major metropolis (as in Beijing Tong-xiang Hui), or even a province (as in Sichuan Tongxiang Hui). Many sending places are not rural but newly urbanized areas or regions marked by parallel trends of internal and international migration. These extended

Table 1.2. Select Ethnic Chinese Organizations in the United States, 2010

Type	Subtotal	Total	Percent
Traditional Organizations			
Family/clan associations		102	7.4
Hometown associations		279	20.4
Village	44		
District	127		
Provincial	65		
Federation	43		
Merchant guilds/tongs		165	12.0
Modern Organizations			
Civic organizations		130	9.5
Cultural organizations		53	3.9
Educational organizations		17	1.2
Music/arts organizations		48	3.5
Sports organizations		19	1.4
Health organizations		12	0.9
Social service organizations		38	2.8
Religious organizations		63	4.6
Political organizations		83	6.1
Economic/business organizations		74	5.4
Alumni associations		142	10.4
High school	28		
College	114		
Professional associations		146	10.6
Total		1,371	100.0

hometown associations are relatively large, with memberships ranging from one hundred to the thousands. For example, Beijing calls itself a new *qiao-xiang*, because many new immigrants hailed from there. However, among the members of Beijing Tongxiang Hui, most are not native Beijingese.

Economic/Business Organizations

Unlike merchant guilds and tongs in old Chinatowns, modern economic organizations and business associations depend heavily on transnational networks to operate and expand their businesses. These organizations express a strong desire to integrate into the American economy while promoting coethnic solidarity for economic purposes and cultural maintenance in the ethnic community. The main purposes of economic organizations are to foster connections among immigrant entrepreneurs, represent and protect their interests in the United States, and facilitate connections with China. These organizations arrange delegations to visit China, seeking economic cooperation and exploring potential business and investment opportunities. They also position themselves at the fore-front of the global economy, acting as transnational agents at the "gateway to the Pacific Rim."

Alumni Associations

Unlike traditional Chinese organizations that are built on kin, village, or place of origin ties, alumni associations are formed on the basis of colleges and universities and, to a lesser extent, high schools which Chinese im-migrants had attended prior to immigration to the United States. Before World War II, most of the Chinese immigrants were low-skilled, unedu-cated laborers from rural areas, so alumni associations were not visible. Since World War II, highly skilled Chinese immigrants have arrived in the United States in three waves. The first wave comprised of war refu-gees when the Chinese civil war broke out in the mid-1940s and the new Communist regime was founded in 1949. This wave included stranded ex-change students, visiting scholars, and members of the Chinese elite. The second wave comprised of students and visiting scholars from Taiwan in the 1960s and 1970s.

The third wave also comprised of students and visiting scholars but primarily from mainland China since the 1980s.[16] Between 1978 and 2008, China sent more than 755,000 students to more than one hundred differ-ent countries. About half came to the United States, and the return rate after graduation was less than 15 percent.[17] Like their Taiwanese counter-parts of the 1960s and 1970s, most of these exchange students and visit-ing scholars were highly selected and came to America to seek advanced training in prestigious graduate schools and research institutions. For a variety of reasons—greater career opportunities, professional freedom of expression, higher income, and more desirable lifestyle—many Chinese students or scholars decided to stay permanently in the United States upon completion of their degrees.

Professional Organizations

Chinese professional organizations generally maintain bilingual websites. Because of the skilled migration from China in the past three decades, these organizations are well represented in various fields of science, engi-neering, medicine, and finance. Organizational membership ranges from a few dozen to several thousand. Some examples include the Chinese Association for Science and Technology USA (New York–based with fifteen regional chapters), Silicon Valley Chinese Engineers Association, and Chinese Scholar Association (Southern California).

Many Chinese immigrant professional organizations have been recognized and courted by the Chinese government in hopes of importing new technology and human capital. These organizations serve multiple purposes: network building among professionals, bridging US-China economic relations, fostering greater diasporic economic exchanges, raising relief funds in the event of natural disasters in the homeland, and protecting the interests of Chinese immigrants in American society.

Modern Chinese immigrant organizations differ from their traditional counterparts in several ways. First, family, kinship, and rural hometowns no longer provide the basis for organization. Merchant associations take the form of economic or business associations that are more specialized and globalized, structurally linked to various networks in the ethnic enclave and in the homeland. Second, the level of organizational density is high, but the organizational structure is horizontal rather than hierarchical and organizational relations are not interdependent, like those in old Chinatowns. There is no equivalent overarching ethnic federation like the CCBA to act as a quasi-government. Third, new ethnic organizations are more oriented toward incorporation in the host society than toward homeland development.

Transnational Organizations

The density and diversity of immigrant organizations in Chinese America indicate a high level of institutional completeness. To what extent do these organizations operate across national borders? Telephone and face-to-face interviews with the leaders of fifty-five well-established Chinese immigrant organizations provide insight into the phenomenon of transnationalism. As Table 1.3 shows, those reported being entirely US-oriented, or having little or no engagement with China, comprise less than one-third (31 percent), while the majority reported being either entirely China-oriented (24 percent) or mixed (44 percent). Among the organizations that are entirely China-oriented, none are traditional associations.[18]

In the old days under Chinese exclusion, various ethnic organizations emerged to assist the Chinese, offering tangible and intangible support to help them fulfill their "gold dream," which entailed a return with gold and glory. The array of family/clan associations, hometown associations, and merchant guilds gave American Chinatowns a distinct structure, which can be unmistakably discerned by the look of the buildings they

Table 1.3. Select Ethnic Chinese Organizations by Orientation, 2010

Organizations	N	Entirely US-Oriented	Entirely China-Oriented	Mixed
Traditional organizations	4	0	0	4
Civic/cultural organizations	17	6	8	3
Social service organizations	4	3	1	0
Alumni organizations	3	0	2	1
Professional organizations	13	6	2	5
Other	14	2	1	11
Total	55	17	14	24
(%)	(100)	(31)	(25)	(44)

still own in Chinatowns. Figure 1.1 provides an illustration in the form of multistory buildings owned by traditional organizations in San Francisco's Chinatown.

For reasons associated with exclusion, traditional organizations prior to World War II were contained and established their roots in Chinatowns. Most of these invested in real estate properties in Chinatown, which are now worth millions of dollars. The organizations usually keep a main hall, an altar, and some space for rituals, meetings, and other activities and rent space on the ground floor and/or basement to ethnic businesses in order to generate a constant flow of income. The rental income is used for operations and various activities.

At present, this ethnic infrastructure has been transformed by broader structural changes in the United States and China. In the United States, the passage of civil rights legislation and liberal immigration reform legislation has created opportunities for social mobility in mainstream American society, allowing immigrants to shift their orientation toward permanent settlement in the United States and making their full participation in American life possible. Traditional organizations have refashioned their missions toward helping immigrants incorporate into American society, preserve cultural heritage, and contribute to the motherland's development. Indeed, the removal of legal and social barriers and freedom for immigrants to incorporate into American society helped ethnic organizations become truly transnational, traversing the two homelands with ease.

Changing Conditions for Transnationalism: The Role of the Sending State

The end of the Cultural Revolution in China ushered in market reforms and social transformation nationwide since 1978. Since the early 1980s,

Figure 1.1. Traditional Chinese Organizations in San Francisco's Chinatown.
Photo by Min Zhou.

the ruling Communist Party of China (CPC) shifted its policy toward the expatriate communities—from viewing overseas Chinese as potential spies and traitors to welcoming them as participants in China's economic reform (Thunø 2001). The emerging Chinese market has attracted investments from overseas Chinese and a significant return migration of highly skilled immigrants (Zweig, Chen and Rosen 2004). While the role of the receiving state in immigrant transnationalism is minimal to none, the role of the sending state is significant. Structural changes in the Chinese polity and the active involvement of the Chinese government greatly influences organizational transnationalism.

State Governance in Overseas Chinese Affairs

The Foreign Ministry of the Chinese state has no jurisdiction over overseas Chinese affairs. Instead, there are two parallel administrative bodies in charge: the Overseas Chinese Affairs Office (known colloquially as *qiao-ban*) at various levels of government, from the State Council to the provincial and local; and the Federation of Returned Overseas Chinese (known colloquially as *qiao-lian*), under the leadership of various levels of the CPC, as indicated in Figure 1.2.

The Overseas Chinese Affairs Office of the State Council (the national *qiao-ban*) is the overarching ministry-level agency supervising all affairs concerning overseas Chinese, their relatives living in China, and returned migrants. The organizational structure is hierarchical, with the national office at the top followed by the provincial ones and each of the lower ad-

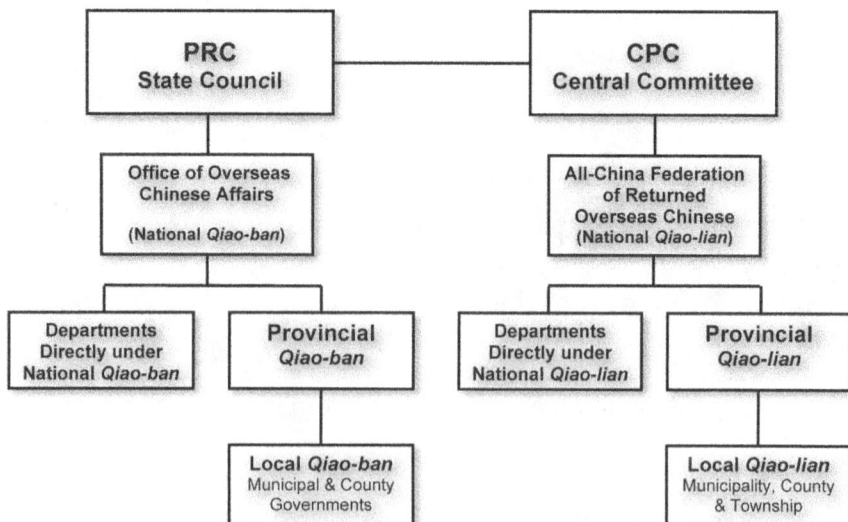

Figure 1.2. Organizational Structure of the Chinese State in Charge of Overseas Chinese Affairs.

Note: PRC: the People's Republic of China; CPC: the Communist Party of China.

ministrative levels—municipality, county, and township—of government. *Qiao-ban* is on the government budget, and its personnel are civil servants.

The All-China Federation of Returned Overseas Chinese (the national *qiao-lian*) is known as a quasi-governmental organization, but it is under the jurisdiction of the CPC and hence has authority. Like *qiao-ban, qiao-lian* has a top-down organization to the lowest administrative level—townships and villages. *Qiao-lian* functions independently from *qiao-ban,* with the following four objectives: (1) to represent and protect the interests and rights of returned overseas Chinese and their families; (2) to unite returned overseas Chinese and their families and encourage them to participate in China's modernization; (3) to improve technological communication with overseas Chinese; and (4) to encourage overseas Chinese to live harmoniously in their host societies.

In addition to *qiao-ban* and *qiao-lian,* the Zhi Gong Party is a public interest party in charge of overseas Chinese affairs. This party is composed of returned overseas Chinese, their relatives, and renowned figures and scholars who have extensive overseas ties. Because of its historical ties to the Chinese diaspora, the ruling CPC and the state both incorporate the Zhi Gong Party into overseas Chinese affairs. Overall, these affairs are highly controlled by the state and the CPC. There are significant structural barriers to the development of nongovernmental organizations (NGOs), including immigrant transnational organizations. Such development requires approval by various levels of the Bureau of Civil Affairs and must be registered with the Ministry of Civil Affairs of the PRC. Other requirements include a significant sum of registered capital, cosponsorship by a government agency, a ban on public fund-raising, and an annual inspection for registration renewal. As a result, the number of state-approved NGOs is very small, bearing no comparison to those found in other immigrant-sending nations.

Major Changes in Government Policies

In May 1989, the State Council reiterated the important role of overseas Chinese in implementing the open-door policy and made it clear that the goal of overseas Chinese affairs is to attract overseas Chinese participation in mainland China's economic development.[19] Since the turn of the twenty-first century, the official policy regarding overseas Chinese has shifted from attracting remittances and capital investment to fostering ties. The policy also emphasizes helping overseas Chinese become naturalized citizens, increase their participation in the mainstream of their host countries, and establish ties in their new homelands. For example, in 2006–7, the strategic plan of the *qiao-ban* of the City of Guangzhou included: support for new overseas Chinese associations; training young individuals to become leaders of local overseas Chinese communities; and organizing summer camps for Chinese youths and teenagers from around the world.

In the 1980s and 1990s, policies regarding Chinese students studying abroad emphasized "return." Starting in the late 1990s, however, the policy changed to recognize that returning to China is not the only way to "serve the country." Now, the state encourages graduates who decide to stay abroad to assimilate into mainstream society and actively participate in politics in their host countries. However, the PRC does not recognize or promote dual citizenship. Based on the PRC Nationality Law, as soon as a Chinese citizen becomes a naturalized citizen of another country, he or she will automatically lose his or her Chinese citizenship. Chinese immigrants who have become naturalized US citizens face bureaucratic hurdles when they attempt to conduct regular transnational activities.[20]

Reaching Out to the Diaspora

The Chinese state not only creates an open environment but is also proactively involved in the transnational field. In this respect, it shares certain characteristics with other sending states, such as Mexico (see Iskander, this volume). Local *qiao-ban* in migrant-sending communities at the county or township level set aside a substantial amount (as high as one million yuan or approximately $164,000) in their operating budgets and raise funds from other government agencies and corporate sponsors to facilitate transnational activities. The Chinese state generally does not get involved in organizational formation abroad, but in recent years, some local governments, from traditional and new *qiao-xiang*, have supported the establishment of immigrant organizations abroad and even provided start-up funds for some organizations. State-sponsored activities may be grouped into six main categories: (1) capital investment and economic cooperation; (2) training and relationship building; (3) philanthropic work and disaster relief; (4) cultural promotion; (5) scientific, technological, and scholarly exchange; and (6) *qiao-xiang* publications.

Capital Investment and Economic Cooperation

In the initial decades of economic reform, the Chinese state aggressively sought support from the Chinese diaspora, exploiting the financial, cultural, and social capital of the Chinese overseas and facilitating investments by setting up special economic zones (SEZs) in the migrant-sending regions in Guangdong (Shenzhen, Zhuhai, and Shantou) and Fujian (Xiamen).[21] Between 1979 and 1987, 90 percent of foreign investments in

SEZs came from the Chinese diaspora, especially Chinese investors and entrepreneurs from Hong Kong, Macao, and Taiwan.[22] By 2000, there were over 200,000 foreign-funded enterprises in China; two-thirds had been launched and were owned or co-owned by ethnic Chinese entrepreneurs. The Chinese state has repeatedly acknowledged the contribution of overseas Chinese for bringing about such a "miracle."

In site visits to various *qiao-xiang,* respondents from the local governments repeatedly said that substantial overseas Chinese contributions can be traced to every landmark structure and every major development project in the 1980s and early 1990s. Since 2000, information technology (IT) and biotech developments have brought about a new era of innovation around the world. Overseas Chinese investors and entrepreneurs have been at the forefront of this development, launching hi-tech industries in China, including electronics and electric machinery manufacture, biological technology and manufacture, and rare metallurgical industries.

Training and Relationship Building

Since 2000, the Chinese government has shifted its policy, moving from attracting foreign capital to nurturing social relations and assisting overseas Chinese to explore potential opportunities in China. The state, provincial, and municipal governments sponsored or cosponsored annual conventions, including symposia, fairs, and training sessions for overseas Chinese interested in investing in or doing business in China. For example, the Training Sessions for Leaders of Overseas Chinese Communities is a state-sponsored program offering advanced and custom training for young overseas Chinese entrepreneurs. In addition, the Chinese state also helps established transnational organizations reach out to existing and aspiring entrepreneurs in the Chinese diaspora.

Philanthropic Work and Disaster Relief

The Chinese government believes that it can count on the support of the Chinese diaspora when China encounters natural disasters. On 12 May 2008, a 7.9-magnitude earthquake hit Sichuan Province, killing about 70,000 people and leaving over 18,000 missing. On the next day (13 May), the national *qiao-ban* launched an emergency disaster relief project called Qiao-ai (Love from the Chinese Diaspora) to coordinate and manage monetary and material donations from concerned overseas Chinese. On the same day, about 68.5 million yuan in cash or materials poured in from the expatriate community. At a press conference in June the national *qiao-ban* announced a "Two-100-Goal"—to build one hundred *qiao-ai* schools and one hundred *qiao-ai* health clinics in the earthquake-affected areas—using donations from overseas.[23] The provincial *qiao-ban* and thirteen municipal ones in Guangdong Province jointly established a Qiao-xin Foundation in 2006 and raised 41.1 million yuan in the first five months to build housing for 2,300 rural earthquake victims.

Cultural Promotion

State-sponsored activities for cultural promotion aim to assist expatriates and their offspring in preserving Chinese cultural traditions and heritage via "inviting in" and "going out." Some of the most remarkable "inviting in" activities are those targeted toward youths and teenagers, such as Chinese-language programs in the United States and China and "root search" trips to China. The main purpose of these programs is to ensure that future generations of overseas Chinese understand and appreciate their heritage. Another state-sponsored activity for promoting culture is "going out" in the form of overseas cultural visits. For example, various levels of *qiao-ban* and *qiao-lian* have allotted budgets for annual visits to the Chinese diaspora. Furthermore, the Chinese state also regularly sponsors consulate parties and receptions for celebrating Chinese holidays, where leaders of Chinese immigrant organizations, prominent Chinese Americans, US government officials, local community leaders and business elite, and foreign diplomats are in attendance.

Scientific, Technological, and Scholarly Exchange

The Chinese state has been keenly aware that many of the thousands of students that it sent abroad for advanced training stayed permanently in the countries of study upon completion of their training. Currently, the Chinese government not only considers returned students and scholars a driving force for the country's economic and social development, but it also supports those staying abroad in the belief that they will make contributions to China in various ways, such as academic exchanges, conducting joint research, bringing in projects and investments, and providing technical information.[24] Since the mid-1990s, the Chinese state has launched a variety of programs to attract the permanent or temporary return of highly skilled migrants in the fields of science and engineering. For example, the National Ministry of Education has implemented several programs to attract scholars to return and to facilitate their careers in their countries of residence. These programs provide financial support to established young and middle-aged scholars in Western countries and invite them back to leadership positions in the academy.

Qiao-xiang Publications

Last, Chinese local governments have actively launched networking activities with overseas Chinese by organizing or sponsoring networking conferences (e.g., the world conventions of hometown associations, hosting homecoming visits, and tours of overseas Chinese organization leaders) and through in print and/or online publications to share news about hometowns and maintain information flows. In *qiao-xiang* in Guangdong and Fujian, most municipal- or county-level *qiao-ban* and *qiao-lian* publish *qiao-kan* (overseas Chinese journals). Even villages and towns publish *qiao-kan*.

Transnationalism in Motion: Engaging the Ancestral Homeland

Chinese immigrant organizations have engaged their ancestral homeland in four main types of transnational activities: (1) hometown projects; (2) philanthropic work; (3) conventions and professional conferences; and (4) cultural events.

Hometown Projects

Hometown projects are usually place-specific. In the past and present, these projects have been based in a sending village or a township that an immigrant organization represents. These projects are typically pragmatic, such as repairing or upgrading a road, a school, or an ancestral hall or building a new temple, park, library, or elderly activity center. But they can be symbolic as well, such as building a new village gate, a statue, or a roadside altar. Traditional family and hometown associations have played a central role in this type of activity. In new sending regions of Fuzhou, Fujian, many villages have witnessed new constructions ranging from extravagant buildings and public facilities to new homes built by migrants. Figures 1.3 and 1.4 illustrate a cultural center and a public park in two different villages in Fuzhou.

Overseas Chinese donations for village-level hometown projects are usually managed by committees consisting of village elders. Because of rapid urbanization, many traditional migrant-sending villages have been incorporated into large towns and cities. In this case, extended hometown associations play a larger role than the village-based associations. They usually work on larger projects, such as schools, hospitals, universities, public libraries, museums, and parks, which are developed in collaboration with local governments. Wuyi University, for example, is a regional

Figure 1.3. Cultural Center, Houyu Village, Changle, Fujian.
Photo by Min Zhou.

university located in Jiangmen, a key hometown of early Chinese immigrants to the United States. Established in 1985, it received substantial overseas Chinese donations (roughly $26 million) that funded a museum, a library, faculty and student dormitories, an athletic facility, an exhibition hall, and equipment.

Philanthropic Work

Philanthropic work includes fundraising for major disaster relief. For example, immediately after the 2008 earthquake in Sichuan Province that claimed sixty-eight thousand lives, the CCBA in New York established the Sichuan Earthquake Relief Program, raising a total of $1.32 million within a four-month period. Within a week after Typhoon Morakot hit Taiwan in August 2009, the CCBA of New York raised nearly $90,000 from its member organizations.

Regular donations also provide aid to families in poverty and scholarships for children in sending villages and in the Chinese immigrant community. For instance, the Baisha Village Association in New York practices *le-juan* (happiness donation) and *xi-juan* (donations by the newlyweds

Figure 1.4. Xiangshan Square, Fuzhou, Fujian.
Photo by Min Zhou.

and people attending the wedding in the name of the newlyweds) to raise funds for philanthropic work, scholarships, and aid to poor families.[25] Both types of donations are deposited into a village fund and bulletin boards are placed in conspicuous places to acknowledge donors' names and the amounts donated.

Conventions and Professional Conferences

Conventions and conferences are important organizational activities, which may be held regularly in the United States, China, or elsewhere. Traditional family, hometown, or merchant associations hold these conventions globally, reflecting organizational efforts to connect to other Chinese communities in the diaspora. Worldwide hometown association conventions have become more and more visible in recent years: some of these conventions are held in China with significant material support from the Chinese government. These events are published in conference proceedings or commemorative editions, in Chinese or bilingually. In contrast, modern organizations, professional organizations in particular, usually hold annual conventions in the United States with distinguished keynote speakers and relevant themes in the profession, such as "Semi-conductor—Embracing Our Life, Leading Our Future" (the theme of the 2011 convention of the Silicon Valley Chinese Engineers Association).

Cultural Events

Cultural events, including major holiday celebrations, are an integral part of ethnic community life in the United States. Chinese immigrant organizations, especially those in Chinatowns, take the lead in planning and organizing cultural events in the form of parades, street fairs, or banquets. During major traditional Chinese holidays, such as the Chinese New Year, the Lantern Festival, and the Mid-Autumn Festival, Chinatowns in major American cities hold parades, blending typical American marching processions and the traditional ritual and festive celebrations of China. Local politicians and community leaders make their presence felt in parades or on center stages at street fairs before cultural performances by Chinese singers and dancers. Many Chinese immigrant organizations participate in major international and domestic cultural events in Beijing as well as in local areas. For example, there is a section in Tiananmen Square in Beijing reserved for distinguished guests and leaders of overseas Chinese organizations to view the parade on National Day (1 October).

How Organizational Transnationalism Matters

Our case study reveals some significant ways in which organizational trans-nationalism matters for the individual, the ethnic community, and the ancestral homeland. Nonetheless, we should emphasize that transnationalism only involves a relatively small proportion of the immigrant population.

Effects on the Individual

First, ethnic organizations serve as actual or virtual sites in which members find opportunities to meet, and transnationalism helps expand these opportunities. Interpersonal relations among coethnics beyond ethnic enclaves can, in turn, strengthen network building across professions and/or class lines. One organizational leader told us: "In my hometown association, we no longer have members from villages. Our members are so diverse that we don't even speak the same dialect anymore. And we have experts in just about any major professional fields."[26]

Second, ethnic organizations function as a symbolic stage for members to validate an ethnic or cultural identity that may be marginalized in the host society and to gain recognition or compensate for lost social status (Min 2008; Li and Zhou 2012). In our field observations, we found that organizational leaders used their symbolic organizational affiliations to assert their status in the community and in the transnational field. Mr. Wang, the president of an alumni association, explained,

> The Chinese are very status-conscious. People's ranks in their work unit or organizations are important status symbols. In business or in contact with government officials, you must use proper titles, never the first name, to address yourself and people you are interacting. So you need to print business cards with your name and some sort of title in Chinese, such as president, director … This not only allows the Chinese to address you properly and comfortably but also shows that you are somebody.[27]

Third, ethnic organizations offer an alternative means for civic participation. Because of language and cultural barriers, Chinese immigrants often find themselves detached from civic organizations in their local community and in mainstream American society. Hence, they are stereotyped as hardworking individuals with little enthusiasm and interest in civic affairs. A Chinese man, the leader of a professional organization, reported: "I have lived in this [white middle-class suburban] neighborhood for fifteen years. Never once have I attended the local association meeting and voted there, and never once have I been to a neighborhood picnic or party. I don't know how to make small talk with my neighbors. … I rarely went to my kids' school."[28] Yet, the same man would drive forty-five miles one way from home to be regularly engaged in formal and informal activities of his professional organization and ethnic events.

Fourth, ethnic organizations serve as incubators for leadership training. The president of an alumni association offered this view: "One cannot just claim to be a leader, one must act like one. Even though my role in this [alumni] organization is purely voluntary, I do have to take initiative and responsibility for planning, organizing, and improvising activities for our members. So the more I got involved, the better I became at it."[29] Successful entrepreneurs or established professionals aspiring to become entrepreneurs are more actively involved. Leaders, rather than members, are using organizations as a means of building transnational business partnerships or "go-betweens" to better capitalize on economic opportunities. In many cases, leaders voluntarily form nonprofit civic organizations and claim leadership roles in order to advance these self-interests. Once they firmly establish a foothold or reputation in the community and earn the trust of Chinese government officials and entrepreneurs, they enter into partnerships with businesses on both shores or offer their services as consultants or brokers. A member of an alumni association put it succinctly:

You think they [the leaders] spend so much time and money for nothing? Oh no. An organizational leadership is a shortcut to power in China. With an organizational title and some legwork, you can get to meet high-ranking Chinese officials up close and personal. Otherwise, you cannot even make an appointment with the secretary of a local official.[30]

Effects on the Ethnic Community

We have argued elsewhere that ethnic organizing is a key mechanism for community building (Zhou and Lee 2013). The Chinese case illustrates how this works. First, immigrant organizations are intrinsically linked to an ethnic enclave or ethnoburb, the physical or symbolic location of the ethnic community. The proliferation of organizations provides building blocks to reinforce the ethnic community's foundation and reaffirm a sense of identity among immigrants. For example, San Francisco's Chinatown, located in a low-income immigrant neighborhood, continues to serve as a focal point for coethnic interorganizational and transnational engagement because of its long-standing institutional presence. When the Chinese government sends delegations, immigrant organizations in Chinatown serve as local hosts to Chinese guests by holding welcoming banquets that draw organizations and their members in or out of Chinatown.

Second, immigrant organizations are well-connected to the enclave economy. Transnationalism leads to better economic opportunities for immigrant entrepreneurs and contributes to local economic development by expanding existing businesses. It also facilitates the influx of Chinese capital, making the enclave economy both local (linking to regional economies in the United States) and global (linking to the Chinese economy and beyond) (Zhou 2009; Zhou and Cho 2010).

Effects on the Ancestral Homeland

There are multiple ways that Chinese immigrants engage with their homeland. In the past, families of overseas Chinese depended on migrant remittances for survival. Today, forms of transnational engagement continue to include sending remittances to support family members and maintaining regular long-distance communications. These activities often reflect individual rather than organizational behavior.

Remittances are a form of conspicuous consumption in migrant-sending villages. Performing family or holiday rituals, such as weddings and funerals, and building large ancestral homes have become big events that cost hundreds and thousands of dollars. Migrant families often find themselves in a race to become the "best" of something—the most extravagant wedding, the most expensive funeral, the tallest/largest house—as a way to display family honor or to regain social status.

Also remarkable are charitable donations for improvement in public works (roads, bridges, drainage, water supply, and other infrastructure), gates, ancestral halls, and schools, assistance to the elderly and the poor, and scholarship to young people. There are also new uses of funds that were rare in the past. These include the construction of office buildings, public parks, libraries, museums, cultural centers, elderly activity centers, and temples and churches. Unlike remittances, these kinds of donations are usually done via organizations. Both remittances and donations have direct and indirect effects on local economic development in local industries or small entrepreneurship.

New patterns of homeland development that are shaped by transnationalism include family or clan-based entrepreneurship or investment in lucrative businesses in other regions all over the country. Other activities of transnational Chinese immigrants include science and technology investment in government-designated zones and parks, biotech and "green" engineering, pharmaceuticals and health-related dietary products, and investment in education (supplementary schools and language schools for preparing students going abroad).

Conclusion

Prior research on Latin American immigrant transnationalism in the United States shows that governments of many sending countries value their compatriots' contributions to the homeland and seek to expand these transnational ties through a series of state-sponsored policies and activities, including matching funds for migrant donations to development projects and granting dual nationality, dual citizenship, and/or voting rights in national elections. China, being a one-party Communist country, is unique, so a systematic study of Chinese immigrant transnational organizations in the United States and their effects on homeland development supplements our knowledge from Latin American immigrant experiences.

Like other sending countries, the Chinese government in Beijing and local governments perceive transnational communities in terms of resources for homeland development. However, the Chinese government is also concerned with national image building and compatriots' commitment to the homeland. While immigrant transnationalism is enthusiastically endorsed and supported by the Chinese state, immigrant transnational organizations tend to operate independently of the Chinese state with the dual purposes of immigrant incorporation into the new homeland and development in the ancestral homeland. Traversing the two homelands entails constant interaction and negotiation between migrants and the sending state via transnational organizations.

Min Zhou, PhD, is currently Tan Lark Sye Chair Professor of Sociology and director of the Chinese Heritage Centre at Nanyang Technological University, Singapore. She is also Walter and Shirley Wang Endowed Chair in US-China Relations and Communications and professor of sociology at UCLA . Her research interests are in international migration, racial and ethnic relations, Asia and Asia America, and the Chinese diaspora. Her recent publications include *Contemporary Chinese America* and *The Accidental Sociologist in Asian American Studies.*

Rennie Lee is a doctoral candidate at the University of California–Los Angeles and is completing a thesis entitled "Coethnic Community Effects on the Educational Attainment of Immigrant and Native-Born Children in the U.S., Canada, and the U.K."

Notes

1. The CIOP originally targeted three immigrant groups—Mexicans, Colombians, and Dominicans—and was later extended to include three Asian immigrant groups—Chinese, Indians, and Vietnamese.
2. Each of the three metropolitan areas has maintained a fairly extensive Chinese-language telephone directory. Even though the ethnic population has grown rapidly in every state since the turn of the twenty-first century, there are familiar settlement patterns of community development that resemble those in the traditional immigrant gateway cities.
3. All interviews were conducted by the authors with the assistance of Junxiu Wang, Lu Xu, and Sallie Lin. Junxiu Wang and Lu Xu also provided valuable assistance in bilingual data collection and transcription.
4. A *qiao-xiang* is defined by the Chinese government as a place where the ratio of returned overseas Chinese and relatives of overseas Chinese to the total population is 10 percent or more. All interviews and fieldwork in China were conducted by Min Zhou with the assistance of Junxiu Wang between July 2009 and September 2010.
5. Guangdong Province had a population of eighty-three million as of 2010, the second most populous province in China. The ratio of returned overseas Chinese and relatives of overseas Chinese in Guangdong to the total provincial population is about 36 percent. It has been one of the two major sources of emigration to Southeast Asia since the twelfth century and the major source

of immigrants to North America since the mid-nineteenth century. More than thirty million people of Chinese ancestry in the world (probably more than half of Chinese Americans) can find their roots in Guangdong Province.

6. Twenty-five interviews were conducted in Guangdong Province, including interviews with various levels of *qiao-ban* and *qiao-lian* of Guangdong Province, Guanzhou, Jingmen, Shunde (an administrative district of Foshan City), and Zhongshan City. Others included leaders or officials of the Guangdong Museum of Overseas Chinese; Jiangmen Museum of Overseas Chinese; Guangzhou Zhigong Party; Zhongshan Historical Society; Guangdong Friendship Association of Chinese Overseas; Jiangmen Overseas Exchange Association; Jiangmen Youth Federation for Overseas Chinese; and villages in Taishan, Kaiping, Shunde, and Zhongshan.

7. Compared to Guangdong, Fujian Province is much smaller, with a population of thirty-five million as of 2010. Nonetheless, its ratio of returned overseas Chinese and relatives of overseas Chinese in Fujian to the total provincial population is about 26 percent. It has been a major source of emigration to Southeast Asia since the twelfth century, but to North America only since the late 1980s.

8. Twenty-five interviews were conducted in Fujian Province, including interviews with officials of various levels of *qiao-lian* of Fujian Province, Fuzhou City, Changle City, Fuqing City, Lianjiang County, Aojiang Town, Guantou Town, Jiangjing Town, Sanshan Town, and Tingjiang Town. Others included leaders or officials of the Institute for the Study of Chinese Overseas of the Fujian Academy of Social Sciences; Changle Association of New York; Changle Museum of Overseas Chinese; Baisha Village; Changxi Village; Gongyu Village; Houyu Village; Xiaqi Village; Yangyu Village; and Zelang Village.

9. Twelve face-to-face interviews were conducted with officials at the Overseas Chinese Affairs Office of the State Council; All-China Federation of Returned Overseas Chinese; National Central Committee of Zhi Gong Party; and Western Returned Scholars Association. Fieldwork also included a focus group with officials at Beijing Federation of Returned Overseas Chinese; and site visits to the Zhongguancun Science and Technology Park.

10. See https://www.cia.gov/library/publications/the-world-factbook/rankorder/2004rank.html?countryName=China&countryCode=ch&regionCode=eas&rank=119#ch (accessed 2 May 2012). By CIA estimates, GDP per capital (PPP) in China was at $8,400, ranked one hundred and nineteenth.

11. Measured at GDP (purchasing power parity, or PPP) in 2011 dollars. The largest economy was the European Union, estimated at $15.39 trillion, and the second largest was the United States, at $15.04 trillion as of 2011.

12. Many of these organizations maintain a Chinese-language website: for example, Yeong Wo (Zhongshan and three other counties), http://www.yeongwo.com/; NingYeung (Taishan), Hainan (Hainan Island, which became a province in 1988), http://www.hainamsca.com/.

13. See http://www.ccbanyc.org/ (accessed 5 December 2009).

14. See also http://www.ccbala.org (accessed 5 December 2009).

15. Village-based hometown associations are no longer common since 1990, except for the Fujianese. Because most of the undocumented Fujianese hailed

from rural villages, many established hometown associations based on the village of origin.

16. The number of students from Taiwan continues to be high. During the 1980s and 1990s, economic development in Taiwan and the Pacific Rim created many opportunities for American-trained students, and the trend of return migration was noticeable. However, the number of Taiwanese students who chose to stay continued to be substantial.

17. Calculated from statistics of Chinese exchange students and scholars published in *Chinese Education*, 23 August 1997, p. 1. The number of 95,000 US-bound students/scholars between 1978 and 1991 was not far off the track. According to the Immigration and Naturalization Service, 62,000 student visas were issued to Chinese between the 1979 and 1987 fiscal years. Of these exchange students, slightly over half were privately sponsored—not nominated or supported by the Chinese government.

18. We should caution that a much higher proportion of Chinese immigrant organizations in the ethnic community are entirely US-oriented, but our data collection focuses only on the ones that are sizable and well-established and have the capacity to be transnational if they choose to do so.

19. Cited in a report "Changes in policy on overseas Chinese affairs and comparison and study between the two sides of Taiwan Straits" by the Overseas Chinese Research Institute of Fujian Social Science Academy. See http://www.ynql.yn.gov.cn/readinfo.aspx?B1=1529 (accessed 23 January 2010).

20. See http://www.chinadaily.com.cn/china/2010-05/22/content_9881622.htm (accessed 9 February 2010).

21. See http://qwgzyj.gqb.gov.cn/qwhg/146/1346.shtml (accessed 22 January 2010).

22. See http://news.xinhuanet.com/politics/2008-06/02/content_8300471.htm (accessed 24 January 2010).

23. See http://www.wyu.edu.cn/fao/index6/jianzhuwubiao.htm (accessed 25 January 2010).

24. See http://ccbanyc.org/enews0809.html (accessed July 2011).

25. *Le-juan* is a kind of donation made by anyone who wants to give, ranging from a small amount ($15 or 100 yuan) to a substantial amount ($7,500 or 50,000 yuan), and *xi-juan* is for newlywed couples, who are members of a hometown association, to donate a lump sum of money, usually in the amount of $500; people attending the wedding may also donate in the name of the newlyweds to their hometown.

26. Interview with Mr. Huang, president of Guangdong Tongxiang Hui, Washington DC, October 2009, in Chinese, translated by Min Zhou.

27. Interview with Mr. Wang, Los Angeles, January 2010, in Chinese, translated by Min Zhou.

28. Interview with Mr. Xin, Thousand Oaks, CA, January 2010, in Chinese, translated by Min Zhou.

29. Interview with Mr. Wang, Los Angeles, January 2010, in Chinese, translated by Min Zhou.

30. Ibid.

References

Basch, Linda, Nina Glick Schiller, and Cristina Szanton Blanc. 1994. *Nations Unbound: Transnational Projects, Postcolonial Predicaments and Deterritorialized Nation-States*. Langhorne, PA: Gordon and Breach.

Chin, Ko-Lin. 1996. *Chinatown Gangs: Extortion, Enterprise, and Ethnicity*. New York: Oxford University Press.

Chin, Ku-Sip, In-Jin Yoon, and David Smith. 1996. "Immigrant Small Business and International Economic Linkage: A Case of the Korean Big Business in Los Angeles, 1968–1977." *International Migration Review* 30: 485–510.

Diaz-Briquets, Sergio, and Sidney Weintraub, eds. 1991. *Migration, Remittances, and Small Business Development: Mexico and Caribbean Basin Countries*. Boulder, CO: Westview Press.

Durand, Jorge, Emilio A. Parrado, and Douglas S. Massey. 1996. "Migradollars and Development: A Reconsideration of the Mexican Case." *International Migration Review* 30: 423–44.

Glick Schiller, Nina, Linda Basch, and Cristina Szanton Blanc. 1995. "From Immigrant to Transmigrant: Theorizing Transnational Migration." *Anthropological Quarterly* 68 (1): 48-63.

Glick Schiller, Nina, and Georges Fouron. 1999. "Terrains of Blood and Nation: Haitian Transnational Social Fields." *Ethnic and Racial Studies* 22 (March): 340–66.

Gold, Steven. 2001. "Gender, Class, and Network: Social Structure and Migration Patterns among Transnational Israelis." *Global Networks* 1: 57–78.

Goldring, Luin. 2002. "The Mexican State and Transmigrant Organizations: Negotiating the Boundaries of Membership and Participation." *Latin American Research Review* 37: 55–99.

Grasmuck, Sherri, and Patricia R. Pessar. 1991. *Between Two Islands: Dominican International Migration*. Berkeley: University of California Press.

Guarnizo, Luis E., Alejandro Portes, and William Haller. 2003. "Assimilation and Transnationalism: Determinants of Transnational Political Action among Contemporary Migrants." *American Journal of Sociology* 108: 1121–48.

Guarnizo, Luis E., Arturo I. Sanchez, and Elizabeth M. Roach. 1999. "Mistrust, Fragmented Solidarity, and Transnational Migration: Colombians in New York and Los Angeles." *Ethnic and Racial Studies* 22: 367–96.

Iskander, Natasha. 2010. *Creative State: Forty Years of Migration and Development Policy in Morocco and Mexico*. Ithaca, NY: Cornell University Press.

Itzigsohn, Jose, Carlos Dore, Esther Fernandez, and Obed Vazquez. 1999. "Mapping Dominican Transnationalism: Narrow and Broad Transnational Practices." *Ethnic and Racial Studies* 22, no. 2: 316–39.

Jones-Correa, Michael. 1998. "Different Paths: Gender, Immigration and Political Participation." *International Migration Review* 32: 326–49.

Kuo, Chia-ling. 1977. *Social and Political Change in New York's Chinatown: The Role of Voluntary Associations*. New York: Praeger.

Kwong, Peter. 1987. *The New Chinatown*. New York: Hill & Wang.

Landolt, Patricia. 2000. "The Causes and Consequences of Transnational Migration: Salvadorans in Los Angeles and Washington DC." PhD dissertation, Johns Hopkins University.

Levitt, Peggy. 1998. "Social Remittances: Migration Driven Local-Level Forms of Cultural Diffusion." *International Migration Review* 32: 926–48.

———. 2001. *The Transnational Villagers.* Berkeley: University of California Press.

———. 2007. *God Needs No Passport: Immigrants and the Changing Religious Landscape.* New York: New Press.

Levitt, Peggy, and Deepak Lamba-Nieves. 2011. "Social Remittances Revisited." *Journal of Ethnic and Migration Studies* 37: 1–22.

Li, Wei. 1997. "Spatial Transformation of an Urban Ethnic Community from Chinatown to Chinese Ethnoburb in Los Angeles." PhD dissertation, University of Southern California.

Li, Xiangyi, and Min Zhou. 2012. "Social Status Compensation through Transnational Practices: A Comparative Study of Cultural Remittances between Two Emigrant Groups from South China." *Sociological Studies* 3: 182–202.

Liu, Hong. 1998. "Old Linkages, New Networks: The Globalization of Overseas Chinese Voluntary Associations and its Implications." *The China Quarterly* 155: 588–609.

Mahler, Sarah J. 1995. *American Dreaming, Immigrant Life on the Margins.* Princeton, NJ: Princeton University Press.

Min, Pyong G. 1986/87. "Filipino and Korean Immigrants in Small Business: A Comparative Analysis." *Amerasia Journal* 13: 53–71.

———. 2008. *Ethnic Solidarity for Economic Survival: Korean Greengrocers in New York City.* New York: Russell Sage Foundation.

Moya, Jose C. 2005. "Immigrants and Associations: A Global and Historical Perspective." *Journal of Ethnic and Migration Studies* 31, no. 5: 833–64.

Østergaard-Nielsen, Eva. 2001. "Transnational Practices and the Receiving State: Turks and Kurds in Germany and the Netherlands." *Global Networks* 1: 261–81.

Piper, Nicola. 2009. "Temporary Migration and Political Remittances: The Role of Organisational Networks in the Transnationalisation of Human Rights." *European Journal of East Asian Studies* 8, no. 2: 215–43.

Popkin, Eric. 1999. "Guatemalan Mayan Migration to Los Angeles: Constructing Transnational Linkages in the Context of the Settlement Process." *Ethnic and Racial Studies* 22: 267–89.

Portes, Alejandro, Cristina Escobar, and Alexandria Walton Radford. 2007. "Immigrant Transnational Organizations and Development: A Comparative Study." *International Migration Review* 41 (Spring): 242–81.

Portes, Alejandro, and Luis E. Guarnizo. 1991. "Tropical Capitalists: U.S.-Bound Immigration and Small Enterprise Development in the Dominican Republic." In *Migration, Remittances, and Small Business Development: Mexico and Caribbean Basin Countries,* ed. Sergio Diaz-Briquets and Sidney Weintraub, 101–31. Boulder, CO: Westview Press.

Portes, Alejandro, Luis E. Guarnizo, and William J. Haller. 2002. "Transnational Entrepreneurs: An Alternative Form of Immigrant Economic Adaptation." *American Sociological Review* 67: 278–98.

Portes, Alejandro, Luis E. Guarnizo, and Patricia Landolt. 1999. "The Study of Transnationalism: Pitfalls and Promise of an Emergent Research Field." *Ethnic and Racial Studies* 22: 217–37.

Portes, Alejandro and Rubén G. Rumbaut. 2006. *Immigrant America: A Portrait* (3rd edition). Berkeley, CA: University of California Press.

Portes, Alejandro, and Min Zhou. 2012. "Transnationalism and Development: Mexican and Chinese Immigrant Organizations in the United States." *Population and Development Review* 38, no. 2: 191–220.

Rouse, Roger. 1989. "Mexican Migration to the United States: Family Relations in the Development of a Transnational Migrant Circuit." PhD dissertation, Stanford University.

Schrover, Marlou, and Floris Vermeulen. 2005. "Immigrant Organizations." *Journal of Ethnic and Migration Studies* 31: 823–32.

Smith, Robert C. 2005. *Mexican New York: Transnational Worlds of New Immigrants.* Berkeley: University of California Press.

Thunø, Mette. 2001. "Reaching Out and Incorporating Chinese Overseas: The Trans-territorial Scope of the PRC by the End of the 20th Century." *The China Quarterly* 168: 910–29.

Waldinger, Roger, Eric Popkin, and Hector Aquiles Magana. 2008. "Conflict and Contestation in the Cross-Border Community: Hometown Associations Reassessed." *Ethnic and Racial Studies* 31, no. 5: 843–70.

Wong, Bernard P. 1988. *Patronage, Brokerage, Entrepreneurship and the Chinese Community of New York.* New York: AMS Press.

Yoon, In-Jin. 1995. "The Growth of Korean Immigrant Entrepreneurship in Chicago." *Ethnic and Racial Studies* 18: 315–35.

Zhou, Min. 2009. *Contemporary Chinese America: Immigration, Ethnicity, and Community Transformation.* Philadelphia: Temple University Press.

Zhou, Min, and Myungduk Cho. 2010. "Noneconomic Effects of Ethnic Entrepreneurship: Evidence from Chinatown and Koreatown in Los Angeles, USA." *Thunderbird International Business Review* 52(2): 83–96.

Zhou, Min, and Rebecca Kim. 2001. "Formation, Consolidation, and Diversification of the Ethnic Elite: The Case of the Chinese Immigrant Community in the United States." *Journal of International Migration and Integration* 2(2): 227–47.

Zhou, Min, and Rennie Lee. 2013. "Transnationalism and Community Building: Chinese Immigrant Organizations in the United States." *The ANNALS of the American Academy of Political and Social Science* 647: 22–49.

Zweig, David, Changgui Chen, and Stanley Rosen. 2004. "Globalization and Transnational Human Capital: Overseas and Returnee Scholars to China." *The China Quarterly*: 735–57.

Chapter 2

Transnational Philanthropy of Urban Migrants

Colombian and Dominican Immigrant
Organizations and Development

Cristina Escobar

Immigrant organizations in the United States have emerged as forces affecting development in countries of origin. In this chapter I provide a comparative analysis of two illustrative cases involving the participation of Dominicans and Colombians, giving attention to the characteristics of Latin American migration to the United States and to defining factors in places of origin and destination. I emphasize the role of the state and civil society in countries of origin and in host countries, arguing that in cases involving migration to the United States, the former is more influential than the latter in shaping organizations and their transnationalism.

Colombian and Dominican organizations share several characteristics. In both cases, nearly half have cultural and civic missions, aiming to preserve immigrant values, traditions, and identity and to provide assistance in countries of origin, especially in the aftermath of natural disasters. There are differences as well. First, with the exception of hometown associations (HTAs), which are a minority in both cases, Dominican organizations carry out far fewer activities and projects in their homeland than their Colombian counterparts. By comparison to the Colombian case, there are a significantly greater number of large, well-financed Dominican organizations in the United States providing services to local communities. Second, Colombians have opened chapters of their organizations in

---

Notes for this chapter begin on page 80.

the United States as 501(c)(3) (nontaxable, nonprofit) entities in order to legally collect donations from patrons. There is no parallel in the Dominican case, which is characterized by organizations connected to active political parties and a large think tank with links to the last Dominican presidency.

A second aim of the chapter is to explain such differences and the significant effect they have on the character of organizational action in home countries. Since both Dominicans and Colombians share a similar context of reception in the United Sates, I argue that differences in their organizational approach and outcomes depend mostly on state and civic dynamics in the context of origin.

A study of Colombian and Dominican transnational organizations adds perspective to the literature on collective remittances, migrant associations, and development that, in Latin America, has mainly focused on hometown associations. Hometown associations tend to be formed by people migrating out of rural environments; Dominican and Colombian immigrants, by contrast, flow mostly out of cities.

A third aim of this chapter is to better understand how the different character of Dominican and Colombian organizations, composed mostly of urban migrants, influences their activities back home. I thus examine the main characteristics of organizations, the type of involvement they maintain in places of origin, and the partnerships they have established with the state and/or other institutions.

Immigrant Organizations and Development

Surges in international migration have increased the likelihood of immigrant involvement in the development policies of countries of origin. Neither market-oriented paradigms (1950s and 1960s)—where the state played a central developmental role—nor dependency models (1970s and 1980s)—which assigned importance to grassroots and self-help mobilization as forces in development—gave much attention to immigrant organizations. It was not until the 1990s, with an emergence of new interest in diasporas and transnationalism, that immigrant associations began to be recognized as agents of development (Faist and Fauser 2011; Kivisto 2011). We now know that migrants contribute to their countries of origin as senders of remittances, as part of professional or business networks, or through hometown associations as senders of collective gifts (Kivisto 2011).

Individual remittances have attracted most attention from scholars and policy makers, but recently immigrant donations—either individual or through organizations—have become central to discussions of development. As stated earlier, however, the emphasis has been primarily on hometown associations (Orozco 2009, 2006, 2005, 2004, 2003), sometimes obscuring the actions of other forms of organizations. The equation of migrant organizations with hometown associations has practical and theoretical implications. From a practical point of view, the work of migrants as agents of development can be quite different depending on whether the organizations have projects in a single locality or in various regions of the home country. Endeavors led by urban professionals share few similarities with projects implemented by hometown associations. Similarly, contacts in home countries or the localities where projects are implemented, as well as the character of exchanges, all vary with the types of organizations involved. Theoretically, equating immigrant organizations with hometown associations does not enable us to distinguish between traditional (the charitable giving that is the most common among migrant organizations and HTAs) and new forms of diasporic philanthropy (where there is an intent to transform and not just to alleviate) (Newland, Terrazas, and Munster 2010).

Another point I aim to broach in this chapter concerns immigrant organizations as embedded simultaneously in the state-civil society dynamics of the context of origin and context of destination because of their movement in transnational space. The goal is to look at places of exit and arrival (at the supranational, national, regional, and local levels), because it is in this overlapping space that migrant organizations and their dynamics are defined.

Research Design and Characteristics of the Organizations

I use data from a large study of first-generation Colombian, Dominican, and Mexican immigrant organizations carried out at the Princeton Center for Migration and Development,[1] the Comparative Immigrant Organizations Project (CIOP). The study includes: (1) inventories of organizations formed by Dominicans and Colombians; (2) face-to-face interviews with leaders of transnational organizations (thirty-two with Colombians and thirty-one with Dominicans); (3) visits to communities, projects, and offices in the countries of origin; and (4) interviews with government officials in the United States and the countries of origin. Leaders interviewed were members of organizations that have active transnational connections and are recognized by their communities, other organizations, or consulates. I complemented the CIOP data with interviews with immigrant leaders, community leaders, and government officials in 2008–9,[2] 2011, and 2012.

General Characteristics

Dominicans and Colombians represent two of the largest groups of immigrants from Latin America in the United States. Both are the result of post-1965 waves of immigration, predominantly of urban origin, and low to middle class. The number of Colombians in the United States is estimated at 1.18 million (35.4 percent of the total 3.3 million Colombians abroad) (DANE 2006). Colombians have higher levels of education than other Latin American groups in the United States (Guarnizo, Sánchez, and Rocha 1999; Portes and Rumbaut 2006: 69). They concentrate in the metropolitan areas of Florida, New York, and New Jersey, but there are also sizable Colombian communities in Chicago and Houston, as well as in Atlanta and the state of California (US Census Bureau 2000; Aysa-Lastra 2008: 32).

There are an estimated one million Dominicans in the United States concentrated mainly in New York, New England, and Florida (Rodríguez and Hernández 2004). They began arriving as political refugees in the 1960s and 1970s but were followed by economically based migration waves in the 1980s and 1990s. Today, the majority of Dominican migrants are working-class, but there are also significant proportions of middle-class professionals and entrepreneurs (Grasmuck and Pessar 1991; Portes and Guarnizo 1991).

Organizational Characteristics

An analysis of the CIOP inventory of immigrant organizations formed by Dominicans and Colombians shows that there is no clear-cut division between transnational and nontransnational organizations. Organizations created with the specific purpose of helping people in home countries are not the only ones that actually maintain permanent relations with the countries of origin. There are organizations that cater to immigrants in places of residence and in the homeland, and organizations oriented mainly toward communities in the United States that have nonetheless developed activities, programs, and connections with their home countries (Escobar 2010). Efficient communication and transportation technologies, the active recruitment by local, regional, and national governments in the home country, and even the antimigrant movement in the United States have all contributed to the increasing transnational orientation of the organizations.

According to the data collected by the CIOP, immigrant transnational organizations are relatively small (the median number of members is twenty-seven for Colombian organizations and thirty-four for Dominican organizations) and, with few exceptions, they do not operate with large

funds (the median annual budget is $20,000 in the case of Colombian or-
ganizations and $24,000 for Dominican organizations). Almost all organi-
zations (99 percent of Colombian organizations and 82 percent of Dominican organizations) depend on volunteers. Their main sources of funding
are direct member contributions and fund-raisers, such as raffles, parties,
galas, bingos, and other events, carried out through members' uncompen-
sated labor (Table 2.1). While some organizations benefit from church contributions or state donations or foundations (most common among Dominican organizations), the more stable sources of income are members'
contributions and the leaders' fund-raising efforts.

For the most part, these organizations involve face-to-face interactions.
People meet to discuss objectives and plan activities and fund-raisers.
Nearly all Colombian (93.5 percent) and Dominican (90 percent) organizations meet at least once a month; all of them meet at least once every
three months. Close to half of Colombian organizations (42.31 percent)
and nearly one-third of Dominican organizations (32 percent) meet socially at least once a month. Slightly more than 85 percent of Colombian
organizations and more than half of Dominican organizations (56 percent)
do so at least every three months. Immigrant organizations not only provide a space for interaction, they also coordinate social events like sports
competitions, parades, festivals, and other cultural gatherings.

Transnational organizations are also, for the most part, self-sufficient.
Half of the Colombian and 60 percent of the Dominican organizations
have incorporated as nonprofit groups and obtained 501(c)(3) status from

Table 2.1. Sources of Support of Immigrant Organizations by Nationality

Sources	Colombian	Dominican	Total
	%	%	%
From members	19.45	31.03	25.24
From raffles, parties, events in US	60.9	21.79	42.02
From raffles, parties, events in Colombia/ Dominican Republic	0	3.25	1.63
From donations/foundations	2.93	7.14	5.04
From local/state/national governments	0	1.25	2.14
From political parties	2.86	0	1.43
From churches	0	3.46	2.25
From businesses	12.03	13.19	12.57
From others	3.21	4.46	3.83
N	30	29	59

Note: Figures do not add up to 100 because individual organizations can receive support
from more than one source.
Source: CIOP data.

the Internal Revenue Service, which exempts them from paying taxes and allows them to receive tax-deductible donations. Access to additional resources is a main reason cited by many organizations for their interest in obtaining a 501(c)(3) status. However, only a small number receive funds from either foundations or governments, even though many have developed programs to serve immigrants in the United States.

Except for social service providers (which have headquarters, hired staff, and significant resources from local and state-level institutions), there is a gap between what most immigrant organizations could potentially obtain as incorporated nonprofits and what they actually receive. Becoming a recipient of additional funds from foundations or corporations involves qualitative changes that not all organizations are willing to undertake. This is especially true for civic and cultural organizations or hometown associations that have operated informally for years. The voluntary, self-sustaining character of many of these organizations makes it difficult for them to change in order to become grant recipients.

Colombian Organizations

Colombian organizations in the United States share two main characteristics. First, they tend to be formed by urban middle-class people and, second, they tend to be cross-regional, that is, their members come from different localities and regions in the country of origin. There are hometown associations among Colombians, but they are not common. Among more than three hundred Colombian organizations included in the CIOP inventory, there are only six HTAs, all from the Colombian western coffee region, an area with high levels of out-migration. Among civic and cultural organizations—which constitute the largest proportion (47.3 percent) of Colombian organizations (Table 2.2)—those created to assist people in Colombia include a wide range of activities. Some reproduce voluntary associations formed by elite women in the home country. Damas Voluntarias in Miami, for example, organizes fund-raising events and supports various nongovernmental organizations (NGOs) in Colombia. Others are networks of friends and acquaintances who contribute to specific projects in Colombia. For example, Corazón a Corazón, founded in 1981, helps children with heart problems get medical care in the United States. Still other groups emerged as a result of community efforts to aid the victims of natural disasters.

Three of these organizations in the New York metropolitan area—Long Island for Colombia, Siempre Colombia, and Comité Divino Niño—were all established in 1999, the year when an earthquake devastated the Colombian coffee-growing region. There are also traditional civic and cul-

Table 2.2. Type of Immigrant Organizations by Country

Type	Colombia		Dominican Republic	
	%	n	%	n
Civic	47.30	149	30.00	51
Cultural	10.16	32	15.29	26
Economic	4.44	14	2.35	4
Hometown	1.90	6	3.53	6
Home Country	0.32	1	1.18	2
Home-Country NGOs	3.17	10	0.00	0
International Philanthropic (Lions, Kiwanis, etc.)	6.98	22	3.53	6
Political—US	3.49	11	4.12	7
Political—Home Country	4.44	14	5.88	10
Professional	8.89	28	14.12	24
Religious	1.59	5	1.18	2
Service Providers	2.86	9	17.06	29
Sports	0.63	2	1.76	3
Student	3.81	12	0.00	0
Total	100.00	315	100.00	170

Source: CIOP data, 2008.

tural organizations mainly oriented toward the immigrant community in the United States, for example, the Centro Cívico Colombiano de New York, created in 1978; the Club Colombia USA, Hackensack, New Jersey, established in1969; the Club Colombia de Dover, New Jersey, created in 1979; and Colombianos en Acción, founded in Paterson, New Jersey, in 1989. These entities have, in recent years, developed new projects and activities in Colombia.

Professional organizations (8.9 percent of the CIOP inventory) generally aim at creating and maintaining social networks formed by highly skilled Colombians in the United States. One of them, Profesionales y Estudiantes Colombianos en el Exterior (PECX), created in 1991, was born as the support network for a Colombian governmental program interested in creating an international electronic network of professionals abroad (Red de Caldas). Today, however, PECX operates independently and sees as its main objective to support Colombian professionals and students in the United States (Escobar 2010).

By comparison to other Latin and non-Latin immigrant groups, excluding Asians, Colombians have formed a significant number of groups belonging to international philanthropic organizations (6.98 percent), such as Lions, Kiwanis, or Rotary Clubs.[3] These cater to both communities in the United States and in the country of origin. Constituents tend to be older and more affluent than the US population at large (Ramakrishnan and Viramontes 2006). For some migrants, membership in these international philanthropic organizations becomes a status symbol that they would not have been able to claim at home. International organizations provide contacts and facilitate relations between clubs, authorities, and other formal groups in Colombia, thus easing the difficult task of selecting, delivering, and monitoring projects in the home country. Specifically, clubs organize *hermanamientos* (brotherhoods), a sort of formal commitment between Colombian organizations in the United States and specific clubs in the country of origin (Escobar 2010).

Recently created development foundations account for the largest amount of resources invested in Colombia—significantly larger than those transferred by all other organizations combined. Such foundations—which mainly include Give to Colombia (since 2003) and Genesis (since 2001)—channel large donations from US corporations to Colombian recipients. Genesis also supports educational programs in the United States.[4] While Genesis was created in the United States, Give to Colombia was promoted by the Colombian corporate sector. Give to Colombia directly connects donors abroad with specific projects carried out by NGOs, which they assist and monitor indirectly through Compartamos, a social branch of the Colombian corporate sector.

In addition to foundations created with the purpose of channeling resources into Colombia, there also are chapters of Colombian NGOs that have branched out into the United States. They represent 3.17 percent of the total number of organizations in the CIOP inventory. Their main goal is to organize fund-raising events to finance projects in Colombia. Worth noting among them is El Minuto de Dios (since 1950), a large and well-recognized Catholic institution that groups together housing, educational, economic, and media agencies working to provide services to people in need. El Minuto de Dios first opened an office in Miami in 2003 and now organizes the popular *banquetes del millón* to raise funds in various American cities (Aysa-Lastra 2007; Escobar 2010).

Immigrants from Colombia have created an array of organizations involved in philanthropic or development activities in their home country. They include (1) civic and charitable organizations, some of which started as disaster relief organizations; (2) chapters of international philanthropic organizations; (3) foundations; (4) chapters of Colombian NGOs; and (5) hometown associations.

Dominican Organizations

Dominican organizations, like those formed by Colombians, tend to be created by middle-class people, but also by more humble workers coming from cities rather than villages. By comparison to their Colombian counterparts, Dominican organizations are mostly oriented toward the United States and less toward the country of origin. As in the Colombian case, Dominicans tend to form civic and cultural organizations. Two other common associational forms among Dominicans are clubs (places for social gathering and recreation) and service providers like Alianza Dominicana, founded in 1987. These are mostly oriented toward the immigrant community in the United States, but a few have contact with places of origin (Escobar 2010).

A distinctive feature of Dominican professional associations (14.1 percent of the total) is the extent to which they maintain close ties with powerful professional organizations in their home country. This is the case with the Association of Dominican Journalists in New York, linked to the Colegio Dominicano de Periodistas (Dominican College of Journalism), and the three chapters of the association of Dominican doctors, linked to the Colegio Medico Dominicano (Escobar 2010).

In contrast to Colombia, there are no Dominican NGOs that have branched into the United States. On the other hand, there is a much more active engagement with political parties and politically oriented institutions in the Dominican Republic. For example, the Fundación Global is an NGO, created by former president Leonel Fernández after leaving office in 2000, that studies, proposes, and promotes policies for sustainable development and democracy in the country. It has a sister foundation in New York, the Global Foundation for Democracy and Development.

As in the Colombian case, Dominican hometown associations represent a small fraction of the total number of Dominican immigrant organization (3.53 percent). Nonetheless, they carry out important transnational activities in a context characterized by a low transnational orientation among other organizations.

To summarize, aside from hometown associations, which are by definition linked to their localities of origin, there are, in the Dominican community, professional associations linked to the island, as well as organizations more oriented toward the United States, such as service providers or sport clubs, that maintain occasional contacts and implement selected activities in the country of origin.

Migrant Organizations and State and Civil Society

The Colombian Case

The Colombian state has been historically weak. By contrast, Colombian civil society has flourished independent and critical of both the state and political parties (Villar 2001). Starting in the 1980s and accelerating in the 1990s and 2000s, immigrant organizations sought counterparts to channel philanthropic contributions at the regional and local levels. Given the already established tradition of circumventing politicians and the state whenever possible, local NGOs, churches, and other institutions appeared more appealing to immigrant groups than government agencies.

In the new constitution of 1991, the Colombian state granted citizens living abroad the right to retain their citizenship when naturalizing in other countries, as well as the right to participate in national elections from abroad. Such rights were granted relatively early by comparison to other Latin American countries, in response to pressures exercised by the expatriate community, assisted by certain political sectors in Colombia (Escobar 2007). Despite such early political concessions, the Colombian state did not reach out to immigrants with a comprehensive program until a decade later, and even then it maintained a low profile in its relations with transnational organizations.

In the early 1990s, the Colombian government became preoccupied with the loss of professionals moving abroad. It then established a pioneer Internet network of expatriate Colombian scientists (Red Colombiana de Investigadores en el Exterior, or Red de Caldas). This network paralleled the creation of a program supporting the return of highly educated Colombians. While a few positive results came out of this effort, the network did not last long, falling short of the high expectations that it had originally created (Meyer et al. 1997; Pineda 2008; *El Tiempo* 1993, 2003).

By 2003, as Colombian expatriates became more visible as senders of remittances, the state developed a more comprehensive program, Colombia Nos Une, designed not just for the highly skilled but also for lower- to middle-class migrants who had made up the bulk of the mostly economic migration since the 1980s. Policies associated with Colombia Nos Une have been designed to facilitate economic transferences, training, credit, and investment from points of destination; they have also resulted in the design of programs to help Colombians abroad (MRE 2006: 19–20, 2008; COMPES 2009). In 2005 and 2006, Colombia Nos Une undertook an effort to coordinate local organizations abroad, but the program was discontinued.[5] Officials of Colombia Nos Une then redesigned their strategy in order to carry out workshops on different topics, according to the needs and requests of communities in various countries of destination.[6]

From the outset, Colombia Nos Une has worked on the technological infrastructure necessary to create virtual networks of Colombians abroad. A virtual platform was initiated in 2007 and is now in operation, although the connections it was expected to promote fell short of expectations due to competition from other social media and the lack of clear benefits for participation. In an effort that continues the tradition of Red de Caldas, the government is also involved in the online enrollment of highly qualified persons, estimated to represent 6.4 percent of Colombians abroad.[7]

To summarize, Colombia has been characterized by a mix of a weak state and a dynamic civil society that has often taken the lead in establishing linkages with communities abroad. Government policy has focused on facilitating remittances, attracting individual investments, providing some services to the expatriate community, and trying to capitalize on the knowledge of the highly skilled. It has not yet offered, however, solid programs to promote or channel the potential contributions of immigrant organizations.

The Dominican Case

A history of patrimonial regimes in the Dominican Republic—including the dictatorship of Rafael Leonidas Trujillo (1930–61) and the authoritarian government of Joaquín Balaguer (1966–78)—limited the development of civic institutions and organizations in that country. During the period of struggle for democracy (1978–96), social organization and mobilization emerged, but the result was a kind of party "infiltration" in which political parties penetrated and politicized other organizations and civil society in general (Hartlyn 1998). The politicized character of Dominican society was transferred to the community in the United States and has influenced its organizations. Dominican political organizations, both US- and home country–oriented, are not proportionally much more numerous than their Colombian counterparts, but they are enmeshed in thick networks linking immigrant leaders with parties and politicians at home, thus influencing the organizations' character (Itzigsohn 2004; Graham 2001). The politicization of the Dominican population, as well as its experience in structured, well-disciplined parties, has benefited Dominican organizations in the United States. The same may be said about civic organizations formed by Dominicans, which have played a pivotal role in training leaders and in the political incorporation of immigrants (Escobar 2010).

In the Dominican case, it has not been the state or civil society but rather the political sector that has been in a position to extend itself beyond territorial boundaries. The Dominican community in the United States was critical in the past to the success of political parties not only as a potential electorate (party bosses used to fly individuals back to the island on Election Day) but also as a means of financing political campaigns (Graham 2001; Sagás 2004). After the enactment of the 1997 Law 275, the role of the expatriate community changed; that piece of legislation established political parties' financing by the state, along with private contributions. The same law made it possible for Dominicans abroad to vote without having to travel back to the island (Escobar 2007).

In his second administration (2004–8), President Leonel Fernández, who grew up in the United States, held as a governmental priority the consolidation of a "strategic alliance" between the Dominican Republic and the Dominican community abroad. In addition to a housing initiative, his government launched, in 2005, a program to create a Presidential Consulting Council of Dominicans Abroad (Consejos Consultivos de la Presidencia de los Dominicanos en el Exterior, or CCPDE), following the Mexican model. The board responsible for the program comprised representatives from the five US regions where Dominicans are concentrated—New York, New Jersey, Miami, Chicago, and New England—and from ten other countries where significant numbers of Dominicans live.

This council, which had its first annual meeting in 2006 under the guidance of the newly created Secretariat for Dominicans Abroad, includes members suggested at regional meetings but officially nominated by the president.[8] Other than limited resources, the major challenges faced by the program have been: (1) the top-down selective approaches of council members, which limit representation and participation; and (2) difficulties in moving the program into something more than a vehicle for the party in power to consolidate a constituency abroad. In January 2008 the National Council for Dominican Communities Abroad (Consejo Nacional para las Comunidades Dominicanas en el Exterior, or CONDEX) was created by law as a formal state entity in charge of Dominicans living outside the island. The idea was to give continuity to a program that up to that time had depended mostly on the president.

In short, the highly politicized character of Dominican civil society has influenced immigrant organizations in the United States, first, because of the immigrants' familiarity with organizational participation; second, because of the political activism and contacts that encouraged some organizations to become service providers with external funds; and third, because political parties continue to be critical transnational actors.

Contributions of Immigrant Organizations

There are some commonalities in the way that Colombian and Dominican immigrant organizations carry out activities and projects in their countries of origin. There are significant variations as well. A crucial, and not always evident, similarity between Colombian and Dominican organizations stems from their location in the United States, where the federal government neither seeks to mold immigrant organizations nor promotes specific programs for immigrants to carry out in their countries of origin. Canada and some European countries enact specific policies to help immigrant communities organize. In several European countries, codevelopment programs have been implemented by governments to aid immigrant incorporation in places of destination and arrest out-migration from points of origin (Bloemraad 2005, 2006; Fauser 2011; Kivisto 2011; Cebolla Boado and López-Sala, this volume). Such incentives are not present in the United States, and that influences decisively the character and reach of organizational activities.

What Do Organizations Do?

A leader of a women's organization in Miami describes how her group decides which projects to support:

> We receive many requests from Colombian foundations with different objectives regarding children, the elderly, or people who really need a hand. [On that basis] we try to determine a specific project we want to work with. We don't just send them the money for them to figure out what to do with it. ... We try to quantify the project and determine if we can help. ... We try to organize between four to five different events each year.

A member of a nearly thirty-year-old Lions Club in Miami that, like similar entities, has twinning relations with Lions Clubs in Colombia summarizes their work as follows:

> We helped in the construction of a health center in Bogotá, in the barrio La Gloria, with the Lions Club of Bogotá-San Agustin; we also worked in Cartagena, with the Lions of Cartagena-Crespo, and Cartagena de Indias. With the Club Medellín-Laurels, we helped an association named Drop of Milk, which is like a day care [center] for children—from newborns to seven or eight years old. With the Club Santa Marta-Rodadero, we collected funds to build a school. With the clubs of three cities in the coffee region, Pereira, Armenia, and Manizáles, we helped them get ophthalmologic equipment.

The leader of a Dominican service organization in New York described their projects as follows:

> We collect here all we can use in the Dominican Republic, mainly in the area of health. We ask for medical equipment, and we send it to clinics and hospitals. There is a program called Nutrition for Life in which we are involved, along with two other institutions in the city of New York. Once a year, a commission of doctors and experts travels to bring medicine to clinics and rural neighborhoods of the Dominican Republic.

A member of another organization located in New York described their contribution to the Dominican Republic:

> We donate medicine to hospitals. ... When we make a donation to the Dominican Republic, a commission goes to give it directly and personally. And, when we receive requests, there is a commission that resides there and goes and verifies if the person really needs it. Only after they give us their report do we make a donation. ... We have also given equipment, instruments. We gave to the maternity ward in the hospital Nuestra Señora de Altagracia, in the capital, beds, some instruments, canes, wheelchairs, sheets, and all that a hospital needs.

Colombian organizations invest their collective remittances in three main areas: almost three-quarters of organizations (71.8) carry out projects helping the sick, the elderly, the disabled, and children; two-thirds (65.6 percent) develop projects on education; more than half (56 percent) on health; one-third (31.2 percent) on economic promotion (including activities of the chambers of commerce and donations for institutions that have economic projects) and housing; and one-quarter (25 percent) have made contributions to victims of the 1999 earthquake (Figure 2.1). In general, Colombian organizations distribute donations of $5,000, $10,000, and up to $20,000 among small projects.

All the projects carried out by hometown associations and civic/cultural organizations can be categorized as philanthropic; they are part of the large trend toward diasporic philanthropy detected worldwide (Newland, Terrazas, and Munster 2010). In contrast, newer and larger foundations, like the aforementioned Genesis and Give to Colombia, can be classified among the new forms of diasporic philanthropy. These foundations deploy greater resources (Genesis reported $1.3 million invested in Colombia in 2011)[9] and implement training programs focusing on particular areas of development—health, basic education, environment, human security—with the intent of producing real social changes (Johnson 2001, cited by Newland, Terrazas, and Munster 2010: 4). They are trying to apply the rigorous methods of business investments to philanthropic ventures and become a "sustainable engine for the country's social and economic development."[10]

The pattern of project distribution among Dominican organizations is different. Almost half of Dominican organizations (48.3 percent) invest in health projects; one-third (35.4 percent) in education; and one-third (32.2 percent) in natural disaster relief. A significant number of organizations made contributions to assist the victims of Hurricane George after it hit Jimani Province, on the border with Haiti. Dominican projects tend to be smaller and less frequent than those implemented by Colombians (Figure 2.1), and all are variants of traditional diasporic philanthropy.

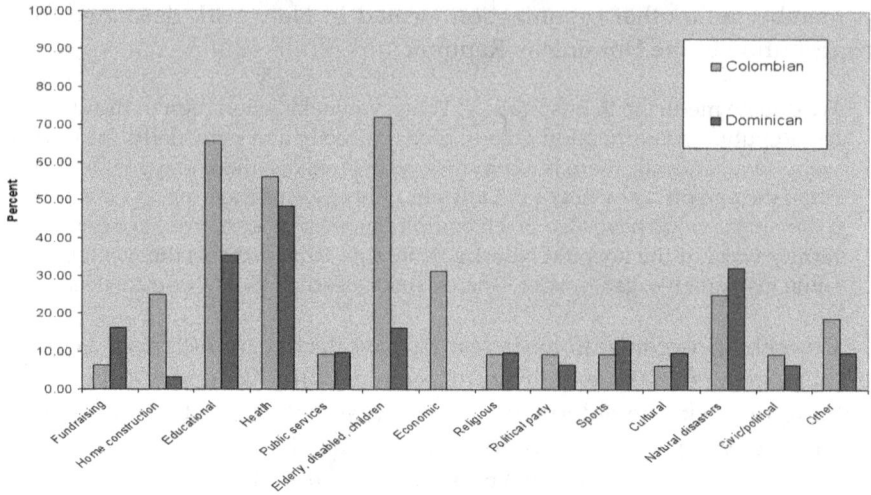

Figure 2.1. Types of Projects of Colombian and Dominican Immigrant Organizations in Their Home Countries

Where and How Do Organizations Carry Out Their Projects?

With the exception of hometown associations, most Colombian organizations include people from different regions, and mostly from cities, since most migrants come from there. As a result, immigrant organizations implement projects in various parts of the country using informal networks formed by relatives, friends, and acquaintances. The decision about where to carry out an activity/project depends not only on the members of the organization, but also on the input they receive from the homeland. As noted earlier, NGOs have an active role in tapping immigrant organizations and requesting funds to implement small projects. These petitions are generally submitted through informal channels, including relatives and acquaintances. On the Dominican side, contacts are also informal, but as the Dominican quotes above show, active professional networks—health professionals, for example—serve as links and conduits for requests between organizations and hospitals, health centers, and neighborhoods on the island.

There are all sorts of individuals and entities serving as counterparts of immigrant organizations in the countries of origin. Members of these organizations look for the best options to guarantee the successful implementation of their projects. As one of the interviewees quoted above told us, some immigrants prefer to do things themselves directly. But this is not an option for many, depending on the type of organization, the legal status of the organization's members (only those with legal documents can travel back home), and the type of project. Some organizations find the right intermediaries only after experiencing serious difficulties.

The data show similar strategic approaches among Colombian and Dominican organizations in pursuit of their goals. They use all sorts of intermediaries, but NGOs and chapters of organizations are most common. There is, however, more reliance on the part of Colombian organizations on church-related institutions, whereas Dominican organizations approach hospitals, libraries, universities, and schools directly. There is also more interaction with political parties in the Dominican case. In both instances, state institutions play a minor role (Figure 2.2).

As mentioned earlier, the state has not been a good partner for Colombian immigrant organizations embarking on development programs in their homeland. By contrast, Colombian civil society, with its numerous NGOs, Lions Clubs, churches, chambers of commerce, public and private orphanages and nursing homes, and philanthropic institutions, continues to be directly involved in programs financed by members of the Colombian diaspora. The only program to attract both collective as well as individual contributions has been Conexión Colombia, a private initiative started in 2003 through an Internet platform that solicits individual donations. Today, Conexión Colombia channels donations from individuals or groups abroad toward an estimated fifty NGOs in Colombia. While its main aim is to serve as a conduit for donations (and guaranteeing the good use of

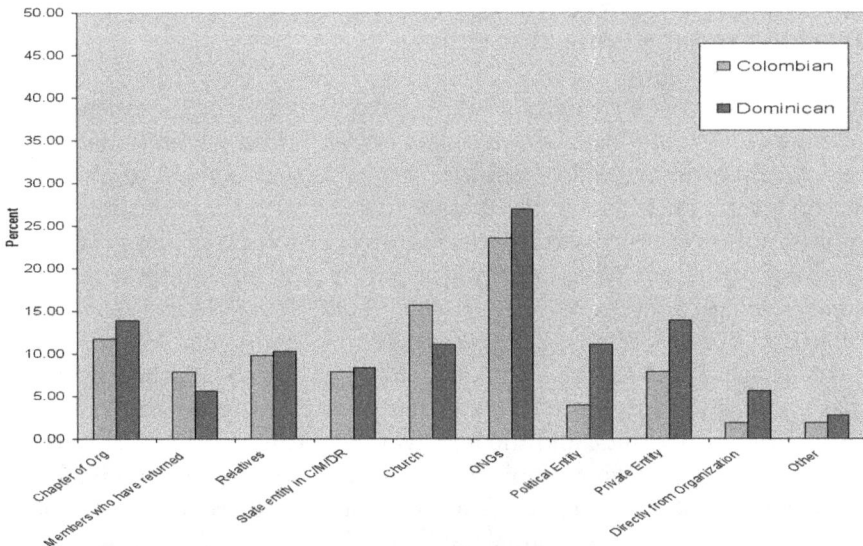

Figure 2.2. Entities in Home Countries Serving as Counterparts of Immigrant Organizations in the United States by Nationality

those donations), Conexión Colombia has also helped to create groups of donors among Colombian entrepreneurs in some cities (e.g., Compromiso Manhattan).[11] Two state entities have followed the lead of Genesis and have become their partners in large projects: Acción Colombia, the social agency of the Colombian presidency, and Bienestar Familiar, the family and childhood government initiative.[12]

In the case of the Dominican Republic, the state has prompted investments, channeled individual remittances, and initiated some housing projects.[13] The consulting boards of CCPDE and CONDEX, mentioned earlier, developed leadership programs for Dominican youths in the United States and exchanges with Dominican elected officials abroad. However, the state initiative to address the contribution to development of the organized community has been reduced to projects that facilitate the entrance of "donations" (such as medical equipment for hospitals) into the country (CONDEX 2008). The private sector has not taken the lead either. Traditional philanthropy is well received, but there are no new alternative development initiatives, private or public. Given the overpowering role of political parties and the fact that civil society is embedded in them (Espinal, Morgan, and Hartlyn 2010), the political agenda continues to dominate the transnational relations of Dominicans. Dominican elected officials in the United States have become important transnational figures, not only as government assets but also as symbolic resources.

Tensions and the Issue of Identity

A final question is why immigrant organizations engage in transnational activities and what is their projection across future generations. When asked, organization leaders named "personal satisfaction" as the main reason for their involvement in these activities: "For Christmas, two years ago we got a very nice card that we will never forget. Imagine, 173 children with different types of physical and mental disabilities holding a huge billboard that read: THANK YOU FOR GIVING US WHAT LIFE DENIED US. So, what else can you want?"

Aside from personal satisfaction, leaders made explicit their desire to share their good fortune with those left behind. After all, most of them are economic migrants, and the best way they can contribute is through philanthropic projects. Members of organizations are also motivated to participate by the opportunities for sociability that these organizations offer. Finally, elements of status and identity are also involved. As the literature on hometown associations has underlined, members of organizations embedded in transnational communities benefit from a redefined status "not readily otherwise available within the context of the United States" (Goldring 1998: 174; Iskander, this volume). Urban immigrants are not as embedded in transnational communities as rural ones. Urbanites are therefore unable to redefine their status at the level of family and community in the same way as their counterparts in hometown associations. Nonetheless, they are still able to improve their status. Members of immigrant organizations, many of which also carry out programs and projects in the United States, receive recognition and assume a representative role in the eyes of local authorities in the United States as well as in the countries of origin.

A strong sense of identity helps explain the transnational character of organizations and is very apparent among civic and cultural groups, which constitute the majority of Colombian and Dominican organizations. These organizations have developed in a post–civil rights multicultural context where immigrants are not forced to shed their culture, as they were in the past, and in a global era when technological facilities make possible intense and frequent contact with places of origin. They are also part of a world in which sending country governments often depend on immigrants' remittances and, therefore, court them as potential allies and contributors. Colombian and Dominican organizations also aim to maintain cultural identity for the benefit of subsequent generations. While hometown associations serve to reinforce local and regional identities, organizations formed by urban migrants, usually from diverse cities, reinforce mostly national identities.

Are these organizations able to instill a sense of belonging and identity in the second generation? Most members of organizations studied were conscious of and interested in the US-born generation, some appealing to them through programs aimed at children and youths. Despite such efforts, most agree that the children do not show much interest in transnational activities. Whether or not some of them participate depends on the parents and how they have managed to bring them, or not, into their circle. Among Colombians and Dominicans, second-generation participants are more the exception than the rule.

Immigrant organizations face opposing forces. On the one hand, first-generation immigrants tend to maintain their relation to countries of origin, thus strengthening their national identity. On the other hand, there are pressures pulling immigrant organizations to adopt pan-ethnic ("Hispanic" or "Latino") identities in places of destination, especially when competing for government resources.[14] This is more the case of organizations with a higher participation of second-generation immigrants. They may retain a sense of identity linked to their parents' homeland; nevertheless, they are less inclined to follow the same models in terms of organization. In lieu of time-consuming fund-raising activities, members of the second generation may opt for more efficient strategies by applying for funds to development agencies or foundations—something they are more inclined and more qualified to do than their parents. They are also more willing to sacrifice national identity for a pan-ethnic or development-oriented self-definition.

Conclusion

In this chapter I have summarized the characteristics of transnational Colombian and Dominican immigrant organizations and their activities in the United States. A comparison of both groups yields similarities and differences. There is more activity on the part of Colombian organizations toward their home country, while Dominican organizations focus much of their efforts on Dominicans in the United States. Both groups include high numbers of urban migrants and, therefore, organizational forms other than hometown associations are present. The different characteristics and histories of migration are therefore important features to bear in mind when analyzing varying forms of transnationalism emerging in diverse immigrant communities. The urban character of the migration, for example, is as important for the transnationalism of immigrant organizations among Dominicans and Colombians as among other national groups, such as Indian immigrants in the United States (see Agarwala, this volume).

Although both the Colombian and the Dominican governments initiated programs for expatriates starting in the early 2000s, in neither case have these programs helped shape or organize the collective remittances of the expatriate community. Instead, migrants organized and became involved in transnational activities/projects by using their own informal contacts. Colombia has a strong and active civil society that has served as a dynamic counterpart for immigrant organizations overseas looking for partners to carry out their projects back home. Moreover, civil society has extended over the border to play an active role in the United States, channeling funds to Colombia. The private sector more than the state has created avenues for expatriates to channel their individual and collective contributions. Conexión Colombia is the main example. Finally, the US-based foundations that channel large resources into extensive, well-planned, sustainable projects are the ones inviting the Colombian state to become a partner. These development programs contrast with more traditional philanthropic activities that have characterized transnational Colombian immigrant organizations.

In the Dominican Republic, where civil society has been very politicized, it has been the vibrant political society and the powerful political parties that have dominated transnational activities. This has facilitated the political incorporation of Dominicans into the United States and allowed for the establishment of immigrant organizations heavily oriented toward American politics. Development activities of Dominican organizations, most of them an expression of traditional philanthropy, have been relegated to a secondary level.

A look at the dynamics of state-civil society in Colombia and the Dominican Republic helps us understand these different patterns, because immigrant organizations in the United States—where there is no policy for immigrant organizations or for their development activities back home—are shaped more by homeland characteristics and policies than by forces in the host society.

Finally, I examined questions of identity and continuity across generations, arguing that some second-generation Colombian and Dominican immigrants may maintain their ancestral identity and even be interested in continuing transnational philanthropic activities. Nevertheless, the means to implement transnational activities by the second generation are likely to assume new organizational forms. While increasing links with countries of origin can reinforce national identities, there are other important forces mitigating that effect. An important one is the pressure to relinquish country-specific identities in favor of a more general Hispanic or Latino self-definition to achieve, among other goals, a stronger political presence in the United States as well as access to a larger resource pool.

Among organizations formed by first-generation immigrants, a way out of that dilemma is to locate alternative sources of funding that only a few possess (Colombian foundations linked to the corporate sector are a clear example). Such affluent organizations not only have enough means to carry out larger transnational activities, setting the agenda and establishing permanent relations with private and state agencies in the country of origin, but they can also implement programs leading to sustainable development. A question for further research is not just the degree of transnationalism among members of the second generation, but whether or not they will subscribe to the philanthropic models used by most of their parents' organizations. Such models aimed to provide assistance to people in crisis back home, but the new generations may want to instead pursue programs of sustained intervention (social investment) with which they expect to effectively contribute to development.

Cristina Escobar is a sociologist who earned her PhD from University of California–San Diego. She has taught at Temple University, Franklin and Marshall College, West Chester University, and Rutgers University–Camden. She did a postdoctorate at Princeton University and worked as a research associate at the same university. She won a postdoctorate research grant from the Social Science Research Council and a Presidential Authority Award grant from the Russell Sage Foundation. She has done research on migration and citizenship, transnational immigrant organizations, and migrants' political participation. Among her publications are "Dual Citizenship and Extraterritorial Political Rights in Latin America," *Latin American Research Review* 42, no. 3 (October): 41–73 (2007), and "Exploring Transnational Civil Society: A Comparative Study of Colombian, Dominican and Mexican Immigrant Organizations in the United States," *Journal of Civil Society* 6, no. 3 (December): 205–35 (2010).

Notes

1. Research for this project was financed by the Russell Sage Foundation and the MacArthur Foundation and directed by Alejandro Portes.
2. These interviews were done thanks to the support of the Presidential Authority Award of the Russell Sage Foundation.
3. Ramakrishnan and Viramontes found these forms of Kiwanis Clubs, which they call "hybrid," among Filipino Americans in Los Angeles (2006: 41).
4. See http://www.givetocolombia.org and http://www.genesis-foundation.org.
5. Personal interviews, Colombian consuls in Miami (January 2006), Los Angeles (September 2005), New York (March 2006), and a representative of Colombia Nos Une in the United States (June 2006).
6. Personal interview, director of Colombia Nos Une, Bogotá (April 2012).
7. This is a French pilot program that involves the creation of diaspora incubators for Latin American knowledge (Création d'incubateurs de diasporas des savoirs pour l'Amérique Latine, or CIDESAL; *incubadora de conocimiento* means "knowledge incubator"). It seeks to facilitate the contributions of highly qualified Colombians to their home country. See http://www.redesco lombia.org/content/listado-de-colombianos-en-el-exterior-con-alta-califi caci%C3%B3n-ya-supera-los-9000-registros (accessed July 2012).
8. Personal interviews, New York (July 2007, May 2008) and Philadelphia (May 2009).
9. See http://www.genesis-foundation.org/ (accessed 5 May 2012).
10. See Give to Colombia's website at http://givetocolombia.org/index.php/en/aboutg2c/foundation (accessed 23 December 2012).
11. CIOP interview, New York (March 2006).
12. See Genesis's website at http://www.genesis-foundation.org/our-allies/ and their spring newsletter at 009:http://www.fundaciongenesis.org/cmsen/pdf/09.04.08%20Spring%20newsletter.pdf (both accessed 17 August 2012).

13. Interview with Dominican consul in New York, 3 August 2007 (CONDEX 2009).
14. State policies and laws (e.g., affirmative action and multiculturalism) that were designed to eliminate racial discrimination have ironically conditioned immigrant incorporation "in ethno-racial terms such as 'Hispanics' or 'Asians'" (Joppke 1999: 155–60; Bloemraad 2006: 140).

References

Aysa-Lastra, M. 2008. "Perfil sociodemográfico de residentes en Estados Unidos Año 2000." In *Presencia colombiana en Estados Unidos: Caracterización de la población inmigrante,* ed. Ana María Bidegain, 27-58. Bogotá: Ministerio de Relaciones Exteriores de Colombia/Florida International University—Colombian Studies Institute and Latin American and Caribbean Center, LACC.

———. 2007. "Diaspora Philanthropy: The Colombian Experience." The Philanthropic Initiative and the Global Equity Initiative, Harvard University.

Bloemraad, Irene. 2005. "The Limits of Tocqueville: How Government Facilitates Organisational Capacity in Newcomer Communities." *Journal of Ethnic and Migration Studies* 31, no. 5: 865–87.

———. 2006. *Becoming a Citizen: Incorporating Immigrants and Refugees in the United States and Canada.* Berkeley: University of California Press.

COMPES (Consejo Nacional de Política Económica y Social). 2009. *Política Integral Migratoria.* Document 3603. Departamento Nacional de Planeación, República de Colombia.

CONDEX (Consejo Nacional para las Comunidades Dominicanas en el Exterior). 2009. *Informe.* http://www.condex.gob.do/condex/docs/condex-2010/CONDEX%20-%20Informe%202009.pdf (accessed July 2012).

———. 2008. *Informe.* http://www.condex.gob.do/condex/docs/condex-2010/CONDEX%20-%20Informe%202008.pdf (accessed July 2012).

DANE (Departamento Administrativo Nacional de Estadística-Colombia). 2006. *Censo Nacional 2005*: Bogotá.

El Tiempo. 1993. "Red para capturar científicos." 13 September, p. 3b.

———. 2003. "Habría acceso a un millón de computadores." 29 November, p. 8c.

Escobar, Cristina. 2010. "Exploring Transnational Civil Society: A Comparative Study of Colombian, Dominican and Mexican Immigrant Organizations in the United States." *Journal of Civil Society* 6, no. 3 (December): 205–35.

———. 2007. "Dual Citizenship and Extraterritorial Political Rights in Latin America." *Latin American Research Review* 42, no. 3 (October): 41–73.

Espinal, Rosario, Jana Morgan, and Jonathan Hartlyn. 2010. "Sociedad civil y poder político en República Dominicana." *America Latina Hoy* 56: 37–58.

Faist, Thomas, and Magrit Fauser. 2011. "The Migration-Development Nexus: Towards a Transnational Perspective." In *The Migration-Development Nexus,* ed. Thomas Faist, Margit Fauser, and Peter Kivisto, 1-26. New York: Palgrave Macmillan.

Fauser, Margit. 2011. "How Receiving Cities Contribute to Simultaneous Engagements for Incorporation and Development." In *The Migration-Development*

Nexus, ed. Thomas Faist, Margit Fauser, and Peter Kivisto, 136–58. New York: Palgrave Macmillan.

Grasmuck, Sherri, and Patricia R. Pessar. 1991. *Between Two Islands: Dominican International Migration*. Berkeley: University of California Press.

Goldring, Luin. 1998. "The Power Status in Transnational Social Fields." In *Transnationalism from Below*, ed. Michael Peter Smith and Luis Eduardo Guarnizo, 165–95. Comparative Urban and Community Research 6. New Brunswick, NJ: Transaction Publishers.

Graham, Pamela. 2001. "Political Incorporation and Re-incorporation: Simultaneity in the Dominican Migrant Experience." In *Migration, Transnationalization, and Race in a Changing New York*, ed. Hector. R. Cordero-Guzmán, Robert C. Smith, and Ramón. Grosfoguel, 11–108. Philadelphia: Temple University Press.

Guarnizo, Luis, Arturo Sánchez, and Elizabeth M. Roach. 1999. "Mistrust, Fragmented Solidarity and Transnational Migration." *Ethnic and Racial Studies* 22, no. 2: 367–96.

Hartlyn, Jonathan. 1998. *The Struggle for Democratic Politics in the Dominican Republic*. Chapel Hill: University of North Carolina Press.

Itzigsohn, José. 2004. "Dominicans in Providence: Transnationalism in a Secondary City." In *Dominican Migration: Transnational Perspectives*, ed. Ernesto Sagás and Sintia E. Molina, 74–95. Gainesville: University of Florida Press.

Joppke, Christian. 1999. *Immigration and the Nation-State: The United States, Germany, and Great Britain*. Oxford: Oxford University Press.

Kivisto, Meter. 2011. "Modernization, Development and Migration in a Skeptical Age." In *The Migration-Development Nexus*, ed. Thomas Faist, Margit Fauser and Peter Kivisto, 204–24. New York: Palgrave Macmillan.

MRE (Ministerio de Relaciones Exteriores de Colombia). 2006. "Memorias segundo seminario sobre migración internacional colombiana y la conformación de comunidades trasnacionales." 15–16 June, Bogotá.

———. 2008. "Cinco años de gestión migratoria: Resultados y proyecciones, diciembre 4." Programa Colombia Nos Une.

16. Meyer, Jean B., Jorge Charum, Dora Bernal, Jacques Gaillard, José Granés, John Leon, Alvaro Montenegro, Alvaro Morales, Carlos Murcia, Nora Narvaez-Berthelemot, Luz Stella Parrado and Bernard Schlemmer. 1997. "Turning Brain Drain into Brain Gain: The Colombian Experience of the Diaspora Option." *Science, Technology and Society* 2, no. 2: 285–315.

Newland, Kathleen, Aaron Terrazas, and Roberto Munster. 2010. *Diaspora Philanthropy: Privte Giving and Public Policy*. Washington: USAID-MPI.

Orozco, Manuel. 2009. "Hometown Associations: Transnationalism, Philanthropy and Development." *Brown Journal of World Affairs* 15, no. 2 (Spring–Summer): 1–17.

———. 2006. "Considerations on Diasporas and Development." Paper presented at the Role of Diasporas in Developing the Homeland conference, 16 June, Georgetown University, Washington DC.

———. 2005. "Transnational Engagement, Remittances and Their Relationship to Development in Latin America and the Caribbean." Institute for the Study of International Migration, Georgetown University.

————. 2004. "Distant but Close: Guyanese Transnational Communities and Their Remittances from the United States." Report commissioned by the US Agency for International Development, Washington DC.

————. 2003. "Hometown Associations and Their Present and Future Partnerships: New Development Opportunities?" Report commissioned by the US Agency for International Development, Washington DC.

Pineda, Claudia. 2008. "Condiciones sociales y educación." In *Presencia colombiana en Estados Unidos: Caracterización de la población Inmigrante,* ed. Ana Maria Bidegain, 185–231. Bogotá: Ministerio de Relaciones Exteriores de Colombia—Florida International University (Colombian Studies Institute and Latin American and Caribbean Center, LACC).

Portes, Alejandro, and Luis Eduardo Guarnizo. 1991. "Tropical Capitalists: U.S.-Bound Immigration and Small Enterprise Development in the Dominican Republic." In *Migration, Remittances, and Small Business Development: Mexico and Caribbean Basin Countries,* ed. Sergio Díaz-Briquets and SidneyWeintraub. Boulder, CO: Westview Press.

Portes, Alejandro, and Ruben Rumbaut. 2006. *Immigrant America: A Portrait.* 3rd ed. Berkeley: University of California Press.

Ramakrishnan, S. Kartrick, and Celia Viramontes. 2006. *Civic Inequalities: Immigrant Volunteerism and Community Organizations in California.* San Francisco: Public Policy Institute of California.

Rodríguez, Maria Isabel, and Ramona Hernández. 2004. *Construyendo alianzas estratégicas para el desarrollo: Republica Dominicana—Estado de Nueva York.* Santo Domingo: Fundación Global Democracia y Desarrollo/Dominican Studies Institute CUNY.

Sagás, Ernesto. 2004. "From *Ausentes* to Dual Nationals." In *Dominican Migration: Transnational Perspectives,* ed. Ernesto Sagás and Silvia Molin. Gainesville: University of Florida Press.

US Census Bureau. 2000. "Hispanic or Latino by Type." Census 2000 Summary File 1 (SF 1) 100–Percent Data.

Villar, Rodrigo. 2001. *El tercer sector en Colombia: Evolución, dimensión y tendencias.* Bogotá: Confederación Colombiana de Organizaciones No Gubernamentales.

Chapter 3

Tapping the Indian Diaspora for Indian Development

Rina Agarwala

Owing to their colonial history and their historic integration with global markets, Indians have been migrating across the world for centuries. Today twenty million Indians live outside India (GOI 2000). They span the spectrum of class, profession, and history—ranging from construction workers in the Middle East and taxi drivers in New Jersey to bank managers in Latin America and information technology (IT) entrepreneurs in Silicon Valley. Given the magnitude and diversity of the Indian diaspora, it is surprising how little we know about their activities and their impact on the country of origin.

This chapter, based on the Comparative Immigrant Organizations Project (CIOP), examines how Indian immigrants in the United States have influenced development in India. Development is defined broadly to include policies and practices that aim to improve well-being in the socioeconomic *and* political realms. Surveys have shown that nearly 95 percent of overseas Indians send money to their families or close friends to support education, health, or other personal concerns in the homeland (Sampradaan 2001). For years, India has been the largest recipient of remittances, estimated at $54 billion per year today (World Bank 2009). Nearly 30 percent of these remittances come from the Middle East (where most Indians are blue-collar workers), and 40 percent come from North America (where the majority are professionals and technicians) (Reserve Bank of India 2010). In this chapter, I examine the connections that Indian Americans forge through transnational organizations. Unlike individual remittances, US-

Notes for this chapter begin on page 105.

based organizations founded and led by Indian Americans create formal, sustained linkages with institutions in the home country.

Prior to the mid-1980s, the Indian diaspora's relations with the homeland were weak. Under British rule, Indians abroad were seen as a labor pool designed to benefit mainly the British Empire.[1] In 1947, the newly independent Indian government pushed the diaspora away by using the state's physical boundaries to define the nebulous limits of national identity. Only those residing within the country's borders were deemed "Indian." This message aimed to protect the hundreds of thousands of new migrants who had left present-day Pakistan to enter present-day India and were viewed with suspicion after the partition of independence.

Since the mid-1980s, the Indian government and the diaspora have altered their stance toward one another. In the United States, for example, there has been an expansion in the number of organizations that Indian immigrants have launched to foster linkages with their country of origin. Concurrently, the Indian government has initiated new policies and institutions to strengthen its bonds with the diaspora. In the mid-1980s, it created new bank accounts that allowed nonresident Indians (NRIs) to invest in their home country. In 1999, it launched two new visa status cards for Persons of Indian Origin (PIO) and Overseas Citizens of India (OCI), which facilitated emigrants' ability to travel in and out of India, invest in property, and hold rupee bank accounts.

In 2000, the Indian government commissioned a high-profile committee to write a report on the diaspora. Based on that report, in January 2003 the government inaugurated its first annual conference of overseas Indians, known as Pravasi Bharatiya Divas (PVD) or Overseas Indian Day. The conference date, 9 January, commemorates the day that Mahatma Gandhi (perhaps India's most famous emigrant) returned from South Africa to launch the independence movement. The PVD conference facilitates networking opportunities between emigrants, the Indian government, and Indian organizations; commemorates emigrants who have contributed to the country's development; and communicates new diaspora policies, such as the recent bill that will enable overseas Indians to vote in their country of origin. Finally, in 2005, India became one of the few nations to create a cabinet-level Ministry for Overseas Indian Affairs (MOIA).

Several factors explain India's recent interest in strengthening transnational linkages with its diaspora. First, the government's early investments in state-funded higher education are translating into a greater share of Indian graduates emigrating to take high-paid jobs across the world. In the United States, the growth of the IT sector has expanded the size and status of the Indian American community, and changed its composition to include more temporary migrants. Today, the annual tax income lost from high-skilled emigration from India to the United States is estimated to be 0.5 percent of India's gross national product (GNP) or 2.5 percent of total fiscal revenues (Desai et al. 2009). To make up for this shortfall, the government is recognizing that it must reach out to its large and potentially circular diaspora by encouraging its members to move back or send money to India through remittances or investments. These options have become increasingly salient given the role of overseas Chinese in the expansion of China's economy (see Zhou and Lee, this volume).

Second, tapping the potential of overseas Indians (in the United States and elsewhere) has been facilitated by the recent liberalization and globalization of the Indian economy, which have reduced the institutional barriers and negative stigma earlier attached to partnering with those living outside the country.[2] Finally, India's recent rise in economic and geopolitical terms has provided emigrants with the dignity that many crave, as their income and skill have proved insufficient in ensuring their full assimilation into their host countries.

To examine the nature of the recent growth in transnational linkages between Indian Americans and Indians, this study examines the following questions:

1. What is the scope of transnational organizations among Indian immigrants in the United States? When and why did transnational organizations emerge? Who participates in them?
2. How do transnational organizations affect homeland development? In what areas are they concentrated? What explains this concentration?
3. How do transnational linkages affect power dynamics between the Indian government and the Indian diaspora, and between Indian and US organizations?

My findings suggest Indian Americans' high status and their transnational linkages are interdependent and mutually constitutive. Indian transnational organizations serve as a two-way bridge between diaspora members' home and host countries. In one direction, emigrants use transnational organizations to transfer funds and ideas from the United States to advance socioeconomic and political development in their country. In such exchanges, their elite status shapes the focus of their development efforts and influences their power over government in India. In the opposite direction, Indian Americans use transnational organizations to transfer symbolic power from the homeland to bolster their identities in the United States.

Such efforts help Indian Americans fill voids in their assimilation that their professional status promised but failed to fulfill. Most importantly, they help Indian immigrants attract second-generation interest in their ancestral country. The effects of these transnational linkages have been mixed. Although attempts to affect Indian development through transnational efforts appear dwarfed relative to other development efforts (especially in a country the size of India), a closer look yields several significant impacts at the national and state levels. Attempts to bolster ideational goals among Indian Americans have been successful among first-generation immigrants, but less successful in the second generation (Fernández-Kelly, this volume).

Methodology

I first compiled an inventory of 624 Indian transnational organizations that operate nationally and in the four metropolitan statistical areas (MSAs) where over 55 percent of the Indian American population resides.[3] All organizations in the inventory were established before 2009, have had at least one project in India since 2005, and were founded and are led by a person of Indian origin. These criteria ensure that the inventory reflects sustained transnational efforts motivated by immigrant logics, rather than those of multilateral organizations staffed by Indian Americans. This inventory is the first of its kind for the US-based Indian population. Drawing from the inventory, I conducted sixty-nine semistructured interviews with organization leaders in the United States. The interview sample roughly represented the distribution of organizations by type (Table 3.1). Inter-

Table 3.1. Distribution of Organization Type in Interview Sample and Total Inventory

Organization Type	Number Interviewed	% of Interviewed Organizations	Number in Inventory	% of Inventory Organizations
Arts/cultural	5	7.2	50	8
Development/ health/education	10	14.5	119	19.1
Ethnic/caste/ linguistic/identity	12	17.4	166	26.6
Human rights	3	4.3	17	2.7
Political	2	2.9	16	2.6
Professional/alumni	13	18.8	51	8.2
Religious	8	11.6	178	28.5
Religious combination	16	23.2	27	4.3
Total	69	100	624	100

"Religious combination" refers to organizations that combine religion with another aim, such as "development," "human rights," or "professional/alumni."

views oversampled "religious combination" organizations (because they yield important insights into the transnational politics and identities of Indian immigrants), and professional/alumni organizations (because they represent a primary focus of the Indian government).

I also conducted sixty-three in-person interviews in India with leaders of the partner organizations interviewed in the United States, government officials, and scholars involved in issues concerning overseas Indians.[4] Interviews and site visits were also conducted in India's capital city of Delhi and in the states of Gujarat and Andhra Pradesh. Unlike in the United States, geographic variation among organizations in India is largely due to the linguistic and cultural boundaries of Indian states. In addition, state-level governments differ in their policies toward their expatriates. For these reasons, the growing Indian American community gradually turned away from initial pan-Indian organizations to form state-based organizations. Both states covered in the study are prosperous, have embraced liberalization and globalization, and have pursued their diasporas as a development resource. Politically and socially, however, they differ in ways that have shaped varying forms of their transnational connections.

The Gujarat government has enacted programs to draw investments from the large overseas Gujarati business community and is one of the few states in India to use homeland associations. In 2000, the Gujarati population in the United States was 150,000, about one-third of the Indian immigrant population in the United States (GOI 2000). A large percentage of Gujarati Americans are business owners. Today, 65 percent of budget motels and 40 percent of all motels in the United States are run by a subsect of Gujaratis (known as "Patels") (Assar 2000). Gujarati Americans, therefore, tend to be permanent immigrants who have recently increased their interest in strengthening relations with their home state. From 1995–2014, Gujarat was ruled by Chief Minister Narendra Modi of the Bharatiya Janata Party (BJP), a party that supports Hindu nationalism; in 2014, Modi became the Prime Minister of India. Overseas Gujaratis support Modi and draw enormous pride from the state's recent economic success, Modi's conservative social tendencies, his recent overwhelming victory in the national elections, and his attention to the diaspora.

Unlike Gujarat, the catalyst of global integration in Andhra Pradesh, Chief Minister Chandrababu Naidu of the local state party Telugu Desam Party (TDP), earned praise in the West but faced opposition at home. During his rule from 1995 to 2004, Naidu hosted visits by Tony Blair, Bill Clinton, and Bill Gates; earned a "Naidu Day" by the governor of Illinois; and won numerous awards, including South Asian of the Year by *Time Asia* (Singh 1999; Monbiot 2004). Underlying the West's praise for Naidu were his investments in the IT sector and private IT colleges (Xiang 2002).

In 1995, Naidu created the Hyderabad Information Technology Engineering Consultancy City (or Hitec City), where he provided investors with exemptions from statutory power cuts and labor inspections and permission for three-shift operations. Under Naidu, Microsoft chose the state's capital, Hyderabad, for its first foreign research and development center. Naidu was also the first Indian chief minister to digitize state government activities and maintain a state government Web portal.

Unlike in Gujarat, politics in Andhra Pradesh have not been dominated by elite Hindus or national-level parties. Muslims have long retained a large presence and dominated the police and military services; local ethnic parties have attained electoral success; and ethnic separatist movements and a strong Maoist insurgency have challenged mainstream power. In this context, public-sector unions and the rural poor in Andhra Pradesh opposed Naidu for ignoring their needs.

Andhra Pradesh's expanding IT sector became recognized by global employers as a secure source for IT professionals. Telugus (as natives of the state are named) have thus become the majority within the Indian American software professional community, and they represent 23 percent of Indian IT professionals worldwide (Xiang 2002). Unlike Gujaratis, Telegu Americans are professionals and hold temporary visas. Although the Andhra Pradesh government continues to create software technology parks to draw overseas Indian IT entrepreneurs to invest in local start-ups or return to India to work, it is now less active than the Gujarat government. Moreover, Andhra Pradesh's investments in education and IT, combined with its countermovement history, have made Telegu Americans' transnational activities more diverse than those of Gujaratis.

Indian American Transnational Actors: New and Elite

Today, nearly 1.9 foreign-born Indians live in the United States, making them the third-largest immigrant group in the United States after Mexicans and Chinese.[5] While a large percentage of the foreign-born Indians in the United States arrived after the mid-1960s, over 40 percent arrived after 2000. Such immigrants are thus fairly new, and they occupy a strikingly high socioeconomic status. These characteristics have affected their transnational activities.

In the early 1900s, a small minority of Muslim and Sikh men from the Indian state of Punjab migrated to California to work as agricultural laborers. Due to the US legal restrictions on marriage across races at the time, these migrants married Mexican women, forming a unique community (Leonard 2007). Despite their small numbers and their diverse family makeup, they launched the first Indian transnational organizations in the United States. Rather than dividing along religious differences, they united along their common language and socioeconomic status. In the United States, they created organizations to fight for "South Asian" representation in local US government *and* for Indian independence. Nearly two thousand of them participated in the Ghadar Movement, going to India to fight British colonial rule.

The second wave of Indian migrants to the United States was highly skilled and arrived in the aftermath of the 1965 liberalization of US immigration laws that targeted professionals and students. Indians were uniquely positioned to take advantage of these legal shifts, because they had been trained in engineering colleges that the Indian government launched in the 1950s to create a cadre of technicians to lead the newly independent nation's industrialization efforts. While many graduates remained in India to advance local development, others migrated to the United States for higher-paying jobs once the borders opened. By the 1970s and 1980s, most had sponsored spouses and extended family members to join them. At first, these migrants formed organizations to create familiar communities and help them assimilate, but they became more involved in transnational activities after the 1980s.

Finally, in the 1990s, a third wave of Indians entered the United States as employers tapped Indian graduates to staff the expanding IT sector. This wave set off an exponential growth in the Indian American population. Significant for transnational linkages, many of these newer immigrants hold temporary visas; Indians have consistently represented 35–55 percent of H-1B visa authorizations that enable US employers to temporarily hire skilled, overseas workers (Terrazas and Batog 2010). Due to the likelihood of their return to India, these migrants have been very active in transnational organizations.

In addition to being one of the largest receivers of Indian immigrants, the United States also attracts the most educated. Seventy percent of Indian Americans over the age of twenty-five (including foreign- and US-born) are college graduates, 67 percent are professionals, their median household income is over $90,000, and their poverty rate is as low as 4.6 percent. Nearly 80 percent report being able to speak English "very well" (American Community Survey 2009). It is this group of highly educated immigrants who I found to be most active in transnational organizations. Six percent of Indian Americans work as taxi drivers, factory workers, newsstand workers, and farmers, and two hundred thousand Indians are estimated to be in the United States illegally (GOI 2000; Terrazas and Batog 2010). Such migrants are active in some religious and ethnic organizations, but they are nearly absent from leadership positions in transnational organizations.[6]

Indian Transnational Organizations in the United States

As shown in Table 3.1, religious groups represent the largest category of Indian American transnational organizations, at nearly 30 percent. As shown in Table 3.2, Hindus, Sikhs, and Christians have the largest share of such entities, which is striking given the relatively smaller population of Sikhs and Christians (in the United States and in India). Equally noteworthy is the low share of Indian Muslim organizations in the United States (2.5 percent) given their sizable population in both India and the United States.

Religious organizations are followed in number by those focusing on ethnic identity, development, and professional and alumni interests. Human rights and political organizations are a minority. Particularly striking when compared to other immigrant groups is the near absence of hometown associations reflecting Indians' professional, urban, and elite status. Their transnational organizations range from small, informal groups to large and high-profile groups. Politically, there are a few organizations that identify as leftist; the majority range from center-left to extreme right. This is noteworthy given the large number of leftist social movements in India.

The majority of Indian American transnational organizations are stand-alone entities operating in one location. Approximately one-third are national (in some cases international) with local chapters, and 10 percent serve as umbrella organizations. Approximately 70 percent have less than one thousand members with no paid staff, operating through volunteers.

Table 3.2. Religious Organizations

Kind	Number of Organizations[a]	Share of Religious Organizations (%)[a]	Share of US Population (%)[b]	Share of Indian Population (%)[c]
Buddhist	3	1.5	0	0.8
Christian	61	29.9	4.8	2.3
Hindu	70	34.3	72	80.5
Jain	2	1.0	1.8	0.4
Muslim	5	2.5	10	13.4
Sikh	62	30.4	5.1	1.9
Spiritual	1	0.5		
Total	204	100	100	100

[a] From CIOP inventory. Includes religious combination organizations.
[b] From Kapur (2010).
[c] From Census of India (2001).

Only one-quarter have an annual budget over $1,000,000.[7] While most of them appeal only to ethnic Indians, 25 percent recruit non-Indian members, volunteers, staff, donors, and board members.

Men are more active in transnational organizations than women. Although women participate in ethnic organizations (where membership is family-based), they are nearly absent from leadership positions (see Zhou and Lee, this volume, for comparison with Chinese immigrant organizations). In my sixty-nine interviews, I encountered only two women leaders. Consistent with other immigrant groups, first-generation Indians are more active in transnational activities than their children, although exceptions are found in religious and some development organizations (see Fernández-Kelly, this volume). Of first-generation Indian immigrants, the younger cohort (of largely IT professionals ages twenty-five to forty) is very active and has more trust in organizations than the older cohort (of traditional professionals, ages fifty and over).

Most Indian transnational organizations in the United States have emerged in the last two decades. This is explained by two sets of opportunity structures that affected different groups of immigrants. The first came during the early 1990s, just after the end of the Cold War, when India ended its participation in the nonaligned movement and began to thaw relations with the United States, enacted its version of neoliberal reforms and opened its economy to global markets, and witnessed the rise of Hindu fundamentalism at the social and electoral levels. These changes gave many Indian Americans just the impulse needed to reconnect to their homeland after spending decades being ignored by the Indian government and resented by nonmigrants. The second spike came in the early 2000s, when the 11 September 2001 attacks suddenly made Indian immigrants uncomfortable and their loyalties to the US suspect. Simultaneously, the IT boom brought in an unprecedented number of young, educated, high-earning Indian IT workers to the United States. Such changes challenged Indian Americans' expectations of their ability to assimilate in their host country and forced them to use transnational linkages to retain the dignity and respect that they felt their skills and income commanded.[8]

Indian Transnational Organizations as Bridges of Development

Transnational organizations serve as a bridge through which Indian Americans can influence socioeconomic and political development in India. Their elite status enables them to transfer financial resources, ideas, and practices to the homeland. This ability as well shapes their support and complicates their relationship with Indian partners and government. Although these efforts have been relatively small, compared to development efforts originating in India, many have been significant.

Socioeconomic Development Support from Host to Home

Many transnational organizations tap diaspora wealth to raise funds for existing organizations in India. Indian university alumni organizations, for example, raise money among diaspora members to support their alma maters, using American university practices as a role model. The Indian government has supported these efforts by offering incentives for US-based professors and graduate students to teach in India. Creating "world-class universities" has now become a central component of India's economic growth strategy. Professional associations (including physicians, entrepreneurs, and hoteliers) are increasingly trying to form partnerships with institutions to transfer knowledge from the United States to their home country. The Indian Government has tried to facilitate such business partnerships by supporting software technology parks and research and development centers (Saxenian 2005).

Religious organizations routinely raise funds for religious bodies (ashrams, gurus, or dioceses) or movements in India. Many have examined the Sikh diaspora's efforts to raise funds in the 1980s to support a separatist movement for Khalistan, a Sikh homeland (Shani 2005; Oberoi 1987; Fair 2005; Biswas 2004). The subject reemerged in the 1990s, highlighting the Hindu diaspora's support for Hindu nationalist movements and political parties in India (Levitt 2008; Kurien 2006; Mathew and Prashad 2000; Rajagopal 2000). Unlike other transnational organizations, religious groups have been able to bypass suspicions of nongovernmental organizations (NGOs) and access Indian Americans' wealth in the form of donations. Indian religious organizations in the United States are large and most enjoy substantial budgets. In my interviews, funding was rarely mentioned as a primary challenge.

Many development organizations in the United States began simply to raise money from expatriates to support a parent organization in India. In most cases, the organization is well-known in India and enjoys substantial capacity. However, Indian NGOs have had to seek alternative funding sources as multilateral and bilateral aid to India has declined. The growing mass of "high net worth" Indians in the United States thus have become an important source of alternative funding for Indian NGOs. In these cases, the US organization serves as a "younger sibling" and is rarely the source of new ideas or strategic visions. The diaspora is used for its money, but it does not exert much influence over the direction of development back home.

In addition to raising funds for a particular organization, Indian trans-national organizations are increasingly raising funds to support direct development projects. Some religious organizations, especially among Muslims, Christians, and Sikhs, have participated in development philanthropy and education in India for decades.[9] Leaders of these religions all spoke of how charity is an important and often articulated part of their practice. In the United States, Indian mosques, churches, and gurudwaras (Sikh places of worship) provide a physical channel through which members can share information about community needs and collect contributions. In 2004, remittances from Sikhs totaled $2–3 billion per year (World Bank 2004).

Although in the past Sikh remittances funded large-scale projects such as building hospitals, memorial archways, and schools, they have recently been used to improve basic civic amenities and sanitation. Dusenbery and Tatla (2009) argue that this change is a function of the improved political and economic status of the diaspora combined with the deterioration of state and economic conditions in the Sikhs' home state of Punjab. More recently, Hindu organizations (in India and the United States) have also engaged in direct poverty-alleviation efforts (Anand 2004). This trend was spurred by an attempt to deflect the negative attention Hindu organizations were receiving for allegedly raising money to support violence against religious minorities in India. Many Hindu organizations now self-classify as "development" organizations. Others call themselves "Indian." Since the controversies, many Hindu organizations have begun to highlight their involvement in community service in India and the United States.

Secular organizations have also been created in the United States to foster development in India. Unlike organizations that raise funds for a parent group in India, these exert more power over their Indian partners. For example, the diaspora has used these organizations to export American ideals of formalized philanthropy, volunteerism, and tax breaks for charitable giving. While surveys of philanthropy in India have shown that traditional forms of individual giving to family members, religious institutions, or beggars is extremely high, institutionalized forms of giving are low (Agarwal 2010).

Underlying these ideals is a strong distrust of government and a privileging of private charity. In my interviews, some NGO leaders in India said that American notions of formalized philanthropy are "un-Indian" and will not spread to the population.[10] Others felt they were necessary, because they could ensure that people give "more wisely" rather than on an ad hoc basis.[11] A number of Indian NGOs are currently working with government officials to decrease the bureaucratic hurdles involved in international philanthropy and to improve the tax incentive to give from abroad.

Unlike religious organizations, almost all the development organizations said they spend most of their time fund-raising through efforts that include online campaigns and galas featuring popular actors and musicians from India. Less common were foundation grants and corporate funding. Several organizations expressed interest in tapping the corporate sphere, especially since Indians are so well represented in that sector. Companies are said to be eager to please their large Indian employee base and display their commitment to India as they expand their businesses into that country's market. In several cases, organizations targeted companies that were led by Indians, the American India Foundation being the most famous, with Citibank and McKinsey as active partners and Bill Clinton as a founding supporter. In addition to tapping American companies, many organizations are also tapping Indian companies moving to the United States.

Indian Americans tend to donate to a limited set of politically noncontroversial causes. Donors are quick to give to natural disaster relief (Gujarat earthquake, tsunami in Tamil Nadu, floods in Punjab), but sustained development efforts are often underfunded. Many groups focus on children. By far the most popular cause for Indian Americans is education in India. Most Indian immigrants in the United States explain their own "success" as a result of education. For first-generation immigrants, their education was mostly completed in their country of origin, and they remain loyal to the teachers and adults who supported them. They see education as the path out of poverty for India's masses and as a politically noncontroversial subject. The focus on education has not only inspired many transnational development organizations in the United States, but has also forced several organizations that address broad-based development to rebrand themselves as "education-oriented."

Transnational efforts to promote socioeconomic development in India have met with mixed success. At the local level, religious philanthropy has assisted development efforts, but it has been criticized for fostering inequality at the macro level. Diaspora donations to build private schools offering English instruction and following the Central Board of Secondary Education (CBSE) curriculum are said to have widened the quality gap between public and private schools and undermined teachers' morale in public schools. Autar Dhesi (2009: 223) critiques the diaspora's role in rural development, arguing that interventions often ignore cultural sensitivities and give "further impetus to caste-based political and social divides by institutionalizing communalism."

Some leaders of development organizations blame donors' distrust of NGOs for the inefficiencies and inequalities stemming from their projects. For example, donors often want all of their money to go to the cause and none to overhead. As a result, many transnational organizations must rely on an enormous, revolving volunteer base and a small full-time staff. Second, donors often want to donate to their own hometown, where they have relatives and friends who can monitor the use of the money and recognize their donation. That has exacerbated inequalities and diverted the work of development organizations.[12]

Still others blame the Indian government for not being as successful as the Chinese in facilitating diaspora investments in the homeland (Saxenian 2005; Zhu 2007). Although India ranks first in terms of remittance-receiving countries, it ranks low in terms of attracting foreign direct investment from overseas Indians (at less than 1 percent).[13] This is surprising given the number of programs the Indian government has recently launched to lure diaspora investments. Some officials blame structural constraints, arguing investments from overseas Indians will remain low relative to overseas Chinese because of the disproportionate share of professionals (rather than businesspeople) in the Indian American diaspora. Others express frustration with the power dynamic involved in fomenting such links. The secretary of the Ministry for Overseas Indian Affairs (MOIA), Dr. Didar Singh, was emotional about this topic:

> Let me make one thing clear. We are not standing with begging bowls asking for diaspora investments. Absolutely not! This is the biggest misconception among the diaspora—that we want their money. We are just as happy if they want to invest their money elsewhere. People are investing in India because it's a good place to invest. We will showcase our growth and opportunities and we will facilitate and welcome any investments that come in. But we won't differentiate between NRI [nonresident Indian] investment and others. We believe we have a tremendous economy.[14]

There is irony in this statement from the secretary of the ministry whose express purpose is to differentiate between NRIs and other investors.

Tensions form when Indian diaspora donors use their resources to recommend changes to Indian institutions. In 1999, for example, wealthy Indian Institutes of Technology (IIT) alumni in the United States responded to an Indian government request by raising millions of dollars for Indian universities. The issue turned controversial when the alumni associations suggested that the IITs be restructured so as to resemble American universities, with differentiated pay and a broader curriculum. Indian politicians and scientists perceived this as an attempt to dictate the activities of the state-sponsored IITs (Lessinger 2003). Government officials also felt immigrant professionals did not give the Indian government enough credit for their success. As Mr. Gurucharan, CEO of the Indian Council of Overseas Employment, explained, "It really is the Nehruvian legacy that laid the foundation for the global IT revolution."[15] The secretary of the MOIA, Dr. Didar Singh, concurred: "We are very proud of our diaspora. We celebrate their success and recognize them at our annual conference. *But* we believe this is the result of their own efforts *combined* with the global brand that is India. As India's economy began to rise and our reputation grew and our importance increased, so the Indians abroad got noticed."[16]

Political Development Support from Host to Home

In addition to raising funds for organizations back home and for economic development projects, Indian transnational organizations also transfer ideas and practices from the United States to support political movements in India. Some religious organizations, for example, advocate secularism and religious equality—principles that are considered foundational to India's constitution but are viewed (especially by members of minority religious groups) as under threat today.[17] Christian organizations in the United States, for example, are involved in raising awareness on anti-Christian violence in India. "When a church in India is burned by Hindutva [Hindu nationalists], we tell the State Department. We want Hindutva to know that these actions will make India poorer," explained Nehemiah Johnson, general secretary of National Association of Asian Indian Christians of the USA.[18] Christian immigrants use their status in the United States and their connections to a global superpower to influence events in their home country.

Others use their own status to directly lobby the Ministry of Education and the prime minister in India. Still others support movements to protect members of religious minorities in the United States and India. Despite the wide variety of Sikh organizations in the United States, for example, the community has worked hard to create a common identity and thus have a stronger voice. The World Sikh Council formed in 1995 in the United States aimed at creating a federation of gurudwaras and Sikh organizations to raise awareness of their culture in America and to fight the dilution of their religion in India.

Muslim organizations also advocate secularism in India, but they do so by raising awareness of the effects of poverty on Muslims.[19] Many Indian Muslim organizations began in the 1980s, but "[t]he massacre in Gujarat pushed people to become more active. It really disturbed us," explained Shaheen Khateeb, founding member and ex–general secretary of the Indian American Muslim Coalition.[20] To this end, they have worked with

Muslim counterparts in India to reframe the anti-Muslim rhetoric from identity and religion to class. Of all transnational Indian organizations, Indian Muslims are unique in their focus on the intersection of culture with class. Like Christians, they use their elite status in the United States to engage in strong advocacy work with the Indian government. They also raise substantial funds for education scholarships for poor Muslims.

Since the 1980s, Indian ethnic and identity organizations have increasingly engaged in bridging functions to support the Indian government's efforts to expand the country's international influence. They do this by offering to "spread Indian culture." As the secretary of the MOIA, Dr. Didar Singh, explained, "The global Indian is a tool of 'soft power.' When the diaspora brings Bollywood and Indian fashion, music, culture, food, etc., to their neighbors, we are converting people to see India."[21] Recently, the Indian government created its first Indian cultural center in the United States as part of the Indian Council for Cultural Relations.

In addition to fostering social and cultural links, identity organizations strengthen India's international influence by shaping its foreign policy agreements with the United States. "We would like to work more with the US and Canada. If the diaspora assists us in making bridges, then India benefits," said the MOIA secretary, Dr. Singh.[22] These efforts began during the Afghanistan war of the 1980s, when India-US tensions heightened as the United States increased support for Pakistan and India turned to the Soviet Union for help. In 1987, relations improved when then Prime Minister Rajiv Gandhi announced a pro-West, pro-business approach that appealed to the US government and to Indian Americans. During his first visit to North America, Rajiv Gandhi explicitly reached out to the Indian diaspora as a bridge to thaw the icy US-India relations that were a vestige of the Cold War.[23] He hosted the first reception for members of the Indian diaspora in the United States, to which the leaders of all transnational organizations were invited. He also hosted the first Indian cultural festivals in Washington DC and Paris.

Since then, Indian identity organizations have encouraged members to pressure their congressmen on US-India foreign policy issues and to bring them to receptions at the Indian embassy. The largest overseas group, Global Organization for People of Indian Origin (GOPIO), was instrumental in shaping the recent nuclear deal between India and the United States. They led countless town hall meetings, spearheaded letter-writing campaigns to local congressmen, and advocated in front of the White House. In return for their assistance in affecting foreign policy and spreading Indian culture, identity organizations have advocated for legislative changes in India to facilitate travel, business, and capital transfers through reduced fees, special credit cards, and bank accounts. These efforts have been very successful.

State-Level Development from Host to Home

Interestingly, some states in India have initiated their own transnational linkages to sub-sections of the Indian diaspora; some of these efforts have been especially visible and effective. Public officials in India have only recently begun to tap transnational organizations to benefit their states. Such gestures have been warmly welcomed by Indian Americans.

This is best exemplified by the previous Chief Minister of Gujarat and now Prime Minister of India, Narenda Modi. Although Modi was famously denied an entry visa to the United States, he intimately connected with the Gujarati diaspora by shifting the focus from eliciting investments to fomenting cultural ties and social contributions. As Gujarat Chief Minister, he sent DVDs of Gujarati cultural programs and a personalized letter to Gujarati organizations on their anniversaries. To encourage transnational philanthropy from overseas Gujaratis, he published a book entitled *Vatan ni Sewa* that showcased projects funded by nonresident Gujaratis (NRGs). He has organized annual conferences that are replete with symbolism and fanfare. After the annual overseas Indians conference in Delhi, for example, the government of Gujarat hosts a smaller gathering for Gujarati diaspora members. "Gujaratis don't feel too connected to Delhi. So it is a brilliant move by Modi to take advantage of the Gujaratis that are in town for the annual conference," explained Ravi Saxena, then acting chief secretary of the NRG Division.[24]

Every year, the Gujarati government also holds a "Vibrant Gujarat" meeting that targets global investors. In 2011, Modi built a massive convention center, called the Mahatma Mandir (named after Gujarat-born Mahatma Gandhi), to serve as a space to negotiate world peace. Its design, where an ornate garden will connect the Mandir to the state parliament, was inspired by the National Mall in Washington DC. Just in time for the 2011 event, Modi asked NRGs to bring with them soil and water from their host countries and rivers to pour into the foundation of the Mandir. In 2010, Modi orchestrated worldwide celebrations for Gujarat's fiftieth anniversary to help the government connect to NRGs. Although the NRG Division and Foundation began before Modi, he expanded their budgets, increased their activities, and cemented relations with Gujarati organizations abroad.[25] As Manikant Patel of the New York Gujarati Samaj explained: "*Now* we are very much connected. Modi has done so much for Gujarat, and our members are very excited about him. He put Gujarat on the world map, and we are so proud to be Gujarati! I have constant contact with Modi by email and phone."[26]

Gujaratis are also among the few Indian Americans who organize hometown associations. Because many Gujaratis come from a farmer caste and grew up in rural areas, they provide contributions to their home villages. I visited several villages in Gujarat that rely almost entirely on diaspora contributions. The villages have extremely well organized and professional leaders and village bodies to attract contributions, manage them, and spend them. With overseas monies, these villages have built hospitals, schools, cardiac research centers, heart surgery facilities (that host international patients), yoga retreat centers, water filtration facilities, and biogas production plants. Most donations are made by individuals. Some, however, are organized through hometown associations. As Mr. Bhanji Khadria, president of the Kadwa Patel Samaj of North America explained:

> At first, I was ... opposed to creating a caste-based organization. I became a member of my college alumni association instead. But I found that caste loyalties [are] what moved people to give. It is difficult to get money from city people who are schooled in an English milieu. I find the lower-class people from rural areas are more giving. So that is what we did. The money raised is not only used for one caste, but we used the shared caste background to motivate people to give.[27]

Recently, Telegu American organizations (from the Indian state of Andhra Pradesh) have also become more active in transnational activities as the Telegu community in the United States has grown. One of the largest Telegu organizations, American Telegu Association (ATA), convinced former Maryland governor Martin O'Malley to accept Andhra Pradesh as a sister state with which to conduct business. Telegu American organizations also hold conferences in India to share knowledge on business, agriculture, IT, and pharmaceuticals. They hold seminars to increase awareness of AIDS and inform parents in India about US universities to which they can send their children. Interestingly, in addition to promoting Telegu culture in the United States (by flying Telegu artists from India), these organizations also promote and preserve their culture *in India*. Every year, they go to that country to support arts and rituals that are no longer commonly practiced. "What we saw as children, we don't see any more in India. So we promote it," explained Telegu Association of North America (TANA) President Jayaram Komati. In other words, Indian emigrants use transnational organizations to sustain the India that they knew when they left.

As the Telegu American community has expanded, the ethnic and cultural divisions present in their home state have been reproduced. The Telangana NRI Association (TeNA), for example, formed in 2007 to resist the perceived cultural domination of the castes of Kammas and Reddys in the largest Telegu American organizations (ATA and TANA). They created a forum where the minority of Telangana immigrants could showcase their unique heritage. According to Venkat Maroju of TeNA, "Although we speak Telegu and we are all of the same economic class, we felt the mainstream Telegu organizations in the US did not represent Telangana culture and food adequately."[28] Transnational groups also supported the Telangana separatist movement in India by helping them articulate a unique identity. For these efforts, Telangana immigrants use websites to spread poetry, fiction, and other written art forms.

Although the government of Andhra Pradesh has been promoting IT development, education, and return migration, it has not been as overt as the Gujarat government in fomenting relations with Telegu organizations in the United States. "These groups have lived in the US for a long time, so they do not send as many remittances or make as much investment as the software engineers or the Gulf workers—who are all on temporary work visas," explained N. V. Ramana Reddy, special secretary to government for political and nonresident Indian (NRI) affairs.[29] Despite their skepticism toward the earlier waves of Telegu emigrants, however, relations appear to be changing, as recent emigrants have more diverse social backgrounds and many of them return to India.

I met with several government officials who had worked with Telegu American organizations and had traveled to the United States to attend their meetings. Officials repeatedly reminded me of the diaspora's interest in Indian real estate. "I would say the entire rise in real estate prices in Hyderabad can be attributed to NRI speculation and investment," said Reddy.[30] Today, the state-level Department of Industries and Commerce provides NRIs with special incentives to invest. Investments beyond real estate, however, have been limited. As Secretary of Industries and Commerce, T.S. Appa Rao, explained, "Telegus in the US are mainly professionals. They are not entrepreneurs, like the Gujaratis."[31]

Indian Transnational Organizations as Bridges for Significance and Identity

In addition to supporting development in India, transnational organizations serve as a bridge to promote the identities of Indians in the United States through the transfer of symbols. For this purpose, India's economic expansion and global presence empowers Indian Americans in ways that their elite status in the United States promised but failed to do. Transnational attempts to bolster the identities of first-generation immigrants have been relatively successful; similar efforts have faced mixed success with the second generation.

Leaders of ethnic and religious organizations stated that transnational linkages were necessary to "preserve their identities," thereby portraying themselves as minorities under threat. Although Hindus are the majority religion in India, they see themselves under attack by the global religions of Islam and Christianity. Sikhs present themselves as threatened in the United States (due to mistaken identity as Muslims) and in India (due to the historically tense relations with the government). Christians think of themselves as under attack in India due to the rise of Hindu fundamentalists. Finally, Muslims (more tentatively and subtly) see themselves as threatened by the war on terror in India and the United States.

Transnational organizations help Indian immigrants boost their legitimacy through ties to the homeland, thus helping to preserve their identities. Scholars have shown how Indian Muslim migrants in the 1960s, who were often connected to the royal family of Hyderabad, tried to maintain their status at home while simultaneously adapting to their new environments through ethnic organizations such as the Hyderabad Foundation (Leonard 2002; Moore 1995). Support for the Sikh separatist movement in India can be partly attributed to the insecurities immigrant Sikhs were feeling in response to the expanding Hindu American community. Organizations such as the Khalistan Council, Babar Khalsa International, and the Khalistan Commando Force emerged during the 1980s to signal support for an independent Khalistan and to enable Sikh diaspora leaders to claim legitimacy and enhance their standing in the US-based community (Biswas 2004).

By the 1970s, many Indian religious organizations had purchased physical structures (a temple, gurudwara, or church) where religious rituals could be formally and publicly practiced. Most of these institutions retain close ties to a parent body back in India. As detailed earlier, they raise substantial funds and other resources to support the parent body back home. In return, they receive symbolic support from the parent organization, which legitimizes their existence in the United States. They also receive assistance from religious leaders who travel to the United States to train local priests. Today these structures serve as "safe" spaces where immigrants can fight invisibility in the United States through community gatherings, education seminars, and public religious practice.

During the 1980s, Indian ethnic organizations used their transnational ties to boost their significance in the United States. Organizations such as GOPIO, National Federation of Indian-American Associations (NFIA), and AIA helped fight discrimination by securing representation in community and political affairs. As Munish Gupta, president of the NFIA

India Council, said, "Color brought these early Indians together. Color matters in the US. ... These people had to struggle for their existence, and they wanted something better for their children. Community centers were created, but they had to be backed by more powerful associations. That is why we started."[32] These large organizations create newsletters on diaspora affairs, organize an annual India Day parade in New York to boost Indian American visibility and promote Indian businesses, and hold workshops on issues concerning the Indian diaspora.

Even alumni organizations have increasingly used their transnational links to bolster Indians' recognition in the United States. In addition to raising funds for their alma maters and offering social and professional networks for their members, these organizations showcase the contributions that Indians have made to the American economy. They fight resentment based on claims such as "American jobs are being outsourced to India" and "Cheap Indian software engineers are taking American jobs." One organization, PAN-IIT, made a list of eight hundred IIT graduates who have significantly contributed to the American economy and presented it to the US Congress. The list included founders, inventors, and patent holders for flat screens, cell phone towers, LASIK surgery, Sun Microsystems, fiber optics, and more.

Perhaps the most important power Indian organizations in the United States achieve through their transnational linkages is attracting the second generation. A majority of leaders said this is the reason they joined an organization, and nearly all said attracting the second generation was their most important future goal. My findings suggest that organizations that retained active linkages with the homeland were more successful in this goal than others.

Hindu and Sikh religious organizations have been the most successful in drawing second-generation Indian Americans. Part of this success is due to their acceptance of the second generation's loyalties to the United States. Religion is presented as something that can span geographic identities and encompass multiple locations. Conveniently, although immigrants are encouraged to embrace their host country identity, they are also encouraged to recognize India as the birthplace of their religion.[33] In addition to conducting rituals and ceremonies, religious transnational organizations educate second-generation youths with the help of leaders from the home country. Hindu organizations, for example, hold weekly *bal vihar* sessions (religious classes) and organize Hindu heritage camps in the summer, where second-generation Indian youths learn yoga, prayers, Hindu history, and Hindu texts. "We want to give them a feeling of who they are and where they come from, so when they go to college they can speak with a degree of confidence [to non-Hindus]," explained Abhaya Asthana, general secretary of Vishva Hindu Parishad (VHP).[34] "We try to give young people clear tips on how they can practice their own religion in their dorm or on a class trip, but also how to explain it to their peers and answer derogatory questions," asserted the director of media relations at BAPS Swaminarayan Sanstha, the New York branch of one of the largest Hindu organizations in the world.[35] The international chapters of BAPS are closely overseen by the head organization, based in Gujarat.

Many development organizations found an increased interest among second-generation Indians to "do some good." Some claimed 50 percent of their volunteer base was from the second generation. Others said they often receive requests to volunteer for their projects in India. Leaders admitted, however, that while they were proud of their ability to attract young people's interest, they found it difficult to incorporate such interests into sustained organizational activity. Ironically, many claimed that parents sometimes held their children back from traveling to India due to concerns over safety and health.

The power that active transnational links with India have in attracting second-generation Indian Americans can also be seen in the relative failure of ethnic organizations to achieve the same goal. Leaders of almost every ethnic organization said their main purpose was to ensure that the young do not lose their language, identity, and rituals. These organizations host holiday celebrations and social gatherings; provide health training; offer financial assistance and education sessions; assist in the assimilation of newly arrived senior citizens who lack English-language skills; and serve as a ready marriage market for Indian immigrants. Despite their efforts, organizations repeatedly decried the apathy that second-generation youths showed for their activities. This failure may, in part, be attributed to the weak transnational linkages ethnic organizations have retained with India.

Conclusion

Indian transnational organizations represent an iconic case illustrating the way immigrants are responding to globalization and economic liberalization in the new millennium. Although migration from India to the United States began at the beginning of the twentieth century, it accelerated after 1965 after the passage of legislation that provided incentives for technical and professional workers to move to the United States. The technological revolution of the subsequent decades further expanded the demand for highly skilled workers and contributed to the growth of the Indian population in America.

While the *causes* of Indian migration to the United States are symptomatic of economic and political changes operating at the international level, its *effects* are still under review and may portend typical forms of adaptation among professional immigrants and their children. In this chapter, I have shown that transnational organizations formed by Indians have aimed at creating stable linkages between the adopted country and the land left behind. Professional and alumni organizations have sought to establish social standing and a vindicated identity in America, while at the same time seeking social and economic advantages in India. Either through direct investment and remittances or by tapping social and political connections in the country of birth, Indian Americans in transnational organizations have built new physical and symbolic terrains that allow them to maintain a presence at both ends of the geopolitical spectrum. By focusing on economic development in India, such organized efforts help to bolster a strong presence in India while at the same time contributing to assimilation in the United States.

Equally important, from a theoretical point of view, are the efforts of transnational organizations with respect to second-generation Indians. Although Indian youngsters tend to show limited interest in the transnational practices of their parents, there is a significant exception: their involvement in organizations that focus on religion. In that sense, religion emerges as a new marker of identity enabling the children of Indian immigrants to retain a connection with their ancestral past while at the same time affirming a distinct identity in the United States. The results in terms of effectiveness in altering economic and political development in India have been decidedly mixed.

Rina Agarwala is an assistant professor of sociology at Johns Hopkins University. Her primary research interests are labor, migration, and international development. Agarwala is the author of *Informal Labor, Formal Politics and Dignifying Discontent in India* (Cambridge University Press, 2013) and the coeditor of *Whatever Happened to Class? Reflections from South Asia* (Routledge Press, 2008). Agarwala has also worked on international development and gender issues at the United Nations Development Program (UNDP) in China, the Self-Employed Women's Association (SEWA) in India, and Women's World Banking (WWB) in New York.

Notes

I wish to thank Anne-Marie Livingstone, Alex Rakow, and Smriti Upadhyay for their invaluable research assistance on this project.

1. This resulted in millions of Indians migrating to the Caribbean, Latin America, and the Pacific Islands to serve as indentured servants, primarily in agriculture. Subsequently, Indian merchants also migrated to these areas.

2. India's efforts to liberalize its economy and open its doors to other economies began in the mid-1980s and were institutionalized in 1991.

3. These are New York City (and northern New Jersey, Long Island, and parts of Connecticut and Pennsylvania); Washington DC and Baltimore (and parts of Virginia, West Virginia, and Maryland); Chicago (and Gary and Kenosha); and San Francisco (and Oakland and San Jose). Other significant MSAs of Indians not included in the study include Los Angeles, Philadelphia, and Houston. This information was drawn from my analysis of the US Census and the Integrated Public Use Microdata Series (IPUMS-USA).

4. Government officials were from the Ministry of Overseas Indian Affairs, the Ministry of External Affairs, the Ministry of Home Affairs, and the Ministry of Minority Affairs in Delhi; the Department of Industries and Commerce, the Overseas Manpower Company of the Department of Employment and Training, and the Special Secretary of Non-Resident Indian Affairs in Andhra Pradesh; and the Non-Resident Indian Division of the Government of Gujarat, the Gujarat State Non-Resident Gujarati (NRG) Foundation, and the Gujarat Chamber of Commerce and Industry in Gujarat.

5. Nearly seven hundred thousand second-generation Indians live in the United States.

6. This finding may be attributed to an attempt to present a particular image among Indian Americans. The set of questions in our survey that inquire about education level, English proficiency, and occupation were extremely sensitive.

7. Note many organizations do not have members per se. In those cases I have used the number of volunteers or the donor base as an approximation of "membership."

8. There was also a smaller but significant jump in the mid-1980s, just after the anti-Sikh riots in India and the arrival of a new prime minister, Rajiv Gandhi, who was pro-West and pro-business.

9. See, e.g., Dhesi (2010); Dusenbery and Tatla (2009); Gayer (2002); Helweg (1983); Kumar (2003); Singh and Singh (2007); Taylor, Singh, and Booth (2007); Thandi (2000, 1994); Voigt-Graf (2004); Walton-Roberts (2005, 2004a, 2004b).

10. Interview with Sanjay Agarwal, principal and founder of AccountAid, 18 January 2011.

11. Interview with Dr. Pradeepta Kumar Nayak, executive director of Sampradaan, 13 January 2011.

12. See, e.g., Lessinger (1992) and Taylor, Singh, and Booth (2007).

13. While remittances can increase consumption levels, counter local business cycles, and provide direct assistance to poor families, a standard economic approach for developing countries that has not yet reached full production capacity is to increase investments.

14. Interview, 19 January 2011.

15. Interview, 25 January 2011. Here, Gurucharan is referring to Nehru's commitment to training Indian youth to participate in India's heavy industrialization.

16. Interview, 19 January 2011.
17. For a more detailed discussion of this trend, see Agarwala Rina. Forthcoming. "Divine Development: Transnational Indian Religious Organizations in the U.S. and India." *International Migration Review.*
18. Interview, 29 April 2011.
19. I found few Indian Christian organizations in the United States supporting a growing movement among Christians in India to include Dalit (or low-caste) Christians in India's reservation quotas (or affirmative action efforts). Many Dalits have been converting to Christianity since the 1920s under the promise that Christianity would offer them a casteless faith. Early Christian leaders fought to exclude Dalit Christians from the reservation quotas provided in the Indian constitution. Despite the immense focus on this issue among Christians in India, the Indian government has not been responsive. In 2006, the Indian government launched a new Ministry of Minority Affairs. It has a small budget and primarily focuses on Muslims. As B. P. Sharma, joint secretary in the ministry, said, "Christians are absolutely fine; they are above the national average on most indicators!" Interview, 26 May 2011.
20. Interview, 27 April 2011.
21. Interview, 19 January 2011. Since 2005, the MOIA has initiated several programs to foster links with Indian identity groups throughout the world. They include a program to host Indian diaspora youths in India, assistance to trace diaspora roots in India, a scholarship program for diaspora youths to study in India, and a welfare fund to assist diaspora members in emergencies.
22. Interview, 19 January 2011.
23. Although then prime minister Indira Gandhi visited the United States in 1983 to improve relations with the US government and Indian Americans, it was not as successful. At that time, many of the Indian identity organizations were formally recognized by the government of India.
24. Interview, 12 March 2011.
25. Additional activities of the Gujarat's NRG Division and Foundation include: working with the University Grants Commission of India to create a Diaspora Research Center in Northern Gujarat University; translating the government of India's guidelines on marrying a nonresident Indian from English to Gujarati and distributing twenty thousand copies to women's organizations; maintaining an updated NRG website of global events; and maintaining a database of seventy thousand NRGs and administering an NRG identity card.
26. Interview, 19 April 2011 (emphasis in original).
27. Interview, 22 April 2011.
28. Interview, 4 May 2011.
29. Interview, 23 May 2011.
30. Ibid.
31. Interview, 14 May 2011.
32. Ibid.
33. Religion is also presented as something that can span class boundaries. Although the leadership and the majority of members of religious organizations were elites, religious organizations showed the largest participation of the minority of working-class Indians.

34. Interview, 7 April 2011.
35. Interview, 29 May 2011; interviewee requested to remain anonymous.

References

Agarwal, Sanjay. 2010. *Daan and Other Giving Traditions in India: The Forgotten Pot of Gold*. New Delhi: AccountAid India.
American Community Survey. 2009. United States Census Bureau. Washington. D.C.
Anand, Priya. 2004. "Hindu Diaspora and Religious Philanthropy in the United States." International Fellowship Program with Center on Philanthropy and Civil Society, New York.
Assar, Nandini Narain. 2000. *Gender Hierarchy among Gujarati Immigrants: Linking Immigration Rules and Ethnic Norms*. Blacksburg: Virginia Polytechnic Institute and State University.
Biswas, Bidisha. 2004. "Nationalism by Proxy: A Comparison of Social Movements among Diaspora Sikhs and Hindus." *Nationalism & Ethnic Politics* 10, no. 2: 269–95.
Desai, Mihir, Devesh Kapur, John McHale, and Keith Rogers. 2009. "The Fiscal Impact of High-Skilled Emigration: Flows of Indians to the US." *Journal of Development Economics* 88: 32–44.
Dhesi, Autar S. 2009. "Diaspora Intervention in Rural Development: Boon or Bane?" In *Sikh Diaspora Philanthropy in Punjab: Global Giving for Local Good*, ed. Verne A. Dusenbery and Darsham S. Tatla. New Delhi: Oxford University Press. 219–35.
———. 2010. "Diaspora, Social Entrepreneurs and Community Development. *International Journal of Social Economics,* 37 (9): 703–16.
Dusenbery, Verne A., and Darsham Singh. Tatla. 2009. "NRIs Are the New VIPs." In *Sikh Diaspora Philanthropy in Punjab: Global Giving for Local Good*, ed. Verne A. Dusenbery and Darsham S. Tatla. New Delhi: Oxford University Press. 3–29.
———. (ed). 2009. *Sikh Diaspora Philanthropy in Punjab: Global Giving for Local Good*. New Delhi: Oxford University Press.
Fair, C. Christine. 2005. "Diaspora Involvement in Insurgencies: Insights from the Khalistan and Tamil Eelam Movements." *Nationalism & Ethnic Politics* 11(1): 125–56.
Gayer, Laurent. 2002. "The Globalization of Identity Politics: The Sikh Experience." *International Journal of Punjab Studies* (7): 223–62.
GOI (Government of India), Ministry of External Affairs. 2000. *Report of the High Level Committee on the Indian Diaspora*. New Delhi: Non Resident Indians & Persons of Indian Origin Division.
———. 2001. Census of India. New Delhi: Census Bureau
Helweg, Arthur W. 1983. "Emigrant Remittances: Their Nature and Impact on a Punjabi Village." *New Community* (10): 435–43.

Kapur, Devesh. 2010. *Diaspora, Development, Democracy.* Princeton, NJ: Princeton University Press.

Kumar, Gopa R. 2003. *Indian Diaspora and Giving Patterns of Indian Americans in the USA.* New Delhi, India: Charities Aid Foundation India.

Kurien, Prema. 2006. "Multiculturalism and 'American' Religion: The Case of Hindu Indian Americans." *Social Forces* 85(2): 723–41.

Leonard, Karen. 2002. "South Asian Leadership of American Muslims." In *Muslims in the West: From Sojourners to Citizens,* ed. Yvonne Y. Haddad. New York: Oxford University Press. 233–49.

———. 2007. "Transnationalism, Diaspora, Translation: Punjabis and Hyderabadis Abroad." *Sikh Formations* 3(1): 51–66.

Lessinger, Johanna. 1992. "Investing or Going Home? A Transnational Strategy among Indian Immigrants in the United States." *Annals of the New York Academy of Sciences* 645: 53–80.

———. 2003. "Indian Immigrants in the United States: The Emergence of a Transnational Population." In *Culture and Economy in the Indian Diaspora,* ed. Bhikhu Parekh, Gurharpal Singh, and Steven Vertovec, London: Routledge. 165–82.

Levitt, Peggy. 2008. "Religion as a Path to Civic Engagement." *Ethnic and Racial Studies* 31(4): 766–91.

Mathew, Biju, and Vijay Prashad. 2000. "The Protean Forms of Yankee Hindutva." *Ethnic and Racial Studies* 23(3): 516–34.

Monbiot, George. 2004. "This Is What We Paid For." *Outlook India,* 20 May.

Moore, Kathleen M. 1995. *Al-Mughtarib`un: American Law and the Transformation of Muslim Life in the United States.* Albany: SUNY University Press.

Oberoi, Harjot S. 1987. "From Punjab to 'Khalistan': Territoriality and Metacommentary." *Pacific Affairs* 60(1): 26–42.

Rajagopal, Arvind. 2000. "Hindu Nationalism in the US: Changing Configurations of Political Practice." *Ethnic and Racial Studies* 23(3): 467–96.

Reserve Bank of India. 2010. "Remittances from Overseas Indians: Modes of Transfer, Transaction Cost, and Time Taken." *RBI Monthly Bulletin.*

Sampradaan. 2001. *Investing in Ourselves: Giving and Fund Raising in India.* New Delhi: Sampradaan Indian Centre for Philanthropy.

Saxenian, AnnaLee. 2005. "From Brain Drain to Brain Circulation: Transnational Communities and Regional Upgrading in India and China." *Studies in Comparative International Development* 40(2): 35–61.

Shani, Giorgio. 2005. "Beyond Khalistan? Sikh Diasporic Identity and Critical International Theory." *Sikh Formations: Religion, Culture, Theory* 1(1): 57–74.

Singh, Gurmail and Sawarm Singh. 2007. "Diaspora Philanthropy in Action: An Evaluation of Modernization in Punjab Villages." *Journal of Punjab Studies* 14(2): 225–48.

Singh, Manmohan. 1999. "South Asian of the Year: Chandrababu Naidu." *TIME Asia,* 31 December. http://articles.cnn.com/1999-12-30/world/9912_30_sd_1_andhra-pradesh-reforms-indias?_s=PM:ASIANOW. Accessed 2013.

Taylor, Steve, Manjit Singh, and Deborah Booth. 2007. "Migration, Development and Inequality: Eastern Punjabi Transnationalism." *Global Networks* 7(3): 328–47.

Terrazas, Aaron, and Cristina Batog. 2010. "Indian Immigrants in the United States." Migration Policy Institute.

Thandi, Shinder. 1994. "Strengthening Capitalist Agriculture: The Impact of Overseas Remittances in Rural Central Punjab in the 1970s." *International Journal of Punjab Studies* 1(2): 239–70.

———. 2000. "Vilayati Paisa: Some Reflections on the Potential of Diaspora Finance in the Socio-economic Development of Indian Punjab." *International Journal of Punjab Studies* 7(2): 323–41.

Voigt-Graf, Carmen. 2004. "Towards Geography of Transnational Spaces: Indian Transnational Communities in Australia." *Global Networks* 4(1): 25–49.

Walton-Roberts, Margaret. 2004a. "Globalization, National Autonomy and Non-Resident Indians." *Contemporary South Asia* 13(1): 53–69.

———. (2004b). "Returning, Remitting, and Reshaping: Non-resident Indians and the Transformation of Society and Space in Punjab, India." In *Transnational Spaces*, ed. Peter Jackson, Phil Crang, and Claire Dwyer. London: Routledge. 78–103.

———. 2005. "Transnational Educational Fundraising in Punjab: Old Practices, New Readings." *Journal of Punjab Studies* 12(1): 129–52.

World Bank. 2004. *Resuming Punjab's Prosperity: The Opportunities and Challenges Ahead*. Washington DC: World Bank.

———. 2009. *Remittances*. Washington DC: World Bank.

Xiang, Bao. 2002. "Ethnic Transnational Middle Classes in Formation: A Case Study of Indian Information Technology Professionals." Paper presented at the 52nd Annual Conference of Political Studies Association (UK) "Making Politics Count" University of Aberdeen, April 5–7, 2002.

Zhu, Zhiqun. 2007. "Two Diasporas: Overseas Chinese and Non-resident Indians in Their Homelands' Political Economy." *Journal of Chinese Political Science* 12(3): 281–96.

Chapter 4

Partners in Organizing
Engagement between Migrants and the State in the Production of Mexican Hometown Associations

Natasha Iskander

The massive historic protests in 2006 against anti-immigrant legisla-tion in the United States have sparked renewed interest in immigrant community mobilization. Analysts have turned to Mexican immigrants in particular, not in the least because Mexicans represent the largest immi-grant group in the United States by far. In this focus, many scholars and policy makers both have trained their attention on one form of Mexican civic organization that played an important, yet somewhat unanticipated role in the pro-immigrant marches of the mid-2000s: hometown associa-tions, often called HTAs (Bada, Fox, and Selee 2006; García-Acevedo 2008; Portes, Escobar, and Walton Radford 2007). Broadly defined as organiza-tions formed by migrants from the same community of origin (Fox and Bada 2009), they have been roundly lauded as structures that provide migrants with a wide array of support (Ramakrishnan and Viramontes 2010). HTAs have been characterized as organizations through which mi-grants not only maintain their cultural identity and sustain their affective connection to their hometowns, but also as structures through which com-patriots from the same community or region of origin can provide one another with social and material backing in the United States (Bada 2011; Orozco 2004).

This recent interest in HTAs has dovetailed with the enthusiasm that economic development practitioners have displayed toward this organi-zational form (Aparicio and Meseguer 2008; Burgess 2008; García Zamora

2005). For over a decade, development proponents of HTAs have described them as vehicles that enable migrants to participate in the economic development trajectories of their communities of origin, and perhaps more pointedly, they have identified them as effective funnels that direct remittances—the monies that migrants send home—toward public goods and business investment (Orozco 2004). Despite their differing concerns with HTAs, scholars of migrant civic engagement and economic development concur that HTAs are organizational structures that embody significant transnational expressions of migrant identity and engagement.

This chapter enters this research terrain and looks specifically at the Mexican HTAs that have become a central object of investigation in both migration and development studies. For the most part, the Mexican HTAs examined represent very specific constructs: with most founded over the last decade, they tend to be registered with the Mexican government as formal civic organizations brought together by their affective ties to a community of origin. In a sense, the emphasis on this brand of HTAs is understandable; registration with state authorities makes them visible as objects of analysis, differentiating them from other types of community mobilization, especially community drives that may be contingent and ephemeral, or those that are organized under the umbrella of other institutions, like a church (Vertovec 2004). By the same token, however, these HTAs are very particular organizational models. They can appear, and are actively represented in the literature, as civic organizations with clearly demarcated boundaries. They are viewed as autonomous and freestanding, even if they have extensive interactions with government authorities. Indeed, it is this supposed organizational independence even in the context of intense deliberations with the Mexican state and, for a time, with United States government authorities as well that observers have identified as critical to the political sway that HTAs have been able to exercise (Smith and Bakker 2008; Waldinger, Popkin, and Aquiles Magana 2008).

My goal with this chapter is to offer a cautionary note, and to suggest that the emphasis on HTAs as freestanding organizational structures may be incomplete. This representation of HTAs leads to an inaccurate gloss of these civic organizations as separate from the state institutions with which they interact. In actuality, they have strong ties with Mexican government actors, and their organizational boundaries are heavily crisscrossed with exchanges between HTA members, government actors, and community members. Thus, I argue that a more useful, and more accurate, way of considering Mexican HTAs is as social fields in which multiple actors negotiate both new expressions of transnational political identity and the possibilities for actions those identities allow. In other words, HTAs, rather than being freestanding civic organizations, are in fact arenas of contestation, where migrants, state officials, and local communities on both sides of the US-Mexico border wrestle with questions of identity, belonging, political power, and resources. Even more pointedly, the HTAs that have featured so centrally in migration and development analyses have emerged as spaces where migrants and state actors together elaborate Mexican policy toward its emigrants. In this respect, HTAs act as incubators for new migration and development policy approaches that are then extended well past the limited sphere of existing HTAs to Mexican emigrants more broadly.

This perspective highlights HTAs as theaters that host a flow of transnational political practices and identities that are contingent, informed by specific times and places (Abbott 1997; Landolt 2008). The negotiations between migrants and the state, as well as the products of those contexts, are shaped by the specific political opportunities and constraints of the moment. Historical factors as broad as shifts in migration policy or changes in national leadership influence the way that migrants and state actors engage in the arenas that HTAs provide, but so too do more localized events such as the outcome of municipal elections, a poor crop, or a dispute over land ownership. In addition to external historical events, however, contests within HTA spaces are also shaped by the previous exchanges they hosted. The very local history of interactions within a given HTA supports but also constrains the possible identities and political strategies that that HTA can spark (Sewell 2008). Tending to the diversity and the historical specificity of the negotiations that occur in the context of HTAs is important, I argue, because these exchanges determine the significance and impact of the migration and development policies that HTAs help produce and enact. The same policy interventions can—and do—have vastly different meanings and outcomes depending on the contexts in which they are enacted and the HTAs that they involve.

To illustrate the role of HTAs as fields of social contest, this chapter relies on a layered research strategy. It focuses squarely on contemporary HTAs, formed within the last five years. It draws first on interviews with presidents of thirty-eight Mexican HTAs primarily constituted in 2007 or later, with the lion's share registered in the last two years, and listed on a public registry maintained by the Mexican federal government. The sample included HTAs that were located in a wide array of US states, both traditional and newer areas of Mexican immigration, and that were based on affiliation to communities of origin in diverse municipalities throughout Mexico.[1] Interviews explored how the HTAs were formed, their current projects, and their interactions with various levels of the Mexican government (see Tables 4.1 and 4.2 for summary statistics on the HTAs interviewed). These discussions were supported by interviews with current

Table 4.1. Summary Statistics of HTAs Interviewed

Mexican State		US State		Year of Creation	
Chiapas	1	Alaska	1	2000	1
Colima	1	Arizona	1	2002	1
Durango	2	California	17	2004	1
Guanajuato	13	Illinois	4	2007	5
Guerrero	1	Minnesota	2	2008	10
Hidalgo	2	Nebraska	1	2009	2
Jalisco	2	Nevada	1	2010	9
Michoacán	3	New York	1	2011	9
Morelos	1	North Carolina	1		
Oaxaca	4	Texas	8		
Puebla	2	Virginia	1		
San Luis Potosí	1				
Sinaloa	1				
Tlaxcala	1				
Zacatecas	3				
Total	38	Total	38	Total	38

officials of various Mexican states and the federal Mexican government, as well as a review of policy documents.

In the second layer of research, the focus turns to HTAs from Zacatecas and Guanajuato, two Mexican states where exchanges between migrants and state actors have evolved in two very distinctive ways. HTAs anchored in Zacatecas have tended to coalesce into large and politically powerful federations, whereas those from Guanajuatan communities have engaged with the state government on a more individual basis. The governments of these two states have some of the longest traditions of crafting policies to engage with migrants in the United States, and their efforts have been robustly documented (Ferandez de Castro, García Zamora, and Vila Freyer 2006; García Zamora 2005; Ramírez 2012; Smith and Bakker 2008). The state-level analysis for this chapter includes interviews with representatives of HTAs or federations and with government officials. It also reviews the local Mexican press for exchanges between migrants and government officials.

The third layer of research situates the cases of Zacatecan and Guanajuatan HTAs in their historical contexts and draws on interviews with actors that participated in the creation of models of engagement between migrants and governments of both states from the late 1980s through the late 2000s; actors interviewed include migrant activists, current government officials, and former bureaucrats and political leaders. After opening

Table 4.2. HTAs in the Institute for Mexicans
Abroad Public Registry by Mexican State

Mexican State	HTAs in Registry
Aguascalientes	13
Baja California	12
Campeche	16
Chiapas	22
Chihuahua	26
Coahuila	6
Colima	8
Distrito Federal	13
Durango	76
Estado de México	15
Guanajuato	453
Guerrero	64
Hidalgo	136
Jalisco	93
Michoacán	125
Morelos	17
Nayarit	10
Nuevo León	16
Oaxaca	84
Puebla	63
Querétaro	29
Quintana Roo	1
San Luis Potosí	66
Sinaloa	15
Sonora	7
Tamaulipas	13
Tlaxcala	14
Veracruz	12
Yucatán	65
Zacatecas	22
Total	1512

Source: See ime.gob.mx (accessed 3 May 2012).

with an overview of the analytic and policy treatments of contemporary HTAs, this chapter offers a discussion of the range of exchanges between migrants and the Mexican government that are contained in the spaces that are opened when new HTAs are founded. It follows with a review of the historical evolution of HTAs in Zacatecas and Guanajuato to illustrate the ways in which HTAs are situated, in place and in time.

A New Brand of Hometown Association?

By and large, analysts of Mexican hometown associations have billed them as new, sometimes pathbreaking, expressions of transnational migrant political identity and as novel vehicles for engaging with the Mexican government. Other scholars, however, have cautioned that contemporary Mexican hometown associations have historical roots in the mutual aid societies that were so prevalent among Mexican immigrants in the early 1900s (Gonzalez 1990). Indeed, hometown associations have existed throughout the history of Mexican migration to the United States, and migrants have for decades donated funds for projects in their communities of origin (Gonzalez 1990; Iskander 2010). For the most part, migrants initiated these philanthropic initiatives independently, without prompting from government officials or other leadership in their communities of origin. However, as historiographers of HTAs point out, migrants often had to interact with government representatives to carry out their projects. Some note the strength of the ties that the mutual aid societies and hometown associations forged with government, coordinating with Mexican consular officials to provide material assistance and cultural support to their members (Gonzalez 1990; R. Smith 2003).

But in a technical sense, observers of contemporary Mexican HTAs are correct in their view that these groups represent a new trend. This is because they are, for the most part, migrant associations formed under the umbrella of a matching funds program that went into effect as national policy in 2002. The program, officially titled the Three-for-One Program for Migrants (henceforth 3x1), matches funds raised by groups of migrants for community projects in their towns and villages of origin. As the program's name suggests, the federal, state, and municipal governments all contribute one dollar for each dollar that migrants raise. In order to participate in the program, migrants must form a hometown association and register their group with the Mexican federal government, either through consular offices or indirectly under the umbrella of existing federations of HTAs.

On its face, the initiative is modest. In 2010, the federal budgetary allocation for the 3x1 program was approximately $50 million. The projects funded under the initiative were relatively small overall, with 2,438 projects completed that year, at an average budget per project of about $20,000. As in previous years, the projects included basic infrastructure projects, such as paving roads or laying down water pipes, the beautification or restoration of cultural spaces like churches and plazas, the construction of sporting arenas, clinics, or other community venues, and, in an emergent trend, investment in facilities to support local industry. In 2010, 881 HTAs formed in 664 municipalities spread across 28 Mexican states participated in the program.

Interpreting what close to nine hundred HTAs means, however, is complicated. Some were quite small, with no more than ten members, whereas others were somewhat larger and belonged to federations from the same Mexican state. A few had membership bases that were quite strong. The HTAs that participated in 3x1 made up close to half of the two thousand HTAs registered with the Mexican government over the life of the program. Estimates of HTA membership taken as a whole vary widely but range between ten thousand to thirty thousand people. In absolute numbers and, relative to the total population of Mexican migrants in the United States, the adherents of the HTAs that have received so much attention represent a miniscule proportion of the Mexican migrant population (Instituto de los Mexicanos en el Exterior 2011).

However, as the voluminous literature on the 3x1 program has documented, the Mexican government's matching funds program and the civic mobilization it has supported has had an outsized impact (García Zamora 2005; García Zamora 2007; Goldring 2004; Kijima and Gonzalez-Ramirez 2012; Lopez 2009; Orozco 2004; Orozco and Garcia-Zanello 2009). The program has been credited with improving the delivery of public goods in municipalities throughout Mexico (Bada 2008; Duquette 2011). Tethering projects to groups with strong interests and ties in specific communities has channeled public monies to some marginalized areas of the country that otherwise have had difficulty attracting public investment (Aparicio and Meseguer 2008). Through their involvement in project design and in the supervision of implementation, HTAs have been identified as catalysts for the emergence of new forms of administration, most pointedly new mechanisms of accountability in local governance (Burgess 2008, 2012). The most provocative outcome of the program is the increase in political influence that migrants have been able to exercise in their communities and in the states of origin (Smith and Bakker 2008). Using the HTAs, and especially federations of HTAs, migrants have created increasingly sophisticated and powerful political lobbies; they have exercised electoral sway, among friends and relatives and, more significantly, in wider political debates; and they have wrested new rights of suffrage and political representation from both state and federal legislatures (Iskander 2010; Williams 2008). So substantial has been their influence that many scholars, invoking Hirshman's (1970) triptych of avenues for political participation, have noted that HTAs have come to embody the vehicle through which migrants exercise "voice" *after* "exit" (Duquette 2011; Fox and Bada 2008).

HTAs created through the framework of the 3x1 program have been equally credited with supporting immigrant integration, advancement, and mobilization in the United States (Somerville, Durana, and Terrazas 2008). Accounts of HTA members informally providing one another with employment leads, donations for emergencies, and other kinds of material support are numerous, as are those of more formalized efforts to raise funds for scholarships and other awards (Bada 2008). More compelling to analysts, however, has been the role that HTAs have played in bolstering immigrant social movements. Mexican HTAs in Los Angeles and Chicago received particular attention because of their success in connecting to broader pan-immigrant activism and to electoral campaigns (Cano 2009; Fox and Bada 2009; Shannon 2006; M. Smith 2007).

Most of these analyses have been attentive to the exchanges between HTAs and the Mexican government, as they have occurred on both sides of the border. These interactions have been described as so intensive that they have supported forms of coproduction (Ostrom 1996) between HTAs and government actors—coproduction in the provision of public goods in Mexico, but also coproduction of the political influence that HTAs have exercised (Cano and Délano 2007; Délano 2010; Duquette 2011). Moreover, scholars have pointed out that there has been notable crossover between migrant leadership and state officials, with migrant leaders of HTAs and federations of HTAs taking elected and appointed positions in diverse instances of the Mexican government (Iskander 2010; Ramírez 2012; Smith and Bakker 2008).

Despite their sensitive observation of the quantity of interaction between HTAs and the Mexican government, however, these perspectives still maintain a separation between the migrant organizations and state actors. HTAs and government may interact, they may collaborate, they may tussle, but they still remain conceptually and actually distinct in this view. The structures that encapsulate the HTAs and their federations are represented as marking the boundary between government and migrant civil society. An examination of the processes through which HTAs are and have been created calls this characterization into question. It reveals that state actors engage in mobilizing and formalizing HTAs, and do so in an ongoing way, proactively and deliberately cultivating organizational strength and forms of political action among these migrant civic groups. This begs the question of whether it is accurate to describe exchanges between HTAs and government actors as coproduction when what is often produced is the migrant organization itself, with government often taking the lead in this endeavor.

Coproducing Hometown Associations

In a 2008 presentation in Mexico City directed at migrant leaders and various offices of government, the Mexican federal government described the 3x1 program as an initiative set up in response to migrant desires to carry out community development projects in their hometowns, but also stressed that its scope stretched far beyond this philanthropic mandate to advance additional priorities. Central among these was the organization and mobilization of migrant communities in the United States. In this vein, the 3x1 initiative was represented as providing an important platform "to motivate migrants to identify with their communities in Mexico and with their country," and to draw on that identity to "foster and strengthen the formation of HTAs in the United States" and "strengthen the organizational capacity of HTAs and migrant organizations in their dealings with the Mexican government and with the government of the country in which they reside" (SEDESOL 2008).

As part of its efforts to further the goals it has around community mobilization, the Mexican federal government has refined the 3x1 program to mandate the formation of formal HTAs. According to program guidelines finalized in 2008, any group of migrants interested in participating in the 3x1 program must formally register with consular authorities and secure a *toma de nota*, a document that certifies their existence and their compliance with certain minimal requirements established by the Mexican federal government. These include an active membership of at least ten persons, "with common interests, living abroad, who, among other activities, carry out initiatives in favor of their communities of origin in Mexico." Members must provide formal identification, preferably a consular identification card (*matrícula consular*), and its board of directors must provide contact information that will be verified for accuracy.

The *toma de nota* must be renewed every two years, both to ensure that the HTA continues to have at least ten active members and that the contact information for its leaders remains correct. The program regulations also lay out procedures for creating a federation of HTAs: groups of HTAs can register as federations if they can demonstrate the association of five migrant groups, and must commit to remaining a nonprofit, autonomous organization, without political affiliation of any kind (SEDESOL and Instituto de los Mexicanos en el Exterior 2012). HTAs that obtain a *toma de nota* are encouraged to list themselves in the public registry maintained by the Institute for Mexicans Abroad. Some HTAs have been more amenable to this suggestion than others, with HTAs that join a federation preferring to be listed under the larger organization's umbrella, rather than as individual groups.

According to officials in the federal government, the requirement for a *toma de nota* was put in place in response to migrant demands for greater transparency in the 3x1 program. Numerous migrant groups complained to the federal government that municipal presidents throughout Mexico, but especially from states where migrant HTAs and their federations were not well established, were submitting community development projects to the 3x1 on behalf of migrant HTAs that did not exist. These were "phantom clubs," as one official termed them, created as an administrative fiction to claim additional state and federal resources under the rubric of the matching funds program.[2] By all accounts, the safeguards provided by the new guidelines have curtailed the most egregious abuses of this type.

Municipal authorities have long played a role in organizing HTAs, often traveling to locations across the border to convene and establish the migrant organizations. But migrant complaints to federal officials in this case represent a forceful statement of their view of what this new form of civic organization—a 3x1 HTA—should represent. Tellingly, their demand was not for full independence from government, but rather a call on government to participate more actively in safeguarding their organizational space. Migrants petitioned that they, at the very least, be the main protagonists in the creation of their own HTAs, and that their membership be robust enough to qualify as a civic group. They demanded that their identity not be co-opted by a shell organization, headed by a migrant figurehead but deployed cynically by municipal governments to pad their budgets. In this sense, these government regulations were the product of exchanges between migrants and the Mexican state over what an HTA should be in practice.

These actions were a reflection of migrants' rejection of the somewhat romanticized notions of HTAs as groups that formed organically and independently around altruistic, if also nostalgic, goals for their communities—notions that even the Institute for Mexicans Abroad embraced in their early consideration of HTAs, portraying them, in early project memos, as "effective social networks" that "provided an excellent vehicle to strengthen the ethical, moral, and civic values of the community" (Instituto de los Mexicanos en el Exterior 2004). Migrants' complaints were also a "realpolitik" reminder to the federal authorities that HTAs were small groups that needed protection from the instrumental appropriation of their identities by others.

In addition to limiting the misuse of the 3x1 program, the guidelines have had two important implications for HTA organizing, shaping them as arenas when migrants and government interlocutors elaborate new forms of transnational civic identity. First, the regulations have provided migrant groups with a solid springboard for organizing and for pushing past inertia or ambivalence among their adherents and potential adherents. One HTA anchored in a community in Durango observed, for example, that "our group was formally established in 2011 after working informally for six years. We were just a few people and then grew to ten so that we could meet the requirement for participating in the 3x1."[3] This experience was echoed by a majority of the HTAs interviewed; indeed, six out of thirty-eight organizations sampled reported that they registered with the consulate in the hopes of putting together a 3x1 project, but had not yet identified the project that they wanted to complete or were still finalizing its design.[4] One leader of an HTA representing a community in Puebla located in the New York metropolitan area noted that he had worked with Mexican community organizations in the city for close to a decade but had found them "very disappointing ... lacking a true community base and lacking leadership, without a true representation from the community," and it was this frustration, rather than a targeted ambition to complete defined 3x1 projects, that motivated him, with others, to start a formal HTA. As he explained, "If you don't get people to come together here, even as they integrate into this society, you cannot achieve development [in the communities of origin]."[5]

The formal registration of an HTA or a federation of HTAs provides a critical point of contact between consular officials and migrants who might otherwise remain unknown to them. While interviews reveal that there is considerable variation among consular offices in the ways they respond to this connection, numerous HTAs reported receiving substantial and ongoing mentorship in organizing capacity. Descriptions that were articulated repeatedly in response to questions about consular offices were that the staff was "very helpful"; HTA presidents reported that their groups were "well received" and they benefited from "good orientation" about how to set up and maintain an HTA.[6] One leader of an HTA rooted in Hidalgo recounted, for example, that she had started an HTA in 2005, but that it was through interactions with staff from the Institute for Mexicans Abroad and staff at the consulate that she learned her HTA could form a federation with other groups from the same state. "The consular office gave us a lot of support with meetings on a monthly basis to guide our experience, to register, to learn the rules ... to prepare paperwork and demonstrate the viability of our projects so that they could be approved. ... The support we received as a federation was really very good."[7]

Based on the limited interview sample used for this chapter, it is difficult to determine conclusively how widespread the consular practice of using HTA registration as the beginning of capacity-building efforts is. Nevertheless, federal government officials report that this is an important thrust of their activities. As explained by a 3x1 official at the federal level, the directory acts as a foundation for consular outreach activities: "The function of the *toma de nota* is first and foremost to give the consulates an opportunity to be familiar with the work of the clubs."[8] "Each consulate uses the directory in its own way, depending on its respective approach and work with HTAs," confirmed an official at the IME. "Some might use it to identify which clubs are in existence in their areas and invite them to come to training at the consulate."[9] In this respect, the *toma de nota* process provides the Mexican government with a crucial optic onto migrant civic organization; it makes the extent and location of migrant organizing efforts visible and legible. The Institute for Mexicans Abroad does not have a census or complete database of migrant groups; indeed, by their own report, they only know how many and which groups have acquired the *toma de nota* under 3x1 regulations.[10]

The outreach use of the registry of the *tomas de nota* mandated by the 3x1 program points to the second function the matching funds program plays in creating spaces for the development of transnational political identities. It is no accident that the Institute for Mexicans Abroad views HTAs as "our reason for being."[11] For the Mexican federal government, HTAs are doorways to the broader migrant population, but they are also spaces where migrant rights and activism around other issue areas beyond imperatives of the 3x1 program are explored. As one staff member explained, HTAs "provide us with a structure through which we can reach the community. HTAs are like 'arms' that extend our outreach capacity." And the outreach that HTA networks support engages with numerous issue areas, such as "financial education, health programming, empowerment, and the protection of migrants' rights."[12]

Moreover, in much the same way that the topical areas the Mexican federal government has addressed with HTAs have expanded, the organizational building efforts have as well. The Institute for Mexicans Abroad has worked with HTAs and held leadership seminars in Chicago, Houston, New York, Washington DC, and San Francisco in collaboration with the American Jewish Committee to draw on the experience of Israel and its engagement with Jewish communities in the United States. It has also offered leadership training in partnership with local universities, most recently with the City University of New York. As a staff member at the Institute for Mexicans Abroad noted, the goal of these training sessions is much broader than to support the functioning of a single government program. Rather, "the aim of these workshops is to develop capacity among Mexican community leaders to create opinion leaders, local functionaries, entrepreneurs, and more skilled community leaders in general, to promote a better understanding of the contribution of the Mexican community in the US, and to advance the image of Mexico."[13]

While the Mexican government has strengthened its efforts to provide a broader platform for migrant organizing and integration in the host society, the focus for migrants who have formed HTAs recently, however, has remained the 3x1 program. Many of the HTA leaders interviewed acknowledged that their organizations provided forms of support to its members that were ancillary to the task of carrying out a matching funds project, and they also noted that the services provided by consular offices were helpful in this respect, as well as in the general support of *el movimiento migratorio*—the immigrant movement.[14] Nevertheless, the main goal of their HTAs was funding and completing development projects, however conceived, in their community of origin. Likewise, their primary expression of transnational civic identity was anchored in the towns and villages from which they heralded.

State Government Engagement with Hometown Associations

As a reflection of their interest in the 3x1 program as a vehicle to express their hometown identities, newer HTAs have been proactive in connecting with state-level government officials. Whereas their involvement with federal-level consular authorities is mandated by program design through the *toma de nota,* HTAs have actively sought out state-level authorities to assist them in submitting projects and securing their approval. While HTAs have had some success in connecting with Mexican state-level government authorities in the United States, their initial contact tends to be in Mexico, and their ongoing exchange with state government takes place in the halls of state government buildings. The physical location of HTAs' engagement with state government officials has had important implications for the leadership structure—both formal and informal—of HTAs. Traveling back to Mexico is more feasible for migrants that have the legal status and the financial means to do so. This creates a selection bias toward more established migrants, who tend to have been in the United States for a longer period of time; it also tends to favor men, for reasons that are not yet well documented. Older HTAs, and especially those that have coalesced into federations, tend to display this membership profile, with the leadership dominated by long-term male migrants with legal status (Ramakrishnan and Viramontes 2010). Newer HTAs, such as those sampled for this chapter, are more likely to have members that are recent and undocumented migrants, with less organizational capacity and less ability to travel to Mexico to follow up on their projects with state authorities.

For the most part, state government authorities have been responsive to migrant outreach around the 3x1 program and have met such outreach with their own efforts to connect with HTAs under the 3x1 program's rubric. However, there has been a notable distinction between state-level instances of federal offices, especially the Secretariat of Social Development (SEDESOL), the federal office responsible for the 3x1 program, and the governments of specific states. SEDESOL has three satellites north of the border, one in Los Angeles, one in Chicago, and a recently established one in New York, but runs training programs around the United States, with most outreach efforts targeting migrants from single hometowns or municipalities. Its exchanges with migrants have hewn closely to program mandates, addressing how to establish and run an HTA within the context of the matching funds program. Recent outreach by state government officials, in contrast, has tended to rely on the 3x1 program as a means of establishing contact with migrant constituents. In a manner similar to consular authorities, state officials have expanded discussions about 3x1 projects to include larger political considerations. This has been especially true of representatives from traditional migrant-sending states in northwest and central Mexico: state governments and political parties in or out of office.

Partly as a response to these political overtures, newer HTAs have joined or consolidated into federations. As several interviewees pointed out, HTAs in a group are more effective at resisting political influence and pressing for the funding and implementation of the projects they propose. "We established a federation," said a federation president from a traditional migrant sending state, "because it gives us the opportunity to have a more official relationship and work directly with our state government." All of the federations from our state send a secretary [representative] that travels back to Mexico to secure funds for our projects through a meeting with the [state] government. The process is like an open negotiation between the secretaries and the state government: '"This is how much we bring to the table. So now, how much are you going to put down?'"[15] And in this endeavor, HTAs have often received tutelage and support from SEDESOL and consular officials. Indeed, HTA presidents reported connecting with other HTAs from their state at training sessions provided by their local consulate.[16] Not infrequently, state government officials have also played an important role in bringing HTAs into federations, in order to access or strengthen the political constituency that supra-HTA organization can represent (Ramírez 2012; Rivera-Salgado, Bada, and Escala-Rabadán 2005; Williams 2008).

In a reflection of the negotiating power that this arrangement affords, federations from numerous states, particularly those with well-established ones like Zacatecas, Michoacán, and Jalisco, among others, have instituted regulations that are informal but binding in practice for all HTAs to participate in the 3x1 program. With tacit agreement with state officials, only projects sponsored by a federation are considered for funding. But as federations have expanded and their political heft has grown, they too have expanded exchanges with state government past the narrow confines of the 3x1 program. They have pressed for legislative changes, including suffrage in national and state elections, and the allotment of state delegates. They have also wrested financial commitments from state governments to increase funding for various projects spearheaded by migrants but that fall outside of the parameters of the 3x1 program. Newer HTAs, while maintaining their keen interest in the 3x1 program, have joined these political efforts. As one HTA president interviewed commented, "Migrants advance through struggle and demands—*a través de luchas y exigencias*. It is a matter of how motivated we migrants are to improve our lives and how we learn how to achieve this."[17]

Municipal Government Engagement with Hometown Associations

Unlike the ongoing exchanges and political negotiations between HTAs and state government, interactions at the municipal level appear far more mercurial and tense. In interviews, a common complaint regarding municipal authorities was that they were nakedly partisan in their selection of projects and were obstructionist with projects that did not improve their political party's political standing. "HTAs receive much more outreach from municipal presidents during an election year. It is a political exchange," said one HTA president. "Our relationship with the municipal government has been antagonistic. It has been really hard to get the mayor [municipal president] to give political support to the project, but a new mayor took office in January so it might get better," reported another.[18]

Because municipal authorities implement the actual project, handling construction and coordination, HTA presidents observed that local authorities often have influence that is greater than the proportion of funds they contribute to any given project. "The municipal president determines the project we do. ... In our view, the [municipal] government is charging us for what each project costs, and we as the HTA are 'contracting' the project with them. ... When a project does not fit the within the 3x1 program, our HTA pays the cost of the project in full, depending on what the municipal government asks for," said an HTA president representing a Guanajuatan HTA.[19] Similarly, an HTA president from Michoacán reported that 3x1 projects were "controlled" by municipal government and complained about price inflation. "The companies that are hired are affiliated with the local government political party."[20] Other interviewees echoed this concern about corruption, voicing frustration that municipal governments were playing fast and loose with 3x1 project budgets. In an account of a paving project, one HTA president explained that the migrant group contributed their portion "in full, but only part of the paving was actually accomplished and the municipal government kept the difference."[21]

In order to exercise greater control over the project budgets and project implementation, many HTAs now work with "mirror committees" — *comités de espejo* — made up of residents in the community of origin. HTAs and federations in states that have a longer and more intensive history with the 3x1 program, like Zacatecas, Jalisco, and Michoácan, have formed citizen supervisory committees to monitor projects, often taking the protective measure of creating an account for 3x1 funds that is separate from any municipal accounts. In 2005, the federal government took up this innovation and sponsored the formation of "mirror committees" as a means to address the problem of "phantom HTAs" created by municipal authorities (Shannon 2006). The HTAs sampled had a favorable view of these committees, considering them essential to effective project implementation. Indeed, for some HTAs, the "mirror committees" did more than increase accountability: they served as an indispensable bridge for migrants to their communities of origin, especially when travel back to Mexico was complicated by migrants' lack of legal immigration status, and facilitated deliberation with local residents about project choice. "We now have a mirror committee," explained one president from an HTA rooted in Hidalgo. "The committee has been indispensable and without it, it would not be possible to do the projects."[22] Some also observed that the mirror committees have taken on their own initiatives to push for improved government service and to author social change, a claim echoed by scholars who have analyzed the effect of the 3x1 program on local mobilization in Mexico (Bada 2008; Duquette 2011).

Overall, presidents of the newer HTAs viewed the 3x1 program as a work in progress. According to them, it has provided migrants with a springboard from which to organize, and has opened up channels for them to engage with the various instances of the Mexican government. "Though there are problems with the program, it is really important because it is the only thing we have," summed up one HTA president. "The concept is excellent, but the structure is deficient."[23] The HTAs, along with the federations that some have joined, have provided a space for the elaboration and strengthening of program structures. In an iterative fashion, the programs have also shaped HTAs and the form and actions they take. Today's HTAs enter an existing flow of forms and actions, with histories, in some cases, that are now decades long.

Hometown Associations: Zacatecas and Guanajuato

In early 2012, the opinion pages of the main local newspaper in Zacatecas were bursting with commentary about political maneuvering by the Institutional Revolutionary Party (PRI) to dominate the organizations that migrants had created. Editorials decried "the attacks against migrant organizations in an effort to maintain and consolidate control over the migrant community—and their leaders—to harvest electoral votes for contests over position in the federal government now and for contests at the state level later" (Columna Reloj de Sol 2012). At issue was the fracture of the Federación de Clubes Zacatecanos del Sur de California, the largest and longest-standing federation of Zacatecan hometown associations in the United States, into two rival federations, one of which displayed a stronger affinity with PRI, which had swept into power at the state level with the election of Miguel Alonso Reyes as governor in 2010.

This was the second instance of a well-established federation breaking apart in as many months: the Federación de Clubes Zacatecanos de Fort Worth split into two factions for similar reasons at the end of 2011. The sense of alarm in the editorial pages of the local daily was bolstered with accusations of vote buying "left and right" in elections by PRI-affiliated migrant groups to determine the governance of these federations, blatant bias by the state agency that vetted potential 3x1 projects in favor of those in municipalities governed by the PRI, and widespread corruption by politicians who were awarding 3x1 construction contracts to weave a clientelistic web.

By contrast, coverage in Guanajuatan dailies of the 3x1 program and of migrant organizations was sparse and staid. The main story during this same time period on the 3x1 program, buried in the back of the local section of the main state newspaper, concerned the matching funds scheme that supported the restoration of the stained glass windows in the state capital's cathedral (Flores 2011).[24]

The contrasting press coverage reflects the difference in significance that migrant hometown associations and the 3x1 program have in both states. In Zacatecas, federations of HTAs have become powerful political actors, shaping the outcome of electoral contests at the local and state levels on both sides of the border. In the state's projected budget for 2012, the 3x1 program represented fully half of the state's funds for public works.[25] In Guanajuato, on the other hand, HTAs remain largely unaffiliated with federations, and the few federations that exist are nascent and weak. In 2012, the 3x1 program represented a smaller fraction of the state's budget for public goods, and, in an indication of how marginal the program is, government officials were hard-pressed to provide even a rough estimate of the contribution the matching funds program made to the state's budget.[26] The new HTAs created under the rubric of the 3x1 program enter these two contrasting political and organizational landscapes.

When Zacatecan HTAs form, they also simultaneously join a federation. Federations have effectively enforced this fusion by insisting that HTAs can only participate in the 3x1 program through federations, a stipulation by which all levels of government abide, even though it contravenes federal guidelines. In an environment where competition for 3x1 program funds is fierce and only 40 percent of all projects submitted are approved, projects that are not vetted and actively pitched by federations receive no consideration whatsoever. When a group of migrants want to form an HTA, the first point of contact is the local federation. The federation files a *toma de nota* with the relevant consulate, and if the federation has non-profit status in the United States, which all the major Zacatecan federations do, it extends this to the newly created HTA. It then acts as a liaison between municipal authorities and the new HTA, mediating the process of defining a viable 3x1 project that the new migrant group can sponsor.

Federations also provide a platform for knowledge sharing among HTAs, holding yearly plenary meetings where insights about strategy are exchanged. Furthermore, in recognition that the membership of newer HTAs is more likely to include undocumented migrants, and that travel thus represents risking deportation, federations are increasingly fostering knowledge exchange through telephone calls and email. Thus, for Zacatecan HTAs, their primary contact with any instance of Mexican government is through the federations. As one federation president summed it up, "The federation is really our universe of operation."[27]

To support these activities, it has been common practice among federations to charge member HTAs an annual fee, which appears to be proportional to the political clout that the federation possesses in Zacatecas. The Federación de Clubes Zacatecanos de la Costa Oeste, which was created in 2003, "specializes" in HTAs in places like Utah and the Carolinas that are geographically isolated from major federations. It charges $150; in contrast, the Federación de Clubes Zacatecanos del Sur de California, which was, until early 2012, the most powerful federation, levied a fee of no less than $2,000. The argument articulated by federations is that this fee and the mandated membership in federations for HTAs is a means to enhance migrant influence. "What this rule is really enforcing is the affiliation of clubs with federations in order to make federations more politically powerful," explained one federation president interviewed. "The federations are the mediators (*vínculo*) between the US government and the Zacatecan government. They serve to strengthen the political power of the Zacatecan and the Mexican state vis-à-vis the US government."[28]

In Guanajuato, HTAs and their emergent federations carry little political weight in either side of the border, and the process through which HTAs are formed both reflects and cements this reality. Groups of migrants from Guanajuato keen on participating in the 3x1 program have tended to organize on their own initiative, relying on the same kinds of assistance from the consulates and, occasionally, from municipal authorities from which HTAs rooted in communities all around Mexico have benefited. Interestingly, Guanajuatan migrants have been exceptionally active in the formation of individual HTAs: of the 1,512 HTAs currently listed in the public registry of the Institute for Mexicans Abroad, 453 claim affiliation to a community in Guanajuato.

This growth reflects in part the proactive stance of the state government in promoting the registration of new Guanajuatan HTAs, designed to create the appearance of collective migrant strength. As part of this effort, the state actively distributes information about registering with the Institute for Mexicans Abroad, publishing on its website contact information of advisors in different regions of the United States who provide one-on-one assistance on how to register (Faret 2004).[29]

Beyond this initial encouragement, however, the state government has offered little additional support and no guidance to HTAs in launching a 3x1 project. It has instead opted for a state-focused outreach strategy, technocratic and top-down, through its Dirección de Atención a Comunidades Guanajuatenses en el Extranjero (DACGE). The centerpiece of this strategy has been creation of Casas Guanajuato, groups of migrants with which the state government works to secure nonprofit status in the United States. The Casas Guanajuato program was designed to create identities among migrants that were fixed on their state of origin rather than on the town and villages from which they came. As the governor who initiated the program in 1994, Carlos Medina, explained, "We wanted [migrants] to look toward Guanajuato and its government for their future. And that's why we decided that the Casas Guanajuato should have a larger state identity, rather than be identified with a given municipality. And anyway, how much can a municipality really do for migrants in any case?"[30]

The Casas Guanajuato program has a mixed track record, with many of the Casas Guanajuato groups collapsing into shell organizations with minimal or no membership (Faret 2006; Iskander 2010). Of late, however, the Casas Guanajuato program has seen increased migrant participation; HTAs have appropriated it to tap into the organizational support that the state government offers and to take advantage of the privileged access to government authorities that the program can afford. Similarly, there has been an incipient movement to forge federations of Guanajuatan HTAs, and new federations report working in conjunction with the Casas Guanajuato program. As one federation president explained, several HTAs can come together under the banner of a single Casa Guanajuato.[31]

The difference in organizational strength between Zacatecan and Guanajuatan migrant groups and the intensity of exchanges with state actors is the product of distinct historical trajectories. In Zacatecas, HTAs along with their federations and the 3x1 program developed together. Both the migrant groups and the program around which they organized emerged out of exchanges between migrants and state officials, and both continued to evolve as that engagement matured and refashioned them. The origin of the 3x1 program was an informal 1x1 matching funds agreement, sketched out on a piece of notebook paper, when a newly elected governor, Genaro Borrego, traveled to Los Angeles in 1986 to meet with Zacatecan migrants there. Said the then governor, "If they contributed a dollar ... well, it just seemed fundamental to me in terms of equity that I contribute a dollar [as well]."[32]

The governor anointed the new state-based federation as a privileged interlocutor and representative of Zacatecan migrants on both sides of the border. He did this in part through various symbolic gestures that migrants found enormously validating, including publicly honoring each of the existing Zacatecan HTAs with a Mexican flag at a large sporting event that the governor attended (Iskander 2010).

This reciprocal recognition, exchange, and collaboration continued over the next twenty-five years, peaking in intensity during each state electoral contest. During the electoral campaign of the next state governor, Arturo Romo, a pledge was made—and kept—to ratchet up and institutionalize the informal 1x1 agreement to a 2x1 program, drawing in an additional dollar from the federal government. The following gubernatorial candidate, Ricardo Monreál, likewise made a promise in 1998 to increase the matching funds ratio from 2x1 to 3x1, drawing municipal funds into the equation, and this trend continued in subsequent campaigns. As the program expanded, so too did migrant organizational activity, and both federations and their membership increased in number and in strength. At times, this growth in migrant mobilization occurred through the direct involvement of state bureaucrats: under the Romo administration, for example, staff from the state planning office traveled to US cities precisely to create one or more HTAs, bringing shovel-ready projects in a briefcase. According to some of the staff members who carried out this organizing north of the border in the mid-1990s, this was done strategically to provide the new HTA with a task around which its members could mobilize, and thus reinforce the group's nascent structure.[33]

These efforts cultivated the ability of federations and state government to coordinate politically, but more importantly, they sharpened the skill of Zacatecan federations to mobilize and lobby in varied political arenas. And mobilize they did: they soon wrested from the state and national legislatures new rights of suffrage and political representation, and secured unprecedented access to presidential administrations in both countries. Until migration reform became an issue too volatile for the presidents of both the United States and Mexico, Zacatecan migrants—émigrés from a poor state in Mexico of a little over one million inhabitants—had audiences with Presidents Fox and Bush (Iskander 2010).

The 3x1 program that originated in Zacatecas became national policy in 2002, illustrating another aspect of the interaction between migrants and the state. The rich and intensive exchanges between migrant and state actors have turned Zacatecas into an incubator for new programs directed at Mexican migrants. They allow for negotiation and incremental refinement of program strictures, such that, once polished, they can be easily extended to other states or to the nation as a whole. There is no more compelling example of this today than the Comité de Validación y Atención a Migrantes (COVAM). According to the rules of operation of the 3x1 program, the COVAM is the committee responsible for the prioritization, allocation, and validation of projects for each state (SEDESOL and Instituto de los Mexicanos en el Exterior 2012). Mandated in 2005, COVAMs have been convening regularly in practice only since 2009.[34] In Zacatecas, however, some version of this oversight committee has been meeting since 1995, and the COVAM itself is largely patterned on the plenary meetings where municipal, state, and federal bureaucrats quarreled openly and vociferously with Zacatecan federations over the allocation of 3x1 monies.[35]

Moreover, in Zacatecas, the COVAM, on its face a bureaucratic instrument to ensure accountability in program implementation, continues to be adapted by migrant and state actors for uses that exceed its technical mandate. Several idiosyncratic practices have been put in place in Zacatecas to ensure that the COVAM acts fairly: for example, one of the four municipal seats on the committee is given to each of the four parties that are most active in Zacatecas, regardless of the number of municipalities they govern, in order to prevent party capture. Likewise, the four seats granted to the federations rotate among the federations (currently seventeen) that are registered with the federal government. The COVAM meetings, held quarterly, either in the United States or Mexico, also act as critical convenings for the federations, regardless of whether they have a seat on the committee that year. At moments of political tension with the state government, federations view a show of strength at the COVAM meetings as important. During the April 2012 COVAM meetings, a federation president commented that all the federations were going, "as a block, to

defend everyone's projects" and "to defend the autonomy of the federations [from the government] and from the designs of its [political] party."[36]

The COVAM in Guanajuato could not be more different in structure
and in process than the 3x1 committee meetings in Zacatecas. In Guanajuato, the COVAM hews very closely to its technical function, as dictated
by the 3x1 program guidelines, and its proceedings, which are more per-
functory and occur seven times a year, are administrative in tone. Moreover, participation in the committee is assigned, with little contestation.
Federal and state functionaries responsible for the implementation of the
3x1 program sit in the COVAM, and municipal presidents are selected
based on their level of emigration. This representation changes from year
to year as out-migration rates fluctuate. HTA and, more recently, federation representatives are selected based on the "level of productivity" that
each candidate organization displayed in fund-raising over the previous
year. "If they become less productive," explained a state official, "they are
asked to step down."[37]

This emphasis on productivity in Guanajuato's policy toward its migrants has historical roots, and new HTAs enter a logic to which migrant
groups have long been subject. Like Zacatecas, Guanajuato has some of
the longest-standing state-level outreach efforts. Alongside its outreach
efforts to migrants through the provision of services and the support for
the Casas Guanajuato program, the state government has strived to make
remittances more "productive." Rather than having them spent on uses
that the government views as consumption, including expenditures on
housing, food, and schooling, the state wants to direct a larger proportion
of the monies migrants send home toward business investment.

To that end, the state created its own version of a matching funds
arrangement for small firms. The scheme, called Mi Comunidad, was
launched in 1996 and functioned as follows: the state government encouraged migrants to raise start-up funds for small firms in their hometown—chiefly clothing *maquilas* on the forceful suggestion of government
bureaucrats—which one or more migrants would return to manage. In
return, the state promised to match their investment with in-kind contributions of installations, machinery, training, and wage subsidies. Thirteen
firms were established under the program, and as the governor of Guanajuato at the time, Vicente Fox, ascended to the presidency in 2000, he
pledged to start one hundred Comunidades firms in his first one hundred
days in office (Iskander 2010).

Unfortunately, the program was a spectacular bust. Firms were located
in isolated communities, far from industry supply chains, and hampered
by deficient road and communication infrastructure, with landline tele-
phones that worked sporadically. Within five years, all but one firm had

failed, with the owner of the remaining firm contemplating migrating back to the United States to raise capital for his failing enterprise (Iskander 2005).

The case of Guanajuato illustrates that without state participation in the development of migrant organizations—without its coproduction of HTAs and their federations—the mobilization efforts of migrants are likely to stay underdeveloped. HTAs remained small, atomized organizations that posed little political threat to the state government and its neoliberal vision of development. By the same token, the HTAs that emerge today through the 3x1 program are less likely to gather the required political strength and exercise the necessary sway.

The Road from Guanajuato to Zacatecas

In Zacatecas, in Guanajuato, and, indeed, in all Mexican states, hometown associations rooted there have not been simply groups of migrants who came together around local identities. Rather, they have been, and continue to be, produced by intensive exchanges between migrants and government interlocutors. It is this interplay between migrants and government actors that gives HTAs their organizational structure, and opens them up as spaces for collaboration and contest over the articulation of transnational civic identity. Attention to the way that HTAs have been produced—and coproduced—shows how variegated the practices are that define their contours and their influence. They differ by level of government, by geographic location in the United States and in Mexico, and by the political controversies within Mexican states.

The evolution of so-called migrant productive projects, supported through matching funds schemes, captures this analytic urgency. In Guanajuato, an early adopter of this kind of project through the Mi Comunidad program, the experiment not only failed, but also caused financial harm to the migrants that participated. Zacatecas borrowed and adapted the underlying idea of supporting small businesses through a 3x1-style initiative. Since 2005, migrants and state officials have been experimenting with various models. A first attempt was a 4+1 program, sponsored by Western Union, where the company would top off 3x1 funding with an additional matching portion for small business investments (Orozco and Diaz 2011). The effort displayed mixed results, suffering from the same issues of value-chain integration and technical capacity that were the downfall of the Guanajuato program. Nevertheless, the program was expanded nationally, and in 2009 was adopted and adapted by the federal government as a 1x1 program for business investment, officially called

Proyectos Productivos para el Fortalecimiento Patrimonial. This federal program matches—at a one-for-one ratio—the investment that a single migrant family makes in a business initiative. The program essentially acts as a vehicle and a subsidy for microcredit, in a credit market that is tight for small and rural entrepreneurs. Ironically, the 1x1 program is favored by migrants from Guanajuato, the state that supplied the original conceptual framework for this policy, precisely because it allows them to bypass municipal and state levels of government and deal instead directly and solely with the federal government.

In Zacatecas, however, the program has taken a new shape: as of the last electoral contest in 2010, it has become the 2x1 program, with additional contributions from the state government. Projects are vetted by the migrant federations, which, in most cases, extend ongoing technical support to the new entrepreneurs. Moreover, through the involvement of the state government, the projects (mescal factories, cybercafes, hair salons, pig farms, dehydration of specialized chilies, etc.) have entered development planning discussions at the state level.

In this instance again, diminutive Zacatecas emerges as a dynamic incubator for innovative policy. This effervescent creativity is the product of the same exchanges that produced HTAs and their federations. In other words, not only do interactions between government actors and migrants coproduce HTAs, but they also coproduce new development trajectories at the local and national levels. Consequently, attention to the quality of these exchanges is vital: they can support the elaboration of new development approaches even as they support migrant mobilization on both sides of the border, or they can hobble, sometimes definitively, migrant efforts at organizing and collaborating with one another and with their governments.

As Mexico now faces a situation where migration has crested and is currently at a steady state, with net migration at zero (Passel, Cohn, and Gonzalez-Barrera 2012), it also enters an era where the benefits of emigration to the country will come less in the form of remittances and more through the ingenuity of its migrants. Looking beyond the organizational boundaries of HTAs to identify which among the many varied and contested interactions that occur within these organizations support creativity, and which have caused migrants instead to retreat from failed exchanges with government and from top-down clientelistic interactions, is arguably more important now than ever.

Natasha Iskander is an associate professor at New York University's Wagner School of Public Service. She is the author of the award-winning book *Creative State: Forty Years of Migration and Development Policy in Morocco and Mexico* (Cornell University Press, 2010) and, more recently, of more than ten journal articles, book chapters, and op-ed pieces on tacit skill development among migrant workers.

Notes

This project was funded by New York University Wagner School of Public Service. Special thanks go to Breana George for her outstanding research support, without which this chapter would not have been possible.
1. Interviews for the chapter were all conducted in Spanish. Interviews in 2012 were conducted over the telephone, but earlier interviews were conducted in person. While some information is provided about the affiliation of the interviewees, identifying information is withheld in order to maintain the confidentiality of the interviewee's identity.
2. Interview, April 2012.
3. Interview, March 2012.
4. Interviews, March–April 2012.
5. Interview, March 2012.
6. Interviews, March–April 2012.
7. Interview, March 2012.
8. Interview, April 2012.
9. Interview, April 2012.
10. Personal communication, April 2012.
11. Interview, April 2012.
12. Interview, April 2012.
13. Personal communication, March–April 2012.
14. Interviews, March 2012.
15. Interview, March 2012.
16. Interviews, March 2012.
17. Interview, March 2012.
18. Interview, March 2012.
19. Interview, March 2012.
20. Interview, March 2012.
21. Interview, March 2012.
22. Interview, March 2012.
23. Interview, March 2012.
24. Newspapers surveyed for this chapter include: *El Sol de Zacatecas*; *El Mirador*; *El Sol de Leon* (Guanajuato); and *Reforma*.
25. Interviews, April 2012.
26. Interviews, April 2012.
27. Interview, April 2012.
28. Interview, April 2012.
29. Interviews, April 2012.
30. Interview, July 2003.
31. Interview, April 2012.

32. Interview, May 2003.
33. Interviews, March–May 2003.
34. Interview, April 2012.
35. Interview, April 2012.
36. Interview, April 2012.
37. Interview, April 2012.

References

Abbott, Andrew. 1997. "Of Time and Space: The Contemporary Relevance of the Chicago School." *Social Forces* 75, no. 4: 1149–82.

Aparicio, Francisco Javier, and Covadonga Meseguer. 2008. *Collective Remittances and the State: The 3x1 Program in Mexican Municipalities.* Mexico City: CIDE.

Bada, Xochitl. 2008. "Sociopolitical Remittances, Rural Development, and Mexican Migrant Hometown Associations: The Shifting Nature of Transnational and Trans-local Connections in the Chicago-Michoacán Corridor." PhD dissertation, University of Notre Dame.

———. 2011. "Participatory Planning Across Borders: Mexican Migrant Civic Engagement in Community Development." *The Latin Americanist* 55, no. 4: 9–33.

Bada, Xóchitl, Jonathan Fox, and Andrew D. Selee. 2006. *Invisible No More: Mexican Migrant Civic Participation in the United States.* Washington DC: Woodrow Wilson Center and UCSC Report.

Burgess, Katrina. 2008. "State-Society Relations Beyond Borders: Migrant Transnationalism in Mexico and El Salvador." Paper presented at the 3rd Coloquio sobre Migración y Desarrollo, 6 November, Heredia, Costa Rica.

———. 2012. "Collective Remittances and Migrant-State Collaboration in Mexico and El Salvador." *Latin American Politics & Society* 54:4. 119–146.

Cano, Gustavo. 2009. "Orale! Politics: Mobilization of Mexican Immigrants in Chicago and Houston." PhD dissertation, Columbia University.

Cano, Gustavo, and Alexandra Délano. 2007. "The Mexican Government and Organised Mexican Immigrants in The United States: A Historical Analysis of Political Transnationalism (1848–2005)." *Journal of Ethnic and Migration Studies* 33, no. 5: 695–725.

Columna Reloj de Sol. 2012. "Descomposicion." *El Sol de Zacatecas.* 23 January, B2.

Délano, Alexandra. 2010. "Immigrant Integration vs. Transnational Ties? The Role of the Sending State." *Social Research* 77, no. 1: 237–68, 424.

Duquette, Lauren. 2011. "Making Democracy Work from Abroad: Remittances, Hometown Associations and Migrant-State Coproduction of Public Goods in Mexico." PhD dissertation, University of Chicago.

Faret, Laurent. 2004 "Implicarse aqui, con la mirada hacia alla: La organizacion comunitaria de los guanajuatenses en los Estados Unidos." In *Clubes de migrantes oriundos mexicanos en los Estados Unidos: La politica transnacional de Ia nueva sociedad civil migrante,* ed. Guillaume Lanly and M. Basilia Valenzuela. Guadalajara: Universidad de Guadalajara. 225–52.

Fernandez de Castro, Rafael, Rodolfo García Zamora, and Ana Vila Freyer, eds. 2006. *El Programa 3x1 para Migrantes: ¿Primera politica transnacional en Mexico?* Mexico City: Universidad Autonoma de Zacatecas.

Flores, Mayra. 2011. "Concluyen en catedral restauración de vitrales: Apoyan migrantes mexicanos." *El Sol de Leon*. http://www.oem.com.mx/elsoldeleon/notas/n1921566.htm. (Accessed 17 April 2012).

Fox, Jonathan, and Xóchitl Bada. 2008. "Migrant Organization and Hometown Impacts in Rural Mexico." *Journal of Agrarian Change* 8, nos. 2–3: 435–61.

———. 2009. *Migrant Civic Engagement*. Research Paper Series on Latino Immigrant Civic and Political Participation 3. Washington DC: Woodrow Wilson International Center for Scholars, Mexico Institute.

García-Acevedo, María R. 2008. "The (Re)construction of Diasporic Policies in Mexico in the Era of Globalization and Democracy: The Case of the Clubes de Oriundos." *Politics & Policy* 36, no. 6: 1066–92.

García Zamora, Rodolfo. 2005. "Mexico: International Migration, Remittances and Development." In *Migration, Remittances and Development*, ed. OECD. Paris: OECD, 81–88.

———. 2007. "El Programa Tres por Uno de remesas colectivas en México: Lecciones y desafíos." *Migraciones Internacionales* 4: 165–72.

Goldring, Luin. 2004. "Family and Collective Remittances to Mexico: A Multi-dimensional Typology." *Development and Change* 35, no. 4: 799–840.

Gonzalez, Gilbert G. 1990. *Mexican Consuls and Labor Organizing: Imperial Politics in the Southwest*. Austin: University of Texas Press.

Hirshman, Albert. 1970. *Exit, Voice, and Loyalty: Responses to Decline in Firms, Organizations, and States*. Cambridge: Harvard University Press.

Instituto de los Mexicanos en el Exterior. 2004. *Clubes de Oriundos*. Instituto de los Mexicanos en el Exterior. Mexico City: Secretaria de Relaciones Exteriores.

———. 2011. *Asuntos Económicos y Comunitarios: Informe 2011*. Mexico City: Secretaria de Relaciones Exteriores.

Iskander, Natasha. 2005. "Social Learning as a Productive Project: The Tres-por-Uno Project in Zacatecas." In *Migration, Remittances and Development*, ed. OECD. Paris: OECD.

———. 2010. *Creative State: Forty Years of Migration and Development Policy in Morocco and Mexico*. Ithaca, NY: Cornell University Press.

Kijima, Yoko, and Horacio Gonzalez-Ramirez. 2012. "Has the Program 3×1 for Migrants Contributed to Community Development in Mexico? Evidence from Panel Data of 2000 and 2005." *Review of Development Economics* 16, no. 2: 291–304.

Landolt, Patricia. 2008. "The Transnational Geographies of Immigrant Politics: Insights from a Comparative Study of Migrant Grassroots Organizing." *Sociological Quarterly* 49, no. 1: 53–77.

Lopez, Sarah Lynn. 2009. "Migrant Remittances and the Mexican State: An Emergent Transnational Development Model?" Institute for the Study of Societal Issues (ISSI) Fellows Working Papers 37, University of California–Berkeley.

Orozco, Manuel. 2004. "Mexican Hometown Associations and Development Opportunities." *Journal of International Affairs* 57, no. 2: 31–52.

Orozco, Manuel, and Katherine Scaife Diaz. 2011. *Partnerships at Work: Western Union's 4+1 Experience in Mexico*. Washington, D.C: Inter-American Dialogue.

Orozco, Manuel, and Eugenia Garcia-Zanello. 2009. "Hometown Associations: Transnationalism, Philanthropy, and Development." *Brown Journal of World Affairs* 15, no. 2: 57–73.

Ostrom, Elinor. 1996. "Crossing the Great Divide: Co-production, Synergy, and Development." *World Development* 24, no. 6: 1073–87.

Passel, Jeffrey, D'Vera Cohn, and Ana Gonzalez-Barrera. 2012. *Net Migration from Mexico Falls to Zero—and Perhaps Less.* Washington DC: Pew Hispanic Center.

Portes, Alejandro, Cristina Escobar, and Alexandria Walton Radford. 2007. "Immigrant Transnational Organizations and Development: A Comparative Study." *International Migration Review* 41, no. 1: 242–81.

Ramakrishnan, S. Karthick, and Celia Viramontes. 2010. "Civic Spaces: Mexican Hometown Associations and Immigrant Participation." *The Journal of Social Issues* 66, no. 1: 155.

Ramírez, Héctor Rodríguez. 2012. "El papel de los migrantes mexicanos en la construcción de una agenda de políticas públicas: El caso del Programa 3x1." *Región y Sociedad* 53: 231–57.

Rivera-Salgado, Gaspar, Xóchitl Bada, and Luis Escala-Rabadán. 2005. "Mexican Migrant Civic and Political Participation in the U.S.: The Case of Hometown Associations in Los Angeles and Chicago." Paper presented at the Mexican Migrant Social and Civic Participation in the United States, 4–5 November, Woodrow Wilson International Center for Scholars, Washington DC.

SEDESOL. 2008. "Progama 3x1." In *56ª Jornada Informativa del IME: Líderes de Clubes de Oriundos y Directivos de Comités Cívicos-Patrióticos.* Mexico City: SEDESOL. 13–17. (there are no editors for this volume).

SEDESOL and Instituto de los Mexicanos en el Exterior. 2012. *Programa 3x1 Para Migrantes Lineamientos para los consulados de méxico 2012.* Mexico City: SEDESOL.

Sewell, William H. 2008. "The Temporalities of Capitalism." *Socio-Economic Review* 6, no. 3: 517–37.

Shannon, Amy. 2006. "Las Organizaciones Transnationales como Agentes de Desarrollo Local." In *El Programa 3x1 para Migrantes: ¿Primera Politica Transnacional en Mexico?,* ed. Rafael Ferandez de Castro, Rodolfo García Zamora, and Ana Vila Freyer. Mexico City: Universidad Autonoma de Zacatecas.

Smith, Michael Peter. 2007. "The Two Faces of Transnational Citizenship." *Ethnic and Racial Studies* 30, no. 6: 1096–1116.

Smith, Michael Peter, and Matt Bakker. 2008. *Citizenship Across Borders: The Political Transnationalism of el Migrante.* Ithaca, NY: Cornell University Press.

Smith, Robert C. 2003. "Diasporic Memberships in Historical Perspective: Comparative Insights from the Mexican, Italian and Polish Cases." *International Migration Review* 37, no. 3: 724–59.

Somerville, Will, Jamie Durana, and Aaron Matteo Terrazas. 2008. *Hometown Associations: An Untapped Resource for Immigrant Integration?* Washington, D.C.: Migration Policy Institute.

Vertovec, Steven. 2004. "Migrant Transnationalism and Modes of Transformation." *International Migration Review* 38, no. 3: 970–1001.

Waldinger, Roger, Eric Popkin, and Hector Aquiles Magana. 2008. "Conflict and Contestation in the Cross-Border Community: Hometown Associations Reassessed." *Ethnic and Racial Studies* 31, no. 5: 843–70.

Williams, Heather. 2008. *From Visibility to Voice: The Emerging Power of Migrants in Mexican Politics.* Fairfax, VA: George Mason University Press.

Chapter 5

Navigating Uneven Development
The Dynamics of Fractured Transnationalism

Margarita Rodríguez

This chapter discusses the results of the first comprehensive study on Nicaraguan immigrant organizations in South Florida. Conceptually, it connects four bodies of literature: (1) studies on the relationship between immigrant organizations and development (Portes, Escobar, and Walton Radford 2007; Portes, Escobar, and Arana 2008); (2) broad approaches focusing on global processes (Robinson 2003; Harvey 2005, 2010; Sassen 1996, 2010); (3) transnational perspectives on immigration (Basch, Glick Schiller, and Szanton Blanc 1994; Glick Schiller 2013; Portes, Escobar, and Walton Radford 2007; Glick Schiller and Fouron 1998; Levitt 1998); and (4) global perspectives on migration (Portes and Walton 1981; Sassen 2002; Gabaccia 2000; Grossfoguel 2003; Cervantes-Rodríguez 2010; Glick Schiller 2013). The study covers a time span of thirty years, from the Nicaraguan revolution of 1979 to 2011.

Methodologically, the study incorporates evidence from ethnographic research in South Florida and Nicaragua from the late 1990s to 2011, when conducted the last in a series of fieldwork stages including Miami-Dade County and several *departamentos* (provinces) in Nicaragua (Managua, Masaya, León, Estelí, and Matagalpa in the Pacific/Central Pacific regions and Bluefields and Corn Island in the Atlantic region). I completed semistructured, in-depth interviews with forty-six leaders or members of immigrant organizations, and twenty-six interviews with mayors of cities and towns in Nicaragua, informed observers, community activists, and leaders of civil society organizations. The research strategy also included

---

Notes for this chapter begin on page 156.

taking part in events organized by some of the entities investigated and conducting on-site observations of their projects.[1] Finally, I also undertook archival research at the Nicaraguan collection of the Otto Richter Library of the University of Miami, with a focus on documents, newspapers, and ads from organizations that were active in the 1980s.

Visualizing Development: Immigrant Organizations in the Migration-Development Nexus

On my last visit to Managua, I saw a prolific display of signs from security companies aiming to sell crime protection to other companies, households, office buildings, and individuals. Strategically located along main arteries in which garbage carts powered by actual horses coexist with high-horsepower SUVs, such marketing devices can be seen close to malls and near high-end residential areas, like Altamira and Los Robles, where the headquarters of prominent nongovernmental organizations (NGOs) and multilateral organizations share space. For the first time, I also witnessed an impressive deployment of government ads from the Frente Sandinista para la Liberación Nacional (FSLN) throughout major city avenues and beyond. These were not selling products or services but a brand. Large billboards featuring succinct messages and the smiling face of the FSLN party leader showed who was in charge. This avalanche of multiple ads coexists with the ever-present images of street vendors, windshield cleaners, and impoverished children defying the government's efforts to keep them hidden from the public eye.

As these images suggest, "uneven development" encompasses seemingly contradictory effects, including the coexistence of wealth and impoverishment in common terrains (Mandel 1975; Harvey 2005, 2006; Robinson 2003; Sassen 2010). The concept also points to imbalances in the price of labor power between rich and poor countries related to large social and economic gaps between labor-exporting and labor-importing nations. Such inequalities are linked to what has been termed "accumulation by dispossession" (Harvey 2006; Mandel 1975) and foster "the uneven and combined development of capitalist, pre-capitalist, and semi-capitalist relations of production, which are nevertheless linked together by capitalist relations of exchange" (Mandel 1975: 70).

Global restructuring associated with neoliberalism and the further deepening of capitalism at a global scale has shaped the collective efforts of immigrants on development-related issues in countries of origin through what, following Foucault, may be called a power-knowledge matrix. Furthermore, uneven development as a global process can only be grasped through the understanding of the state as a relevant actor holding control of resources, institutions, and immigration policies affecting the rights and responsibilities of citizens. Governments play a critical role at the national and local levels when supporting or obstructing the efforts of immigrant organizations.

NGOs have also played a key part in development on a global scale both as abiding followers of or counterhegemonic forces opposing international financial organizations. As Harvey (2010, 253) has noted, NGOs range from those with agendas that build upon critiques of the systemic faults of capitalism to those that are "actively neoliberal, engaging in the privatization of welfare functions or fostering institutional reforms to facilitate market integration of marginalised populations..." He calls attention to the limited problem-solving capacity of NGOs and their restricted "ameliorative" impact on the problems they target concerning development.

Nicaraguan immigrant organizations are a particular type of NGO that exhibit the general characteristics described above, including a complex and often ignored embeddedness in global structures through their involvement in transnational fields. Class locations and identities and patterns of development, cultural characteristics, and racial differentiations, some of which can be traced to the colonial period, have been among the critical forces shaping the formation and modus operandi of Nicaraguan organizations, including interactions and their transnational involvement. I thus give attention to social class, understood as the personification of economic relations (Harvey 2006) often involving "contradictory locations" (Wright 1985).

Immigrants' social position and repositioning strategies are also altered by gender, race, and other political variables that become constitutive elements of social mobility and power. Writings on international migration, especially those addressing transnationalism as "the process by which immigrants forge and sustain multi-stranded social relations linking together their societies of origin and settlement" (Basch, Glick Schiller, and Szanton Blanc 1994: 7), have extensively documented the elements that mold identities, social hierarchies, and power relations as part of the immigrant experience. This chapter emphasizes the heterogeneity of the immigrant population and experience as part of the reconstitution of the local and the global through power relations.

Fieldwork in Nicaragua, including my more recent research on transnational organizations, sheds light on the centrality of NGOs, their tense history of cooperation and conflict with the Nicaraguan state, and the institutions that have advanced alternative development paradigms. According to the International Center for Non-for-Profit Law (2014), there

are approximately 5,985 associations, foundations and similar organizations in Nicaragua. A cursory search of NGOs based in the United States
with projects in Nicaragua yielded nearly three hundred. Those entities
share several characteristics. Poverty eradication has been a common mission in the vast majority of cases. In addition, relief efforts, health services,
international economic development, education, religion and spiritual development, and community improvement are among the most frequent
issues targeted by these organizations.

Women, immigrants, children, orphans, poor people, farmers, and those
who cannot afford health care tend to be among the targeted beneficiaries.
In Nicaragua, civil society organizations (CSOs) are also widely known
for their relief efforts at critical moments, such as during natural disasters
and subsequent recovery stages. They are also known for their involvement
in projects financed by regional and global development agencies, and
for the edgy relationship many have had with administrations of varying
ideological persuasions.

During interviews, my respondents tangentially referred to national
development, mostly to emphasize that Nicaragua is one of the poorest
countries in the Americas. Yet as they explained their specific goals and
actions, development-related issues rose to the forefront, but with a focus
on individuals, specific groups, and communities. This was telling given
broader state-centric approaches to "national development" dominant
during the 1980s. A closer look at the historical context in which immigrant organizations were formed, their mission, and their functions led to
an initial typology that maps their location in global structures and illustrates the influence of differing development paradigms.

The first type, transnational humanitarian organizations and organizations with pro-development projects, provide medical services, school
materials, clothes, food, and similar services to impoverished individuals
and households in Nicaragua. The "human development" framework in-
forms their approach. These organizations are heterogeneous in terms of
the social class of their leaders and members, regions of origin, the role of
women, their ability to command resources, and their reach in Nicaragua.
Some are oriented toward the immigrant community, having been system-
atically involved in assisting Nicaraguans in Miami establish networks to
access social services, training opportunities, or immigration services.

The second type, business-centered and professional organizations,
work as a platform to facilitate recognition and status and form social
networks among their members and with other entities. They enable
social actors to reconfigure their class position. Members are concerned
with gaining access to markets and expanding their investment potential
or normalizing their participation as professionals in labor markets. The

nurses' association is the only professional organization that has a well-established assistance program in communities of Nicaragua.

The third type, civic/political organizations, focus on immigration and citizenship rights and voice opposition against nondemocratic and corrupt actions and events in Nicaragua. They are instrumental in the reconfiguration of political identities. Some articulate state hegemonic narratives and interventions and others challenge them. Occasionally the same organization can perform the two functions simultaneously or at different times. With few exceptions, they are actively involved in transnational projects.

The fourth type, cultural organizations, maintain and re-create the "cultural memory" of groups outside Nicaragua through the exaltation of nationalist themes and figures, such as the great poet Rubén Darío. They have been instrumental in the reformulation of nationhood and national identity of Nicaraguans in the United States, and have promoted a sense of Hispanic belonging—*Hispanidad*—through cultural initiatives. They also tend to operate in transnational fields.

Despite their specific focus and strong philanthropic tendencies, self-interest and, in some cases, for-profit rationale cut across organizations. All of them secure or make an effort to secure revenues in the form of grants, as NGOs have become an important source of legitimate employment and income-generating activity. All organizations have also been involved in humanitarian efforts during natural disasters in Nicaragua. And all kinds of organizations have played a role in sustaining and remaking identities. The above typology, however, shows key differences in terms of expressed goals, class-related strategies, and transnational engagement. Next, I discuss these organizations in greater detail and use other forms of classification to capture diverse aspects of their operations.

Nicaraguan Immigrant Organizations in South Florida since 1979

Table A.1 shows the names of organizations included in this study and currently operating in South Florida, the year in which they were formed, whether they are registered as nonprofits, and whether they are regularly engaged in transnational activities. Of the forty Nicaraguan immigrant organizations identified as being operating in South Florida when the study was concluded, thirty-three were formally registered as 501(c)(3) not-for-profit organizations and seven had no formal incorporation. Thirty-four had developed sustained links with institutions, associations, and/or communities in Nicaragua. Tables A.2 and A.3. display the organizations by type and those formed in the 1980s respectively. Most of the organizations formed since the 1990s (over 40 percent) have been focus on civic/humanitarian goals, followed by organizations with professional or business promotion concerns (20 percent) and cultural goals (10 percent). Table A.3 shows that 50 percent of the organizations formed during the 1980s focused on political goals or had a civic and/or military focus. The rest were equally divided into organizations addressing humanitarian aid and civic engagement, culture and sports, or they were alumni associations, which combine different objectives. A contrast of Tables A.2 and A.3 reveals that out of the eighty-one organizations identified, fifty-one were operating at some point in the 1980s; of those, only ten survived to the present, while new ones have emerged since 1990.

During the 1980s, Nicaraguans formed more than fifty organizations in Miami, most of them pursuing political objectives, but some also devoted to humanitarian, professional, and cultural goals. The vast majority of the political organizations and associations with a militant profile did not survive the 1980s. Most were dismantled after the defeat of the Sandinistas in the election of 1989. Most professional organizations survived to the present day, as did alumni, cultural, and civic organizations. Some professional and civic entities changed their names, usually as they broadened their scope or modified their immediate goals to adjust to new realities.

Professional organizations formed during the 1980s advanced instrumental goals such as social mobility, incorporation into the labor market, and professional recognition. Many empowered Nicaraguan professionals and facilitated collective bargains before state and federal authorities, and facilitated connections with strong Cuban American organizations and the emerging Cuban American lobby. In the process, members of Nicaraguan organizations underwent a transition. They claimed a sense of belonging to specific groups and reinforced professional and regional identities forged in Nicaragua through immersion into a new and highly dynamic social environment. This process involved the adoption of new identities (e.g., "exile," "refugee") and a sense of membership in entities such as the "Nicaraguan community" or the "Hispanic community." Immersion into American society did not necessarily hinder the forging of transnational networks and the advancement of transnational projects; in some cases domestic immersion and transnational engagement were two sides of the same coin.

Transnationalism was truncated for Nicaraguan migrants during the 1980s. Some remittance agencies operated "underground," and transnational households adopted piecemeal strategies toward Nicaraguans studying abroad who had close relatives in the home country. Some forms of transnationalism were related to the survival of a few segments of the private sector in Nicaragua. Nicaraguans launched transnational strategies that were not restricted to Nicaragua, mostly in Central America, as was the case of many South Florida–based Nicaraguans.

Immigration, Class Differences, and the Formation of Associations

After being dislodged from their class positions in the country of origin, Nicaraguan professionals sought to reconstitute social ties and networks and reposition themselves in the receiving society by forming associations. The Nicaraguan Bankers Association (NABA) is a case in point. According to a prominent member of that group:

> The first thing the Sandinistas did was to take over the banks. The bankers left to the United States, although they developed substantive businesses and made important innovations in the industry throughout Central America. Miami became the mecca of Nicaraguan professionals. In 1983 we founded the Nicaraguan American Bankers Association (NABA). At some point we had a roster of about one thousand members, both bankers and workers; lending officers, stockbrokers, etc. Our first goal was to create a professional network to share experiences and support each other. NABA also assisted in the opening of job opportunities for Nicaraguans in the banking industry and in the provision of training.[2]

By supporting causes that were beyond their immediate instrumental goals, such as immigrants' rights, NABA secured a position of leadership among Nicaraguans and Hispanics in general (Cervantes-Rodríguez 2006). As they became further immersed in US society, they also acted transnationally. The growing internationalization of the financial sector offered a suitable platform to achieve that objective (Robinson 2003; Cervantes-Rodríguez 2006).

Other professional organizations also blossomed in the 1980s; they included two major endeavors, the Asociación Médica Nicaragüense en el Exilio (Nicaraguan Medical Association in Exile) and the Asociación Nicaragüense de Ingenieros y Arquitectos (Nicaraguan Association of Engineers and Architects, or ANIA). The first focused on accreditation and, through a strategic alliance with Cuban American organizations, allowed Nicaraguan physicians access to a special program that facilitated preparatory training at the University of Miami.

This benefit was not extended to all immigrant professionals, but, like Cuban doctors, Nicaraguan physicians in exile benefited from it. They also received ample support from other organizations, including ANIA, which assumed the presidency of the Federation of Nicaraguan Professional Organizations in Exile (FANPE), investing the Nicaraguan medical organization with still more leverage. ANIA was involved in accreditation and in helping its members find jobs. It cooperated with the California Department of Transportation by establishing a link with Nicaraguan engineers and architects to meet the department's demands for Hispanic professionals in San Francisco.[3] Like other professional associations, ANIA also assisted colleagues in their attempts to regularize their immigration status and win contested asylum cases.

Since the 1980s, Nicaraguan professionals have faced difficulties finding employment. The most obvious problem arose when their knowledge of English did not meet prevailing standards. According to Martha Borgen, president of ANIA:

> We had architecture, design and engineering firms in Nicaragua prior to 1979 that were concerned with the introduction of new trends and techniques. But we went back in terms of the development for about fifty years during the Sandinista regime. ... Then we came here. This is an industrialized country and technologically very advanced. If the professionals in the field didn't catch up, they would be left behind. So we had language and technological gaps that we had to overcome.[4]

By the time Nicaraguan professionals organized, thousands of Nicaraguans of lower education and very modest economic means were arriving as well (Cervantes-Rodríguez 2006). Their individual and social needs substantially differed from those of the economic elite. Their pressing issues included how to find affordable dwellings and jobs, temporary aid for food, public schools, and programs in which they could learn English and other useful skills. Their experience was fraught with drama, because many poor Nicaraguans had crossed the border illegally and most could not afford good attorneys to assist them. Many peasants and poor people who had fought with the opposition (Contras) in Nicaragua or were displaced by the war started to arrive in Miami as refugees.

Accordingly, the 1980s and 1990s witnessed the foundation of humanitarian and civic organizations that assisted Nicaraguans by facilitating access to legal counsel and incorporating them into the Cuban American safety net. The Comité de Nicaragüenses Pobres en el Exilio (Committee of Poor Nicaraguans in Exile, or CONIPOE), Fraternidad Nicaragüense, Centro Asistencial Nicaragüense, and Hogar Amor y Esperanza, among other organizations, focused on poor Nicaraguans in need of assistance. Cristóbal Mendoza, founder of CONIPOE, aptly summarized the rationale behind the foundation of these organizations: "We founded CONIPOE on June 27, 1985. I told myself, 'the rich people are here already, the middle class is leaving Nicaragua but we also have poor people leaving through the border and coming to Miami. The rich live in another world.

They have their own world and we have ours. The world of the poor is the world of unsatisfied necessities.'"[5]

There have been strong symbolic unifiers across all organizations—such as the "exile" or "refugee" identities—but the rationales leading to their formation, their membership, and their interaction with other similar groupings reflect profound class divisions. Furthermore, organizations themselves re-created such divides through the deployment of symbols of status and distinct patterns of communication.

Between 1990 and 2006, Nicaraguan society underwent important transformations. Under President Violeta Chamorro's government, Nicaragua started an intense rearticulation with the global structures of capitalism, which included the systematic intervention of international financial institutions, such as the World Bank and the International Monetary Fund, and the increased presence of the US Agency for International Development. The initiation of structural adjustments in the 1990s went hand in hand with a call for the financial and human capital accumulated by the exiles in South Florida. Personal calls from members of ministerial cabinets, tax incentives, the presentation of the master plan for the city of Managua, and all sorts of strategies and incentives were used at different points between 1990 and 2006 to attract Nicaraguan investors and to reverse the effects of the brain drain suffered during the 1980s.[6]

Some former exiles were hired in high-ranking Nicaraguan government and private sector positions; many made strategic investments in finance, real estate, and other increasingly profitable activities, while many others opened car repair shops, cafeterias, restaurants, motels, beauty parlors, and pet shops, sometimes hanging bilingual signs or even signs in Spanglish at the entrance of their businesses. A legal framework was created to address claims for compensation for expropriations and the return of real estate property and other assets to exiles and other Nicaraguans who had been affected during the 1980s.[7] This period witnessed an unprecedented involvement of Nicaraguan migrants in transnational activities and projects (Cervantes-Rodríguez 2006). The deep changes that Nicaraguan immigrant organizations in South Florida experienced in the 1990s and early 2000s, during the administration of Violeta Chamorro and the subsequent administrations of Arnoldo Alemán and Enrique Bolaños, were part and parcel of regime change and the expansion of transnational social fields connecting Nicaragua with the United States.

Table A.2 shows that most of the organizations and hometown associations formed between 1990 and 2010 focused on humanitarian and pro-development issues in Nicaragua. In addition, most civic/political and cultural organizations and alumni associations had some type of transnational engagement. The new political context affected organizations in

other ways as well. Some professional organizations saw their membership shrink either nominally or in terms of their effectiveness as a result of
the return of professionals and business owners to Nicaragua, their relocation to other states, or their retirement. Second-generation Nicaraguans
tend not to be involved in transnational organizations. Only the leader
of the Nicaraguan American Civic Task Force is a second-generation migrant, the daughter of a prominent leader of the exile community. Florida
International University in Miami also has a Nicaraguan American student association, which has been involved in some humanitarian efforts
in Nicaragua.

Changes in Immigration Laws and Their Aftermath

In the United States, the period spanning the last decade of the twentieth
century and the beginning of the twenty-first saw regressive changes in
immigration and welfare-related laws with the passage of the Personal Responsibility and Work Opportunity Reconciliation Act of 1996 (PRWORA)
and the Illegal Immigration Reform and Immigrant Responsibility Act of
1996 (IRRIRA). These two laws curtailed immigrant access to social services, particularly health care, and further criminalized unauthorized
immigrants.

These laws prompted a strong reaction from pro-immigrant groups
and immigrant organizations. The struggle to override the new provi-
sions and stop deportations brought Nicaraguans together as never before. Some organizations, including the Nicaraguan Fraternity and the
Nicaraguan Committee of Poor Nicaraguans, actively mobilized, but
most organizations also became widely involved. This was done, as emphasized by the leaders of one of the most vocal organizations, by "following the rules of the game."[8] This led to the passage of the Nicaraguan Adjustment and Central American Relief Act (NACARA) in 1997.
NACARA eventually led to the adjudication of permanent legal status
to over seventy thousand Nicaraguans, allowing many to travel to their
home country and return to the United States. Arguably, Nicaraguans
exemplified what has been described as three key aspects of successful
civic engagement: "literacy," or knowledge of community affairs and political issues, "skills," or competency in achieving group goals, and "civic
attachment," or a feeling or belief that individuals matter in community
affairs (Stepick et al. 2001).

Nevertheless, as noticed by many of those interviewed for this study,
NACARA did not translate into significant political power for Nicaraguans.[9] Deportations increased dramatically from 2006 to 2011. Nora

Sándigo, the founder and president of American Fraternity (known as Nicaraguan Fraternity until the passage of NACARA), explained that the organization focuses on promoting immigration reform, stopping deportation, and assisting children whose close relatives have been deported or are in detention centers.[10] However, an effective civic mobilization similar to the one experienced prior to the passage of NACARA has not yet taken place.

Profiles and Specifics of Organizations with Transnational Projects

Most organizations involved in humanitarian and development-related issues were established between 1990 and 2006. The American Nicaraguan Foundation (ANF) is the best known and the one with the greatest impact in Nicaragua. ANF was founded by the Pellas family, one of the wealthiest groups in Nicaragua and Central America. The Pellas family has a history of emigration to the United States after the Sandanista revolution of 1979, and ANF is linked to the same history. It has its development and financial headquarters in downtown Miami and Washington DC and manages several field operations in Nicaragua. The team in Managua includes experienced as well as young engineers and other supporting staff. Their capacity to raise funds and target several projects simultaneously has grown over time: "In 1992, ANF distributed $2 million in food, cloth, medicine, and classroom materials; by 1998 we were distributing $53.2 million after Hurricane Mitch, which placed us among the main providers of assistance to the affected families."[11]

ANF has distributed educational materials and basic medicines to hundreds of clinics and other medical facilities since then. Food assistance to schools has also been a top priority. ANF representatives reach out to more than three hundred thousand low-income and poor individuals in Nicaragua. ANF collaborates with governmental entities such as the Nicaraguan Low-Income Program of the Institute of Urban Development, the Water and Drainage Ministry, and the Health and Education Departments. ANF's connections beyond Nicaragua include early cooperation, since 2001, with United Way International and partnerships with NGOs such as Food for the Poor and La Colmena. ANF's multilayered fund-raising strategy also includes Nicaraguan corporations—such as the Pellas Group, ESTESA, Nicaraguan Sugar Estates, and the CiSa/Mercon Coffee Group—plus fund-raising activities in the United States, prominently in Miami. The organization has evolved from the design of programs for assistance to the poor to full-fledged community development projects. According to a prominent ANF official:

Originally, we had a focus on humanitarian activities including the distribution of goods—such as food, medicines, school supplies, and the like to the neediest people in different areas of Nicaragua. Then we developed our department of projects. Currently, we work with sixteen hundred organizations. As of today, we provide sixty thousand families with daily meals. Sustainable development projects involving agricultural production do not have as impressive an impact. However, once they start growing, a single project may impact two hundred families who receive training. Assistance in terms of sustainable development means that they will have their own farms and will become self-sufficient in the near future.[12]

In 2010, ANF was ranked by *Forbes Magazine* (n/d) among the two hundred largest US-based philanthropic organizations. During my fieldwork trips to Nicaragua, I visited five ANF development projects: a housing and community project in the municipality of Pueblo Nuevo in Estelí; the ANF-Taiwan International Cooperation and Development Agricultural Project in León; the ANF-ICDF Agricultural Training and Production Project in Tipitapa; a housing and community project in El Hular, Matagalpa; and a water purification project in the community of La Mona, León.[13] A project involving agricultural activities related to papaya and guava plantations in León incorporated women into market-related activities for which they received payment. Housing, water sanitation, and community-building projects have had a tangible impact on poverty alleviation and the empowerment of individuals and families throughout the country.

In 2005, a group formed by Nicaraguan women from wealthy families in Miami created a committee in support of the Instituto Técnico Especializado Juan Pablo Segundo. Located in Managua, the institute offers technical education, including carpentry, culinary training, cloth making, and computer training, to young Nicaraguans from poor families. The organization is led by artist Rosario Ortiz de Chamorro and is staffed by women volunteers. They provide funds to cover year-round scholarships (about $375 per student) and some of the institute's regular expenses. Between 2005 and 2008 the committee raised more than $100,000. Projects have included the construction of a kitchen and a bakery, the construction of a center for the design and production of clothing, and a computer lab.

The institute receives partial support from Nicaraguan immigrants living in other US cities as well.[14] The same group of Nicaraguan women who support the institute also make contributions to the Asilo de Ancianos de León. These women are part of families that have developed a transnational lifestyle, including frequent trips to Nicaragua where they have investments and often second homes. Some of the members of this committee and the leadership of the ANF are linked to each other through kin and friendship networks.

The Nicaraguan American Nurses Association (NANA) was founded in 1996 to support the professional efforts of Nicaraguan nurses in Miami and to formalize their assistance to communities in Nicaragua.[15] Most members of this organization are immigrant nurses from the Nicaraguan Atlantic coast; in fact, the history of NANA is intertwined with a strong nursing tradition rooted in missionary efforts to deliver health services to Atlantic coast communities in earlier centuries. Those efforts concentrated on the Honduran-Nicaraguan border, in places like Bilwaskarma, separated from Honduras by the River Coco, and the cities of Puerto Cabezas and Bluefields. The Moravian School of Nursing was founded in Puerto Cabezas in the 1930s. The first president of NANA and many other members are from Bilwaskarma. Most constituents of the organization have been in the United States for more than a decade and have been working as registered nurses in South Florida for many years.[16]

The Nicaraguan American Nurses Association works in close partnership with the Women's Group on the Community Presbyterian Church. These two organizations tend to focus on marginal neighborhoods and rural areas in the Managua-Masaya-Granada corridor, and many of them have retained personal links to the Atlantic coast, assisting with remittances and other family transfers. Their projects in Nicaragua are coordinated with the Vicentine Sisters religious order through family, friendship, professional, and religious connections. According to Martina Bolaños, vice president of the International Association of Charities, the Voluntarias Vicentinas is a lay association founded in France by Saint Vincent de Paul that currently has more than 150,000 volunteers in twenty-one countries.[17] When asked about their impact in Nicaragua, representatives of the Vicentinas noted that the communities they work with are extremely poor and unable to raise funds locally.[18] Under such circumstances, monies sent from Miami by women's groups make a big difference. According to the coordinator of the Presbyterian Church Women's Group:

> Our work is also important for the children. Many Nicaraguan children don't even have birth certificates. The women's group goes [to Nicaragua] once a year and the nurses go at least twice every year and we alert families to the importance of having children registered to have greater access to social services and things like that. We also bring medicines and sanitary products and help provide school meals.[19]

Concerns about extreme poverty in the Atlantic region led to the foundation, in 1998, of Costeños Unidos Pro-Desarrollo de la Costa Atlántica (CUPROC; People United for Development of the Atlantic Coast), but, because it had no consensus concerning priorities, it eventually disappeared. Some of CUPROC's members, however, have continued their transnational efforts through hometown associations (HTAs) or by connecting with international volunteer organizations like the Lions Club. Currently, there are five registered nonprofit groups working in the region: the Nicaraguan Nurses Association, Friends in Action for the RAAN (Región Autónoma de la Costa Norte), the Alumni Association of El Colegio Moravo, the Alumni Association of El Colegio Cristobal Colón, and the Bluefields Caribbean Lions Club.

Having had its traditional economy destroyed by a combination of predatory actions by multinational companies, natural disasters, and out-migration, the Atlantic coast in Nicaragua faces many problems at present. Main cities such as Bluefields, but also small towns, have become heavily dependent on immigrant remittances and investments. The mayor of Corn Island explained:

> We have a lot of people living outside Corn Island. Only a few of my childhood friends stayed here; most are now in Miami and Washington. They help by sending money, which has become a main source of income. We depended on fishing but that's mostly gone [as a result of resource depletion]; tourism is in diapers. Most people mostly depend on remittances.[20]

Among organizations founded between 1990 and 2006 are the Nicaraguan American Chamber of Commerce and the American Nicaraguan Chamber of Commerce—the second entity created by disaffected members of the first. Both cater to Nicaraguan business owners interested in expanding in South Florida, Nicaragua, and beyond under new free trade agreements. Another organization, EXPONICA, started as a key promoter of grassroots trade by Nicaraguan artisans specializing in the sale of ethnic products in Miami. The EXPONICA Fair was well established by the late 1990s, bringing together craft makers and food producers from Masaya and other areas in Nicaragua. EXPONICA has evolved into a Latin American Fair in Miami-Dade County, under the leadership of the same Nicaraguan entrepreneurs that initiated it many years ago.

Cultural organizations include the Instituto Cultural Rubén Darío, Fundación Internacional Rubén Darío, the Círculo de Escritores y Poetas Iberoamericanos, and organzations that promote local cultures in the form of festivals. In addition to their expressed functions, these organizations contribute to relief efforts during natural disasters in Nicaragua.

The Present Scene

The period between 2007 and 2012 has witnessed a deep recession in the United States, unprecedented numbers of deportations, reductions in Official Development Assistance (ODA), and a slowdown in the growth of the value of remittances. Some of these trends were in the making years before the onset of the recession. Development assistance, which exceeded $1.2 billion in 2004, declined dramatically in recent years as a result of the overall global decline of ODA and the cuts made by some donors after the left-wing Sandanista Front came back into power. These are important trends considering that Nicaragua is classified among the countries that most heavily depend on ODA and remittances. Remittances are estimated to be the equivalent of about 13 percent of Nicaragua's gross domestic product (GDP) (ECLA 2010).

According to census data, nearly 105,000 Nicaraguans reside in Miami-Dade County. This is the largest concentration of Nicaraguans in a metropolitan area outside their native country and 30 percent of the Nicaraguan population in the United States. Interviews and informal conversations revealed that many Nicaraguan families are facing great challenges, including the risk of deportation and family separation. Many children have been left stranded as a result of harsh deportation practices in the past years. This situation has been compounded by the recession, which has affected not only manual laborers but also a segment of the well-educated and fully bilingual members of the group. Many have faced long periods of unemployment; others now work intermittently in low-paid jobs that do not offer health insurance or accident protection. Miami-Dade County has been deeply affected by rising poverty rates since the recession that started in 2007. Between 2010 and 2012, family and individual poverty rates increased to 18.9 and 20.8 percent, respectively; in 2012, 13.6 percent of the country children were living below 50 percent of the poverty line; a condition known as "deep poverty" (2012 American Community Survey data, cited in Miami-Dade County, 2013). In 2012, the poverty rate reached 20.9 and 27.3 percent for the foreign born population and its non-naturalized segment, respectively (ibid.). Many Nicaraguans rely on charities for basic social assistance and health care. Local churches have been another important source of support for Nicaraguans. Religious institutions like Our Lady of Divine Providence Church, located in Miami, have been at the lead of this relief effort.

Simultaneously, the installation of Daniel Ortega, the FLSN leader, as president of Nicaragua marked the beginning of a period characterized by the formation of new civic and political organizations in South Florida. Since 2007, shortly after the Sandanistas came back to power, many of these organizations started to denounce corruption and the antidemocratic nature of the Sandinista government. Some civic organizations in Miami are currently involved in transnational advocacy related to citizenship. Two issues that are gradually capturing their interest are immigrant rights in the United States and, simultaneously, the way immigrants' lives are being affected by regulations enacted by the Nicaraguan state.

Nicaraguans in South Florida at the onset of the century are confronting a complex situation marked by the counterpoint between philanthropic transnational activities by different groups, including members of the exile elite, professional organizations, alumni associations, and groups of diverse class composition, along with an increasingly precarious economic situation both among poor immigrants in Miami and large segments of the Nicaraguan population at home. The advent of the Sandinista Front to power in 2007 again politicized Nicaraguan transnationalism, reenergizing anti Sandinista sentiments. In this context, relations between the home government and its expatriates, while not severed, have acquired an increasingly adversarial character. Nicaraguan transnationalism is certainly fractured along multiple ways, giving rise to a complex context and unpredictable future concerning the transnational engagement of immigrant organizations and its implications.

Conclusion

This chapter has shown that the formation of Nicaraguan organizations and their transnational engagement since 1979 have been framed by global social and economic processes and globally dominant discourses and forms of intervention on development. Since the 1990s, Nicaraguan immigrant organizations have displayed an increasing propensity toward engagement in transnational projects. However, this involvement has been uneven. Important differences exist across organizations in terms of access to material and nonmaterial resources. Nicaraguans in South Florida are sharply differentiated in terms of social class. The social class of leaders, access to donations from the private sector, and the institutional articulation of organizations with US-based institutions associated with philanthropic structures prove to be main factors explaining differential access to resources and the scope and impact of transnational activities. Such disparities have been accentuated by recent global economic trends. ANF is singular in two important respects. First, it is an immigrant organization that displays characteristics of global nonprofit organizations, including a sophisticated corporate structure. Second, it relies on personal relationships and strong ties with philanthropic organizations directly involved in the human development/global development framework, but also with members of Nicaragua's economic elite.

Nevertheless, organizations that differ in terms of goals, social class, and resources often share certain commonalities in practice. The commitment and skills of the leaders of the organizations and their social recognition and ability to mobilize volunteers and command resources have been critical aspects associated with greater transnational reach. In addition, most organizations have effectively mobilized to raise funds during moments of crisis, especially those prompted by natural disasters.

Although the success of Nicaraguan grassroots organizations regarding development in the home country is limited, tens of thousands of individuals, as well as social service, educational, and religious institutions in Nicaragua, have benefited from the support they have received from community-based groups in South Florida. Such entities have had an ameliorative impact on Nicaraguan underdevelopment. Can immigrant organizations do more? The continuation of power relations that perpetuate underdevelopment and an increasingly adversarial relation with the regime in Nicaragua suggest they can only have partial success assuaging poverty and dispossession.

Finally, this chapter does not support the argument that transnational involvement and incorporation into US society operate as a zero-sum game. The idea that transnational immigrant involvement slows down integration into the receiving polity has no basis of fact. In the 1980s, several branches of the American government supported and even incited the involvement of exile organizations to support specific US security objectives. Increasing acquaintance of immigrants with institutions in the United States has, in turn, increased their ability to tap resources necessary to maintain transnational projects.

Nicaraguan immigrant organizations have embodied strategies, values, and norms that have been informed by neoliberal approaches to the world economy particularly influenced by US-based institutions. The discourses that envision immigrant organizations as a unified group operating in opposition to the structures of capitalism or as a threat to "the basic unit of the nation" miss these complexities. Cyclical shifts in the dominant conceptualizations of development on a global scale since the 1960s have led to the current stage in which the migrants tend to be rationalized as "agents of development."[21] Nicaraguan immigrant organizations have tended to operate within these parameters. Their transnational involvement and impact are far from being antisystemic.

Prior research has shown that immigrants do not generally become involved in transnational activities until a certain threshold of economic and legal security is reached (Portes, Escobar, and Arana 2008; Guarnizo, Portes, and Haller 2003). To be sure, the precarious situation that many immigrants in South Florida face makes difficult the expansion of such ties. These immigrants are torn between their own unsatisfied needs and the claims for help by kin and friends back home. They are further conflicted by their awareness of growing inequalities, escalating violence, and a precarious democracy with authoritarian tendencies in Nicaragua. This complex scenario suggests that uneven transnationalism between Nicaragua and the United States will continue to have only very limited ameliorative effects on the precarious situation in which many Nicaraguans live.

Margarita Rodríguez, PhD, is a Lecturer at the Department of International Studies, University of Miami. She is the author of *International Migration in Cuba: Accumulation, Imperial Designs and Transnational Social Fields* (Pennsylvania State University Press, 2010) and coeditor of *Caribbean Migration to Western Europe and the United States: Essays on Incorporation, Identities and Citizenship* (Temple University Press, 2009). She has studied the Nicaraguan community in the United States and Spanish migration in earlier periods, publishing articles and book chapters on these and other topics. Her research interests focus on migration issues, including global aspects related to labor migration, migration of health care professionals, and the transnational strategies launched by migrants to access health services.

Notes

A preliminary version of this chapter was delivered in May 2009 as a research report to the Center for Migration and Development (CMD), Princeton University. I would like to express my appreciation to Alejandro Portes for his interest in the Nicaraguan case and for inviting me to address it. My appreciation also goes to Nancy Doolan from the CMD and Bruce Bagley from the Department of International Studies at the University of Miami for the support received in terms of logistics; and to graduate students Ali Adolfo Bustamante and Randy Salazar, who assisted me with the gathering of some of the data from secondary sources. I conducted all fieldwork, including all interviews and observations in South Florida and Nicaragua. The precious time of other participants who were interviewed is greatly appreciated as well.

1. An interview schedule comprising twenty-five questions was sent to a subsample of twelve organizations as a supplement to in-depth interviews and has been used for the characterization of the organizations. The most relevant information was captured through in-depth interviews and on-site observations.
2. Interview with Roberto Arguello, founder and former president of the Nicaraguan Bankers Association, Miami, 16 July 2008.

3. Email communication with Martha Borgen, current president of the Association of Nicaraguan Engineers and Architects (formerly known as ANIA), Miami, 15 April 2009.
4. Interview with Martha Borgen, current president of the Association of Nicaraguan Engineers and Architects (formerly known as ANIA), Miami, 5 April 2009.
5. Interview with Cristobal Mendoza, president of CONIPOE, Miami, 15 February 2009.
6. For a detailed analysis of transnationalism among Nicaraguans in the 1990s, see Cervantes-Rodríguez (2006).
7. Although some people have benefited from this approach, the mechanisms to address these issues and the political and economic aspects of the process have made it extremely difficult, and Nicaraguans are still struggling with the issue of compensation and the return of properties.
8. Interview with Cristobal Mendoza, president of CONIPOE, Miami, 15 February 2009.
9. The interview with attorney Mario Lovo (Miami, 17 June 2009) was particularly revealing on this issue.
10. Interview with Nora Sándigo, Miami, 22 June 2009.
11. Interview with Ariel López, general manager, 5 February 2009.
12. Interview with Alvaro Pereira, executive director of ANF, Nicaragua, 4 March 2009.
13. Pictures and additional information about the organizations can be seen at http://nicaraguanssouthflorida.wordpress.com/ (Accessed 10 March 2009).
14. Interview with Rosario Ortiz de Chamorro and other members of the organization. Data from the 2005–9 report provided to the author by the coordinator of the group.
15. Interview with Alice Blandford, president of NANA, Miami, 21 February 2009.
16. Interview with Arleen Bloomfield, first president of NANA, Miami, 15 May 2009. See also the newsletter *Moravian Missions* 12, no. 10 (November 2003).
17. Interview with Martina Bolaños, vice president of Asociación Internacional de Caridades, and Mercedes Bolaños Martínez, national president of Vicentine Volunteers Nicaragua, Managua, 10 March 2009.
18. Ibid.
19. Interview with Melinda Brown, coordinator of the Women's Group on the Community Prebysterian Church, Miami, 12 February 2009.
20. Interview with Cleveland Webster, mayor of Corn Island, Corn Island, 6 March 2009.
21. Emphasis on the financial mainstreaming of remittances and the positive outcomes of "social remittances" has been part of these efforts. For example, it has been argued that "social remittances … are potential community development aid" under the rationale that "[b]ecause they travel through identifiable pathways to specific audiences, policymakers and planners can channel certain kinds of information to particular groups with positive results" (Levitt 1998: 927).

References

Basch, Linda, Nina Glick Schiller, and Cristina Szanton Blanc. 1994. *Nations Unbound: Transnational Projects, Postcolonial Predicaments, and Deterritorialized Nation-States.* Langhorne, PA: Gordon and Breach.

Cervantes-Rodríguez, Margarita. 2006. "Nicaraguans in Miami-Dade County: Immigration, Incorporation, and Transnational Entrepreneurship" *Latino Studies* 4, no. 2 (Spring): 232–57.

———. 2010. *International Migration in Cuba: Accumulation, Imperial Designs and Transnational Social Fields.* University Park: Pennsylvania State University Press.

ECLA (Economic Commission for Latin America and the Caribbean). 2010. *Nicaragua.* http://www.eclac.cl/publicaciones/xml/4/41974/Nicaragua_eng_mar ch_11.pdf. (Accessed 11 March 2010).

FORBES, n/d. "The 200 Largest U.S. Charity List (fiscal year ending in 12/31, 2010)." Retrieved from: http://www.forbes.com/lists/2011/14/charities-11_American-Nicaraguan-Foundation_CH0233.html

Gabaccia, Donna. 2000. *Italy's Many Diasporas.* Seattle: University of Washington Press.

Glick Schiller, Nina. 2013. "A Global Perspective on Migration and Development." In *Migration, Development and Transnationalization,* ed. Thomas Faist and Nina Glick Schiller. New York: Berghahn Books. 22–41.

Glick Schiller, Nina, and Georges Fouron. 1998. "Transnational Lives and National Identities: The Identity Politics of Haitian Immigrants." *Comparative Urban and Community Research* 6: 130–61.

Grosfoguel, Ramon. 2003. *Colonial Subjects: Puerto Ricans in a Global Perspective.* Berkeley: University of California Press.

Guarnizo, Luis Eduardo, Alejandro Portes, and William Haller. 2003. "Assimilation and Transnationalism: Determinants of Transnational Political Action among Contemporary Migrants." *American Journal of Sociology* 3, no. 108 (May): 1211–48.

Harvey, David. 2005. *A Brief History of Neoliberalism,* New York: Oxford University Press.

———. 2006. *The Limits of Capital.* London: Verso.

———. 2007. "Neoliberalism as Creative Destruction." *Annals of the American Academy of Political and Social Science* 610 (March): 22–44.

———. 2010. *The Enigma of Capital and the Crises of Capitalism.* New York: Oxford University Press.

International Center for Non-for profit Law. "NGO Law Monitor: Nicaragua" (last updated June 16th, 2014) Retrieved from: http://www.icnl.org/research/monitor/nicaragua.html

Levitt, Peggy. 1998. "Social Remittances: Migration Driven Local-Level Forms of Cultural Diffusion." *International Migration Review* 32, no. 4 (Winter): 926–48.

Mandel, Ernest. 1975. *Late Capitalism.* New York: Verso.

Miami-Dade County, Department of Regulatory and Economic Resources. "Miami Dade-County at a Glance" (October 2013).

Portes, Alejandro, Cristina Escobar, and Renelinda Arana. 2008. "Bridging the Gap: Transnational and Ethnic Organizations in the Political Incorporation of

Immigrants in the United States." *Ethnic and Racial Studies* 31, no. 6 (September): 1056–90.

Portes, Alejandro, Cristina Escobar, and Alexandria Walton Radford. 2007. "Immigrant Transnational Organizations and Development." *International Migration Review* 41, no. 1: 242–81.

Portes, Alejandro, and John Walton. 1981. *Labor, Capital and the International System.* New York: Academic Press.

Robinson, William. 2003. *Transnational Conflicts: Central America, Social Change, and Globalization.* London and New York: Verso.

Sassen, Saskia. 1996. *Losing Control? Sovereignty in an Age of Globalization.* New York: Colombia University Press.

———. 2002. "The Repositioning of Citizenship: Emergent Subjects and Spaces for Politics." *Berkeley Journal of Sociology* 4: 4–26.

———. 2010. "A Savage Sorting of Winners and Losers: Contemporary Versions of Primitive Accumulation." *Globalizations* 7, nos. 1–2 (March–June): 23–50.

Stepick, Alex, Carol Dutton Stepick, and Philip Kretsedemas. 2001. "Civic Engagement of Haitian Immigrants in Miami-Dade County." Research report prepared for the Hatian American Foundation Inc. Human Services Coalition of Miami Dade County, Kellog Foundation (October 2001).

Wright, Erik O. 1985. *Classes.* London: Verso.

Chapter 6

Breaking Blocked Transnationalism
Intergenerational Change in Homeland Ties

Jennifer Huynh and Jessica Yiu

Migrant-homeland ties are the subject of much contemporary interest from scholars focusing on post-1965 immigration from Latin America and Asia. The profile of Vietnamese emigration is different from that of other Asian countries because the vast majority of overseas Vietnamese fled the country as refugees. The transnationalism of political refugees has been undertheorized; home country networks are likely to be different for forced versus voluntary migrants. Unlike most immigrants, refugees are generally barred from returning to their home countries, and hence their capacity to engage in transnational activities is more restricted.

For these reasons, refugees and political exiles—such as the Vietnamese—represent an interesting case study for understanding the continuity of, and constraints on, the maintenance of active homeland ties for immigrants and their children. While the transnational literature has largely focused on the occurrence of transnationalism, there has been comparably scant discussion about the factors that may hinder or curtail transnational involvement, despite the immigrants' yearnings to maintain ties. One of the first attempts to theorize about the limitations of transnational engagement is "blocked transnationalism," which argues that the political and social realities on the ground prevent interests and concerns about the home country to be translated into an effective presence (Portes and Rumbaut 2006).

In the case of Vietnam, from 1975 to 1994, exiled Vietnamese in the United States could not legally travel to, invest in, or send large sums of

Notes for this chapter begin on page 182.

remittances (Espiritu and Tran 2002). Following *Đổi Mới*, the economic liberalization reforms that were enacted in 1986, which were eventually followed by the normalization of US-Vietnam relations in 1995, formal restrictions against Vietnamese immigrants' active homeland ties were lifted. In turn, this series of reforms spearheaded the diaspora's visible philanthropic initiatives back in Vietnam.

In studying the unique case of the Vietnamese immigrant community in the United States and its transnational organizations, we address several broader key themes in the literature on transnationalism and development, and we raise further questions as an extension to better understanding these key themes. First, what is the incidence and intensity of organizational membership in the respective immigrant communities, particularly in the context of blocked transnationalism? Second, who are the key actors involved and how do they interact? As elaborated in our analysis below, the Vietnamese case illustrates how transnationalism represents the complex interplay between the diaspora (including immigrants and their offspring), sending and receiving states, and various parts of civil society.

Third, and on a related note, what are the tensions and points of conflict that can be identified among the different stakeholders in the transnational field? In the Vietnamese case, the relationship between a sizable portion of first-generation immigrants, who fled their country because they were persecuted by the Communist regime, and the present-day Vietnamese state remain considerably strained and tense. Given that formal state-enforced restrictions on homeland involvement circumscribe the first generation's ability to openly engage in transnational activities, as well as create a psychic barrier between the origin state and the exiled immigrants, how is the nature of homeland involvement among the first generation influenced by formal barriers being lifted? Furthermore, is the contentious relationship between first-generation immigrants and the Vietnamese state replicated by the second generation in their relationships with the Vietnamese state?

Fourth, what are the real and the potential contributions of transnational organizations to development at the local and national levels? Furthermore, are there generational distinctions in the kind and scope of contributions to development? And, finally, what is the interplay between organizational efforts directed at improving the living conditions of migrants and their offspring in the host societies and their mandate of transnational development?

Guided by these key common themes in the literature on transnational organization and development, this chapter seeks to redefine transnationalism in the context of political refugees, probing the ways in which this unique category of migrants engages in the *actual* and *affective* aspects of transnationalism. Blocked transnationalism upends conventional notions of transnationalism as a linear phenomenon; as a concept, it emphasizes the constraints placed upon the capacity of individuals and even communities to be transnationally involved. Of particular interest is whether these structural and psychic constraints affect the transnational engagements of the first and second generations in a similar or different manner.

Viewing Blocked Transnationalism through Actual and Affective Ties

The literature on transnationalism has been differentiated into two distinct schools of thought. On the one hand, there is the perspective advocated by Alejandro Portes, Luis Guarnizo, and Patricia Landolt (1999) that conceptualizes transnationalism as a form of practice or *actual* ties. By their definition, the transnational domain is narrowed to include "activities that require regular and sustained social contacts over time across national borders for their implementation" (219). The connotation is that transnationalism only occurs in the actualization of cross-border linkages—most likely, in the form of direct contact—through observed and enumerable practices (for example, visits back home, remittances, and contact with kin living there). Grassroots projects can include the construction and support of schools and roads in one's hometown or the funding of annual scholarships for underprivileged students.

On the other hand, other scholars such as Nina Glick Schiller, Linda Basch, and Cristina Szanton Blanc (1995) and Peggy Levitt (2004) offer another perspective that conceptualizes transnationalism as a *process*. They see transnationalism as manifested not so much in the actual cross-border activities of migrants but instead in the lived experiences of being a "transmigrant," who is defined as an "immigrant whose daily life depends on multiple and constant interconnections across international borders and whose public identity is configured in relationship to more than one state" (Glick Schiller, Basch, and Szanton Blanc 1995: 48). The transnational process depends upon the affective ties—real or imagined—that immigrants maintain through the reinforcement of ethnonational identities and the preservation of homeland loyalties. In the case of Vietnamese refugees, this could include commemorative events that celebrate the Fall of Saigon in 1975, a community ban against the Vietnamese flag, or a protest against purchasing goods made in Vietnam.[1]

The Scope of Transnationalism and Its Stakeholders

In terms of the empirical basis of transnationalism, past research shows that not all immigrants are transnational, and that in actuality only a small number participate (Portes, Haller, and Guarnizo 2002; Portes, Escobar, and Walton Radford 2007). This is especially true for the second generation, which is properly defined as children born in the United States to immigrant parents. One of the first quantitative studies to examine the scope and characteristics of transnational activity by immigrant groups in the United States was the Comparative Immigrant Organizations Project (CIOP), conducted by Alejandro Portes and his associates (Portes, Escobar, and Walton Radford 2007; Portes and Rumbaut 2006: chap. 5), which first compared three first-generation immigrant nationalities. Results from the study showed that married adult males take part in transnational activities more frequently than all other sociodemographic groups, and that the more highly educated tend to report higher levels of transnational involvement. Furthermore, contrary to expectations, immigrants who are more well-integrated into the United States — as measured by their acquisition of US citizenship and their years of residence — are equally, if not more, likely to engage in transnational activities than their "less integrated" counterparts.

Compared to research on first-generation transnationalism, studies on transnational engagement among the children of immigrants are relatively scarce. Empirical studies that seek to measure second-generation transnationalism ask if the maintenance of homeland ties is either part of the migration experience in which only immigrants partake, or if it transcends the generational boundary to affect the lives of their children. Most studies find that the majority of the second generation is not actively engaging in any form of transnational practice (Kasinitz et al. 2002; Rumbaut 2002). In addition, levels of transnational involvement decline rapidly between the first and second generations (Boyd and Yiu 2007). Specifically, Rubén Rumbaut (2002) finds that, in his San Diego sample, the level of transnational attachments, whether affective or actual, is quite low — always less than 10 percent — across a diverse set of national origin groups. Similarly, Phillip Kasinitz and associates (2002) find in their New York sample an equally minute proportion of their second-generation respondents who report having sustained commitment to parental homelands.

Studies based on ethnographic research, rather than survey data, yield parallel findings. In her study of Guatemalan immigrant children living in Los Angeles, Cecilia Menjívar finds that there are "only few opportunities and spaces that may foster the children's ties to the communities of origin"

(2002: 17). Given this dearth in transnational opportunities, she finds that the second generation is not nearly as inclined as the first to remain linked to the origin communities. Interestingly, how this plays out for children born to refugee parents has not been explored in-depth.

Thus, this body of literature brings to bear several important questions, including: How do the first versus second generations initiate and maintain transnational engagements, whether actual or affective? In particular, how do individuals and transnational organizations, whether in the first or second generation, interact with other stakeholders in the transnational social field, including the state and civil society?

Of particular importance in investigating the phenomenon of blocked transnationalism are the roles of religious organizations, which are an important part of civil society, and the origin state, whereby the former offers a conduit for carrying out homeland engagements in spite of the institutional and bureaucratic barriers erected by the latter against transnational activity. With respect to religion, Rubén Rumbaut (2002) finds that religiosity is a potential predictor of transnational participation among individuals and across generations. Rumbaut speculates that religious participation fosters the transmission of ethnicity and ethnic socialization from the parental generation to the offspring's, which in turn influences the level of transnational engagement.

At an organizational level, religious groups, in both host and home countries, provide an important bridge for facilitating transnational practices (Levitt 2003; Levitt and Glick Schiller 2004). As the study by Rina Agarwala (this volume) on the Indian diaspora shows, religious groups are among the most instrumental and powerful players in the transnational social field. In the case of the Vietnamese, it is particularly interesting to witness how the first generation collaborates with religious groups in the home country to circumvent interactions with the Vietnamese state, which refugees still harbor a deep sense of mistrust toward.

State actions and policies also directly and indirectly influence transnational participation. In many instances, the sending state plays a strong and active role in encouraging and facilitating the transnational activities of its émigré community. Two of the best examples are China and Mexico, whose state policies and initiatives to reach out to and partner with their expatriates have served as "best practice" models on transnational developmentalism for neighboring countries in their respective regions (see Zhou and Lee, this volume; Iskander, this volume).

However, the sending state may not necessarily develop the kind of positive relationship with its émigré community that is conducive to transnational partnerships. As Cecilia Menjívar argues, "the nation-state, through its policies to limit movement across borders, is still a powerful actor that leads immigrants and their descendants to focus on the host countries" (2002: 19). In other words, state policies and political bureaucracies are able to dampen—or *block*—the transnational engagements of immigrants and their offspring. The most immediate and obvious barrier to transnational involvement is travel restrictions. Even after the removal of institutionalized barriers by the state, noninstitutionalized barriers— whether real or imagined—still curtail the direct transnational involvement of immigrant organizations. This is particularly true for sending countries where mass emigration has largely been politically motivated, as in the case of refugees from Vietnam and Nicaragua (see Rodríguez on Nicaraguan immigrant organizations, this volume).

Varying Contexts of Exit and Blocked Transnationalism: The Vietnamese Case

The Vietnamese American population is internally diverse. Their divergent contexts of exit tell a complex story of immigrants with not just varying levels of human capital, but also a wide spectrum of experiences in and memories of Vietnam. Many endured dangerous conditions while leaving Vietnam, waited for years in refugee camps in Southeast Asia, and spent years in prison before their departure for permanent settlement abroad. Others, who fled to the United States more immediately and did not endure such protracted transit times, came from the privileged rungs of Vietnamese society, including intellectuals and the exiled elite of the former South Vietnam regime.

Migration from Vietnam to the United States can be characterized by three distinct periods and waves (Truong 2001; Zhou and Bankston 2001; Zhou 1998). The first substantial outflow of Vietnamese immigrants— comprised of mainly former military and government officials from relatively privileged class backgrounds who were sponsored by US government programs—began in 1975 (Bloemraad 2006). An estimated 20 percent of immigrants from the first wave had a college education, compared to just about 1 percent of the population in South Vietnam (ibid.). Linguistic isolation, economic marginalization, and the loss of their country led most early Vietnamese immigrants to turn to their coethnics for support, thereby building the strong foundation for the tight-knit and flourishing Vietnamese communities that exist across the contemporary American landscape (Bloemraad 2006; Zhou 1998).

A second wave of refugees, comprising approximately half a million individuals, began in 1978. They fled Vietnam aboard small rickety boats or by foot into neighboring Thailand and Cambodia. Motivated to leave Viet-

nam as a result of the new government's implementation of drastic political, economic, and agricultural policies, many immigrants from the second wave were also compelled to leave after having witnessed comrades
being arrested and held in detention in prison and reeducation camps
(Bloemraad 2006). The US Congress passed the Refugee Act of 1980 to
assist Vietnamese refugees, which greatly decreased restrictions on their
entry into the United States. The forced closing of businesses owned by
ethnic Chinese living in Vietnam, in addition to the nationalization and
redistribution of land, created a mass displacement of Chinese who also
left the country.

Migrants who escaped Vietnam and made it into neighboring countries, such as Cambodia and Thailand, by trekking through the treach-
erous jungles and escaping by boat were processed in refugee camps in
Malaysia, Indonesia, the Philippines, and Hong Kong. The conditions of
the camps varied with refugees spending anywhere between 20 days to
six months to more than ten years waiting to be processed to their final settlement destination in the United States, Australia, and Canada (Vo 2000;
Chan 2006; Espiritu 2014).

A third wave of Vietnamese immigration began in 1979 through a
variety of government-sponsored programs. Given the dangerous and
dramatic exodus of the "boat people" of the second wave, over three
hundred thousand Vietnamese were admitted into the United States and
provided with resettlement assistance under the Orderly Departure Program (ODP) (Zhou 1998). Established in 1979 by the United Nations, in
agreement with the government of Vietnam, the ODP provided a safe
and legal means for the departure of immigrants and refugees, rather
than clandestinely by boat. Under the ODP, Vietnamese could travel to
the United States as immigrants following normal US visa issuance procedures if they fell under the family reunification or economic migrant
categories, or as refugees.

In 1989, the US State Department and the Vietnamese government established an agreement to create the Humanitarian Operation (HO) program, which facilitated the immigration and resettlement of South Vietnamese who were part of the former defeated regime or worked for the
United States. Between seventy to eighty thousand people immigrated to
the United States under the HO program. By the end of the third wave, institutionalized channels for Vietnamese immigration to the United States
had been established, and by the 1990s, Vietnamese out-migration dwin-
dled to relatively low levels as ODP registration closed (Aguilar-San Juan
2005; Thai 2008).[2]

For all three waves of Vietnamese immigrants, the relationship between
the sending state and the diaspora has been problematic. In earlier times,

the relationship was marred by mutual hostility but, over time, this animosity dissolved into cautious engagement (Chuyen, Small, and Vuong 2008). Certainly, the state has made a deliberate effort to reconcile with its emigrant population. Over time, the official stance toward its emigrants has evolved from labeling the emigrants as "traitors" to the more neutral "those living far away from the fatherland" to the highly inclusive *"our* Vietnamese abroad" (Dang Nguyen 2005). Not surprisingly, the timing of these labels coincided with the political and economic developments that the country has undergone since the mid-1980s, as well as recognition by the state of the developmental potential of migrant remittances and foreign investment (ibid.). While the refugee population residing overseas comprises only 3 percent of the Vietnamese population, they contribute close to 10 percent of the country's gross domestic product (GDP) in remittances and investments (Pham 2010).

Recognizing its diaspora as a resource, the state dismantled the two-tiered pricing system for Vietnamese versus non-Vietnamese nationals. In addition, it abolished the 5 percent tax on remittances. The Committee for Overseas Vietnamese estimates that between 350,000 and 400,000 Vietnamese expatriates return each year. Typically, they bring back cash and gifts that range between $2,000 and $5,000 (Sidel 2007). Policies such as dual nationality, a visa waiver program, and housing purchases facilitate investments in Vietnam by the overseas population. Special organizations such as the Overseas Vietnamese Business Association and government branches at the national, provincial, and local levels have been established to conduct affairs exclusively with the expatriate community. State-sponsored delegations also visit overseas Vietnamese communities to explain various homeland opportunities.

Despite this positive reception of emigrants, first-generation immigrants have proven to be much more reluctant to reciprocate, as their view of the state is still marked by fear and suspicion carried over from the Communist era. Even though the government is actively encouraging investment via state-sponsored policies, expatriate investments remain concealed under informal joint ventures with family members and friends in Vietnam (Chuyen, Small, and Vuong 2008; Sidel 2007; Thai 2010). These informal ventures are intentionally created without state recognition and intervention because, as one Vietnamese university professor explained: "It's the fear of Communists. People are still uncomfortable in doing business here because many believe the government will decide to nationalize." In addition, as one Vietnamese American lawyer put it, "There are members of the community who are still very passionately anti-Communist and who view any normalization of relations with Vietnam as a betrayal not only of their ideals, but also of all the soldiers who died defending a democratic Vietnam." Social connections and informal ties are the most common ways that expatriates make investments.

Yet, the staunch opposition of first-generation immigrants to the Vietnamese state has softened over time. This is evident in the evolving nature of community associations across the United States. In addition to their immediate focus on integrating and assisting newly arrived immigrants, the original objectives of these associations often included plotting revolutionary change in Vietnam. By comparison, at present, antigovernment sentiments have waned after forty years living abroad. Community associations have developed new priorities that focus on assisting elderly Vietnamese Americans and the integration of the second generation. Moreover, homeland development has become a greater priority than effecting political change; community associations have focused their efforts on raising donations from overseas Vietnamese to construct schools and provide scholarships back in Vietnam.

The second generation appears to have accepted the Vietnamese state's outreach to the émigré community and have engaged in strategic partnerships with the state. In fact, since the normalization of US-Vietnam relations, the Vietnamese government has implemented programs and policies that attempt to attract remittances from the children of immigrants and even the return of the highly skilled to Vietnam.[3] Among organizations under second-generation leadership, a new brand of political activism has emerged whereby activists are less interested in effecting revolutionary change and instead opt to engineer peaceful transformation.

A growing number of economic organizations are slowly emerging despite people's tendency to engage in business on an individual basis. Chapters of the Vietnamese American Chamber of Commerce operate in several areas of high ethnic concentration. These groups, if active, try to maintain an apolitical stance to appease the conservative members of the community. Table 6.1 provides information on the basic social, demographic, and economic characteristics of Vietnamese and Vietnamese immigrants in the United States.

Data Collection in the United States

Our study involved creating a national database of Vietnamese American organizations, administering a survey to the leaders of the principal ones, and conducting in-depth interviews with selected groups.[4] Due to budget and time constraints, the focus of the study was limited to three sites: Orange County and Santa Clara County, both in California, and Harris County in Texas. These sites were chosen because California and Texas are the states with the largest concentration of Vietnamese immigrants

Table 6.1. Socioeconomic and Demographic Profile of the Vietnamese and Vietnamese American Population

Vietnam[a]	
Population	86.9 million
Percent urban	27.8%
GDP per capita	US$1,160[b]
Gini index of inequality	35.6****
Average years of education among urban population	9.9 years
Labor force participation rate (% of total population, aged 15+ years)	65%
Percent below poverty line	14.5%
Capital city	Hanoi
Vietnamese Population in the United States[c]	
Population	1.55 million
Percent US-born	22.2%[d]
Percent in professional occupations	28.5% [d]
Percent who hold a university degree or higher	23.7% [d]
Median household income	US$59,129
Percent below poverty line	13.8%
Primary types of immigration	Primarily legal entry with refugee status or under family reunification
Principal areas of concentration	Orange County/Los Angeles and Santa Clara County, CA; Harris County, TX

Sources: [a] All statistics on Vietnam are derived from 2010 World Bank data, unless denoted otherwise; [b] 2008 World Bank data; [c] All statistics on the US Vietnamese population are derived from 2010 US Census data, unless denoted otherwise; [d] 2007–9 American Community Survey data.

(US Census Bureau 2010). Lion Plaza and the newer Grand Century Plaza in San Jose are the cornerstones of the Northern California Vietnamese community. Little Saigon, a bustling commercial belt in Orange County, serves over two hundred thousand Vietnamese, with a large concentration of Vietnamese-operated enterprises. Although Phuoc Loc Tho, or the Asian Garden Mall, represents the social center of Little Saigon, the area spans across multiple cities in Orange County, including Westminster, Santa Ana, Garden Grove, Midway City, and Fountain Valley. Houston hosts another large Vietnamese community, with vibrant business districts found along Bellaire Boulevard and Milam Street.

A database of transnational organizations located in the three counties was created based on information collected from local Vietnamese-language business directories, commercial data-mining companies (including GuideStar database and Melissa Data), and discussions with informants by email, phone, or in person. A total of 632 organizations were included in our directory. Most have the dual objectives of initiating and implementing domestic and overseas projects in Vietnam. We then categorized them by organizational type. Table 6.2 presents this classification.

Additional field observations were conducted by visiting Vietnamese enclaves in California to speak with leaders of the community, ethnic news media, and consular officials; various organizational activities were attended as well. These activities included two street protests in California, a trade forum with the California-Asia Business Council, fund-raising dinners, and visits to Buddhist temples. Vietnamese celebrations, such as the New Year, or *Tết*, Festival in Orange County, provided an open venue for meeting and speaking with leaders and members of many organizations. Following the CIOP methodology, the organizations were not chosen at random, but rather as "emblematic" of their principal types. Transnational organizations selected for the sample must have existed for at least five years and be currently engaged in one or more projects in Vietnam.

The results were analyzed by first classifying the organizations based on their type. Then, organizations were classified as first or second generation. Second-generation organizations are those in which 60 percent or more of their board members and/or permanent members were born in the United States.[5] These groups ranged from a Lions Club, which

Table 6.2. Distribution of Vietnamese Transnational Organizations by Organizational Type (N = 77)

Organization Type	Percent of All Organizations
Religious	35.5
Hometown associations	24.4
Political	13.0
Civic/cultural	9.5
Social service agencies	5.9
Professional	4.4
Education	2.5
Alumni	1.7
Economic development	1.1
Sports	0.8
Music/arts	0.3

sponsors mobile eye clinics in Vietnam, to youth groups advocating for Vietnam to be reinstated on the list of Countries of Particular Concern for Religious Freedom. By default, first-generation organizations refer to the remaining organizations in our sample in which the majority of board members and/or permanent members were born in Vietnam. Tables 6.3 and 6.4 present summary statistics and examples of first- and second-generation organizations.

Table 6.3. Summary Statistics of Vietnamese Transnational Organizations (N = 77)

Percent of sampled transnational organizations in which at least 60% of board members are second-generation Vietnamese	13.0
Percent of "second-generation organizations" by organizational type	
Civic/cultural	65.4
Religious	14.4
Political	20.2
Hometown association	0.0
Percent of "first-generation organizations" by organizational type	
Religious	31.5
Hometown association	26.0
Civic/cultural	16.7
Political	16.3
Other	10.5

Source: Transnational Organization Project (Huynh 2010).

Table 6.4. Examples of Vietnamese Transnational Organizations by Generation

			Generational type	
Type	Location	Number of members	Percent of permanent members who are second-generation	Classification of organization by generation
Political	Northern CA	5000	0	first
Civic	Houston, TX	55	90	second
Civic	Southern CA	16	62	second
Hometown association	Southern CA	3000	0	first
Religious	Southern CA	2200	0	first
Civic	Houston, TX	100	65	second

Source: Transnational Organization Project (Huynh 2010).

Between January 2009 and January 2010, the survey of transnational Vietnamese organizations was conducted. Table 6.5 presents data on characteristics of members of these organizations, as reported by their leaders.

Data Collection in Vietnam

Following CIOP methodology, organizations that were interviewed in the United States led us to interview their counterparts in Vietnam. Fieldwork in Vietnam took place between July and October 2009, with a focus on selected transnational organizations and governmental agencies involved in overseas Vietnamese affairs at the national, provincial, and local levels.

Table 6.5. Characteristics of the Members of Vietnamese Transnational Organizations as Reported by the Organizational Leaders (N = 77)

Average age composition among members of the organizations	%
Less than age 20	5.0
Ages 20–29	11.2
Ages 30–39	19.2
More than age 40	64.6
Average level of educational achievement among members of the organizations[a]	
Completed elementary schooling or less	9.8
Completed secondary schooling or vocational training	14.3
Attained a postsecondary degree	35.2
Received a postgraduate degree	40.7
Occupational types among members of the organizations	
Professional	54.0
Business owner/self-employed	15.6
Manual laborer	7.4
Other	23.0
English proficiency among members of the organizations	
Not proficient	4.3
Somewhat proficient	28.4
Fully proficient	67.3
Members of the organizations who are US citizens	86.8
Nativity status and average length of residence among members of the organizations	
US-born	13.4
Foreign-born, in the US for more than 10 years	80.0
Foreign-born, in the US for 5–10 years	6.6

Source: Transnational Organization Project (Huynh 2010).

Interviews with the Ministry of Foreign Affairs and other relevant ministries in Hanoi were also conducted, as were interviews with provincial departments in Hai Phong, Hue, and Ho Chi Minh City. Site visits were carried out with fourteen counterparts of US organizations in Vietnam, and additional interviews were conducted with leaders of quasi-governmental organizations that are involved with the overseas community, such as the Association for Liaison with Overseas Vietnamese (ALOV).[6]

Interviews were based on a bilingual instrument that asked leaders of selected organizations and government officials in Vietnam about how transnational projects are initiated, developed, and implemented. Mass organizations in Hue and Ho Chi Minh City, such as ALOV, which operates under the joint supervision of the Fatherland Front, various People's Committees, and the Department of Finance and Investment, were interviewed in order to understand how state directives operate at the provincial and local levels.

Measuring Blocked Transnationalism: The Transnational Ties of First- and Second-Generation Organizations

The strength of transnational ties is indicated by cross-border connections that go beyond the occasional trip home or sending of remittances (Guarnizo 1994). In the Vietnamese case, transnational ties, unlike the Latin American cases studied previously (see Guarnizo, Portes, and Haller 2003), are not formally institutionalized, although myriad organizational linkages exist.[7] Rather, for both first- and second-generation Vietnamese organizations, projects are generally carried out through personal networks of family and friends. The existence of these organizations partially challenges the hypothesis that political refugees and asylum seekers, as well as their descendants, experience blocked transnationalism. Both first- and second-generation Vietnamese find different ways to interact with their country. First-generation activities tend to be more informal, working with hometown associations and religious groups, whereas second-generation organizations use their human capital to create more formal ties with Vietnam through government channels. However, the forms of transnational practice for both first- and second-generation organizations may be less institutionalized than what is common for other immigrant groups.

Second-generation organizations focus on both national and local development, instead of relying upon regional and local ties. These organizations are more likely to interact with local and national governments, and their members travel to Vietnam much more frequently compared to their counterparts in first-generation organizations. Over half of the members of second-generation organizations visit Vietnam at least three times per year. Nearly 44 percent remain in contact with central, local, and provincial governments, compared to less than 15 percent of first-generation organizations. Second-generation organizations rely more on hiring Vietnamese nationals to implement projects and the aid of local government—given their regular contact with all levels of government and other nonprofit institutions—and they rely less on monetary support from the coethnic community.

The US-centered activities of second-generation organizations include an emphasis on culture camps focused on retaining Vietnamese culture through language or artistic expressions for immigrant youth. Participation in NGOs and educational summer trips where young adults use their skills to travel and teach in Vietnamese universities is common. Many youths also return to Vietnam through the sponsorship of business organizations, including internships at large multinational firms such as Intel, or exchanges with international law firms.

First-generation immigrants who are members of transnational organizations tend to lack experience working with organizational counterparts in Vietnam. This is, in large part, because the development of NGOs in Vietnam is a much more recent phenomenon and highly regulated in comparison to the United States. Before Vietnam's liberalization, most associations and organizations operated informally or were a branch of the government. Vietnam's political-economic system yielded few opportunities for people to form voluntary organizations. Only since the implementation of the new renovation policies in the late 1980s and early 1990s did the government provide enabling regulations for the establishment of NGOs (Kerkvliet, Heng, and Koh 2003). Nevertheless, even at present, many organizations, such as the Women's Union and the Youth Union, still operate under the Fatherland Front, an umbrella group of pro-government mass movements that has close links to the Communist Party and the Vietnamese government.

Organizations led by the second generation have taken advantage of the more open space for NGOs to operate in Vietnam in recent years. Between 1992 and 2010, the number of international NGOs increased from 183 to approximately 800 as governmental restrictions relaxed. Thousands of small informal grassroots organizations exist in partnership with local communities, even though many of them are not officially supported by the government. As one member of a first-generation political organization explains:

> I definitely commend the organizations that are able to work in Vietnam, as there is a lot of red tape, corruption, and hoops to have to go through. Many of

these groups are working with the Communist government, and I am sure that the government of Vietnam is not necessarily too fond of these groups either, but they allow them for one reason or another.

Second-generation youths perceive the Vietnamese state as a partner in their various developmental projects, despite being cognizant of their parents' opposition. In the words of a second-generation lawyer: "Many of us grew up in the [United] States and we view history from a different perspective than our parents, who still have a lot of resentment toward Vietnam. In that sense, we try to balance our interests. We try to stay very noncontroversial." A young second-generation woman who volunteered with an international NGO noted:

> When I returned home, the first thing my dad said was, "Why do you sound like a Communist?" This is because I was based in Hanoi. He followed up by saying, "Your accent has changed." … I think he has a lot of pride and a lot of fear and misunderstandings about how Vietnam is—modern Vietnam, that is—and the Vietnam that he left. I would never invalidate his feelings. There is a lot of pain still for him and for our community. I realize that I'm in this weird no man's land where he and his friends think of Vietnam in a certain way. With some members of the community, I talk very candidly about my work, but I don't talk too much about homeland politics.

The legal organization that the Vietnamese American lawyer cited above belongs to sponsors judges and attorneys from Vietnam to visit the United States, in addition to implementing a fellowship program that allows second-generation law students to work as summer associates in Vietnam. Another second-generation NGO successfully implements newborn care initiatives that are approved by the government. The Vietnamese second generation thus finds itself walking a fine balance between respecting their parents' wishes and memories of Vietnam and forging their own understandings of the country. Historical memory still transmits to youths, who grew up hearing stories about their parents surviving the war, followed by their exodus to the United States.

Regardless of the relationship with the state, religious groups have proven to be an important practical resource for most organizations operating in Vietnam. Forty-four percent of second-generation organizations and 33 percent of first-generation organizations are in regular contact with religious groups in Vietnam. Religion tends to operate as a legitimate institution that is independent of the state; therefore, religious groups and leaders garner trust from the diaspora as a conduit for transnational activities. Buddhist temples in Vietnam are linked to temples in the United States. A registry of Vietnamese temples around the globe is published annually, listing Buddhist temples in the United States, Australia, Canada, Norway, and New Zealand. One abbot based in the United States explained that he is frequently contacted by temples in Vietnam requesting assistance—typically monetary—for building temples or for disaster relief. Religious leaders from Vietnam also make visits abroad to personally request support for various projects, including funding orphanages and building houses, schools, and libraries.

The causes and activities that are funded by religious groups are selected on an informal basis, oftentimes at the discretion of individual monks. For example, one Vietnamese American monk took $10,000 in cash with him on a visit to Central Vietnam to donate to his home temple for building a new library. Another monk described how he travels to Vietnam to visit various temples while passing as a local traveling monk. He takes money from his temple in Northern California and then donates it to projects that he deems most worthy.

Making Sense of Blocked Transnationalism:
The Affective Ties of the First and Second Generations

The previous section describes the actual cross-border characteristics and behaviors of first- and second-generation organizations. This section aims to complement this by explaining transnationalism as an affective process. While all organizations serve a role in fulfilling affective ties, not all organizations engage in actual cross-border activities. Transnationalism, when understood as affective ties, describes the lived experiences and connections—real or imagined—that immigrants maintain with the homeland. Moreover, these ties exist at both the individual and collective levels. Members of the diaspora still practice many rituals taken from the homeland in order to preserve their ancestral connections. For instance, Vietnamese American families place altars in their homes to honor their ancestors and continue to practice *đám giỗ* (ancestor worship). The expatriates still commemorate the Fall of Saigon (or Black April), which marked the end of the Vietnam War and the full Communist takeover of South Vietnam, and ensure that their US-born offspring recognize the significance of this event by sending them off to school wearing black ribbons.

How individuals think about and understand these events and their sentiments toward Vietnam represent the emotional and psychic spaces that immigrants inhabit. The sights and sounds of coethnic neighborhoods constantly reinforce homeland ties and identities among their inhabitants. Local radio stations broadcast the news of incarcerated human rights activists in Vietnam, while newspapers commemorate important dates in Vietnamese history. Patrons walk through a replica of a famous garden in

Central Vietnam in their local shopping mall; a string of war memorials dot the landscape in parks and strip malls.

Beyond the coethnic neighborhood, many transnational organizations embody a focal point and a tool for empowerment for the exiles to remember and reimagine their home country. Members of these organizations are able to retain and reassert their social status prior to migration. The most illustrative example of this is when former army officers don garb and reenact ceremonies that reproduce the social hierarchy of the Vietnamese military. Many former leaders of the South Vietnamese military have amassed cult figure status and a sizable following in Vietnamese American communities. Similarly, hometown associations reproduce the social relations and hierarchies of their corresponding villages—village leaders are often selected as distinguished guests at fund-raising dinners and are granted various privileges.

Vietnamese American organizations led by the first generation often celebrate important events in Vietnam's history, such as the reenactment of the famous Tru'ng Sisters revolt in 39 AD, in which two sisters organized a national rebellion against the Chinese that ultimately failed but inspired subsequent rebellions. The ARVN Rangers, a special military group, participate in various war memorial events in Orange County annually, proudly wearing their military garb and berets. Another popular event is the screening of the independent film *The Truth about Hồ Chí Minh* across US cities with large Vietnamese populations. During a screening in California, several hundred men stood to salute both the American flag and the former South Vietnamese flag, singing the national anthem of the old regime.

The strength of affective ties that connect the first generation's imaginary and emotions to their homeland wanes by the second generation, although they still endure as part of their parents' legacy. Vietnamese youths acknowledge their parents' experiences during wartime and their resentment toward the Communist state, although they simultaneously forge their own understandings of Vietnam. As a second-generation Vietnamese American recalled:

> My mom was a lawyer in Vietnam. I think it was hard for her when she first came. She worked at a nail salon and had to learn how to cook and wash dishes. … When I describe to my mom what Saigon is like now, she often doesn't believe me. I tell her that I can buy Levi's jeans, eat KFC, and watch CNN. She only talks about the Communists taking everything.

Interviews with leaders of hometown associations based in San Jose indicate a lingering fear among some first-generation immigrants of being detained at a Vietnamese airport upon arrival. On the contrary, members of the second generation are confident of their freedom to move within the country and to exploit various opportunities, including the prospect of collaborating with the Vietnamese state to conduct transnational activities. A Vietnamese American leader of a second-generation organization explains this intergenerational rift:

> The previous president of this organization was in a situation of upsetting a lot of people when we helped organize a statewide trade mission of a Vietnamese delegation. We later tried to participate in a Vietnamese community event for *Tết* [New Year] and were stopped. We would be invited to attend only if the president retracted his statement and apologized. It put us in a difficult situation.

As illustrated by this incident, controversies often arise within the ethnic community when second-generation organizations attempt to actively and publicly conduct outreach programs in Vietnam. Compared to first-generation organizations, it is less important for second-generation groups to garner trust and support from the Vietnamese American community; instead, they are able to capitalize on their knowledge of how civil society works in the United States to establish partnerships with other American institutions. Tellingly, while no leader of a second-generation organization reported that they perceive the Vietnamese government to be a significant hindrance to their operations, almost 60 percent of first-generation organizations did.

The "open" transnationalism practiced by the second generation in comparison to the more "covert" transnationalism practiced by the first is largely due to the fact that second-generation organizations are not as strongly embedded in the ethnic community. By publicly engaging with business leaders and officials back in Vietnam, youths are actively promoting a revitalized Vietnamese American identity. One second-generation business leader described his decision to open membership in their Chamber of Commerce to people living in Vietnam and to negotiate with the new Vietnamese consulate in the United States. He said his mission was to bring free enterprise to Vietnam. According to him, "It's time to move forward. This is a Vietnamese American Chamber of Commerce and I don't want to place my American citizenship above my loyalties to Vietnam. The opportunities in Vietnam are immense, so why not take advantage [of them]?"

Second-generation members describe the transnational activities as opportunities for personal career development; in an era of market reform, they can capitalize on their bilingualism and cultural fluency in both the United States and Vietnam to work for an international corporation or pursue transnational entrepreneurship. Another second-generation organization member who works for a development agency in Vietnam describes how his involvement is largely due to financial necessity: "Given the economic climate in the US, I would not be able to use my college degree the way I can here. I can contribute to the socioeconomic development of the country. My work in Quảng Nam (a province in Central Vietnam) means that I can help people directly through microfinance and housing initiatives, planning with local government officials and project funders." The interest among second-generation organization members to take advantage of this emergent opportunity structure has recently been reciprocated by the Vietnamese government, which has enacted a policy designed to attract the "gray matter" of this generation.[8]

Opinions about the objectives and activities of transnational organizations among the Vietnamese American community are mixed, although they have grown progressively more positive. In the words of an immigrant Buddhist monk: "Some older people say that we are helping the Communist blood to flow but really, we want those who have education to have a voice on how people will change their society. Change can only happen through education." First-generation leaders often say that their goal is to help Vietnam because they are Vietnamese, whereas leaders of second-generation organizations tend to couch their activities in terms of a process of self-discovery. As a US-born leader states: "Growing up, my parents never talked about Vietnam. We weren't allowed to buy anything with the label 'made in Vietnam.' I came here to see it for myself, to see where my parents came from." Put simply, transnational involvement allows the first generation to *be* Vietnamese—that is, to reaffirm their national identity and reestablish ties with their home country. By contrast, for the second generation, transnational participation allows members of the second generation to *become* Vietnamese, such that through their involvement in homeland projects, they learn more about their origin society and, in doing so, they start to identify with being Vietnamese.

Discussion and Conclusion

The Vietnamese represents an interesting case study for understanding the continuity of, and constraints on, transnational involvement among exiled immigrants and their offspring. Our analysis of the group's transnational activities reinforces and refines the analytical utility of the concept of "blocked transnationalism," which emphasizes the broader political and social factors that may hinder or curtail transnational involvement, particularly among forced migrants such as refugees and asylees (Portes and Rumbaut 2006). Results from our analysis show that although the cross-border activities of exiled immigrants and their children are circumscribed by various institutionalized and psychic barriers, the affective and actual transnational ties of first- and second-generation Vietnamese Americans are far from limited; instead, the ties that crosscut the United States and Vietnam are strong and extensive.

Returning to the key questions related to the broader literature on transnationalism and development, the case of "blocked transnationalism" among Vietnamese Americans provides interesting insights. First, what is the incidence and intensity of organizational membership in the Vietnamese immigrant community? Although we do not have exact statistics on the proportion of individuals in the Vietnamese population who are transnationally active, the fact that there are over six hundred Vietnamese organizations in just three US counties is a testament to how expansive the transnational network spanning the distance between the United States and Vietnam has become. Hometown associations and religious organizations dominate the organizational landscape for the first generation.

As for the extent to which second-generation Vietnamese Americans are involved in transnational activities, even though they represent a small minority in the membership base of the organizations in our sample (less than 4 percent), they are keen on taking leadership roles and forming their own associations with agendas that diverge from those of organizations led by the first generation. Moreover, although the incidence of transnational involvement among second-generation Vietnamese Americans appears to be substantially lower than in the first generation, the intensity of their involvement is arguably higher: compared to the first-generation organizations surveyed, second-generation associations reported having far more regular communication with all levels of the Vietnamese government and sending members to Vietnam on a regular basis for organizational purposes.

A second set of questions asks about key actors involved in the transnational field and the nature of their interactions, particularly the points of tension and conflict that can be identified among the different stakeholders. Points of tension between transnational actors become apparent when generational distinctions interact with relations with the Vietnamese government. Despite the series of liberalization reforms in Vietnam, members of the first generation still harbor a deep sense of mistrust of the state; thus, instead of working with state agencies to conduct homeland activities, they prefer to work surreptitiously, often in partnership with religious organizations or personal contacts in Vietnam. The story of the traveling Vietnamese monk from the United States allocating donations to local projects that he deems most worthy illustrates the informality of how most transnational activities of first-generation groups are conducted. For first-generation philanthropists, a sharp division is drawn between "helping fellow Vietnamese at home" and supporting the Vietnamese state.

A third set of questions in the transnationalism literature asks about the impact of transnational organizations on the sending society as well as on the migrants and their offspring themselves. Although our study does not directly address these questions, the findings have some relevant implications. Certainly, the organizational efforts of Vietnamese Americans have brought about substantial changes in their homeland. As reported by leaders of our sampled transnational organizations, their organizations are engaged in diverse activities and initiatives that are intended to improve their compatriots' quality of life and to develop the social infrastructure, including the health care and educational systems.

Organizations led by the second generation are particularly likely to identify national development as a top priority, which is why they are open to partnering with the Vietnamese government. In turn, with the country's economic growth rates among the highest in the world, the Vietnamese government has enacted policies aimed at attracting the skills and capital of young Vietnamese Americans, who are deemed valuable assets to the country's developmental strategy.

Aside from the stated objectives of the organizations to improve the socioeconomic standing of their community, their participation in transnational organizations provides them with the opportunity to socialize with coethnics, which in turn helps them to reassert their identities and reconnect with their homeland. Based on field observations, organizational events that involve celebrating Vietnamese holidays and commemorating important historical events are particularly significant in the lives of the first generation. For them, the chance to re-create these important rituals serves to remind them of their past lives; in particular, those who came from privileged backgrounds are given the opportunity to reassert their former social status.

For the second generation, their participation in organizational activities and initiatives provides them with the opportunity to discover their ancestral roots and to experience modern-day Vietnam, while attempting to remain impartial to their parents' misgivings about the state of affairs in the country when they were forced to flee. Ultimately, the generational dynamics seen in the case of Vietnamese Americans undermine our assumptions about the interplay between first- and second-generation transnationalism, which predict the unilateral transmission of attitudes and behaviors between parents and children.

Jennifer Huynh is a doctoral student in the Department of Sociology at Princeton University and a visiting scholar at the Center for the Study of

Social Movements at the University of Notre Dame. She is currently writing her dissertation on the integration of second-generation Vietnamese in Southern California.

Jessica Yiu is a PhD candidate in sociology at Princeton University. Her most recent publication is an article in the *International Migration Review* entitled "Calibrated Ambitions: Low Educational Ambition as a Form of Strategic Adaptation Among Chinese Youth in Spain."

Notes

1. The concepts of actual versus affective transnational ties are somewhat analogous but not identical to the conceptual distinction of "ways of being" versus "ways of belonging," respectively, as put forth by Glick Schiller, Linda Basch, and Cristina Szanton Blanc (1995). According to their definition, "ways of being" refer to the actual social relations and practices that individuals engage in, as opposed to the practices that signal or enact identities that demonstrate a conscious connection to a particular group, which is referred to by the concept "ways of belonging." Note that while "actual" and "affective" ties represent distinct forms of transnationalism, "ways of being" and "ways of belonging" represent nested forms of transnationalism, such that "ways of being" provide the precursor to "ways of belonging," which combine action and an awareness of the kind of identity that action signifies.

2. This time period also includes approximately ten thousand Vietnamese who arrived under the Amerasian Homecoming Act of 1987, which targeted the offspring of Vietnamese women and US servicemen. Due to their special set of circumstances, Amerasians can be characterized as a fourth wave (see Gold 1999; McKelvey 1995; Yarborough 2005; Root 1992). Unlike the aforementioned three groups, Amerasians are geographically dispersed and tend to not to be as organizationally active given their small size relative to the three other waves, and are not included in this analysis. There has been some disagreement about how many waves should be counted (Valverde 2013). Those migrating for family reunification, primarily economic migrants under the Orderly Departure Program, have been analyzed as a distinct group in some studies (Vo 2006; Chan 2011; Valverde 2013) but not in others (Gold 1992). Economic migrants have varying motivations for departure compared to political refugees and as such have been identified and theorized as qualitatively different (Cortes 2004; Charles 2006). The latest wave of immigrants from Vietnam includes the growing population of women marrying US citizens, Erasmus students, and the elderly (Thai 2010).

3. It is also important to remember that transnational relationships are not unidirectional. The Vietnamese state actively encourages overseas investments

and philanthropy, as well as cultural exchanges for youth—all of which are objectives that second-generation organizations are also committed to (for instance, the Communist Party of Vietnam Politburo's Resolution 36/NQ-TU).

4. Jennifer Huynh, the principal investigator for the Transnational Organization Project, conducted the data collection in the United States and Vietnam.

5. The data neither identified the age at migration nor the year of arrival among first-generation immigrants. No organization reported leadership by third-generation (or later) immigrants.

6. Organizational development in Vietnam is growing because of changing attitudes toward international organizations. Although Vietnamese American NGOs are not well represented among the entire roster of registered NGOs, the strength of Vietnamese American NGOs lies in their ability to gain support from local governments and other nonprofit institutions. During the 1990s, the number of international NGOs (INGOs) working in Vietnam increased from approximately eighty-six registered INGOs in 1992 to over five hundred registered INGOs today. The director of the People's Aid Coordinating Committee (PACCOM) said in an interview that overseas Vietnamese NGOs account for only about 6 percent of all registered INGOS. He also noted that "most Vietnamese American NGOs have smaller projects like for sums of US$2000 or $3000. The strength of Vietnamese American NGOs is that when they implement projects 70 to 80% have the support of local partnerships" (VUFO 2003a, 2003b).

7. Another important theme that emerges from our quantitative results as well as interviews is the informality of transnational exchanges, as practiced by both the first and second generations. There is still lingering mistrust toward Vietnamese banks and other formal monetary institutions, and therefore collective and individual monetary transfers to Vietnam from the United States are significantly underestimated (Sidel 2007). Religious organizations are the most popular conduit for charitable giving in Vietnam; therefore, further examinations of religious institutions as chief tools for development are warranted. Moreover, it is widely recognized that remittances serve as an important impetus for development, as they are invested in the creation of small and medium-sized enterprises and the expansion of public infrastructures in the migrants' hometowns (Portes, Haller, and Guarnizo 2002). Following this line of research, future studies should examine the role of migrant-owned businesses in Vietnam given the context of blocked transnationalism.

8. Examples of national policies and initiatives that target the return migration of second-generation Vietnamese who are living abroad are aplenty. In 2003, the Fund for Persuading the Overseas Community was initiated by the Ministry of Foreign Affairs to include projects that provided Vietnamese language training for overseas youths in addition to cultural exchange programs and conferences on investment opportunities aimed at second-generation Vietnamese. In 2004, the Politburo Resolution 36 was enacted to not only attract foreign investment from overseas Vietnamese but to also lure overseas brainpower by offering incentives and rewards to highly skilled expatriates who return to Vietnam. In 2007, the national government enacted a visa waiver program that provided overseas Vietnamese (both first and second genera-

tions) with a five-year travel visa that allowed them to enter and leave the country without restrictions. In 2009, overseas Vietnamese were granted dual citizenship.

References

Aguilar-San Juan, Karin. 2005. "Staying Vietnamese: Community and Place in Orange County and Boston." *City & Community* 4, no. 1: 37–65.

Bloemraad, Irene. 2006. *Becoming a Citizen: Incorporating Immigrants and Refugees in the United States and Canada*. Berkeley: University of California Press.

Boyd, Monica, and Jessica Yiu. 2007. "Ties That Bind or Ties That Wane? Transnational Practices across Immigrant Generations." Paper presented at the Annual Meeting of the American Sociological Association, 10 August, New York City.

Chan, Sucheng. 2006. *The Vietnamese American 1.5 Generation*. Philadelphia: Temple University Press.

Chuyen, Truong thi Kim, Ivan Small, and Diep Vuong. 2008. *Diaspora Giving: An Agent of Change in Asia Pacific Communities?* San Francisco and Beijing: Asia Pacific Philanthropy Consortium.

Dang Nguyen, Anh. 2005. "Enhancing the Development Impact of Migrant Remittances and Diaspora: The Case of Vietnam." *Asia-Pacific Journal* 20, no. 3: 111–22.

Espiritu, Yen Le. 2014. *Body Counts: The Vietnam War and Militarized Refugees*. Berkeley, CA: University of California Press.

Espiritu, Yen Le, and Thom Tran. 2002. "Viet Nam, Nuoc Toi (Vietnam, My Country): Vietnamese Americans and Transnationalism." In *The Changing Face of Home: The Transnational Lives of the Second Generation*, ed. Mary C. Waters and Peggy Levitt. New York: Russell Sage Foundation, 367–398.

Glick Schiller, Nina, Linda Basch, and Cristina Szanton Blanc. 1995. "From Immigrant to Transmigrant: Theorizing Transnational Migration." *Anthropological Quarterly* 68, no. 1: 48–63.

Guarnizo, Luis. 1994. "Los Dominicanyorks: The Making of a Binational Society." *Annals of the American Academy of Political and Social Science* 533, no. 1: 70–86.

Guarnizo, Luis Eduardo, Alejandro Portes, and William Haller. 2003. "Assimilation and Transnationalism: Determinants of Transnational Political Action among Contemporary Migrants1." *American Journal of Sociology* 108, no. 6: 1211–48.

Huynh, Jennifer. 2010. *Transnational Organizations and Development in Vietnam*. Unpublished manuscript, Princeton University, Princeton, NJ.

Kasinitz, Philip, John Mollenkopf, Mary C. Waters, and Merih Anih. 2002. "Transnationalism and the Children of Immigrants in Contemporary New York." In *The Changing Face of Home: The Transnational Lives of the Second Generation*, ed. Mary C. Waters and Peggy Levitt. New York: Russell Sage Foundation, 96–122.

Kerkvliet, Benedict J., Russell Hiang-Khng Heng, and David Wee Hock Koh. 2003. *Getting Organized in Vietnam: Moving In and Around the Socialist State*. Singapore: Institute of Southeast Asian Studies.

Levitt, Peggy. 2003. "'You Know, Abraham Was Really the First Immigrant': Religion and Transnational Migration." *International Migration Review* 37, no. 4: 847–73.

———. 2004. "Redefining the Boundaries of Belonging: The Institutional Character of Transnational Religious Life." *Sociology of Religion* 65, no. 1: 1–18.

Levitt, Peggy, and Nina Glick Schiller. 2004. "Conceptualizing Simultaneity: A Transnational Field Perspective on Society." *International Migration Review* 38, no. 4: 1002–39.

Menjívar, Cecilia. 2002. "Living in Two Worlds? Guatemalan-Origin Children in the United States and Emerging Transnationalism." *Journal of Ethnic and Migration Studies* 28, no. 3: 531–52.

Pham, Andrew T. 2012. "The Returning Diaspora: Analyzing Overseas Vietnamese (Viet Kieu): Contributions toward Vietnam's Economic Growth." DEPOCEN Working Paper Series No. 2011/20, 2012.

Portes, Alejandro, Cristina Escobar, and Alexandria Walton Radford. 2007. "Immigrant Transnational Organizations and Development: A Comparative Study." *International Migration Review* 41, no. 1: 242–81.

Portes, Alejandro, Luis E. Guarnizo, and Patricia Landolt. 1999. "The Study of Transnationalism: Pitfalls and Promise of An Emergent Research Field." *Ethnic and Racial Studies* 22, no. 2: 217–37.

Portes, Alejandro, William Haller, and Luis E. Guarnizo. 2002. "Transnational Entrepreneurs: An Alternative Form of Immigrant Adaptation." *American Sociological Review* 67, no. 2: 278–98.

Portes, Alejandro, and Rubén Rumbaut. 2006. *Immigrant America: A Portrait*. 3rd ed. Berkeley: University of California Press.

Rumbaut, Rubén. 2002. "Severed or Sustained Attachments? Language, Identity and Imagined Communities in the Post-Immigrant Generation." In *The Changing Face of Home: The Transnational Lives of the Second Generation*, ed. Mary C. Waters and Peggy Levitt. New York: Russell Sage Foundation, 43–95.

Sidel, Mark. 2007. *Vietnamese-American Diaspora Philanthropy to Vietnam*. Boston, MA: Philanthropic and Global Equity Initiatives.

Thai, Hung Cam. 2008. *For Better or For Worse: Vietnamese International Marriages in the New Global Economy*. New Brunswick: Rutgers University Press.

———. 2010. "Special Money in the Vietnamese Diaspora." Paper presented to the Center for Transpacific Studies at the University of Southern California, 2 April, Los Angeles.

Truong, Hoa T. 2001. "Vietnamese Young Women from the Third Wave of Immigration: Their Struggle for Higher Education." PhD dissertation, University of Massachusetts–Amherst. http://scholarworks.umass.edu/dissertations/AAI3027265/. [Accessed 10 March 2012]

US Census Bureau. 2010. "2010 Demographic Profile (Table DP-1)." http://factfinder2.census.gov/bkmk/table/1.0/en/DEC/10_DP/DPDP1/0400000US06I040 0000US12I0400000US13I0400000US48I0400000US51I0400000US53. [Accessed 10 March 2012]

Vo, Linda. 2000. "The Vietnamese American Experience: From Dispersion to the Development of Post-Refugee Communities." In *Asian American Studies: A Reader*, ed. Jean Yu-Wen and Min Song. New Brunswick, NJ: Rutgers University Press, 290–305.

VUFO (Vietnam Union of Friendship Organisations). 2003a. *10 Years of Partnership between Vietnam and International NGOs*. Hanoi: NGO Resource Centre.

———. 2003b. *Lessons Learned from a Decade of Experience: A Strategic Analysis of INGO Methods and Activities in Vietnam 1990–1999*. Hanoi: NGO Resource Centre.

Zhou, Min. 1998. "'Parachute Kids' in Southern California: The Educational Experience of Chinese Children in Transnational Families." *Educational Policy* 12, no. 6: 682–704.

Zhou, Min, and Carl L. Bankston III. 2001. "Family Pressure and the Educational Experience of the Daughters of Vietnamese Refugees." *International Migration* 39, no. 4: 133–51.

Immigrant Organizations in Europe

Chapter 7

Moroccan and Congolese Migrant Organizations in Belgium

Marie Godin, Barbara Herman, Andrea Rea, and Rebecca Thys

Researchers have tried to determine whether development projects managed by immigrant organizations are a sign of integration into host societies (Bousetta and Martiniello 2003) or the effect of discrimination in contexts of reception (Amoranitis and Manço 2004). That opposition, found in numerous international publications (Basch, Glick Schiller, and Szanton Blanc 1994; Portes, Guarnizo, and Landolt 1999; Guarnizo, Portes, and Haller 2003; Lacroix 2005, 2009), has incited further research on *how* migrant organizations develop transnational activities and not so much as to *why*. In this chapter we investigate both questions with a focus on Moroccan and Congolese organizations in Brussels involved in development cooperation.

There are reasons why we have opted for a comparison of those two groups. First, both represent important immigrant communities in Brussels. Moroccans make up the largest non–European Union (EU) foreign community in Belgium, and the Congolese are the third largest after Turkish immigrants. Second, Moroccan and Congolese migration history to Belgium differs significantly, making a comparison of the two groups all the more interesting. While the Congolese community is smaller in terms of population, it is the largest in terms of the relative number of organizations in Brussels: the organizational density (population divided by number of bigger organizations) among the Congolese is about ten times bigger than in the Moroccan community (Thys forthcoming). Not all migrant organizations are involved in transnational activities, but the proportion

Notes for this chapter begin on page 209.

of organizations involved in development projects is higher in the overall Congolese organizational space as compared to the Moroccan one (Thys 2013). Organisation density refers to the proportion of ethnic minority organisations relative to the size of the ethnic minority population. It can be expressed in two ways; by dividing the number of organisations by the size of the corresponding population, or the other way around; by dividing the size of the population by the number of organisations. The number of inhabitants is calculated for every ethnic minority organization. In this case study:

Moroccan ethnic community:	132,983 (population born with a foreign nationality in Brussels in 2009)
Number of organisations:	658
Organisation density:	0.005
Congolese ethnic community:	13220,722 (population born with a foreign nationality in Brussels in 2009)
Number of organisations:	656
Organisation density:	0.005
Moroccan ethnic community:	132,983 (population born with a foreign nationality in Brussels in 2009)
Number of organisations:	658
Organisation density:	0.032

A main research question in this chapter concerns the differences between the two groups in terms of how the transnational character of organizations has developed over time. By looking at modes of immigrant incorporation and the mobilization of institutional tools, and by relating these dynamics to characteristics of migration history in the two groups, we will obtain a better understanding of their transnational activities. Furthermore, we will position the two groups in regard to the specific migration-development-integration nexus. Immigrant organizations have been active for a long time in development cooperation, but public institutions have only recently considered them as proper "transnational development agents" (Faist 2008). This new approach to the migration-development-integration nexus, often referred to as codevelopment (Naïr 1997), has resulted in favorable judgments with respect to migrants in Belgium. Taking into account these three fields of public policy and how they interact with one another, we will examine how they may have shaped migrants' initiatives. By comparison to the transnational activities of migrant organizations in the United States, which are mostly self-supported, those in Belgium are often buttressed, in financial and logistic terms, by public agencies at the national, regional, and municipal levels.

Historical Context

After World War II, several sectors of the Belgian economy (mainly in coal and steel production) experienced labor shortages (Martens 1976). Labor migration to Belgium accelerated with the signature of a bilateral agreement between Belgium and other countries, starting with Italy in 1946 and continuing with Spain (1956), Greece (1957), Morocco (1964), Turkey (1964), Tunisia (1969), Algeria (1970), and eventually Yugoslavia (1970). Many Moroccans first arrived in the industrial cities of Wallonia and afterward in the deprived urban areas of Brussels and Antwerp. Moroccan workers, regarded as "birds of passage" (Piore 1979), found employment in the secondary sector of the labor market (steel production, construction, transport). This migration corresponded to a guest worker model (Castles and Miller 2009). Nevertheless, worsening economic conditions and rising unemployment rates in the late 1960s called for a new response. On 1 August 1974 the Belgian government decided to stop new immigration altogether. Despite such measures, the number of Moroccan migrants increased sharply between 1974 and 1980 due to dynamics of family reunification and high birth rates in Moroccan families.

The history of Congolese immigration to Belgium differs significantly. Unlike other European countries, Belgium did not at first experience labor immigration from its former colony (Young 1968). The Belgian government never encouraged Congolese emigration before Congo gained independence in 1960. Prior to that event, Congolese immigrants originated mainly in the upper classes, and after independence Congolese student migration increased. Bilateral agreements between educational institutions located in both countries and Belgian cooperation programs allowed Congolese students to pursue their education in cities like Brussels (Kagné and Martiniello 2001). During the 1980s, migration to Belgium increased and diversified. The beginning of the 1990s was characterized by an increasing number of asylum seekers and refugees due to political instability in the country of origin and the decline of the Mobutu regime. Also, many students who had first planned to move temporarily finally settled in Belgium. This led to the formation of a Congolese community, which now includes a significant second generation.

Major migration flows of Moroccans (1970–80) and Congolese (1990–2000) occurred at different periods of time in response to various causes. Belgian integration policies of the mid-1980s were mainly based on an open citizenship law and the adoption of jus soli, which facilitated access to Belgian nationality. Such policies reduced the number of persons retaining their Moroccan and Congolese nationality. In 2010, the percentages of Moroccans and Congolese living in Belgium who had opted for Belgian citizenship were estimated at 70.8 and 64.4 percent, respectively (CEOOR 2012).

There have been at least four steps in the formation of Moroccan immigrant organizations (Ouali 2004; Bousetta and Martiniello 2003; Bousetta 2010). The first step is related to emigration. Early settlement was marked by two types of organizations, some related to the Moroccan consulate and others hostile to the Moroccan political regime. The first, called Fellowships (Amicales), aimed to control the Moroccan immigrant population, guaranteeing allegiance to Hassan II and his regime on the one hand and the noninvolvement of Moroccan immigrant workers in Belgian social and political life on the other hand.

A second type of organization was born in opposition to the regime of Hassan II. By the 1970s and 1980s, as temporary migration of Moroccan immigrants diminished, these two types of organizations started to lose their influence. Those two decades marked the second stage in Moroccan associative efforts, during which strong ties between migrant workers and Belgian trade unions were forged. The main Belgian trade unions— Socialist and Christian—created internal groupings for Moroccan workers. Moroccan immigrants thus began to focus on domestic labor, addressing a law against racism and the right to vote in local elections, as well as welfare benefits.

A third stage saw the establishment of new entities built by second-generation immigrants. Their activities became more focused on issues of integration (cultural activities, school support, vocational training, actions against racial discrimination, etc.). Some organizations also provided space for training future social and political leaders, some of whom became local politicians in the late 1990s. During those years, public policies also supported the institutionalization of Moroccan immigrant organizations, providing them with financial support for running their activities (Rea 2003).

A fourth stage in the formation of Moroccan organizations has recently been observed in relation to transnational activities in the field of development cooperation. Relying initially on local and/or familial solidarity, organizations are now being created to promote international solidarity in areas like education, health, citizenship, human rights, and humanitarian affairs. Policy changes in Belgian cooperation made Morocco a priority country, thus providing institutional support to organizations working in development.

Congolese organizations have followed different pathways. Although Congolese immigrants have been in Belgium since the independence of the Democratic Republic of Congo (DRC) in 1960, formal organizations did not develop until the 1990s (Kagné and Martiniello 2001; Gatugu 2004). It is possible to distinguish three phases in their development. The first, from 1960 to 1990, was characterized by the emigration of Congolese students who settled in the areas where the three French-speaking universities are located. They set up organizations aimed at supporting newcomers. During the same period, Congolese migrant organizations were also engaged with the Congolese political regime by constituting political parties in opposition to Mobutu's government (1965–97).

A second phase, since the 1990s, saw the increase in the number of newcomers and second-generation migrants involved in organizations. Political instability pushed Congolese to emigrate as asylum seekers not only to Belgium but also to France and the United Kingdom. Congolese nationals resided in Belgium intermittently, especially in urban areas like Brussels. Inauspicious conditions for settlement and integration led to the emergence of new kinds of organizations, mainly focusing on immigrants' difficulties in fitting into society: some focused on the incorporation of youths (school support, parental support, youth criminality prevention, etc.), and others on the incorporation of women. Such efforts were possible thanks to integration policies that provided funding to these new migrant organizations. At the end of the 1990s, many Congolese organizations had been formalized and professionalized, following the "predictable developmental process" of ethnic organizations that was outlined by Werbner (1991). Congolese churches also played an important role in support and mutual help.

The third phase in the establishment of Congolese organizations was mainly characterized by the implementation of development projects. Since the beginning of Congolese immigration in Belgium, migrants have financially supported their families at home. Nowadays, Congolese organizations are becoming more and more structured and tend to have projects funded by development cooperation policies. Developmental actions have also been increasing since the 2006 democratic elections in the DRC.

The Migration-Development-Integration Nexus

International organizations (such as the International Organization for Migration [IOM] or the United Nations Development Programme [UNDP]) are at the forefront of a new debate on migration as a tool for development. That debate centers on the large size of remittances sent by immigrants to families back home. The notion of "codevelopment" first appeared in France and was developed by the scholar Samir Naïr (1997). In Belgium, the same idea entered the political debate in the late 1990s. As in France, the first program that considered migrants as agents of development was oriented toward voluntary return to and reintegration of migrants in their countries of origin. That program was not successful and was quickly replaced by a new initiative called Migration and Development, which established a new but still tenuous connection between migration, development, and integration. The requirement for cofinancing imposed on young migrant organizations made their participation difficult.

The main project receiving funding as a result of the new arrangements was the Migration for Development in Africa (MIDA) Great Lakes program implemented with the assistance of the IOM. That program targeted three countries—the Republic of Burundi, the DRC, and the Republic of Rwanda—and supported capacity building of local institutions through the mobilization of individuals in the diaspora. That project has been in operation since 2001 and is often presented as a major achievement of Belgium's pioneering strategy to link migration, integration, and development policies.

Belgium, in fact, has a complex institutional landscape that makes it almost unmanageable to implement a homogenous policy of codevelopment. As a federal state, it includes three physical territories (the Brussels-Capital Region, the Walloon Region, and the Flemish Region) and three linguistic communities (the French Community, the Flemish Community, and the German-speaking Community). Whereas migration policies are a unique prerogative of the federal state, both the federal state and federated entities have authority in the field of integration and international solidarity. Moreover, different philosophies toward migrants' integration among the federated entities prevail.

The case of the Brussels-Capital Region is the most complex, since different public authorities (regional, municipal, and at the community level) have powers that they concomitantly apply on the same territory. Although still very limited, the bilingual (French and Dutch) status of Brussels offers migrants' organizations a variegated set of institutional opportunity structures to engage in the field of development cooperation. On the one hand, migrant organizations registered in the Brussels-Capital Region can get some support through Flemish institutions such as the Flemish Community Commission. On the other hand, migrants' organizations can also apply for funding at the Wallonia-Brussels International (WBI), which represents Wallonia and the French-speaking community in Brussels in the field of development cooperation. In 2010, as result of intense advocacy work on behalf of the General Coordination of Migrants for Development (CGMD), a new annual budget to help migrants' organizations was created by the WBI.

At the Brussels-Capital Region level, authorities have not yet developed a specific policy in the field of codevelopment. In fact, international solidarity matters have been mainly managed at the municipal level either through their own budget or through a decentralized federal program of development cooperation. Those programs are mainly institutional and based on best practices exchanges between civil servants located in the North and in the South. Some municipalities, however, have implemented a special budget for local migrants' organizations willing to engage in the field of international solidarity.

As a consequence, immigrant organizations based in Brussels have access to a range of public funding at the federal, regional, municipal, and community levels to implement development projects in their country of origin. As will be shown, Congolese and Moroccan organizations have varying perceptions of those institutional political structures and rely on them differently.

Methods and Data Collection

Between February and April 2012, we interviewed forty-five leaders of Moroccan and Congolese nonprofit organizations, (23 and 22, respectively) by using semistandardized questionnaires. The main criterion for selection was the transnational character of the migrant organizations: they had to have at least one project or one activity in operation in either Morocco or the DRC over the previous two years. These organizations were surveyed by different sampling methods. First, we decided to capitalize on an ongoing research project on the political participation of ethnic minority organizations in the Brussels-Capital Region (Thys 2013). The focus of that research is on Moroccan, Congolese, and Turkish organizations, either oriented toward the host country or the homeland. The mapping of Moroccan and Congolese organizations in the Brussels-Capital Region done as part of that research project served as a starting point for the application of a snowball sampling method.

Selected organizations were asked to provide information on other organizations that had developed at least one activity in their country of origin over the last two years and that had a majority of members of Congolese or Moroccan origin on their administrative board. This snowball method was used to enlarge the initial sample but also to update the information obtained previously, since the ethnic associative reality in Brussels is known for its ephemeral and mutable character. Information on transnational organizations was collected through communication with local authorities. Each municipality provided a recent list of Moroccan and Congolese transnational development organizations. *Last but not least,* several lists used by different stakeholders involved in the field of migration and development were used to further enhance the sample.

Our sample may seem small compared to other international studies on transnational migrant organizations (see Portes, Escobar, and Arana 2008; Portes and Zhou 2011). In the Belgian context, however, our sample for the Brussels-Capital Region is representative of the Congolese and Moroccan organizations involved in international activities in Belgium. In light of the regional associative landscape, our sample is even close to completeness. A strong indication of the quality of our sample can be found in the combination of mapping methods used. The three different entries in the field complement one another and thus allow us to avoid major holes in our field knowledge.

In addition to the quantitative data collected, twelve semistructured interviews were conducted from January 2012 to April 2012 with different stakeholders involved in the field of international development and migrant organizations. The information collected was used to better interpret quantitative data. The results of this study are therefore based on a combination of quantitative and qualitative methods. This mixed methods approach allows us to present a comprehensive overview of the networks of development of Moroccan and Congolese migrant organizations in Belgium.

Our comparative focus of Moroccan and Congolese organizations raises questions about how their respective transnational activities, although developed in the same area of settlement, are differently shaped by the characteristics of immigration history. Second- and even third-generation Moroccan immigrants in Brussels are now strongly involved in associative life. Congolese organizations, by contrast, are still to a large extent led by first-generation migrants. How does this difference in terms of length of settlement in Brussels influence the transnational activities of both groups? How do different selectivity processes shape not only the intensity but also the type of transnational involvement of Congolese and Moroccans? A comparison of Moroccan and Congolese organizations demands an examination of the specific incentives and constraints in the two countries of origin, and of the differential access to political opportunity structures in Belgium, the country of reception.

The first phase of our comparison focuses on the intergenerational transmission of practices and ideas that may affect the character of transnational organizations—what Fernández-Kelly (this volume) calls the *vertical* vector. A second stage in this comparison dwells on a *horizontal* vector that encompasses the actions of organizations aiming to connect interests at both ends of a geographical spectrum by adjusting to host country and homeland constraints and incentives. To account for these two vectors of comparison, we consider several aspects of transnational activities on the part of Moroccan and Congolese organizations in Brussels.

We first address the interplay between homeland-oriented activities mainly concerned with migrants' integration and transnational-oriented activities. Second, we discuss development projects as established by migrants and their descendants in the country of origin. Thirdly, we look at the differences between Congolese and Moroccan migrant organizations in terms of access to public funding. We then explore differentiated social networking in both groups and its impact on development activities. Finally, we discuss how diaspora policies developed by the homeland governments may also affect the transnational development activities of both Moroccan and Congolese migrant organizations by encouraging or arresting their efforts.

Interplay between Host and Homeland Activities

As previously mentioned, all organizations in our sample were selected for their transnational character. Therefore, international solidarity was not surprisingly most frequently invoked as the main associational goal on the part of organizational leaders. Not all of them, however, selected that item to the same degree—a commitment to transnationalism was referenced more often by Congolese organizations than by Moroccan ones. Next to international solidarity, sociocultural as well as civic activities in Belgium were frequently stressed as most important in defining an association.

Moroccan and Congolese transnational organizations in Brussels are not only active in the two countries of origin; in many cases, they combine international solidarity with activities oriented toward integration into local ethnic minority communities. In fact, several Moroccan organizations were first involved in activities that promote the social incorporation of migrants before becoming involved in international solidarity projects. They supported social cohesion programs and/or "permanent learning" programs aiming to ease migrant settlement (Ouali 2004: 311). International solidarity grew out of those efforts at a later time. Congolese organizations, on the other hand, were involved in the South before engaging in the North, so to speak—they began by connecting with the country of origin and only later focused on integration in the adopted nation.

The two different paths followed by Moroccan and Congolese organizations in relation to host and home countries can be better understood in reference to historical differences affecting both groups and their associations. For example, the timing of each migration was different: the peak of Moroccan migration to Belgium dates back to the 1960s, whereas Congolese migration accelerated only in the 1990s. Thus, the Congolese community and especially its associative elite encompass mostly first-generation immigrants. In the Moroccan case, on the other hand, second- and even third-generation immigrants are involved in associative life.

Second, Moroccan migration to Belgium encompassed mostly humble workers, while Congolese migration originally comprised students, many of whom planned to return to their country of birth to gain standing and recognition, partly as a result of their instruction in Belgium. First-generation Moroccans, by contrast, never had similar professional aspirations. Return aspirations among them, if they exist, are mainly conceived in terms of retirement, vacations, or visits to family members for a short period of time. Thus, the transnational activities of the Moroccan first generation follow an informal logic: to support family and kin, invest in small businesses, buy or build homes, and enjoy holidays or retire back home. Paradoxically, the intergenerational transmission of practices and ideas regarding transnational involvement is less apparent among Congolese, whose first generation is still trying to achieve incorporation into the host society. Younger Congolese in Belgium have few connections with the country of their parents, partly because of lack of resources and protracted conflict in the DRC. Young Moroccans in Belgium, in turn, appear bent on perpetuating transnational involvement on a more formal level than their elders. By comparison to the difficulties faced by Congolese in maintaining bonds with the country of origin, connections with Morocco have been more easily maintained not only because of a shorter and more easily bridged distance, but also because of a greater political stability in the country of origin.

Activities in the Country of Origin

There are similarities in the actions of Moroccan and Congolese organizations in their respective countries. Moroccan as well as Congolese organizations are predominantly engaged in projects concerning education or health, or are organized around the advocacy of causes such as human rights and women's rights (see Table 7.1).

A recent project implemented by Dar El Ward (House of Roses) illustrates the kind of small development enterprise that is typically put in place by Moroccan organizations. That project also illustrates the interplay between homeland and host country activities. Dar El Ward was created fifteen years ago by a group of Moroccan women aiming to provide assistance to newly arrived women from the same country. As their efforts succeeded, they began to turn their attention toward development back home. They worked to build a well and a barn for the Inmel mu-

Table 7.1. Types of Activities of Transnational Organizations

	Congolese		Moroccan		Total	
	N	%	N	%	N	%
Cultural (youths, sociocultural, religious organizations)	7	31.8	8	34.8	15	33.3
Civic (human rights, women's rights, and social/juridical organizations)	4	18.2	4	17.4	8	17.8
International solidarity (international cooperation and humanitarian issues)	10	45.5	7	30.4	17	37.8
Economic (including professional organizations)	0	0	2	8.7	2	4.4
Health	1	4.5	2	8.7	3	6.7
N	22	100	23	100	45	100

nicipality. In Brussels, Dar El Ward collected €13,000 from private donors (mainly through fund-raising activities) and €13,000 from the region of Meknès-Tafilatet. A group of retired citizens of Meknes agreed to supervise the project. Regional authorities in Morocco also supported the efforts of Dar El Ward to bring electricity to remote areas of the country (Delcroix and Bertaux 2012). Despite its involvement in transnational development activities, Dar El Ward's main focus is still on Belgium, with a variety of programs, especially for homeless people.

The association Solidarity with the Moms of Manianga from Belgium (Solimambe) is a good example of the type of transnational development project Congolese immigrants are implementing. As in the previous example, the association was created by women migrants in 1995 to assist newly arrived Congolese women in their efforts to seek employment in Belgium. From the outset, however, the association was also raising funds to meet the needs of equipment or medication for women hospitalized in Kikenge Hospital (Bas-Congo Province). The organization obtained public funding in 2007 (in the framework of a pilot project for a new budget for "codevelopment") for its project for children with disabilities at the Kikesa Center in Kinshasa (Boulc'h 2008).

Although Congolese and Moroccan organizations share some common interests, they differ in the extent to which specific initiatives are implemented. More than half of the projects of Congolese organizations take place at the local level, whereas more than half of the projects of Moroccan organizations occur at the national level (see Table 7.2). Those variations are partly linked to state structures in Morocco and the DRC, and the physical distance spanning the transnational space. As indicated before, Congolese organizations are still predominantly run by people from the

Table 7.2. Scope of Projects in Country of Origin of Transnational Organizations

	Congolese		Moroccan		Total	
	N	%	N	%	N	%
Local	12	57.1	6	28.6	18	42.9
Regional	3	14.3	1	4.8	4	9.5
National	6	28.6	14	66.7	20	47.6
N	21	100	21	100	42	100

Note: N does not add up to forty-five because of missing responses.

first generation. Belgian Congolese embarking on a civic project tend to originate in the same region. By contrast, Belgian Moroccan associative projects are often initiated by second- or third-generation immigrants who meet at school, in their neighborhood, at work, or in sport clubs and who, although sharing a Moroccan background, do not necessarily stem from the same town or village. Having heterogeneous local attachments leads to a lesser obligation to get involved in philanthropic activities that involve family members or villages of origin.

In the Congolese case, moral obligations toward those left behind are still strongly present. Although intergenerational transmissions continue to take place informally among second- and third-generation Moroccans in Belgium, elite members have become structural actors in transnational exchanges. When establishing projects at the local level, they are less involved with family members than their Congolese counterparts, who still depend strongly on kinship networks not only to get started, but also to be successful. Thus, Belgian Moroccan transnational activities are more dependent on bridging weak transnational links, while Belgian Congolese use more bonding or strong links spanning both ends of the transnational space.

The state of the DRC is weaker than the Moroccan state. It is therefore easier to establish a transnational development project with local partners known to migrants before their departure or with members of family or social networks. Finally, looking at the frequency of travel by members or representatives of Moroccan organizations, we notice that they are moving back and forth more often than Congolese representatives. The lack of physical contact between people on the ground and members of the diaspora could explain why for Congolese organizations collaboration with local actors seems to be more difficult and why for them it is easier to rely on kinship relations. This lack of physical contact has led several Congolese organizations based in Belgium to create their own local organizations in the DRC to allow for better management of their projects.

Access to Public Funding, Social Networks, and Homeland Initiatives

Both groups rely on different channels to fund their transnational development activities. This differentiation in the use of what can be called institutional opportunity structures can be understood in reference to distinct migration histories, which have led to differentiated modes of immigrant incorporation. Congolese and Moroccan organizations confirm that they receive public funds in Belgium to finance their transnational practices of development. To obtain funding for a transnational migrant organization in Brussels, different public channels must be mobilized (policy lines concerning integration, migration, and development). Moreover, a variety of political levels need to be addressed at the local, regional, communitarian, federal, and even European levels. Our study reveals that institutional opportunity structures are being used differently by the two migrant communities to sustain their development initiatives. Qualitative data show significant differences in the character of public funding channels. Moroccan organizations tend to rely more extensively on local sources embedded in local politics and communitarian integration policies established by both the French Community Commission (COCOF) and Flemish Community Commission (VGC) in the Brussels-Capital Region. Congolese organizations are absent from these two funding circuits; they seek support through more traditional actors of development cooperation that are active at all levels of power.

Table 7.3. Sources of Funds of Transnational Organizations

	Congolese (N = 22)		Moroccan (N = 23)		Total (N = 45)	
	N	%	N	%	N	%
Belgian government (public funding at several levels)	10	45.5	15	62.2	25	55.6
Private dues	16	72.7	17	73.9	33	73.3
Members' dues	18	81.8	13	56.5	31	68.9
Organization activities (sales, fund-raising activities)	15	68.2	15	65.2	30	66.7
Home country government	0	0	4	17.4	7	8.9
Company sponsorships	4	18.2	7	30.4	11	24.4
Churches/mosques	3	16.6	0	0	6	6.7
European institutions	1	4.5	1	4.3	2	4.4

Note: Percentages do not add up to 100 because organizations may receive multiple sources of funds.

Over the last fifteen years, Belgium has witnessed numerous changes in the field of political representation, including the increased visibility of immigrant-origin citizens (Teney et al. 2010). Their increase in political involvement dates back to the local elections of 2000, but immigrant-origin citizens only acquired the right to vote in Belgium in local elections in 2006 under the Treaty of Maastricht. Some foreign-born political participants were better positioned than others. In Brussels, mainly politicians of Moroccan descent are active (Teney and Jacobs 2007). Multiple factors explain their strong participation, especially at the local level. First, they are far more numerous than other non-European communities, including the Congolese. Second, the Moroccan community is strongly concentrated in some areas of Brussels, whereas the Congolese are more dispersed throughout the metropolitan area. Finally, electoral law, especially the preferential mode of voting within electoral lists, affects Moroccan political representation, since it is a precondition of what could be called an "ethnic vote" or "ethnic voting." A recent study has also revealed that Moroccan migrants tend to have a higher level of intention to vote and participation in political actions than Congolese (Herman forthcoming).

As a result of a stronger presence of politicians of Moroccan descent at the local level, most partnerships within the Municipal International Cooperation program funded by the federal state are being established with municipalities with a high Moroccan density. Such partnerships often result from initiatives on the part of local politicians of Moroccan descent or, to a lesser extent, local leaders or Moroccan migrant organizations acting as pressure groups. Other than such local partnerships, side projects supported by Moroccan migrant organizations sometimes occur but are far from typical. For instance, at the time of the earthquake in Al Hoceima in 2004, there was a huge wave of ethnic solidarity facilitated by municipal ties between Schaerbeek and Al Hoceima, which had existed since 2001 and therefore represent one of the oldest such partnerships. After the disaster, a series of Moroccan student exchanges took place. They were welcomed in different local schools in Schaerbeek and elsewhere in Brussels. Youngsters from Al Hoceima also came to Brussels under the initiative of the Federation of Hopes from Al-Hoceima (Fédération des espoirs d'Al-Hoceima). They received support from both municipalities.

Although Moroccan transnational organizations do not use many public development programs to secure financing for their activities, they resort to specific budget areas whose main objective is to facilitate the integration of immigrants. This is because Moroccan organizations have often engaged in transnational activities after having first worked on immigrant integration at the local level. Access to integration and social cohesion programs were previously established, thus making it easier for the same financing channels to support development projects at a later stage.

The Cactus, a Moroccan Belgian organization, illustrates that evolution. It organizes trips to Morocco as part of its permanent learning program under the French Community administration. The association realized that women who came to their literacy classes did not in fact put into practice the knowledge they acquired. As a result, the instructor decided to organize a trip to Morocco so that participants could meet other Moroccan women and talk to them about their experiences. The Cactus is thus active in international cooperation without using subsidies, but it takes advantage of the institutional landscape it earlier configured on the basis of integration and social cohesion.

Because there are fewer Congolese migrants in Belgium, and because they are dispersed throughout various municipalities in Brussels, they have less representation at the local level. In addition, Congolese seek Belgian nationality to a lesser extent than Moroccans, partly because they have resided in the adopted country for a shorter period of time and still maintain hope of returning to their nation of birth. Some travel to the DRC in an effort to assist family and friends. The DRC government does not recognize dual citizenship; that may be another reason why Congolese are less inclined to opt for Belgian citizenship.

Nevertheless, when a commune has a deputy of Congolese origin—as in the case of the Brussels municipality—partnerships with Congolese counterparts like Kinshasa do occur. Yet Congolese migrant organizations mainly draw on Belgian public funding from the development cooperation sectors at the federal and regional levels. Because first-generation Congolese tend to be highly educated, they seek recognition as experts in the development cooperation field. Their efforts, however, have met with limited success given drastic declines in government spending on foreign development aid. Recently, a small budget set up by the WBI has provided new opportunities for Congolese immigrant organizations.

Impact Sud was one of the beneficiaries of such actions. Following protracted conflict in the eastern territories of the DRC (in the territory of Mwenga, South Kivu province), there are increasing numbers of widows, single mothers, and women abandoned by husbands who have gone to work in the small-scale artisanal mining sector. Stand Up My Mother (Debout ma mère), a project implemented by Impact Sud, focuses on improving the lives of sixty rural women, heads of households and victims of sexual violence. The project aims to develop an agricultural cooperative in which traditional peanut butter (*Kinda Kinda*) is produced by local women. Debout ma mère will allow these women to increase their production and market their wares, substantially improving their economic and social conditions.

Social Networking: Bonding versus Bridging Social Ties

In terms of social networking, Moroccan organizations succeed more easily in mobilizing their community to raise private funds than their Congolese counterparts. The level of intraethnic mobilization among the Congolese seems to be less vigorous, especially in terms of the level of funds that can be raised. By comparison, Congolese transnational organizations are establishing strong ties with other social actors, especially with the Belgian civil society sector but also with trade unions and members of political parties. The mobilization of economic and human resources is more significant among Moroccan organizations than among their Congolese counterparts (Tables 7.3 and 7.4). Moroccans appear to be more effective at raising private funds, especially in the municipalities where they are strongly established. Inhabitants Beni Malloul in Europe, for example, aims to support Beni Malloul in northern Morocco. Its members originate in that village. Thanks to private donations and membership fees, the association was able to collect around €60,000 to encourage development.

Religion does not appear to play a major role in regard to the financial support that migrant organizations can secure; funding through local mosques or churches is rare. On the other hand, the fifth pillar of Islam, the *Zalakt,* encourages and mobilizes the Moroccan community in various solidarity projects, especially during Ramadan, the holiest month in the Islamic calendar. According to Islamic Relief, a transnational Moroccan organization, increased private donations occur during that period. In the summer of 2012, Dar El Ward launched a campaign entitled A Sacrifice for Two to enable poor families to celebrate Eid Kabir (The Feast of the Sacrifice). The cities of Meknes, Fez, Ifrane, Tangier, and Tetouan took part in

Table 7.4. Networks in Belgium

	Congolese (N = 22)		Moroccan (N = 23)		Total (N = 45)	
	N	%	N	%	N	%
Public institutions in Belgium (any level) and EU	19	86.4	21	95.5	40	90.9
Media	11	52.4	18	78.3	29	65.9
Coordination network	12	54.5	20	87,0	32	71.1
Civic organizations	22	100	21	91.3	43	95.6
Congolese/Moroccan embassy in Belgium	11	50	13	59.1	24	54.5
Political party	9	40.9	12	52.2	21	46.7

Note: Percentages do not add up to 100 because organizations may be involved in multiple networks.

this project. Dar El Ward served as a conduit for Moroccan families living in Belgium to buy a sheep for a poor family in one of the partner cities.

Although Congolese transnational organizations are less connected to local administrations, media, and communities, their ties with Belgian civil society are strong, as is the degree of social inclusion of Congolese organizations within coordination networks and even umbrella structures. This is especially true for Congolese women's organizations. Several included in this study (Forum Inter-Régional des femmes congolaises [FIREFEC], Action des femmes pour le développement [AFEDE], Le Mangier en Fleur, and ASSOCITURI) are part of an action platform called All Together for the Cause of Women in the Democratic Republic of Congo, which has been active since 2008 in response to the increase of violence in that country. That initiative has managed to bring together more than eighty organizations from different backgrounds, including Congolese women's organizations, feminine and feminist Belgian organizations, several NGOs, trade unions, and academics.

These "bridging ties" helped Congolese women's organizations to realize their common goals. The same ties allowed them to become involved in the preparation of the Third International Action of the World March of Women that took place in Bukavu (South Kivu) in the DRC on 14–17 October 2010 (Godin and Chideka 2010). Such interactions between feminist groups and Congolese groups at the local level, acting together within a broader transnational female movement, indicates that Congolese women are not acting in closed circuits; instead, they interact with social actors both in their proximate and broader environment (Garbin and Godin 2013).

Local Networks, Private Sector, and Diaspora Policies in Belgium

The interaction between home country authorities and transnational organizations differs greatly for Moroccan and Congolese organizations. Very few Congolese groups in our sample receive funding from authorities back home, via the embassy or directly from the government. By contrast, several Moroccan organizations have received strong support from Moroccan institutions, both public and private (see Table 7.5). The Moroccan community in Belgium counts on more assistance from authorities in the sending country, who are trying to implement programs to promote the involvement of the diaspora in Morocco's development. In addition, the Moroccan community in Belgium receives support from individual Moroccans toward the development of their projects. In contrast, the DRC does not recognize the role that the diaspora plays in the country's development, and the Congolese community in Belgium does not receive public funds from the DRC.

In addition, the policies of the two home states are radically different in the way they consider their nationals living abroad. While Moroccans are allowed to vote in their home country, Congolese living abroad do not have that right. Similarly, Morocco recognizes dual citizenship, but the DRC does not. After the first Congolese democratic elections in 2006, a vice minister was appointed for Congolese living abroad. This post was then removed during Kabila's first mandate. Morocco, on the other hand, has attempted to strengthen institutional ties with its communities living abroad, especially since the events of September 2011. Such communities are now commonly recognized as a diaspora by authorities in Rabat (Bousetta 2010). Since 2007, several institutions have been created to reinforce links with the Moroccans residing in other countries, including a Ministry in Charge of the Moroccans Living Abroad and the Council for the Moroccan Community Abroad.

A project developed by the organization Belgo-Moroccan Skills Forum (Forum des Compétences Belgo-Marocaines) is a good example of the mix of private and public support stemming from Morocco. It involved setting up a management committee for organ and tissue transplantation first in Rabat and later in other Moroccan locations. Exchanges between Moroccan and Belgian academics are planned to overcome the lack of training of local surgeons. The association has so far collected €5,500, mainly from the sponsoring company Royal Air Maroc. Belgo-Moroccan Skills Forum also works closely with the ministry in charge of Moroccans living abroad, as well as with several hospitals in Belgium and Morocco.

Social ties of Moroccan and Congolese groups are better developed in Belgium than in the home countries. Significant differences between the

Table 7.5. Networks in the Home Country

	Congolese (N = 22)		Moroccan (N = 23)		Total (N = 45)	
	N	%	N	%	N	%
Public institutions in DRC/Morocco (any level)	11	50.0	15	68.2	26	59.1
Other organizations (church, mosque, and nonprofit organizations)	11	52.4	17	65.1	28	65.1
Media	10	47.6	15	68.2	25	58.1
Coordination network	11	50.0	12	54.5	23	52.2
Belgian embassy in DRC/Morocco	2	9.1	11	50.0	13	29.5
Political party	2	9.1	3	13.6	5	11.4

Note: Percentages do not add up to 100 because organizations may be involved in multiple networks.

two groups concern links with nonprofit organizations, with the Belgian embassy in the home country, and/or with the embassy of the country of origin in Belgium. Moroccan organizations are more connected with public authorities than Congolese organizations. It is also worth mentioning that the Congolese diaspora is characterized by a strong political opposition movement to the Kabila regime, and as a result relationships with institutions in the host country are strained. An illustration of that are the regularly held demonstrations in Brussels organized by the Congolese diaspora in front of the Congolese embassy.

Conclusion: Incentives for and Constraints on Transnational Activities

In this chapter, we accounted for the location of transnational development organizations founded by Moroccans and Congolese in Belgium within the migration-development-integration nexus. By elucidating diverse modes of immigrant incorporation, different uses of institutional tools, and varying migration histories we clarified variations as well as similarities in the trajectories of the two groups and their transnational organizations. In particular, we showed the importance of migration history in shaping the fates of Moroccan and Congolese people in Belgium.

Among Moroccans, development activities are the outgrowth of earlier efforts at social integration in the adopted country. Moroccan organizations were first developed to improve the lives of migrants and their descendants in Belgium, especially with regard to social disadvantage and racial discrimination. Although they still face overt and subtle attempts at exclusion, Belgians of Moroccan origin involved in development activities are relatively well integrated socially, economically, and politically. Activities related to development have also arisen from durable partnerships with public institutions, especially when local governments have implemented them. Also, the different development projects initiated by Moroccan organizations do not often entail relatives or neighbors; they involve institutional exchanges. The high involvement of second- and third-generation Moroccans in Belgium may also explain the level of affective detachment in development cooperation. Among younger Moroccans, the objective is to create new kinds of ties, whether cultural, social, economic, or symbolic, with the ancestral land.

Congolese organizations are also shaped by the specific facts of migration from the DRC. Higher levels of education among Congolese immigrants and, in many cases, the involuntary character of their departure from the homeland has led to the creation of organizations focused on the future of the country of origin, which remains uncertain and unstable. In this case, ties with the homeland are much stronger and vivid than among Moroccans. The hope of returning back home at some point to take part in the development of the homeland is widespread among first-generation Congolese migrants. Although many organizations offer services to Congolese and their descendants to assist in incorporation into the host society, actions toward the DRC have been, from the outset, more numerous and more intense. Congolese voice a moral obligation toward those who stayed behind more often than Moroccans; this may represent a case of bounded solidarity.

It would be erroneous to analyze Congolese and Moroccan transnational practices only in terms of their own agency; they have had at their disposal institutional resources that have helped them in their transnational efforts. Our analysis shows that Moroccan organizations are better incorporated into Belgian social and institutional structures and face fewer obstacles in the implementation of projects. By contrast, Congolese organizations face barriers that hamper them as effective development agents, including a lack of trust in host institutions, a paucity of resources, limited information, and insufficient recognition. As a result, and by comparison to Moroccans, Congolese are less able to mobilize resources and raise funds to implement projects.

The significant number of politicians of Moroccan origin elected at the municipal level in Belgium, as well as the stronger social integration of Moroccans into social networks in the adopted country, provides them with advantages not available to the Congolese community. That too explains why Moroccan organizations sometimes rely on integration programs to support their actions in their country of origin and why they are more involved in international solidarity through local institutions. Their transnational practices are, in fact, bolstered by their strong integration in the host country.

Congolese organizations, on the other hand, have had limited success in their attempts to incorporate their transnational activities into the social field of Belgian development cooperation. Paradoxically, foreign affairs, development cooperation, and academic exchanges have historically joined the two countries. The DRC has been a main focus of Belgian development cooperation since its accession to independence in 1960. It would seem logical to expect Congolese development activities to rely on traditional institutional instruments of development cooperation between Belgium and the DRC; however, that is not the case. Increasingly, Congolese organizations are attempting to be recognized as legitimate actors of development in several platforms that involve traditional approaches to international development and for which integration of immigrants is not the main priority. The current political discourse on codevelopment and on the value of migrants' capacities in relation to international development remains vacuous and is rarely followed by effective action.

Marie Godin is a doctoral candidate at the University of East London affiliated with the Centre for Research on Migration, Refugees and Belonging (CMRB) and a research associate at the Group for Research on Ethnic Relations, Migration and Equality (GERME) at the Université Libre de Bruxelles. She holds a master of science in forced migration from the Refugee Studies Centre, Oxford University.

Barbara Herman is a PhD candidate at the Université Libre de Bruxelles affiliated with the Group for Research on Ethnic Relations, Migrations and Equality (GERME). She holds a master of social sciences from the Université Libre de Bruxelles. The title of her doctoral dissertation is "Political Participation and Associational Membership among Ethnic Minority Groups in Brussels."

Andrea Rea, PhD, is professor of sociology and director of the Group for Research on Ethnic Relations, Migration and Equality (GERME) at the Université Libre de Bruxelles. He is coeditor (with Bonjour and Jacobs) of *The Others in Europe* (Presses de l'Université de Bruxelles, 2011) and (with Timmerman, Martiniello, and Wets) *New Dynamics in Female Migration and Integration* (Routledge, forthcoming 2015). His research interests focus on the integration of migrants into the labor market, the political participation of ethnic minorities, and the European policies of immigration and integration.

Rebecca Thys is a doctoral candidate at the Université Libre de Bruxelles and a research member of the Group for Research on Ethnic Relations, Migration and Equality (GERME). She is completing a dissertation entitled "Social Capital and the Political Participation of the Turkish, Moroccan and Congolese Community in Brussels" under the direction of Dirk Jacobs.

Notes

The authors would like to thank the students Maria Papadakis and Emilie Franco for their valuable help during the fieldwork.

References

Amoranitis, Spyros, and Altay Manço, eds. 2010. *Migration et développement en Europe: Politiques, pratiques et acteurs.* Brussels: EUNOMAD.

Basch, Linda, Nina Glick Schiller, and Christina Szanton Blanc, eds. 1994. *Nations Unbound: Transnational Projects, Postcolonial Predicaments, and Deterritorialized Nation-States.* New York: Gordon and Breach.

Boulc'h, Stephane. 2008. "Evaluation externe de l'expérience pilote d'appui à des projets de coopération internationale menés à l'initiative de personnes issues de la migration et actives en Région wallonne et en Communauté française Wallonie-Bruxelles." Rapport définitif. Cota ASBL.

Bousetta, Hassan. 2010. *Belgo-Marocains des deux rives: Un pas plus loin Analyse et mise en perspective de l'étude visant à mieux connaître les communautés marocaines vivant en Belgique.* Brussels: Fondation Roi Baudoin.

Bousetta, Hassan, and Marco Martiniello. 2003. "Marocains de Belgique: Du travailleur immigré au citoyen transnational." *Hommes et Migrations* 1242: 94–106.

Castles, Stephen, and Mark Miller. 2009. *The Age of Migration: International Population Movements in the Modern World.* 4th ed. Basingstoke, UK: Palgrave Macmillan.

CEOOR (Centre for Equal Opportunities and Opposition to Racism). 2012. *2011 Annual Report on Migration.* http://www.diversite.be. (Accessed 16 March 2015).

Delcroix, Catherine, and Daniel Bertaux. 2012. "Les activités transnationales des femmes immigrées: L'exemple d'une association de Marocaines de Bruxelles." *Revue européenne des migrations internationales* 28, no. 1: 85–105.

Faist, Thomas. 2008. "Migrants as Transnational Development Agents: An Inquiry into the Newest Round of the Migration-Development Nexus." *Population, Space and Place* 14: 21–42.

Garbin, David, and Marie Godin. 2013. "'Saving the Congo': Gendered Politics of Development and Diaspora Engagement across the Congolese Black Atlantic (USA-Europe)." *The African and Black Diaspora: An international Journal* 6, no. 2: 113–30.

Gatugu, Joseph. 2004. "L'enjeu associatif des nouveaux migrants d'Afrique subsaharienne." *Osmoses* 32: 17–18.

Godin, Marie, and Mado Chideka. 2010. "Congolese Women Activists in DRC and Belgium." *Forced Migration Review* 36: 33–34.

Guarnizo, Luis Eduardo, Alejandro Portes, and William Haller. 2003. "Assimilation and Transnationalism: Determinants of Transnational Political Action among Contemporary Migrants." *American Journal of Sociology* 108, no. 6: 1211–48.

Herman, Barbara. Forthcoming 2015. "Participation politique et vie associative parmi les groupes de minorités ethniques." PhD dissertation, Université Libre de Bruxelles.

Kagné, Bonaventure, and Marco Martiniello. 2001. "L'immigration subsaharienne en Belgique." *Courrier hebdomadaire du CRISP* 1721:.

Lacroix, Thomas. 2005. *Les réseaux marocains de développement: Géographie du transnational et politiques du territorial.* Paris: Les Presses de Sciences Po.

———. 2009. *Migration, développement et co-développement: Quels acteurs pour quels discours?* Paris: Institut Panos.

Martens, Albert. 1976. *Les immigrés: Flux et reflux d'une main-d'œuvre d'appoint.* Brussels: Editions Vie Ouvrière.

Naïr, Samir. 1997. *Rapport de bilan et d'orientation sur la politique de co-développement liée aux flux migratoires.* Paris: Rapport au gouvernement, mission interministérielle "Migrations/codéveloppement."

Ouali, Nouria, ed. 2004. *Trajectoires et dynamiques migratoires de l'immigration marocaine de Belgique.* Louvain-la-Neuve: Academia-Bruylant.

Piore, J. Michael. 1979. *Birds of Passage.* Cambridge: Cambridge University Press.

Portes, Alejandro, Cristina Escobar, and Renelinda Arana. 2008. "Bridging the Gap: Transnational and Ethnic Organisations in the Political Incorporation of Immigrants in the United States." *Ethnic and Racial Studies* 31, no. 6: 1056–90.

Portes, Alejandro, Luis Eduardo Guarnizo, and Patricia Landolt. 1999. "The Study of Transnationalism: Pitfalls and Promise of an Emergent Field." *Ethnic and Racial Studies* 22, no. 2: 217–37.

Portes, Alejandro, and Min Zhou. 2011. "The Eagle and the Dragon: Immigrant Transnationalism and Development in Mexico and China." Paper submitted as part of the Comparative Immigrant Organizations Project (CIOP) supported by grants from the Russell Sage Foundation and MacArthur Foundation.

Rea, Andrea. 2003. "Les politiques publiques et les associations immigrées." In *Politiques d'immigration et d'intégration: De l'Union européenne à la Wallonie*, ed. Alberto Gabbiadini, Marco Martiniello, and Jean-Francois Potelle. 189–223. Namur: Institut Jules-Destrée.

Teney, Céline, and Dirk Jacobs. 2007. "Le droit de vote des étrangers en Belgique: Le cas de Bruxelles." *Migrations Société* 19, no. 114: 151–68.

Teney, Céline, Dirk Jacobs, Andrea Rea, and Pascal Delwit. 2010. "Ethnic Voting in Brussels: Voting Patterns among Ethnic Minorities in Brussels (Belgium) during the 2006 Local Elections." *Acta Politica* 45, no. 3: 273–97.

Thys, Rebecca. 2011. "De mobilisatie van etnische verenigingen rond armoede in Brussel." In *Armoede en sociale uitsluiting: Jaarboek*, ed. Danielle Dierickx, Jan Vranken, Jill Coene, and An Van Haarlem. Leuven and Leusden: ACCO.

———. Forthcoming 2015. "The Political Role of Ethnic Minority Organizations in Brussels." PhD dissertation, Université Libre de Bruxelles.

Werbner, Pnina. 1991. "Black and Ethnic Leaderships in Britain: A Theoretical Overview." In *Black and Ethnic Leaderships: The Cultural Dimensions of Political Action*, ed. Pnina Werbner and Muhammad Anwar. 15–37. London and New York: Routledge.

Young, Crawford. 1968. *Introduction à la politique congolaise.* Kinshasa and Brussels: Editions Universitaires du Congo/CRISP.

Chapter 8

Moroccans in France
Their Organizations and Activities Back Home

Thomas Lacroix and Antoine Dumont

Moroccans constitute one of the largest immigrant groups in France, whose presence in that country dates back to the early twentieth century (De Haas 2005). By contrast to other North African states, Morocco has made emigration a key tool of its development policy. Against this backdrop, Moroccan authorities have maintained a continuous and often confrontational dialogue with Moroccan organizations abroad (Iskander 2010). Since the 1960s, they have played a key role in representing the overseas diaspora. But far from being a mere transmission belt of state policies, the Moroccan organizational field has generated a large array of political, cultural, and social connections. While public authorities have for long regarded Moroccan organizations as agents of development, they have become genuine political actors in both the place of settlement and the society of origin.

This chapter analyzes the composition and evolution of Moroccan organizations in France along the two "vectors" identified in the conclusion of this book: namely, a horizontal vector of voluntary work and a vertical vector of intergenerational transmission (Fernández-Kelly, this volume). In this regard, the notion of "transnational organizational field" is a useful tool. This concept sheds light on the functioning and evolution of networks of organizations interlocking in a transnational sphere. A study of transnational organizational fields mirrors the evolution of immigrant communities, including their arrival and consolidation in points of destination and their will to maintain cross-border ties with countries of origin. It provides a lens through which it becomes possible to highlight the mul-

---

Notes for this chapter begin on page 233.

tiplicity of cross-border social fields or observe their making, becoming, and unmaking.

The Moroccan organizational field has traversed half a century of history, affected by policy shifts, changing migration patterns, and the slow pace of integration processes. In this chapter, based on quantitative and qualitative data, we show that development practices are, more than ever, at the core of voluntary work, but this "developmentalist turn" paralleled a political reconfiguration of the voluntary sector. Drawing on a systematic analysis of Moroccan organizations, our intent is to reveal the relations that may exist between seemingly apolitical philanthropic endeavors and political trends.

In France, the creation and functioning of associations is regulated by Law 1901. The right to create associations was extended to nonnationals in 1981. Administrative procedures for the establishment of an organization require that a list of trustees and their status be registered before the authorities and subsequently published in the *Journal Officiel*. This document is accessible online for all associations created since 1996.

We compiled an inventory of Moroccan organizations by combing the online *Journal Officiel*.[1] For each association, information on the type of activities, contact details, and a short description of the objectives are given. The data have been updated through Internet searches. The database compiled includes 1,605 organizations and provides information about the type of organization, the year of its creation, and the place and nature of its activities. In addition, an online/telephone survey of thirty-five organizations provided additional information about the activities of organizations studied, their partnerships in France and abroad, and the socioeconomic profiles of their members. Finally, quantitative information has been complemented by face-to-face interviews with leaders of the main organizations.

The first section of this chapter presents information on Moroccan organizations in France, their evolution since independence of the sending country, their activities, and their cross-border commitments. In the second section, we seek to shed light on the development practices of these organizations. Development practices surged in the context of democratization of the Moroccan regime. It was conducive to a growing claim for political voice among members the diaspora. That process is analyzed in the third part of the chapter.

Types and Activities of Moroccan Organizations in France

An analysis of the database encompassing Moroccan organizations in France—1,605 have been identified—sheds light on their composition. There are 2.4 associations per 1,000 immigrants in France,[2] a figure close to that found in the Netherlands (Gery Nijenhuis and Annelies Zoomers, this volume), but lower than the average organizational density (16 associations per 1,000 inhabitants in 2006).[3] Among associations investigated, the majority have between ten and fifty members, although eight organizations enjoy over two hundred fee-paying members and up to two thousand occasional supporters (in the case of the association "Cap Sud"). Volunteering is, accordingly, widespread among Moroccans in France.

The main types of organizations are civic and sociocultural, on the one hand, and development and hometown associations, on the other (Table 8.1). In the next section, we present the fifty-year history of Moroccan volunteer activism in France. We show that migrant volunteer work emerged to cater to the needs of local communities in the 1970s against a backdrop of long-distance nationalism. Things changed in the 1990s with the surge of a volunteer sector dedicated to transnational development. This shift paralleled the emergence of new expatriate elites willing to make us of their multiple social and economic contacts in France and Morocco.

Political and Sociocultural Associations of Moroccans in France

The origins of the Moroccan organizational field are to be found in the context leading up to the country's independence. In the 1960s and 1970s, the repression of the leftist opposition in Morocco led to the departure of a large number of political activists, mostly to France, but also to Spain, Belgium, Germany, and the Netherlands. In 1962, various political strands coalesced into the Association des Marocains en France (AMF). The primary purpose of this organization was to support left-wing political parties at home. However, heavy repression during what is now called "the years of lead" impeded any effective support (Rollinde 2002). At the same time, the problems faced by labor immigrants in the receiving countries provided a

Table 8.1. Types of Moroccan Organizations in France

Type	Number of Creations (1996–2012)	Percentage
Civic	199	12%
Cultural	87	5%
Development	534	33%
Hometown	188	12%
Professional	95	6%
Religious	81	5%
Sociocultural	373	23%
Sport	30	2%
Political	12	1%

new field of involvement for leftist activists. In 1982, a factional conflict led to a split and the subsequent creation of the Association des Travailleurs Marocains de France (ATMF). Throughout the 1980s, the ATMF was at the forefront of industrial actions involving North African workers (Daoud 2002). Its involvement at the local level led the association to widen its target groups and membership basis to other North African groups. In 2001, it acknowledged this shift by replacing the term "Marocain" (Moroccan) with "Maghrebin" (North African) in its name (Association des Travailleurs Maghrébins de France).

In order to combat the growing influence of leftist activists among immigrants in France and Europe at large, Moroccan authorities put in place a network of associations under the supervision of their consulates. The first so-called Amicales des Travailleurs et Commerçants Marocains was created in 1973 in the Paris metropolitan area. The competition between supporters and opponents of the Moroccan regime produced a spiral of violence. Activists identified by consular authorities were arrested on their return to Morocco.

The AMF, the ATMF, the Amicales, and their respective networks in France have been the main service providers to the immigrant community. Our database includes forty-nine Amicales, sixteen Associations des Travailleurs Marocains de France, and three Associations des Marocains en France. These associations have animated sociocultural life through the organization of festivals, Independence Day celebrations, parties, and religious gatherings. They also have provided support for problems immigrants face in daily life, either at the workplace or in their relations with administrators, landlords, and so forth. The Amicales act as mediators between immigrants and the consulates, facilitating administrative procedures such as passport renewals.

From the outset, community life was heavily influenced by the country of origin (Catani and Palidda 1987: 29). A climate of surveillance restricted the development of an autonomous organizational field. Very few associations were created during the 1980s. Hometown associations, produced by the chain migration of the 1960s, existed as informal networks, sometimes mobilized around collective endeavors such as the digging of a well or the building of a mosque (Lacroix 2005). A social movement emerged around the claims of children of immigrants born in France for a new social contract, the so-called *mouvement beur*. But this remained disconnected from the activism of their parents, with little or no interest in the country of origin. The memory of political rivalries still marks the Moroccan organizational field today. It partly explains the limited number of officially declared political organizations, which were created in the 1990s.

Only twelve (1 percent of the total) of the listed organizations are labeled as "political." (See table 8.1) Among the latter, one-third support or oppose Moroccan policies in Western Sahara; one-third deal with the democratization process in Morocco; and the rest are branches of political parties (Istiqlal, Parti Socialiste Unifié). The overtly declared "political organizations" are, therefore, those that focus on homeland issues. Another factor explaining the low number of such organizations is the French republican model, which condemns the expression of community interests in the public sphere. Associations reflecting the political interests of the diaspora present themselves as "civic" or even "sociocultural."

Since the mid-1990s, 199 civic and 373 sociocultural associations have been created, second only to the number of development organizations founded in the same period. Sociocultural organizations provide a space for community life and primarily target local populations. They consolidate solidarity networks and foster local integration. For example, Karavan (Toulouse) seeks to promote cultural and artistic activities among youngsters, hoping to favor their professional integration. Other sociocultural associations organize intercultural events to encourage contact between Moroccan and non-Moroccan populations. Civic organizations defend Moroccans' rights. Their activities range from the installation of sociocultural exhibitions to the provision of welfare services to their members, and they sometimes border on political engagement. The Association de la Tribue Sahraouie aims to defend the interests of the Sahraouian community in France, but also coordinates cultural exhibitions on Sahraouian culture and conferences on the so-called Moroccan Sahara.

Other civic associations do not represent the vested interests of a specific group, but seek to promote the political, cultural, or professional integration of the Moroccan population at large. They escort and provide guidance to people facing administrative procedures, organize after-school classes and Arabic language courses, provide support in case of economic hardship, and counsel people who wish to invest in France or Morocco. In fact, civic organizations do not form a homogeneous category; instead, they bridge sociocultural (and apolitical) associations catering to local groups and political organizations addressing homeland issues.

Development Organizations and Hometown Associations

Transnational development may be regarded as the factor that most significantly brought about the renewal of the Moroccan organizational field in the 1990s. If we add up all organizations partaking in development activities, the total is 950, representing 59 percent of all associations created since the mid-1990s,[4] and 1,005, or 63 percent, if we take all forms of cross-border engagement into consideration. In this section, we review three main organizational groups participating in long-distance development: hometown associations, migrant nongovernmental organizations (NGOs), and other types of organizations that are only partially geared toward development activities.

Figure 8.1 shows the transnational turn of Moroccan overseas volunteering. The recent evolution of the Moroccan organizational field in France is marked, on the one hand, by the sheer increase in the number of development organizations and hometown associations (HTAs) and, on the other, by the decline in the number of organizations focusing on local migrant communities. One association out of three registered since 1996 is involved in development; this becomes one out of two if HTAs are taken into account. HTAs invest in infrastructure and other development projects for the benefit of their places of origin. They are to be found in a wide array of immigrant groups throughout the world (Moya 2005). They have been extensively studied in the context of Mexican immigration to the United States (Smith 2006; Zabin and Radaban 1998; Iskander, this volume), or Malian immigration to France (Daum 1998; Gonin 1997; Quiminal 1991). HTAs were initially created to ease the settlement of people from the same home villages into the host societies, but they lost their raison d'être with the drying out of chain migration and the growing integration of migrants into receiving countries. In the 1990s and at the beginning of the twenty-first century, they found new life through their involvement in development efforts (Lacroix 2010).

As will be shown in the second part of this chapter, this "developmentalist turn" has been supported by a growing number of migration and development schemes implemented by both the French and Moroccan authorities. Most hometown groups come from Berber areas where traditional community structures and a sense of cultural distinctiveness remain more vivid than in other parts of Morocco. Our database includes

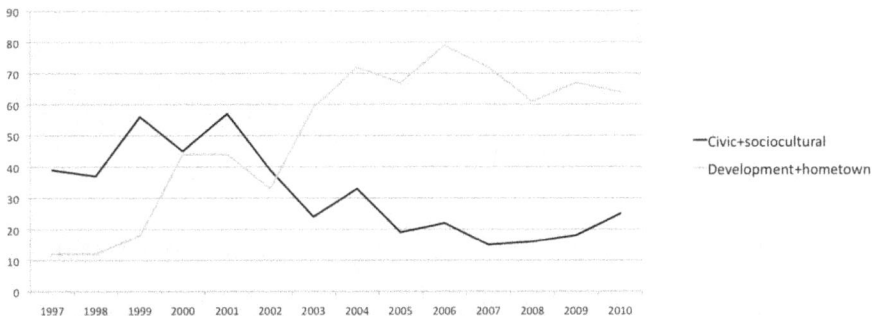

Figure 8.1. Evolution of the Moroccan Organizational Field (1997–2010)

188 organizations, a figure slightly inferior to an earlier estimate of 250 based on the number of projects carried out by government-sanctioned organizations in Morocco (Lacroix 2009). The discrepancy is consistent with the fact that a large proportion of hometown associations are not registered.

By contrast with hometown associations, other migrant NGOs do not necessarily conduct direct work in the home country, but they also contribute to homeland development. They cover a wide array of activities, from building infrastructure to shipping clothes, medications, and school supplies and support for cultural events. We have identified 534 organizations of this kind—the largest category of Moroccan associations in France. They engage at either the regional or national level, relying on a wide spectrum of local and countrywide funding sources. Large organizations mention public subsidies as their primary source of revenue (from the French Foreign Office, local municipalities, and the European Union), above corporate donations and membership fees.

Smaller charities, whose annual budget is under €1,000 per year, mostly rely on membership fees, the collection of goods and money, and the organization of parties and other events. Migrant NGOs are created by migrants who do not exclusively focus on their place of origin. In that sense, their emergence is related to the maturation of the Moroccan organizational field and the evolution of migration trends. While hometown associations are mostly a product of past migration links between villages of departure and places of arrival, migrant NGOs include people of different regional origins settled in France.

Beyond HTAs and migrant NGOs, long-distance development includes a large number of associations that primarily target local communities, but also dedicate part of their resources to occasional cross-border initiatives. This is the case of Asshab (Tours), created in 2008 with the goal of facilitating the insertion of youngsters into local political and economic life. Asshab recently participated in a university twinning operation linking the University of Tours and the University of Rabat. Their organization also partook in the creation of a project of commercialization of aromatic herbs cultivated in Morocco. Such associations seek to combine local and transnational objectives: their activities in Morocco support the local integration of North African youngsters in Tours.

The Development Impact of Overseas Moroccan Organizations

Moroccan organizations committed to homeland development (hometown organizations, migrant NGOs, and other migrant organizations) are extremely varied in their type, size, membership profile, and types of activities, and it is difficult to precisely assess their actual impact on development. There is, nonetheless, a body of evidence showing that their impact is real, at least at the local level. Table 8.2 below shows a breakdown of various types of transnational activities undertaken by the three categories of associations described above.

Development activities are at the core of the transnational agenda of migrant NGOs and hometown associations, and represent over half of the expressed commitment of other types of organizations. Nevertheless, the content of "development" may vary a great deal from one category to the next. Hometown associations are mostly committed to infrastructure projects (building of roads, water systems, health centers, electrification, schools, etc.). That form of engagement is rooted in the *Tiwizi,* that is, the customary code in Berber areas that regulates the collective maintenance of public infrastructure (traditionally, religious buildings and agricultural resources). In addition, three branches of the Moroccan government have channeled collective remittances toward infrastructure projects. Their impact is largely positive: in 1996, 18 percent of households in rural areas had access to electricity; fifteen years later, rural villages were entirely electrified.[5] This impressive result and its swift achievement would not have been possible without the support of overseas hometown associations.

Social projects, such as the creation of nurseries, literacy courses, community centers, and so forth, are not rare. They mostly target the living and schooling conditions of children. By contrast, economic projects represent a tiny proportion of HTAs' cross-border activities. They require high levels of technical skills and infringe upon the private interests of individuals. Leaders interviewed admit that it is very difficult to obtain consensus among villagers regarding economic projects insofar as they

Table 8.2. Main Types of Activities Undertaken in the Origin Country per Type of Organization

	HTAs	Migrant NGOs	Other
Civic/rights/politics	0%	0%	11%
Cultural/religious/sport	2%	1%	24%
Economic	1%	4%	19%
Development	97%	96%	46%
Schooling/childhood	10%	33%	0%
Humanitarian	4%	16%	18%
Health	3%	15%	2%
	N = 188	N = 534	N = 206

(World Bank, 2011).

raise issues of ownership, risk, and profit sharing. The few existing examples include the creation of agricultural cooperatives, tapestry-making
outfits, and tourist hostels.

By and large, the successful engagement of hometown groups in
long-distance development is linked to the diversification of financial and
technical resources. The most successful associations have managed to collect funding from public and private, local and international partners. In
doing so, they have become a key player in the development of rural areas.
Attacharouk is a case in point. That HTA has been formally registered
since 1998. Its role was initially to coordinate the participation of expatriate villagers in the funding of a water system for homes—a project originally initiated by the United Nations Educational, Scientific and Cultural
Organization (UNESCO). In subsequent years, Attacharouk electrified the
village within the framework of a cofunding program with the Moroccan
Office National d'Electricité. In 2003, it built up a public library with the
financial support of the French Foreign Ministry (Programme Coopération Maroc) and the technical support of another migrant organization,
Immigration Développement Démocratie.

Migrant NGOs do not form a homogeneous group; they differ in terms
of their work methods. The majority are constituted by small charities, created for one-shot operations. They collect and ship materials for schools,
orphanages, hospitals, or deprived families. Half (48 percent) of NGOs'
activities target poor children and health issues. Another widespread associational form relies on existing institutions to foster social cooperation
through a twinning of French and Moroccan cities or universities. Others
support (or are overseas branches of) Moroccan associations, hospitals, or
orphanages (Toit au Maroc in Tours, Association pour le développement
de la Fondation Norsys in Lille). Finally, the most visible organizations
do not only undertake their own development agenda in Morocco, but
also support other overseas Moroccan associations. They offer platforms
of exchanges between actors in France and Morocco (Solidarité Culture
et Développement Nord-Sud in Clichy) and connect project owners and
funding bodies (Migrations et Développement in Marseilles, Immigration
Démocratie Développement in Paris).

Finally, the Moroccan organizations for which cross-border commitments are not a primary aim engage in more diverse practices. Development remains a major area of activity (46 percent). The shipping of goods
for humanitarian purposes is a common endeavor (18 percent). But this
type of initiative remains limited in scope and time. Organizations that
sustain contact with Morocco are those for whom transnational engagement is an extension of their local work. Examples of this are cultural organizations that promote Moroccan culture in France and Moroccan art-

ists in France and Morocco (Tanger in Dream in Fontaine de Vaucluse), professional organizations that invest in the sending country (Association Marocaine d'Economie Financière in Paris, Club des Investisseurs Marocains de l'Etranger in Mérignac), and civic organizations that facilitate the integration of youngsters through cross-border projects in the place of origin (Association Humanitaire et Solidaire Union Franco-marocaine in Sotteville-lès-Rouen, Association Montpellieraine Citoyenne et Culturelle in Montpellier, Association Culturelle et Sportive Franco-Marocaine in Belfort).

Most of these organizations work in principal out-migration points in Morocco—the Souss Massa Draa, the Oriental, El Haouz, Taza Al Hoceima, and the Tadal Azilal—which are also the main targets of development efforts (Table 8.3). It is worth noting that the main beneficiary areas are not the largest senders of migrants, but the oldest. The Souss Massa Draa has been producing emigrants since the colonial era. The significance of historical areas hints at the importance of length of settlement and, therefore, integration in cross-border engagement. This is also the case in those areas where one observes a long-standing tradition of collective organization. For example, hometown associations abound among people originating from southern Morocco (Lacroix 2005).

Table 8.3. Geographical Distribution of Development Projects and Other Cross-Border Practices (N = 319)

Moroccan Provinces	
Chaouia-Ouardigha	2%
Doukkala-Abda	3%
Fès-Boulemane	5%
Gharb-Chrarda-Beni Hssen	3%
Grand Casablanca	3%
Guelmim-Es Semara	5%
Laâyoune-Boujdour-Sakia El Hamra	1%
Marrakech-Tensift-Al Haouz	10%
Meknès-Tafilalet	8%
L'Oriental	11%
Oued Ed-Dahab-Lagouira	1%
Rabat-Salé-Zemmour-Zaer	3%
Sous-Massa-Drâa	29%
Tadla-Azilal	6%
Tanger-Tétouan	3%
Taza-Al Hoceima-Taounate	8%

Moroccan Associations and French and Moroccan "Codevelopment" Policies

The focus on development is related to incentives implemented by sending and receiving states to support migrants' projects. Emigration and remittances have been two key elements of the Moroccan toolkit for development. In 2010, the country received $6.4 billion in remittances, representing 6.6 percent of the country's gross domestic product (GDP).[6] In the early 1990s, in the wake of a financial crisis, Moroccan authorities reformed their emigration policy. In the span of three years, the government created a Ministry of Moroccans Abroad, meant to implement a new policy toward migrants; the Foundation Hassan II, to give a new impetus to the relationships between authorities and the expatriate community; and the Bank Al Amal, to support the economic investments of expatriates.

These new policies aimed at enhancing migrant remittances and investment. In 1996, the government undertook a new cofunding scheme meant to support local associations willing to electrify their village. The Programme d'Electrification Rurale Généralisée (PERG) provided a framework of cooperation between the state, the Office National d'Electricité, and village organizations. The state defrays 55 percent of the expenses, the rest being shared by the municipality and the villagers. Migrations et Développement, the largest migrant NGO in France, partook in the preliminary consultations preceding the implementation of the scheme (Iskander 2010). The goal was to encourage the collaboration and financial contributions of migrants and HTAs. PERG proved to be successful in southern Morocco, where hometown associations are particularly active. Between 1996 and 2002, 7,050 villages were electrified. Four of the five provinces that benefited most from the program are located in southern Morocco, the historical emigration area (Taroudannt, Tiznit, Ouarzazate, and Zagora) (Lacroix 2005: 162). Two similar schemes were implemented in the mid-1990s: one for the building of roads (Programme National Concerté des Routes Rurales, or PNCRR) and the other for connecting rural homes to a tap water system (Programme d'Acces Généralisé à l'Eau potable, or PAGER). These three Moroccan schemes are the only examples of programs relying on migrant philanthropy. They favored the participation of hometown associations in translocal projects.

In France, codevelopment policies have had a wider outreach since 1997, when they were formalized and named (Naïr 1997). Their central aim is to support development in out-migration areas, hoping to lower out-migration pressures. They promote all kinds of cooperation with origin areas in partnership with migrants. Codevelopment is, therefore, not an independent government program, but rather a generic term qualifying a myriad of state and local projects. Under this category fall the technical and financial aid provided to returnees, "brain gain" programs, twinning of cities and universities, development programs sponsored by NGOs and hometown associations, and more (Lacroix 2008). To rationalize the participation of migrant organizations, the Forum des Organisations de Solidarité Internationales issues de la Migration[7] (FORIM) was created in 2002. This federative institution aims to buttress the migrant organizational field, to encourage their professionalization, and to insert them into the wider network of development NGOs in France. FORIM includes over seven hundred members, including twenty-eight Moroccan organizations.

Codevelopment policies marked the structuration of the Moroccan associational field. It favored the emergence of government-sanctioned migrant NGOs that mediate the relationships between large funding bodies (national and European institutions), on the one hand, and small project holders (such as hometown associations), on the other. The two main organizations falling under this category have already been mentioned in this chapter: Immigration Développement Démocratie (IDD) and Migrations et Développement (MD). Both were created by former unionist and political activists. MD was founded in Marseille in 1986. It is the oldest and largest Moroccan immigrant NGO, supporting over two hundred hundred projects, mostly in southern Morocco, the area of origin of its leader. It is does not have a development agenda of its own, but supports hometown associations (Daoud 1997; Mernissi 1998). IDD was created in 1998 by former members of the ATMF. It is a platform gathering fourteen smaller associations with a strong leftist leaning. Its first sizable action was to support the building of public libraries in rural areas thanks to funding from the Foreign Office (Programme Concerté Maroc). Both associations partake in government-level discussions and international platforms. For example, they are part of the European Network on Migration and Development (EUNOMAD), which gathers seventy migrant and nonmigrant NGOs from eight European countries.[8]

The surge of interest in migration and development efforts and the creation of new funding schemes in France and Morocco parallel the creation of an increasing number of migrant associations committed to transnational development. There is a wealth of local and national organizations now dealing with issues related to development and benefiting from an array of local, regional, and national funding. Some have successfully mustered financial resources from membership fees and public and private funding in France, Morocco, and even the larger European community. As a result, the subject of transnational development has attracted a new generation of community leaders in search of public legitimacy. The

Moroccan organizational field stands at a crossroads between a surge of interest in migration and development issues and the pace of integration of overseas Moroccans.

Two Portraits of Community Leaders

Kamel and Mohamed both epitomize archetypical profiles of activists navigating in the different spheres of the organizational field, between the local and the transnational, between development and politics, and between hometown networks and cosmopolitan federations. Mohamed was born in 1945 in Tamanart, in the province of Tata. He left his hometown at the age of fourteen to work in Fqih Ben Salah, at the grocery store of a relative. In 1965, he migrated to Gennevilliers, a notorious "Moroccan" suburb in the western area of Paris. Like his relatives already living in that city, he became a worker in the auto industry. He discovered political and union engagement during the May 1968 demonstrations, later enrolling in the Confédération Générale du Travail (CGT) and joining the AMF. During his years of radical activism, he was known as Larbi Toss. As a union delegate, he bore witness to industrial actions of the 1970s and 1980s: Chausson in 1975, Citroën in 1984, and the Collieries of North Pas de Calais at various points during the same period.

In 1982, the AMF split and Mohamed joined the newly created organization, the ATMF. His wife arrived in France the same year and, subsequently, they had two children. He lived two parallel lives: one characterized by his political engagement with the ATMF and the union; the other one marked by his "hometown" engagement with his family and relatives. Like other village fellows, he built a new house and made contributions to the hometown association of Tamanart for it to install a new collective well and refurbish the mosque or madrassa of his village. In the late 1990s his two lives converged with the creation of Immigration Développement Démocratie (IDD), a platform formed by migrant organizations committed to development in the home country. Attacharouk, Tamanart's hometown association, was a founding member of that platform. Most of its members are related to leftist organizations such as the ATMF and the AMF. By 1998, Mohamed retired. He now dedicates all his time to various voluntary activities.

Kamel, our second example, has been participating in association activities since his adolescence. The film club of his hometown, managed by a leftist association, was a rallying point for him and his friends. In the 1980s, it was a central point for local cultural and political life. In 1984, after receiving his baccalaureate, he enrolled in a French institution, the University of Rouen. There, he became an active member of the local branch of the Union Nationale des Etudiants Marocains (UNEM). After two years, he left Rouen to go to Paris, where he survived by taking small jobs and receiving a stipend from his father. During the same period, he trained in computer engineering and got married in 1990.

It was not until 1994 that he returned to voluntary work. He joined the hometown association of his place of origin, which, once a year, organizes a party to collect funds on behalf of deprived children. Among other things, the same organization shipped computers to a school and furnished a dialysis center in the town. It collaborated with the United Nations Development Programme (UNDP) and the municipality of Saint-Denis to set up a sanitation system. In 2003, it joined IDD, the federation of migrant NGOs.

In 2004, Kamel abandoned his participation in hometown development to join a political organization, the Conseil National des Marocains de France (CNMF). The organization was created to claim parliamentary representation for overseas Moroccans in Rabat, the capital. Kamel is still an active member of the leftist circles of Saint-Denis. He volunteered, for example, to take care of the Internet website of the World Social Forum, which took place in Saint-Denis in 2003. Finally, in 2010, Kamel founded his own association, Transferts et Compétences, which aims to ease the circulation of skilled workers between France and Morocco. The association functions as a platform of contacts between French and Moroccan businesses, on the one hand, and Moroccan skilled workers, on the other.

These two portraits synthesize the evolution of the Moroccan organizational field—from membership in associations that take charge of problems faced by immigrant communities in their places of settlement to those that support long-distance development initiatives in the country of origin. Civic and sociocultural associations constitute the first group; development and hometown associations form the second. Both groups are tightly connected. Community leaders navigate this universe by joining different associations and/or alternating different types of involvement at different times. It is therefore important to pay attention to the profile of leaders accounting for these two overarching categories.

Beyond Development: The New Faultlines of the Moroccan Organizational Field

The development turn of the Moroccan organizational field is part and parcel of the general sociological transformation of the immigrant population in France and of the emergence of a new middle class in particular. The slow (albeit, in many regards, segmented) assimilation in the host society has less diminished than transformed their mode of transnational engagement. This dynamic has produced new social, associational and political faultlines, but also a redefinition of the place of migrants in the french-moroccan transpolitical space. We examine this evolution through three key issues: the stratification of the associational field, the role of children of immigrants in the volunteer sector and the claim for external voting in Moroccan elections system.

The Vertical Vector: New Faces in the Moroccan Organizational Field

Our survey of associations reveals a strong polarization of the organizational field with, on the one hand, entities with low annual budgets (less than €1,000 per year), mostly relying on the voluntary work of their members, and, on the other, organizations with very high annual budgets (over €10,000 per year, see figure 8.2).

The bottom level of the Moroccan volunteer sector is a heterogeneous ensemble comprising small local groups as well as national organizations. Most hometown associations are found in that sector. They rely on internal resources to carry out local projects. But "low budget" does not necessarily mean "small and local." For example, the Association d'Ici et d'Ailleurs (founded in 2008 and based in Thiais) boasts six hundred members and beneficiaries living in different parts of France. Its aim is to assist Moroccans who have invested in housing projects in Morocco. Even if they monitor large financial flows, the association itself maintains only one website and organizes few informational meetings for its members.

At the opposite end of the organizational spectrum stand organizations that enjoy substantial financial resources. This relatively high number of successful associations is linked to the Franco-Moroccan elite. The majority of board members in the organizations we surveyed have university degrees. Engineers and professionals are followed by employees and,

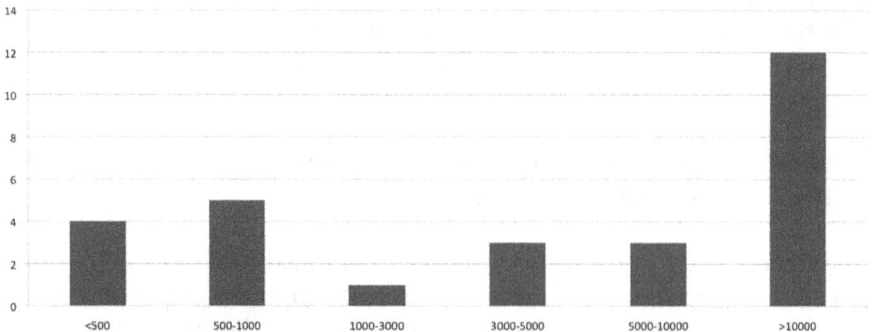

Figure 8.2. Distribution of Organizations According to Their Annual Budget (in euros)

finally, by entrepreneurs and traders. Low-skilled and manual workers are least represented. Another measure of integration of community leaders is their fluency in French and length of stay in France. All the board members interviewed stated that they have a "perfect" or "very good" command of French, and most of them have been in France for more than ten years.

Another finding of this survey concerns the embedding of the Moroccan volunteer sector into French society. This is reflected in the composition of boards of trustees. We were able to gather information on the governing bodies of seventy associations, either through online and telephone contacts or through Internet searches. A large proportion (fifty-three out of seventy) of surveyed organizations present a mixed board, with people of both Moroccan and French (or other) origins. This is particularly true for migrant NGOs. For example, the association Qui m'aime me suive (founded in 2005 in Octeville) is headed by two women, one born in Morocco, the other married to a Moroccan man. Members and supporters are of Moroccan and French origin and they live in the same area. A shared interest[9] in Morocco and interpersonal relations in France account for the presence of people of French origin in Moroccan associations. Mixed membership widens their support base and provides complementary skills and resources. French people are usually in charge of exchanges with local authorities and other partners in France and Europe, while immigrants take on the relations with their Moroccan partners.

Further evidence suggesting the embeddedness of the Moroccan volunteer sector in French society concerns the variety of funding sources. Of course, internal assets such as member fees, those resulting from fundraising events, and the selling of products and services are the primary source of revenue for many associations, but over one-third of those surveyed receive subsidies from public local and national authorities, private businesses, or civil society organizations.

Integration is, therefore, a key factor accounting for the structuring of the Moroccan organizational field. The mushrooming of Moroccan organizations in France during the 1990s and in the 2000s is linked to the emergence of a middle and upper middle class of North African origin: the so-called Beurgeoisie (Leveau and Wihtol de Wenden 2001). This new community elite relies on high levels of human and social capital. They enhance their capacities by navigating through different social and cultural universes and pursue activities in the national and transnational public spheres. Such educated elites contrast with historical leaders in the Moroccan organizational field, who were former unionists, members of Amicales, and political activists active in the voluntary sector for twenty to thirty years. The new elite participates in the transformation of the

France-based Moroccan voluntary sector, a sector more open to the host and origin societies, more cosmopolitan, and more motivated by philanthropic concerns than by political stakes.

Evidence shows that transnational commitments and national integration are not in a zero-sum relation. The incorporation of immigrants in areas of destination has provided them with social and economic resources to engage in cross-border activities. Similarly, as integration problems become less pressing, immigrants find time to invest in homeland concerns. Are the same interests present among the children of immigrants born in France? We are inclined to respond, "Yes, but ..." There is a real interest in transnational issues among members of the new generation, but that interest is framed by existing incentives or by their absence.

The Difficult Transmission of Transnational Linkages

Community leaders generally deplore the lack of commitment of the children. For example, members of hometown associations see development projects as an opportunity to transmit their cultural and family legacy and to present places of origin in a positive light. Despite this intent, neither hometown groups nor other types of organizations undertake specific strategies to attract the second generation. As noted above, the vast majority of youngsters engaged in transborder associational activities were born in Morocco (the so-called 1.5 generation). Members or leaders of associations born in France are more likely to participate in associations that work at the local level: in sports, religious, cultural, and civic activities. However, two themes have spurred interest in cross-border activities among second-generation Moroccans. The first one is development. Crépuscule in Angers, for example, promotes the civic, economic, and political insertion of youngsters in overseas development through the implementation of several projects in Morocco. Participants visit the country of origin, comparing it to the "imagined Morocco."

This dialectical process is key to their reappropriation of identity and strengthens the will to fill a transgenerational gap. By participating, they harmonize different dimensions of their life project: being a child of immigrants, receiving a familial legacy, being a parent transmitting the same legacy, and being a legitimate French citizen active in mainstream society. This approach—tackling personal integration through the reappropriation of genealogical roots—is a common experience among all Moroccan second-generation actors involved in development projects.

The second domain of commitment is business and politics for highly skilled youngsters. Once again, key organizations working in this area, such as Maroc Entrepreneurs, count only a minority of second-generation members in their ranks. The Alliance of Mediterranean Women Abroad (AMEWA), whose aim is to train women leaders and defend the rights of highly skilled workers, is an exception confirming the rule. A woman who owns an IT company in the Parisian area leads the association.

Intergenerational differences are central to the understanding of divergent engagement in cross-border activities. Parents use the skills and resources acquired in the host society to fulfill their duties as transnational villagers, while their children use their links with the place of origin to harmonize and legitimate their role as citizens. The old pattern is rooted in an émigré ethos, associated with family connections that form adult identities (Lacroix 2005: 74–81). First-generation transnationalism tends to produce translocally delimited linkages, in contrast to youths involved in migrant NGOs, which tend to establish wider bonds with the country of origin.

Another implication is that village organizations rely on community structures and mostly remain informal. That is not the case for newer associations, which rely on the shared interests of people whose relationships do not necessarily precede their involvement and, consequently, need formal structures to subsist. Finally, whether immigrant involvement is directed toward the country of origin or toward European society, it expresses a commitment to dual belonging and integration in two distinct societies. Thus, children of immigrants are endowed with a multilayered identity. Transnationalism is a matrix of articulated multiple belongings; it fosters hybridity.

The Debate on the Voting Rights of Emigrants: A Missed Opportunity?

The low level of transnational commitment among children of immigrants is not in the agenda of voluntary organizations. Similarly, it has not been part of the discussions surrounding the voting rights of expatriate Moroccans in the country of origin. Moroccan citizenship is based on jus sanguinis, and anyone who has a Moroccan parent can ask for a Moroccan passport. The debate emerged in response to the pressing appeal made by Moroccan authorities to overseas economic and development actors. Organizations pointed out a growing concern regarding administrative obstacles and political difficulties. Against this backdrop, a claim for political voice emerged among Moroccans abroad. The absence of the right to vote and of parliamentary representation[10] was presented as a threat to Moroccan identity and nation building in the new generations. Activists argued that disenfranchisement is in contradiction to the inalienable character of Moroccan nationality.

A campaign started just before the 2002 general elections to the Moroccan parliament and was transmitted through social media and newspapers. Overseas organizations painstakingly described the difficulties—legal, economic, administrative, and logistical—faced by expatriates: the long lines under the sun in Algeciras or Tangiers for crossing the Strait of Gibraltar during summer holidays and the obstacles to financial investments. Claims for civic rights were conceived as the reward for the work migrants do on behalf of Morocco at the local, regional, and national levels.

For example, in his open letter to the king of Morocco on 23 June 2002, a leader of a small association based in southern France writes, "To deprive us of the right to vote, is to imply that citizens living in the country are more Moroccan than we are. I do not dare say to my children that we want their remittances, but neither their votes nor their citizenship!"[11] This quote in a newspaper article caused great sensation in public opinion. Activists attempted to refer the matter to the Supreme Court, but the claim was rejected. The emphasis put on remittances and the economic role of emigrants is part of a new strategy. This discourse refers to a transnational conception of citizenship, whose exercise derives neither from residency nor from nationality but from dual belonging and dual citizenship.

In 2002, a new endeavor was initiated by Friends of Morocco, a sociocultural association in Versailles. Its aim was to set up a representative body of the Moroccan population living in France, the Conseil National des Marocains en France (CNMF). This initiative echoed a statement of the Moroccan government, which brought to the fore the absence of a democratic representative body within the diaspora. Over a hundred Moroccan associations took part in this project. The network included a wide array of activists from various political backgrounds and various generations. It is headed by a high-level civil servant working at the Fond d'Action Social pour l'Intégration et la Lutte contre les Discrimination (FASILD).[12] In 2006, another network was created with about thirty associations from Belgium, France, Italy, the Netherlands, and Spain. They gathered in Paris on 5 January 2006 to found the so-called Al Monadara network. Their goal was to start a national debate in Morocco about the diaspora. In their final statement, members mentioned the establishment of "transnational citizenship" along with the recognition of the role of expatriates in the economic and social development of Morocco.

The "right to vote" campaign has delineated new lines of cleavage that do not reproduce the long-standing opposition between leftists and members of the Amicales. In France, the debate opposes, on the one hand, the Conseil de la Communauté des Marocains de l'Etranger (CCME), the consultative body reflecting the foreign policy of the Moroccan government, and, on the other, the various organizational networks that campaign in favor of the right to vote: the CNMF in France and Al Monadara at the

European level. These coalitions move beyond historical oppositions and rally former Amicales members, leftist activists, unionists, women, and young community leaders of various political (and religious) leanings, with a strong representation of professionals, civil servants, and business owners.

The presence of new community leaders is conducive to tighter inter-relations with the host society (the head of the CNMF is an administrator at the FASILD). But the lack of grassroots embedding in the immigrant community weakens these networks' capacity for mobilization. This is particularly true for children of immigrants, who hold a marginal place in the debate. Their limited presence in representative organizations reflects this exclusion. Their voice is eclipsed by that of the "1.5 generation" and of recent, highly skilled immigrants. In the debate, the second generation mostly serves to swell the figures of nationals abroad or to flag the threat of loosening national ties. The debate on political rights of emigrants, despite the subsequent reconfiguration of the associational field, has not opened a space for the children of immigrants.

Conclusion

This chapter describes the slow transformation of the Moroccan organizational field in France. It explored the horizontal vector of gradual mutation of associational practices and the transnational orientation of voluntary work. In line with anticolonial struggles prior to independence, the Moroccan voluntary sector abroad emerged with a strong nationalist ethos. The early activism of the 1960s and 1970s was strongly polarized between pro-government and leftist factions. As the Moroccan community abroad grew in size and settled in France, the voluntary sector evolved to cater to the needs of local communities. Since the mid-1990s, a third generation of associations has emerged, more committed to homeland development but also strongly embedded in the host society. This third generation of associations includes migrant NGOs of all kinds working in the fields of education, health, and economic cooperation and hometown associations that have institutionalized long-standing collective practices. Two factors explaining this recent evolution have been noted: first, the appearance of a new generation of educated community leaders, willing to reap the fruits of their upward social mobility; and second, the multiplication of public cofunding and codevelopment schemes on both sides of the Mediterranean Sea.

Beyond this reorientation from local to transnational issues, the contemporary organizational field is generating new political tensions. New political alliances have formed to claim the right to vote and to seek representation in the Moroccan parliament. While working-class organizations used to directly confront state authorities, the new coalitions endorse a consensus-based approach to improve the rights of emigrants within the Moroccan political system. In Myrdal's terms, leftist organizations until the 1980s were protest groups (Myrdal, Sterner, and Rose 1962); in contrast, the new organizational networks appear as accommodators more willing to seek agreement with the authorities. Groups campaigning in favor of absentees' right to vote are heterogeneous ensembles, gathering community leaders from diverse age and political backgrounds.

Despite broad consensus on the legitimacy of this claim, the Moroccan state has postponed the actual implementation of the right to vote for the new generation. Seen from Rabat, the threat is that the diaspora may translate its economic capital into political influence. The creation of the Conseil Consultatif des Marocains de l'Etranger has maintained the illusion of a proactive approach. This lure is coming to an end. The head of the CCME resigned without publishing the recommendations he was mandated to craft. Indeed, these expected recommendations seem to be of little interest at a time when the right to vote of overseas Moroccans has been carved in constitutional stone. Critics of the CCME have multiplied.

At a time of profound evolution of the Moroccan expatriate community, we may ask what these claims are the symptom of. Strong claims for the right to vote under the lens of nationalist resurgence is at odds with field observations of a growing openness of migrant organizations toward the host society. As shown above, a growing number of Moroccan organizations count members with a French background in their boards of trustees. In addition, recent social movements in North Africa and the Middle East have attracted sympathy among community leaders. Diaspora organizations do not seem to have played a decisive role in the outcome of the Jasmine Revolution that shook the other side of the Mediterranean Sea (Gonzales-Quijano 2011).

These two elements (broadening of the membership in the host country and limited political engagement in the country of origin) support a transnationalist rather than a nationalist explanation of recent trends. In other words, the Moroccan organizational field (and its political reconfiguration) are the result of searches for social recognition on *both* sides of the Mediterranean Sea. Voluntary actors assert through long-distance development practices the distinctiveness of their dual embedding. Community leaders engaged in upward social mobility are confronting political scenes both in France and in the country of origin. In response, they use the resources of their integration in France to build up transnational engagement. The growing density of cross-border activities among voluntary organizations accounts for such deep transformation of the Moroccan community as a whole.

The place of the second generation remains in question; it is generally absent from organizations engaged in cross-border activities. The so-called 1.5 generation turns out to be the real force of the vertical evolution in the organizational field. In other words, the generational transmission of transnational linkages is imperfect. It mostly concerns those who arrived at a young age in France. Children of immigrants produce their own linkages, attuned to the concerns of their generation. Their exclusion from the political debates around the right to vote of nationals abroad reveals the lack of interest and, most likely, of understanding of this population. This absence suggests that the future of the Moroccan transnational social space depends on the continuous inflows of new immigrants. Younger leaders raised in France or arrived recently will gradually replace the generation of political activists of the 1970s and 1980s. In the absence of participation from the younger generations, linkages are likely to shrink over time.

Thomas Lacroix, PhD, is a CNRS research fellow at Migrinter, University of Poitiers, and research associate at the International Migration Institute, Oxford University. He teaches courses on migration and development at Science Po, Paris, and is associate director of Migrinter at the University of Poitiers. He published *Les Réseaux Marocains du Développement* at the Presses de Sciences Po in 2005 and recently coedited with Elena Fiddian Qasmiyeh the special issue "Diasporic and Refugee Memories" in the *Journal of Intercultural Studies* (2013). His research focuses on migrant organizations, transnational engagements and temporality, and integration and development.

Antoine Dumont is research associate at Migrinter (CNRS-University of Poitiers). His work focuses on the transnational politics of North Africans abroad. He published in 2008 "Representing Voiceless Migrants: Moroccan Political Transnationalism and Moroccan Migrants' Organizations in France" in *Ethnic and Racial Studies* 31, no. 4.

Notes

1. See http://www.journal-officiel.gouv.fr/association. (Accessed 8 March 2015).
2. There were 663,985 Moroccan-born people in France in 2009 (INSEE RP 2009, IMG1B).

3. Note by the Ministry of Youth, Sports and Associational Life. See http://www.associations.gouv.fr/IMG/pdf/dp-conf-vie-associative_230106.pdf (accessed 6 August 2012).
4. This figure includes organizations that declare having partaken in activities in the domain of development, humanitarian aid, childhood and education, health, and economic cooperation.
5. See http://www.one.org.ma/fr/pages/interne.asp?esp=2&id1=6&id2=61&t2=1 (accessed 8 August 2012).
6. World Bank *Remittances Factbook* 2011.
7. See www.forim.net. (Accessed 8 March 2015).
8. See http://migrations.enda-europe.org/presentation-du-projet-eunomad (accessed 9 March 2015).
9. Very often spurred by tourist trips among French members.
10. A parliamentary representation of Moroccans abroad existed between 1984 and 1988. This experience was stopped, officially, for technical reasons (the difficulty of organizing elections outside of the Moroccan territory) (see Belguendouz 2003). Likewise, Moroccans living abroad participated in the 1996 and 2011 constitutional referendums.
11. See http://www.bladi.net/lettre-ouverte-a-monsieur-le-premier-ministre.html (Accessed 8 March 2015).
12. The FASILD is one of the main institutional bodies in charge of implementing integration policy in France.

References

Belguendouz, Abdelkrim. 2003. Marocains des ailleurs et Marocains de l'intérieur. Rabat: Beni Snassen.
Catani, Maurizio, and Salvatore Palidda. 1987. *Le rôle du mouvement associatif dans l'évolution des communautés immigrées.* Paris: Fas, Ministère des Affaires Sociales.
Daoud, Zakia. 1997. Marocains des deux rives. Paris: Editions de l'Atelier.
———. 2002. *De l'immigration à la citoyenneté, itinéraire d'une association maghrébine en France: L'ATMF (1960–2003).* Houilles: Mémoire de la Méditerranée.
Daum, Christophe. 1998. *Les associations de Maliens en France: Migrations, développement et citoyenneté.* Paris: Karthala.
De Haas, Hein. 2005. "Morocco: From Emigration Country to Africa's Migration Passage to Europe." In Migration Information Source. Washington DC: Migration Policy Institute. http://www.migrationpolicy.org/article/morocco-emigration-country-africas-migration-passage-europe/. (Accessed 8 March 2015).
Gonin, Patrick. 1997. "D'entre deux territoires: Circulations migratoires et développement entre le bassin du fleuve Sénégal et la France." HDR dissertation, Université des sciences et techniques, Lille.
Gonzales-Quijano, Yves. 2011. *La jeunesse arabe et les nouveaux réseaux de la mondialisation: De la sous-culture globalisée à la contre-culture révolutionnaire?* Damas, Institut français du Proche-Orient. http://halshs.archives-ouvertes.fr/docs/00/61/49/87/PDF/jeunesseafkarOk.pdf (accessed 23 October 2012).

Iskander, Natasha. 2010. *Creative State: Forty Years of Migration and Development Policy in Morocco and Mexico.* Ithaca, NY, and London: ILR Press.

Lacroix, Thomas. 2005. *Les réseaux marocains du développement: Géographie du transnational et politique du territorial.* Paris: Presses de Sciences Po.

———. 2008. "Politiques de codéveloppement et le champ associatif immigré africain: Un panorama européen." *The African Yearbook of International Law* 16: 79–98.

———. 2009. "Transnationalism and Development: The Example of Moroccan Migrant Networks." *Journal of Ethnic and Migration Studies* 35, no. 10: 1665–78.

———. 2010. "The Migrant Organizations of Development: Unveiling the Metastructures of Transnationalism." IMI Working Papers, International Migration Institute, University of Oxford.

Leveau, Rémy, and Catherine Wihtol de Wenden. 2001. *La beurgeoisie: Les trois âges de la vie associative issue de l'immigration.* Paris: CNRS éditions.

Mernissi, Fatima. 1998. *ONG rurales du Haut-Atlas: Les Aït débrouille.* Casablanca: Le Fennec.

Moya, Jose C. 2005. "Immigrants and Associations: A Global and Historical Perspective." *Journal of Ethnic and Migration Studies* 31, no. 5: 833–64.

Myrdal, Gunnar, Richard Mauritz Edvard Sterner, and Arnold Marshall Rose. 1962. *An American Dilemma: The Negro Problem and Modern Democracy.* New York and London: Harper & Row.

Naïr, Sami. 1997. *Rapport de bilan et d'orientation sur la politique de codéveloppement liée aux flux migratoires.* Government report. Paris: Mission Interministérielle Migrations/Codéveloppement.

Quiminal, Catherine. 1991. *Gens d'ici, gens d'ailleurs.* Paris: Christian Bourgeois.

Rollinde, Marguerite. 2002. *Le mouvement marocain des droits de l'Homme: Entre consensus et engagement citoyen.* Paris: Karthala, Institut Maghreb-Europe.

Smith, Robert C. 2006. *Mexican New York: Transnational Lives of New Immigrants.* Berkeley: University of California Press.

World Bank, 2011. *Remittances Factbook.* World Bank. http://data.worldbank.org/data-catalog/migration-and-remittances (accessed 7 March 2015).

Zabin, Carol, and Luis Escala Radaban. 1998. "Mexican Hometown Associations and Mexican Immigrant Political Empowerment in Los Angeles." Working paper, Aspen Institute.

Chapter 9

Transnational Activities of Immigrants in the Netherlands
Do Ghanaian, Moroccan, and Surinamese Diaspora Organizations Enhance Development?

Gery Nijenhuis and Annelies Zoomers

Globalization is commonly assumed to have important implications for development processes, including opportunities for poverty alleviation. Globalization connects people and places that are distant in space but linked in ways such that what happens in one place has direct bearing on the other (Giddens 1990: 64; see also Harvey 1989). According to Appadurai (1996: 192), globalization creates landscapes of translocalities:

> Such localities create complex conditions for the production and reproduction of locality in which ties of marriage, work, business and leisure weave together various circulating populations, with kinds of locals to create neighborhoods that belong in one sense to particular nation-states, but are from another point of view what might be called translocalities.

In a globalizing world, local development is increasingly played out in a matrix of links that connect people and places with people and places elsewhere.

An important driver for creating landscapes of translocalities is international migration. Increasing numbers of people around the world are on the move: it is estimated that there are currently between 175 and 200 million labor migrants (GCIM 2005; Farrant, MacDonald, and Sriskandarajah 2006), representing 3 percent of the world population. Although the

Notes for this chapter begin on page 260.

majority of international migration takes place within the Global South (to neighboring countries, the Gulf states), considerable numbers travel north to the classic immigration countries (the United States and Canada) and, more recently, a number of European countries (France, the UK, Germany, Spain, and Italy). Between 2000 and 2010, nearly fourteen million immigrants entered the United States, mainly from Mexico, India, the Philippines, and China. In 2010, 9.4 percent of the total European Union (EU) population comprised people who were born outside the EU (9.4 percent = 31.4 million people). According to Eurostat (2011), the largest absolute numbers of people born outside the EU were in Germany (6.4 million), France (5.1 million), the UK (4.7 million), Spain (4.1 million), Italy (3.2 million), and the Netherlands (1.4 million) (Eurostat 2011; see also Zoomers 2006).

Much has been written about the link between migration and development (De Haas 2007; Van Naerssen, Spaans, and Zoomers 2008; MPI 2008; IFRI 2008; Adepoju, Van Naerssen, and Zoomers 2008), focusing in particular on the importance of the transfer of various types of remittances (such as goods, money, ideas), which establish new connections between people in home and host communities. At the same time, studies in the fields of diasporas and transnationality have called attention to the very limited involvement of immigrant communities in transnational activities and the remaining importance of the state (Portes 1995, 1996). Others (Basch, Glick Schiller, and Szanton Blanc 1994) have showed the importance of "new mobilities," not as binary flows but as a new type of spatial and social configuration, that is, dispersed people being attached to various localities at the same time. According to Basch and colleagues (1994: 6):

> Transnationalism can be defined as the processes by which immigrants forge and sustain multi-stranded social relations that link together their societies of origin and settlement. We call these processes transnationalism to emphasize that many immigrants today build social fields that cross geographic, cultural, and political borders. ... An essential element is the multiplicity of involvements that transmigrants sustain in both home and host societies. We are still groping for a language to describe these social locations.

We refer to a diaspora when a considerable proportion of a country's population lives outside its own territory; the population is dispersed, but maintains intensive and cross-border contacts via social, economic, and political networks (Lucas 2004). Sheffer (2003) made a useful distinction between different types of diasporas. He showed that some diasporas are stateless (such as that of the Gypsies) while others are state-linked. He also distinguished between historical and modern diasporas. Some diasporas are concentrated and others dispersed (Sheffer 2003: 241; Zoomers 2006).

> Diasporas are formed from and include complex mixes of people who have arrived at different times, through different channels (labor migration, asylum, family union, for education, for professional advancement), through different means (legal entry, illegal entry, smuggling, overstaying ...) and with very different statuses (citizen, resident, student ...). (Van Hear, Pieke, and Vertovec 2004: 3)

Populations increasingly affiliate themselves translocally, in other places and time (Shapiro 2000: 83; see also Zoomers and Van Westen 2011). We can speak in this respect of many new forms of nonterritorial affiliation and solidarity (Appadurai 1996: 165).

In the migration literature, much attention is paid to exploring private, individual, person-to-person remittances. Less attention is paid to collective types of transfers. Even though "the extent to which migrants cluster can be seen as a measure of collectively expressed and collectively ascribed identity" (Schrover and Vermeulen 2005: 824), the study of migrant organizations is a relatively new field. "The character, number and size of organizations indicate the extent to which immigrants want to profile themselves as being different or how they are seen to be different by others" (ibid.), but little is known about migration as an organizational field, namely, the factors that play a role in shaping these organizations, and their relationship with processes of integration, transnational engagement, and development.

Concerning the link between transnational engagement and integration, recent studies counter the dominant view that migrants who have close ties with their countries of origin are not integrating into their countries of settlement. A Migration Policy Institute (MPI) study (2008) shows that migrant organizations in the United States, besides stimulating migrants' transnational activities, offer all kinds of services to help their members integrate into American society. The findings of Portes, Escobar, and Arana (2008) are in line with these results. At the European level, research on the contribution of migrant organizations to the integration of transnational migrants in Europe is still in its infancy. Studies focusing on the integration of individual migrants show the same results as the American studies on migrant organizations, that is, migrants' transnational activities are not a barrier to political incorporation. Snel, Engbersen, and Leerkes (2006) argue that those migrant groups that are generally less integrated (e.g., Moroccans, Antilleans) are not engaged in more transnational activities, nor do they feel a stronger identification with their countries of origin than better integrated groups.

Empirical knowledge on the contribution of migrant organizations to development in the countries or regions of origin is still relatively scarce, in both the United States and Europe. Studies by Portes and colleagues

(2007, 2008) and MPI (2008) show that migrant organizations make a fair contribution to development in the regions of origin. According to Portes, Escobar, and Walton Radford (2007), who initiated research on migrant organizations in the United States, these collective efforts played important roles in generating local development in Mexico, the Dominican Republic, and Colombia, having an impact on different modalities and types of development. Within the European context, some studies pointing toward the transformative role of migrant organizations have been completed (Beauchemin and Schoumaker 2009: 1910; Østergaard-Nielsen 2009, 2011; Lacroix 2011).

The aim of our research is to contribute to a better understanding of migration as an organizational field by analyzing whether and how migrant organizations affect development. Instead of exploring private, individual, person-to-person remittances, we focus on collective types of transfers carried out by migrant organizations in the Netherlands. When analyzing the link between diaspora and development, we follow Mohan's (2002) distinction between three types of development, namely, development *in the diaspora* (how people within the diasporic communities use their connections to secure economic and social well-being, i.e., integration into the "host area"), development *through the diaspora* (how diasporic communities utilize their networks beyond the locality to facilitate economic and social well-being), and development *by the diaspora* (how diasporic flows and continued connections "back home" facilitate the development of these "homelands"). According to Van Hear, Pieke, and Vertovec (2004), these three forms of development are interdependent. The present chapter analyzes migrant organizations in the Netherlands, with a specific focus on Ghanaian, Moroccan, and Surinamese migrant organizations, which constitute approximately 40 percent of all migrant organizations in the Netherlands. The Netherlands is home to 3.4 million migrants, who make up approximately 20 percent of the country's total population. Half of these are second-generation migrants (CBS Statline 2011); that is, they were born in the Netherlands.

In this chapter, we look at the extent to which migrant organizations can be seen as important and powerful instruments of change "here" (encouraging integration in the Netherlands), "there" (development and poverty alleviation in the areas of origin), and "in between" (bridging/expanding networks to third destinations). This is based on extensive fieldwork we carried out in the Netherlands in 2010 and 2011, during which we interviewed the sixty most important migrant organizations. We then carried out further fieldwork in Morocco, Ghana, and Suriname. We first describe the methodology and then present an analysis of the "context of exit" and the "context of reception." After this, we provide a typology, and give an in-depth description of the size, age, and focus of the twenty most important migrant organizations of each group. This is followed by an analysis of their activities in the country of origin, an assessment of their contributions to development, the conclusion, and final reflections.

Study Design: Selection of Migrant Organizations from Suriname, Morocco, and Ghana

We first selected representative migrant organizations in the sense that they both represent a large part of the Dutch migrant community and show the diversity of the various groups. We decided to focus on migrant organizations run by people from Suriname (former colony; Dutch speaking/Dutch nationality; no major integration problems); Morocco (ex–guest worker program plus family reunion; integration problems); and Ghana (more recent groups of spontaneous labor workers, mostly low skilled). Together, these groups represent 38 percent of all non-Western migrants in the Netherlands (CBS Statline 2011). We then made an inventory of migrant organizations from the three groups in the Netherlands since the 1980s by consulting several databases and inventories[1] (Van Heelsum 2004; Van Heelsum and Voorthuijsen 2002; Van Naerssen, Kusters, and Schapendonk 2006). For our three nationalities, we found a total of 1,789 migrant organizations.

From these, and focusing on those that were still operational,[2] we selected those that maintain relations in transnational space, that is, we omitted migrant organizations that focus only on the Netherlands and do not develop activities in their respective home countries. We only considered formal migrant organizations, that is, those that were registered as foundations or associations with the Chamber of Commerce. For each of the three groups, we selected the twenty top organizations using a multiple entry points approach, through existing inventories, interviews with experts and leaders of umbrella migrant organizations, and officials of the consulates/embassies of the respective countries. Two additional criteria guided this selection: an organization must have been founded by migrants, and it must have existed for at least three years.

The selection of the twenty most important organizations per group was a challenge, first because despite the presence of inventories, it was difficult to contact certain organizations.[3] Second, not all the organizations in our preliminary selection were involved in transnational activities. Third, and this applied in particular to the Ghanaian and Surinamese organizations, we encountered a certain "point of saturation" at which the multiple entry points approach no longer produced new organizations.

We interviewed the representatives of these organizations—generally the leader or, in three cases, one of the other board members—in order to gain a better understanding of the origin of the organizations, their activities in the Netherlands and in the countries of origin, and their views on development. Each interview lasted 1–1.5 hours; in some cases, two meetings were held, in order to discuss additional matters.

After these interviews, we collected data on the countries of origin in order to gain a better understanding of the activities of the organizations and their partner organizations, and their development impact. We selected a subsample of seven partners per migrant group, covering a varied group of organizations at different locations in Morocco, Ghana, and Suriname. Over a period of four to six weeks per country, we visited the project sites of each of the seven case studies and interviewed leaders, staff, and members of the partner organizations and other local stakeholders, such as the beneficiaries, the local government, and traditional authorities. This implied that we spent time at each location, and were thus also able to make some observations with respect to the activities implemented.[4] The analysis of the data was carried out using NVivo for qualitative information. More factual information was stored and analyzed through an Excel database.

Migration from Suriname, Morocco, and Ghana: Different Contexts of Exit and Reception

In analyzing the functioning of the migrant organizations and the dynamics of the organizational field, we first wanted to explore the "context of exit" and the "context of reception," to see whether these play decisive roles. We looked at the extent to which these backgrounds play a role in the functioning and role of the selected migrant organizations.

The Outflow of Migrants: Contexts of Exit

For a long time, Suriname itself was an immigrant society: its population originated from Ghana, China, Indonesia, and India.[5] Out-migration to the Netherlands started under colonial rule and reached its peak around 1975, when Suriname gained independence. Migration continues today, not only to the Netherlands but now also to Miami, the Antilles, and India. If one includes second-generation migrants, the majority (over 70 percent) of the Surinamese population now lives abroad. The diaspora is very fragmented, being made up of various ethnic groups (Creoles, Maroons, Javanese, Hindustanis, Chinese).

The Surinamese government has not been active in reaching out to its diaspora and regards with some distrust the Surinamese who live in the Netherlands. Until recently, the government had shown hardly any interest in the diaspora, and migrants were generally considered "deserters" rather than heroes. Last year, however, President Bouterse said in a speech about the Surinamese diaspora: "We should change the way we deal with them and they will change the way they deal with us" (DevSur 2011).

In the case of Moroccans who left their homes to become guest workers in various European countries (Germany, France, the Netherlands), the situation is very different. The majority of these migrants were poor farmers, predominantly from the mountainous Rif region; the immigrants were initially mainly males who left their country temporarily to work as guest workers (Van Amersfoort and Van Heelsum 2007). After some time, however, many of these guest workers decided to stay, although a considerable proportion did return home.[6] Morocco is currently experiencing rapid economic growth, and the opportunities for social mobility are greater than in earlier periods.

The Moroccan government plays an active role in reaching out to the diaspora, obliging people to keep dual citizenship and maintain relations with their home country. In the 1970s and 1980s, the main objective of the Moroccan government was to control its citizens abroad: it wanted to prevent integration into the host societies, as it feared a reduction in remittances. Moroccan migrants, on their part, did not feel welcome in Morocco, where they faced corruption, distrust, and lack of protections (De Haas 2007). Since the late 1990s, there has been a shift, with increasing efforts by the government to reach out to the diaspora. For this purpose, several programs and institutions have been established in which the diaspora is granted the status of an active economic and social actor (see also Bilgili and Weyel 2012). The Moroccan state, however, continues to control its emigrants. In this regard, De Haas (2007) refers to a transition from "hard" to "soft" control mechanisms.

Finally, Ghana has had to deal with enormous out-migration since the early 1980s, initially mainly to neighboring West African countries, such as Nigeria. In the 1990s, this flow was also accompanied by a large outflow of Ghanaians to long-distance destinations, such as the United States and the United Kingdom. Due to a relatively large number of people in irregular status, it is difficult to give a precise number of Ghanaians living abroad, but estimates range from 1.5 million (8 percent of the total population) to 4 million (20 percent) (Mazzucato 2009).

Ghana, like Morocco, is currently experiencing rapid economic growth and rapid urbanization. The Ghanaian situation contrasts sharply with that of Morocco, however, as Ghana has hardly any diaspora engagement policies. In 2001, the Ghanaian government organized a Homecoming Summit in which individuals and organizations abroad participated, discussing how to tap and mobilize migrant resources for development (Kleist 2011). But although the 2010 budget foresaw the establishment of a formal national migration policy, this was not implemented. Interest in the diaspora seems to have waned over the years, although Ghanaian embassies and consulates are quite active in the channeling of information to the Ghanaian community (Vezzoli and Lacroix 2010).

The Inflow of Migrants into the Netherlands: Contexts of Reception

The Surinamese, Moroccan, and Ghanaian migrants arrived in the Netherlands in very different periods and under very different conditions and policy regimes. When the Surinamese arrived, the context of reception was rather favorable: the majority did not have language problems, since the Surinamese are Dutch speaking, and there were no restrictions with respect to legal status. Most of them settled in Amsterdam's Bijlmer district. Surinamese migrants are relatively highly educated, particularly in comparison to other migrant groups (CBS Statline 2011). Although the majority of the Surinamese in the Netherlands can be considered integrated, their labor participation is relatively low, particularly among the young (Bosma 2009), and unemployment rates among young Surinamese, especially among the Creoles, are high. In general terms, when migration from Suriname took place, the Netherlands was a rather hospitable country, and integration went relatively smoothly.

The flow of Moroccans into the Netherlands (which started in the 1960s, replacing earlier migration flows from Italy and Spain) took place in the context of guest worker programs. The guest workers were provided with hardly any facilities, as the majority were supposed to return to their home countries at the end of their contracts. No effort was initially made to promote integration, and interventions by the Dutch government were mainly to prevent exploitative relations. It was only in the 1970s and 1980s, when it became clear that the temporary workers were here to stay, that new policies were made for family reunification. Being confronted with a large inflow of poor (Berber) people from rural zones who were generally low skilled or unskilled, had a Muslim background, and lacked language skills, the Dutch government became increasingly involved in developing new tools to facilitate integration (alphabetization, "civic integration).

Another field of action was trying to stimulate return through development programs, such as the REMPLOD program (Reintegration of Emigrant Manpower and Promotion of Local Opportunities and Development), initiated in the 1970s in Morocco. However, the results were disappointing, since only a few people returned and the development impact was small. Today, this Muslim group is increasingly seen as problematic, with high unemployment rates and relatively high rates of criminality. The emphasis has shifted to restrictive policies and how to stimulate "return migration."

The majority of the Ghanaian migrants entered the Netherlands in the 1980s and 1990s, seeking economic opportunities.[7] A large proportion of this group settled in Amsterdam's Bijlmer district, similar to the Surinamese, and to a lesser extent in The Hague. Although part of the Ghanaian community is medium or high skilled (belonging to the middle classes in Ghana), the majority is employed in the lower segments of the economy, such as cleaning. This can be traced to their relatively low proficiency in Dutch. A minority is found in the entrepreneurial sector. Overall, the Ghanaian community is considered relatively close and well organized, with a strong visual presence, in the form of Ghanaian churches, shops (food, video, clothing), radio broadcastings, and magazines. Ghanaians are not explicitly mentioned as a target group—that is, as a "problematic" group—within the framework of Dutch integration policies, and as such there are hardly any specific governmental programs or projects aimed at their integration.

Linking "Exit" and "Reception": The Emergence of Codevelopment Policies

The Netherlands changed from a rather hospitable country offering all kinds of facilities to enable the integration of migrants (housing, subsidized language courses) into a country with an emphasis on restrictive controls. Migrant groups are increasingly forced to meet requirements for integration (such as language requirements), but there is less and less support. Government subsidies in favor of integration and/or possibilities for family reunion are becoming more restrictive, and it is increasingly difficult to stay. The Dutch government plays an important role in the process of integration, a role that Rath (2009: 679) labels "neo-etatism." This is also expressed in the attempts of the Dutch state to establish "umbrella entities," such as the Surinaams Inspraak Orgaan (SIO; Surinamese Consultative Body) and the Samenwerkingsverband van Marokkaanse Nederlanders (SMN; the Moroccan equivalent) to represent all migrant organizations in encounters with the Dutch government.

Parallel to this tendency toward more restrictive policies, there are attempts to align the migration and development agendas, resulting in the formulation of codevelopment policies. These policies are a consequence of the "fear of invasion" (and the limitations of a multicultural society) and a reaction to the discovery of remittances as a source for development (as an alternative to foreign aid). However, a close look at these policies and their budgets reveals that migration management, via circular and return migration programs, continues to dominate (Ministry of Foreign Affairs 2010; Nijenhuis and Broekhuis 2010). Nevertheless, some funds are available to migrants and their organizations to finance development

Table 9.1. Characterization of Migration into the Netherlands and Contexts of "Exit" and "Reception"

	Suriname	Morocco	Ghana
Number of migrants in the Netherlands	344,734	355,883	21,376
Arrived	1970s–1980s	1960s–1980s	1980s–1990s
Characteristics	Ethnicly diverse; highly skilled; well integrated	Temporary guest workers; low skilled; some integration problems	Economic migrants; low skilled; entrepreneurs; some integration problems
Diasporic dispersion	Netherlands, Miami, and the Caribbean	Concentrated in Europe (France/Spain/Germany/Italy)	Globally dispersed, mainly United States/United Kingdom
Size of diaspora as share of total immigrant population	70 percent	10 percent	8–20 percent
Organizational density (no. org/no. migrants*1,000)	2.6	2.2	7.5
Perception of emigrants in country of origin	Negative: emigrants as deserters	Positive: remittances and family reunion	Generally positive: remittances
Outreach by the government	No	Yes: dual citizenship and various programs to link up with the diaspora	A few recent initiatives
Dutch policies	Creation of SIO	Various programs aimed at integration; governmental programs aimed at sustainable return and development; creation of SMN	Access to codevelopment programs

Sources: IOM (2009); CBS Statline (2011).

activities in their countries of origin. Some of these funds are managed by cofinancing agencies, which receive money from the Dutch Ministry of Foreign Affairs. An example is the Linkis initiative, which is a joint effort between several large cofinancing agencies to facilitate the low-threshold funding of private actors. A third of this funding is made available to (collective and individual) immigrant initiatives (Linkis n.d.).

Migrant Organizations: Toward a Typology

In this section, we present the basic characteristics of the migrant organizations and divide them into four groups. We then present an analysis of their main activities "here" (in the Netherlands), "there" (in the home countries), and "beyond" (linking up with global networks).

Table 9.2 shows the basic characteristics of the organizations, all of which are registered with the Dutch Chamber of Commerce. Overall, they are relatively young organizations, with 53 percent having been established in 2000–8.[8] The majority are located in the Randstad area, the Netherlands' main urban agglomeration, comprising the cities of Amsterdam, The Hague, Rotterdam, and Utrecht.[9] These cities are also home to the majority of the migrant groups studied for this research.

Migrant organizations are led by a board of approximately five members, generally all with a migrant background, although some boards have a mixed composition. In practice, there is often one person who can be considered the "engine" of the organization. This, of course, makes the organization very dependent on this person, and therefore vulnerable. Most of these individuals are highly skilled males, with a professional or academic background. Only 21 percent of all organizations are led by women; female leadership is more common among Surinamese organizations, however.

Based on the main focus, activities, and budget of the organizations, we divided them into four categories (Table 9.3). First, *charitable organizations* function as fund-raising organizations that aim to support charities "there," often with the help of migrant voluntary labor. Activities are focused on promoting development in their countries of origin. Second, *civic organizations* focus on the Netherlands ("here") by representing the interests of their group and offering services to the immigrant population. However, civic organizations simultaneously implement activities aimed at development in the countries of origin. Third, *hometown associations* (HTAs) are membership organizations. Typical of these organizations is that the focus is on a certain locality (village, community, "hometown"), and activities are focused on supporting a group of directly involved peo-

Table 9.2. Main Characteristics of the Organizations Interviewed

Number of Organizations Interviewed	60
Year of Establishment	
– Before 1990	15%
– 1990–99	32%
– 2000–8	53%
Board's Educational Background	
– Low (primary/uncompleted secondary)	8%
– Medium (secondary/uncompleted tertiary)	26%
– High (professional/academic)	66%
Gender of Board Leaders	
– Male	79%
– Female	21%
Salaried Employees (in the Netherlands)	
– 0	92%
– 1	5%
– 2–5	3%
– >5	0%
Main Focus	
– Netherlands	24%
– Origin	54%
– Mixed	22%
Activities	
– Fund-raising for activities in country of origin	60%
– Social, aimed at integration in receiving areas	11%
– Capacity building	6%
– Social projects, service provision	17%
– Other	6%
Origin of Capital (several options could be mentioned)	
– Membership dues	12%
– Private donations	45%
– Ministries	8%
– Subsidies of foundations/NGOs	46%
– Municipalities	24%
– Enterprises (Rabobank/Shell)	25%
– EU	4%
Budget (in €)	
– <5,000	19%
– 5,000–49,999	48%
– 50,000–100,000	14%
– >100,000	19%
Average Budget (in €)	58,000

ple (the people with roots in this locality). Activities are focused either "here" (integration) or "there" (philanthropy). Fourth, *development organizations* aim to be more professional and are closely linked to official funding agencies, such as the Dutch Ministry of Foreign Affairs and/or cofinancing agencies and nongovernmental organizations (NGOs). Along with the discovery of remittances as a source of funding development, new initiatives have been undertaken by the state to stimulate codevelopment (programs for capacity building, return migration).

Most (38 percent) of the organizations are charitable organizations; they are predominantly focused on the country of origin, where they implement projects, generally on an ad hoc basis. "Doing something good" is the main motive, and the majority of the activities are focused on fund-raising. Funds are obtained in various ways. Giving lectures to the public, explaining the need for more funds and persuading the audience to make a financial contribution, is one of the most popular instruments, as is organizing cultural and charity events. These include the annual soccer match organized by the Suriprofs, during which Surinamese soccer professionals (many of whom play at a high level in Dutch and European soccer competitions) play a benefit match. Most of charitable organizations' budgets (average: €45,000 per year) is derived from donations and foundations.[10]

The second largest group (one-third) is composed of civic organizations. These aim to represent the interests of their immigrant population in the Netherlands, but are also involved in activities in the country of origin (see Table 9.2). Also in this category are network organizations—such as the Ghanaian Recogin and the Moroccan NISM—whose activities are aimed at supporting self-help associations in the Netherlands. These organizations carry out fund-raising and other activities, most of which are focused on social services (examples include homework supervision, the establishment of food banks, lobbying and advocacy, language courses, environmental education, and advisory activities). The average annual budget of these organizations is €78,300, which is derived from a large variety of sources: donations, local governments, cofinancing agencies, the Ministry of Justice, and private foundations.[11]

Hometown associations direct their transnational activities toward a village or specific region or province in the country of origin. In this category, we distinguish between Ghanaian HTAs on the one hand and Moroccan and Surinamese HTAs on the other. The focus of Ghanaian HTAs is predominantly on the Netherlands. Examples of such organizations are the Okyeman Foundation, the Okuapeman Association, the Kwahuman Association, the Kwahu Youngsters, and the Stichting Ghana-Haarlem. Their main aim is to support the respective communities in adjusting to

Dutch society by informing members about such matters as the Dutch secondary school system, the introduction of the chip card for public transport, and national and local elections.

HTAs are membership organizations, numbering from twenty to seventy households.[12] They meet regularly, often every other weekend, and many hold a special end-of-year event. The bimonthly meetings are generally guided by an agenda and are concluded with drinks. Members pay a fee, ranging from €5–10 a month. These fees are used to rent the venue, to pay for the catering, and for a credit fund for all kinds of specific—and urgent—events: illness, funerals, and weddings. Members who do not pay the monthly dues are still welcome at the meetings, but access to financial support via the credit fund is denied. Compared to the other organizational types, the budget of HTAs is relatively small (€3,600 per year) and based mainly on membership fees and other donations.[13]

The Moroccan and Surinamese HTAs differ from the Ghanaian HTAs in one important respect: although the former organizations also consist of a group of people from the same area of origin, their main focus is on the region of origin, and their activities in the Netherlands are focused on fund-raising. As such, integration of the migrant community hardly plays a role in their activities in the Netherlands.[14]

The last category is composed of development organizations, many of which evolved from civic organizations. They are supported by considerable donor funds (average: €147,600 per year) from a wide range of sources: government ministries and cofinancing agencies, as well as the EU, foundations, and private donations.[15] Ghanaian organizations are overrepresented in this category, because in contrast to the Moroccan and Surinamese organizations, they have access to specific codevelopment programs. They implement development projects on a relatively large scale, often have various projects at different locations, and in some cases also extend their work to other countries. A certain degree of professionalization is common among these organizations, which is also expressed in the number of paid employees (one to three) compared to other types of organizations, facilitated by their larger budgets. They maintain up-to-date websites on which project summaries and annual reports are freely available.

We asked the organizations about their networks, such as contacts with other migrant organizations, NGOs, and national and local governments. Although most organizations are part of a wider network, the intensity and frequency of contacts differ greatly. Three observations can be made. First, of the three migrant groups, the Ghanaian organizations have most contacts with others. Leaders of the HTAs explained that they invite other

Table 9.3. Main Features of the Four Types of Organizations

	Charitable	Civic	HTAs	Development
% of all organizations	38%	32%	20%	10%
Background	Mainly Surinamese	Mainly Moroccan, some Ghanaian	Mainly Ghanaian, some Moroccan	Mainly Ghanaian
Main focus	"There"	"Here" and "there"	"Here"	"There"
Main activities: Netherlands	Fund-raising	Integration; Fund-raising	Integration	Fund-raising
Average annual budget (in €)	45,000	78,300	3,600	147,600
Examples of funding agencies	Private (ad hoc) donations; Wilde Ganzen; Oranje Fonds; Oxfam-Novib	Cordaid; Wilde Ganzen; Ministry; Shell; Rabobank; foundations; NCDO; local governments	Membership dues	European Union; Ministry of Foreign Affairs; cofinancing agencies; NCDO; local governments

Ghanaian HTAs—including all the members—to funerals and weddings. Most Ghanaian HTAs and civic organizations are also members of REC-OGIN, a Ghanaian umbrella organization based in Amsterdam.

Second, both Moroccan and Ghanaian organizations participate in national-level networks, some of them specifically aimed at migration and development, such as the Diaspora Forum for Development (DFD) and the Migrant Consortium. Also, Moroccan organizations participate in events organized by the Morocco Fund. Most well-established Moroccan organizations know the organizational picture quite well, and have good contacts with local governments and certain government ministries. Surinamese organizations, in contrast, appear to have the least contacts: apart from contacts with funding "channels," only a few meet with other Surinamese groups and most operate in relative isolation.

Third, participation in international or global networks is relatively scarce among all organizations interviewed, except for one of the Ghanaian HTAs, the Kwahu Association, which is a founding member of Kwahu Europe, a network organization of six organizations in Europe established in 2010.

Bringing Development "Back Home"

A first glance at the type of activities promoted by the sixty migrant organizations in their areas of origin shows that most activities are focused on improving the infrastructure of health and educational systems, often in combination with the sending of goods. There are numerous examples of projects that support the construction of schools, health clinics, and orphanages. In addition, old school furniture, secondhand or unwanted clothing, and written-off computers and hospital equipment are frequently shipped to the home countries. A more detailed look reveals some interesting differences between the types of organizations with respect to the activities implemented, the approach, and the institutional arrangements/partnerships set up (see Table 9.4).

Types of Activities and Partnerships

All the organizations collaborate on the implementation of their projects with local counterparts, but with different types of partners and in different intensities. The focus of charitable organizations is more often on social activities, on shipping goods, and to a lesser extent on economic projects and capacity building. Compared to other organizations, they collaborate more with mirror organizations (26 percent), which are organizations in the area of origin that are established (by the Netherlands-based organization) to facilitate the implementation of projects. Due to the distance and sometimes limited communication opportunities, migrant organizations experience or foresee difficulties in implementing their projects. They need an executive organization at the local level to coordinate projects and communicate with local stakeholders. Establishing a mirror organization appears to be the most appropriate strategy.

Table 9.4. Main Type of Activities Implemented in the Country of Origin, per Type of Organization

	Charitable	Civic	HTAs	Development
Social services	75%	15%	58%	33%
Economic development	8%	10%	0%	33%
Shipping of goods	12%	25%	42%	17%
Human/civil rights	0%	15%	0%	0%
Capacity building	5%	15%	0%	17%
Other	0%	20%	0%	0%
N	22	20	12	6

Collaborating with mirror organizations in the country of origin is practiced by 17 percent of all migrant organizations we interviewed. An example is the Surinamese Laat een container varen (Let a container sail), which established Laat een container komen (Let a container arrive) in Suriname to facilitate the clearance and distribution of goods. Other partners are local NGOs, as well as municipalities (e.g., the municipality of Dar El Kebdani, the partner of Twizafonds) and regional and national governments.

Civic organizations perform a wide variety of activities, with 60 percent of the activities focused on economic development, human rights, capacity building, and a large category of "other" projects. This last category comprises activities in the field of network services and research and development. Examples of projects are the Muddawannah initiative to support women that are left behind and the school meals project of the Women Concern Foundation (Table 9.5). Partners of these organizations are local NGOs, local, regional, and national health and education institutions, and mirror organizations (15 percent).

The HTAs exclusively focus their activities on social services and on shipping goods. The majority (58 percent) collaborate with a mirror organization, such as the Friends of Tazaghine and the Stichting Ghana-Haarlem. The rest have rather extensive collaboration networks with local entities in the country of origin, such as a local hospital or school. Although their main focus is on the Netherlands, they also want to make a contribution to the village or region of origin. During a holiday visit home, they contact schools or hospitals and ask these whether they need something. They then collect funds from their members to purchase the goods and pay for the shipping.

Contact with the receiving entity is limited, although most organizations pay a visit a year later to see whether the goods are actually being used. Goods are acquired by contacting hospitals and schools in the Netherlands to see whether there are any "leftovers." An example of such an HTA is the Kwahu Youngsters, based in The Hague, who asked the staff of a local hospital whether they needed some hospital beds. The hospital indeed needed more beds, so the HTA arranged the shipping and, a year later, one of the board members visited the hospital to see whether they were in use.

Finally, development organizations are involved in a rather broad range of activities. Besides social sector activities, they have a relatively strong focus on projects aimed at economic development. The poultry project— an EU-funded project implemented by Sankofa, a Ghanaian development organization—is a good example: women in rural communities are given thirty chickens, and they sell the eggs to generate additional income. Most development organizations collaborate with several partners in the countries of origin. During our fieldwork, we observed that most of their partners collaborate with and receive funds from other donors. In some cases, this means that the contribution of the Netherlands-based migrant organization is pooled with funds from other donors. In other cases, there are individual projects. The presence of several donors implies that these partners are less dependent on the Dutch-based migrant organizations.

Contrary to the migrant organizations, the partners in their home countries often have paid staff, ranging from one part-time coordinator to nine full-time employees. This applies particularly to NGOs, but is also observed in the case of mirror organizations, whose staff in some cases tend to receive a fee for their involvement. This is so because incomes in the countries of origin are low, and to make things happen, there needs

Table 9.5. Examples of Projects and Partners, According to Organizational Type

Migrant Organization	Project Description	Partner in Area of Origin
Charitable		
Surflandria (Suriname)	Distribution of meals among poor children	Schools, local welfare organizations
Daar et Atfaal (Morocco)	"Foster parents": material and mental support to orphans	Orphanage and local NGO
Civic		
Muddawannah (Morocco)	Support to women that are left behind by migrants abroad	Service office Berkane (mirror organization)
Women Concern Foundation (Ghana)	Construction of school canteen and toilets; participation in school meals program	Baranton Development Foundation (local NGO)
HTAs		
Okuapeman Association (Ghana)	Goods (hospital beds, computers, TVs)	Hospitals, schools
Vrienden van Nickerie (Suriname)	Scholarships for students, computers, support to elderly and disabled people	Vrienden van Nickerie Suriname/WiN-groep
Development		
Stichting Kantara (Morocco)	Environmental education	Local NGOs, Wereld Waternet, universities
Sankofa (Ghana)	Poultry project to generate income for women	GAPNET, ADFOM (local NGOs)

to be a financial incentive, as reported by several Dutch-based migrant organizations.

Institutional Links "There"

Besides direct partners in the countries of origin, migrant organizations collaborate with other entities at both the local and national level in the country of origin. Examples of such collaborations are other local NGOs, local governments, national governments, and private companies. The type of collaboration varies: in some cases, it is limited to funding or issuing of permits, but network activities were also mentioned, for example, for lobbying in the case of Moroccan NGOs. As for Surinamese organizations, they collaborate with the Surinamese government, with the objective of avoiding paying import duty on shipped goods, and to facilitate the distribution of goods. Some Surinamese partner organizations also receive partial funding from the Surinamese government. The government, for instance, pays part of the salary of the employees of one of these organizations. However, there are also some migrant organizations that merely inform the government about their development interventions. These groups state that they "passively cooperate" with the government, because they have to. Government permission is needed, for instance, to build schools or other structures.

As one of our informants told us: "Who else is going to pay the teachers and donate a piece of land? We're able to recruit teachers and build a school, but for the rest we need the government." Other organizations do not want to involve the national government as a stakeholder. According to them, the government works slowly and is corrupt and bureaucratic. Most importantly, though, there is no funding available. Some migrant groups avoid contact with the government and do not even ask for permission to, for instance, renovate schools, which is officially a government task.

In the case of local governments, collaboration cannot be avoided, as the organizations need permits to construct schools or health posts. However, these official contacts are seen as mainly a necessary evil. Organizations in all three home countries were very critical about the role of the local and national governments. Another informant reported: "Nothing happens until you give them some money. So in case we really need some things done, we give them some money."[16] However, positive collaborations with the local government were also mentioned, such as the partnership of Twizafund with the municipality of Dar El Kebdani in Morocco, which coordinates the use of a garbage truck and the distribution of other goods donated by Twizafund.

Development in, by and through the Diaspora: What Difference Do Migrant Organizations Make?

As stated in the introduction, much has been written about the link between migration and development at the individual level, but little is known about how individuals could benefit from remitting "collectively" by making use of migrant organizations. We looked at the extent to which migrant organizations can be seen as important and powerful instruments of change, encouraging integration (in the Netherlands), development and poverty alleviation (in the areas of origin), and/or expanding networks to third destinations.

By making a distinction between development in the diaspora, by the diaspora, and through the diaspora, our analysis first shows that migrant organizations contribute to development in the diaspora by performing the role of broker: they facilitate the migrant's access to services in the field of integration, and in some cases also provide these services. Examples of such activities are language courses, homework groups, day care activities for the elderly, and information meetings around elections.

Some organizations, in particular the network and umbrella organizations such as RECOGIN, also perform the role of broker by channeling information from the community to the local government and vice versa. As such, they contribute to capacity building and the empowerment of the migrant groups concerned. The role of broker is mainly performed by civic organizations and HTAs. Charitable organizations and development organizations are, by the nature of their activities, less focused on this role, and their fund-raising activities contribute to integration mainly indirectly.

Second, activities in the countries of origin (development by the diaspora) are the most important activities of a very large proportion of the migrant organizations. Of course, this is partly because these organizations were selected on account of their transnational activities. Nevertheless, a wide range of initiatives are implemented in the regions of origin. The desire to show solidarity with the home country is the main driving force for most of these organizations.

Third, development through the diaspora is hardly present among the sixty organizations we studied. There are few systematic efforts to push the Dutch diaspora in the direction of global connections, apart from the already mentioned initiative to establish a European Kwahu umbrella organization. We observed very few connections with similar diasporic groups in other countries. Overall, the contacts and networks of migrant organizations are mainly bilateral, and as such most are not integrated in any global network.

Assessing the contributions of Netherlands-based migrant organizations to development "there," we observed certain interesting elements. First, during our fieldwork we asked partner organizations, target groups, and other local stakeholders (such as local governments) how they evaluate the activities implemented by the migrant organizations. Not surprisingly, we received very positive feedback, although sometimes these could be interpreted as socially desirable answers. We heard few critical comments with respect to the initiatives and roles of organizations abroad.

Second, despite this, some negative comments were made. Some interventions are paternalistic, with initiatives taken in the Netherlands implemented in a top-down manner. Control in these cases lies completely with the Dutch-based organization. This is particularly the case in those partnerships that involve a mirror organization. In addition, due to limited collaboration with local authorities, the projects offered are not always in line with local priorities, and might conflict with existing government plans. However, most organizations point to the absence of the government in the provision of local services, and add that they only fill the gap thus created.

Third, many activities seem to be rather ad hoc and do not address structural changes over time. This applies particularly to many of the charities whose purpose is to transfer "luxury goods," namely, leftovers/secondhand goods from the Netherlands. Fourth, in those cases where migrant organizations collaborate with local NGOs, it is interesting that these partner organizations are sometimes more professional than the migrant organizations themselves. These NGOs often have a small paid staff and many also receive funding from other international NGOs in addition to the support they receive from organizations in the Netherlands, which makes them rather autonomous and not dependent on Dutch funding.

Looking at our results in general, it is interesting that despite the many differences in the contexts of "exit" and "reception" of the Surinamese, Moroccan, and Ghanaian diasporas, the transnational migrant organizations have much in common: there are numerous migrant organizations, and they receive considerable support from Dutch NGOs and the Dutch government. In the Netherlands today, despite its rapid transformation from a hospitable country (friendly to migrants) into a country of restrictive policies, migrant organizations continue functioning in a relatively favorable environment, with ample opportunities for official subsidies and fund-raising.

This is also reflected in the main challenges indicated by migrant organizations. Although several organizations mentioned lack of funds as a problem, and most of them would welcome more resources, there are other issues that are more important to them. In the first place, there is the question of the second generation and its participation in the organizations. Particularly the Ghanaian and Moroccan organizations reported that it is hard to get young people involved, and they expect that this might impact their activities in the longer term. Some Ghanaian HTAs have already implemented projects to involve youths, such as special events around Christmas or a weekend at a campsite. However, the majority of HTAs were skeptical about the results of such activities. Other issues mentioned were lack of people who are willing to invest time in the organization, lack of good venues for their meetings, lack of storage facilities (this applies to organizations that ship goods), and lack of a good, reliable partner in the country of origin.

The power of migrant organizations in the Netherlands to stimulate development in Suriname, Morocco, or Ghana is rather fragmented and heavily dependent on fund-raising and subsidies. However, in light of the total number of people who are directly or incidentally involved and/ or the total amount that has been transferred by various projects, their impact should not be underestimated. Starting from the average amount collected by the various organizations, a total annual transfer of approximately €1–2 million to Suriname, Morocco, and Ghana takes place. Rather than looking at the direct effect of specific projects, it might be better to look at their more indirect impact: the fact that migrant groups collaborate in implementing projects, and the stimulating role that migrant organizations may play in enhancing civil society, not only "there" but also "here," by supporting their members to integrate into the host society.

Conclusion

This chapter has presented an analysis of the strengths and weaknesses of migrant organizations in shaping transnational space, that is, helping migrants to transfer goods, ideas, and capital for the purpose of development. We also tried to understand migration as an organizational field, to comprehend how the contexts of exit and reception play a role in the functioning of migrant organizations and the activities that they implement.

Our study showed that there are a considerable number of migrant organizations in the Netherlands, even though two of the three migration flows concerned (Suriname and Morocco) are relatively old. Most of these organizations are run by male professionals who are relatively well educated, well integrated, and successful in Dutch society. This is very much in line with the situation in the United States, where Portes, Escobar, and Walton Radford (2007) found a similar pattern.

We developed a distinction between four types of organizations, based on their focus, activities, and budget: charitable organizations, civic organizations, hometown associations, and development organizations. Each can also be classified on the basis of its level of "transnationality," focusing on either "integration here" or "enhancing development there," or both simultaneously. Most of the organizations are not linked to particular home communities, are mainly focused on charity, are driven by voluntary workers, and are dependent on fund-raising.

When looking at the role of migrant organizations as agents for change, we found some interesting differences between the different groups, and the corresponding contexts of exit and reception. Most substantial is the contribution the diaspora makes by transferring goods and funds to various kinds of charities in their home countries (development by the diaspora). A wide range of activities and projects are implemented, varying from shipping of goods to the training of nurses specialized in diabetes. While Moroccan organizations have the most varied portfolio of activities and also include more complex interventions, Surinamese organizations mostly focus on social services and the shipping of goods. This also applies to Ghanaian HTAs.

The contribution to integration (in the diaspora) is an important field for Ghanaian HTAs, which help their members integrate into Dutch society, and also for Moroccan organizations. In contrast, this role is very limited for Surinamese organizations; they are mainly oriented toward Suriname, a trend that can be traced to the fact that Surinamese are already well integrated in Dutch society.

In conclusion, migrant organizations play an important role in keeping Netherlands-based migrant communities alive and linking them to the countries of origin, by raising funds in the Netherlands for their areas of origin. However, the diaspora's development impact "on the ground" is rather limited. The main critical comments heard in the home countries were that many projects are not contributing to structural change, due to their relatively fragmented implementation and the relative unfavorable context of reception "there," where local governments are not very open to initiatives from abroad. At the same time, the sustainability of such initiatives will very much depend on whether second-generation migrants are willing to keep these initiatives going.

However, when analyzing the total amount of funds being transferred and the willingness of people to contribute either money or labor, the potential "mobilizing power" is considerable. There are some important leveraging effects, such as the contribution to civil society building through the creation of mirror organizations and partnerships established for the implementation of the organizations' activities, awareness raising in the areas of settlement, contributions to agenda setting, and the "role model" of migrant organizations that have evolved into more professional development entities.

Final Reflections

In a global world, local development is increasingly played out in a matrix of links that connect people and places with places and people elsewhere; migration has some potential to bring new linkages between areas of origin and area of destination. Our study shows that diasporas are formed from complex mixes of people who arrived at different times, through different channels, with different intentions, and with different statuses, and that migrant organizations have some potential to strengthen links among them (Van Hear, Pieke and Vertovec 2004).

At the same time, however, by defining transnationalism "as the processes by which immigrants forge and sustain multi-stranded social relations that link together their societies of origin and settlement," (Basch, Glick-Schiller and Szanton Blanc 1994: 6) we observe that the involvement that migrants sustain in both home and host countries is limited. Involvement is rather symbolic, driven by people's desire to help others in their home country. As such, the "multiplicity of involvements that transmigrants sustain in both home and host societies" hardly exists (Basch, Glick-Schiller and Szanton Blanc 1994: 6).

In studies about transnationalism, the suggestion is made that "increasingly, populations affiliate themselves translocally—in other places and time" (Shapiro 2000: 83; see also Zoomers and Van Westen 2011). According to Appadurai (1996: 165), "we can speak in this connection of many new forms of non-territorial affiliation and solidarity." Based on our study, however, we see that, rather than facilitating time-space compression (Harvey 1989), migrant organizations are "locking in" certain groups and localities. Rather than "on-going series of cross-border movements in which immigrants develop and maintain numerous economic, social and cultural links in more than one nation" (Mitchell 2000, cited by Crang, Dwyer, and Jackson 2003: 446), we find that migrant organizations mobilize funds and collective action on an ad hoc basis and that their support is closely linked to one particular country, being rather unilateral. In this sense, it would be more appropriate to speak about translocal instead of transnational activities. Rather than acting in a "transnational space," migrants operate in a network of different localities, each of which is highly focused in nature (Zoomers and Van Westen 2011).

Gery Nijenhuis is a human geographer and assistant professor of international development studies (Department of Human Geography and Planning, Utrecht University). Relevant publications include: "Embedding International Migration: The Response of Bolivian Local Governments and NGOs to International Migration," *Environment and Urbanization* 22, no. 1 (2010): 67–79; "Leads Migration to Development? Or Is It Contributing to a Global Divide?," *Societies* 2–3 (2012): 122–38 (with A. Zoomers); and "Institutionalising International Migrants' Activities: The Impact of Co-development Programmes," *International Development Planning Review* 32, nos. 3–4 (2010): 246–65 (with A. Broekhuis).

Annelies Zoomers, PhD, is currently chair of LANDac and professor of international development studies in the Department of Human Geography and Planning at Utrecht University.

Notes

The authors would like to thank Annelien Meerts for her collaboration.

1. See also the CGM 'Centrum voor de Geschiedenis van Migranten' database on migrant organizations in the Netherlands: 5 March 2015).
2. We carried out a more detailed check on the 759 Moroccan migrant organizations that we had in our inventory: approximately 640 organizations were still traceable.
3. Not all organizations have up-to-date websites, and phone numbers were sometimes no longer in use.
4. Special thanks go to Annelien Meerts, who carried out the fieldwork in Morocco, Suriname, and Ghana, as well as large parts of the interviews in the Netherlands.
5. In addition to the indigenous population (who comprise only 3 percent of the total population), there is a mix of various immigrant groups: the Creoles (33 percent) came to Suriname from western regions of Central Africa, such as Ghana, as slaves in 1621–1818. The Hindustanis (35 percent of the population) migrated from India to become laborers in 1873–1916). Other groups include the Chinese (who settled as early as 1853) and the Javanese (who arrived in 1890–1939).
6. In Germany, over nine of the twelve million guest workers who migrated to Germany between 1960 and 1993 returned home (Faist 1997).
7. Few Ghanaian migrants in the Netherlands can be considered political migrants.
8. This study only considered organizations that had existed for longer than three years.
9. Except for the Ghanaian GTTK and the Foundation Kwahu Ghana, which are located in Almelo and Eindhoven, respectively.
10. N = 19, as four organizations could not/did not want to disclose their budgets.
11. N = 16, as four organizations could not/did not want to disclose their budgets.
12. All HTAs had noted a decrease (sometimes by as much as 50 percent) in the number of members during the previous five years. Economic problems as

well as migration to the UK (where migrant feel more at ease) were mentioned as possible explanations for this reduction.

13. N = 10, as two organizations could not/did not want to disclose their budgets.
14. Also, they do not have a fixed group of members; they rather speak about donors. We put them in this category because they focus their activities on a sharply demarcated village or region in Morocco/Suriname and not on an arbitrary location, and they do so in an organization that almost exclusively comprises people from this region.
15. N = 5, as one organization could not/did not want to reveal its budget.
16. Interviews with Ghanaian organizations.

References

Adepoju, Aderanti, Ton van Naerssen, and Annelies Zoomers. 2008. *International Migration and National Development in Sub-Saharan Africa: Viewpoints and Policy Initiatives in the Countries of Origin*. Afrika-Studiecentrum Series 10. Leiden and Boston: Brill.

Appadurai, Arjun. 1996. *Modernity at Large: Cultural Dimensions of Globalization*. Vol. 1. Minneapolis: University of Minnesota Press.

Basch, Linda G., Nina Glick Schiller, and Cristina Szanton Blanc. 1994. *Nations Unbound: Transnational Projects, Post-colonial Predicaments, and De-territorialized Nation-States*. Langhorne, PA: Gordon and Breach.

Beauchemin, Chris, and Bruno Schoumaker. 2009. "Are Migrant Associations Actors in Local Development? A National Event-History Analysis in Rural Burkina Faso." *World Development* 37, no. 12: 1897–1913.

Bilgili, Özge, and Silja Weyel. 2012. *Diaspora Engagement in Morocco: Understanding the Implications of a Changing Perspective on Capacity and Practices*. Maastricht: Ministry of Foreign Affairs/IS Academie/Maastricht University.

Bosma, Ulbe. 2009. *Terug uit de Koloniën, Zestig jaar Postkoloniale Migranten en hun Organisaties*. Amsterdam: Uitgeverij Bert Bakker.

CBS Statline. 2011. *Bevolking*. http://statline.cbs.nl/. (Accessed 7 November 2011)

Crang, Philip, Claire Dwyer, and Peter Jackson. 2003. "Transnationalism and the Spaces of Commodity Culture." *Progress in Human Geography* 27, no. 4: 438–56.

De Haas, Hein. 2007. "Between Courting and Controlling: The Moroccan State and 'Its' Emigrants." COMPAS Working Paper 54, University of Oxford.

DevSur. 2011. "President Bouterse: Don't Forget the Diaspora." 3 July. http://www.devsur.com/president-bouterse-dont-forget-the-diaspora/2011/07/03/ Accessed 8 February 2012).

Eurostat. 2011. Population and Migration Statistics: http://epp.eurostat.ec.europa.eu/portal/page/portal/eurostat/home/ (Accessed 10 February 2012).

Faist, Thomas. 1997. "The Crucial Meso-level." *International Migration, Immobility and Development*, ed. Tomas Hammer, Grete Brochmann, Kristof Tamas, and Thomas Faist, 187–217. Oxford and New York: Berg.

Farrant, Macha, Anna MacDonald, and Dhananjayan Sriskandarajah. 2006. "Migration and Development: Opportunities and Challenges for Policymakers." Paper prepared for the IPPR and IOM.

GCIM (Global Commission on International Migration). 2005. *Migration in an Interconnected World: New Directions for Action.* Geneva: GCIM.

Giddens, Anthony. 1990. *The Consequences of Modernity.* Cambridge: Polity Press.

Harvey, David. 1989. *The Condition of Postmodernity.* Oxford: Blackwell.

Institut Français des Relations Internationals (IFRI). 2008. *Co-development Policies in Europe: Objectives, Experiences and Limits.* Paris: IFRI.

International Organization for Migration (2009). "Migration in Ghana. A country profile." Geneva: IOM.

Kleist, Nauja. 2011. "Let Us Rebuild Our Country: Migration-Development Scenarios in Ghana." DIIS Working Paper 30.

Lacroix, Thomas. 2011. "The Indian and Polish Transnational Organizational Fields." IMI Working Paper 40, International Migration Institute, University of Oxford.

Linkis (Laagdrempelige Initiatieven en kennis centrum voor internationale samenwerking). n.d. Database on private initiatives based in The Netherlands. http://www.linkis.nl/nl-NL/Content.aspx?type=content&id=12 (Accessed 22 June 2010).

Lucas, Robert E. B. 2004. "International Migration Regimes and Economic Development." Report prepared for the expert group on development issues (EGDI) in the Swedish Ministry of Foreign Affairs.

Mazzucato, Valentina. 2009. "Small Is Beautiful: The Micro-politics of Transnational Relationships between Ghanaian Hometown Associations and Communities Back Home." *Global Networks* 9, no. 2: 227–51.

Ministry of Foreign Affairs. 2010. *Kamerbrief inzake Voortgangsrapportage Internationale Migratie en Ontwikkeling 2008.* The Hague: Ministry of Foreign Affairs.

Mohan, Giles. 2002. "Diaspora and Development." In *Development and Displacement,* ed. Jenny Robinson, 77–139. Oxford: Oxford University Press/Open University.

MPI (Migration Policy Institute). 2008. *Hometown Associations: An Untapped Resource for Immigrant Integration?* Washington DC: MPI.

Nijenhuis, Gery, and Annelet Broekhuis. 2010. "Institutionalizing Transnational Migrants' Activities: The Impact of Co-development Programs." *International Development Planning Review* 32, nos. (3–4): 37–58.

Østergaard-Nielsen, Eva. 2009. "Mobilizing the Moroccans: Policies and Perceptions of Transnational Engagement among Moroccan Immigrants in Catalonia." *Journal of Ethnic and Migration Studies* 35: 1623–41.

———. 2011. "Codevelopment and Citizenship: The Nexus between Policies on Local Migrant Incorporation and Migrant Transnational Practices in Spain." *Ethnic and Racial Studies* 34, no. 1: 20–39.

Portes, Alejandro. 1995. *The Economic Sociology of Immigration: Essays on Networks, Ethnicity and Entrepreneurship.* New York: Russell Sage Foundation.

———. 1996. "Globalization from Below: The Rise of Transnational Communities." In *Latin America in the World Economy,* ed. Roberto Patricio Korzeniewicz and William C. Smith, 151–68. West Port, CN: Greenwood Press.

Portes, Alejandro, Cristina Escobar, and Renelinda Arana. 2008. "Bridging the Gap: Transnational and Ethnic Organizations in the Political Incorporation of Immigrants in the United States." *Ethnic and Racial Studies* 31, no. 6: 1056–90.

Portes, Alejandro, Cristina Escobar, and Alexandra Walton Radford. 2007. "Immigrant Transnational Organizations and Development: A Comparative Study." *International Migration Review* 41, no. 1: 242–81.

Rath, Jan. 2009. "The Netherlands: A Reluctant Country of Immigration." *TESG* 100, no. 5: 674–81.

Schrover, Marlou, and Floris Vermeulen. 2005. "Immigrant Organizations." *Journal of Ethnic and Migration Studies* 31, no. 5: 823–32.

Shapiro, Michael. 2000. "National Times and Other Times: Re-thinking Citizenship." *Cultural Studies* 14, no. 1: 79–98.

Sheffer, Gabriel. 2003. *Diaspora Politics: At Home Abroad.* Cambridge: Cambridge University Press.

Snel, Erik, Godfried Engbersen, and Arjen Leerkes. 2006. "Transnational Involvement and Social Integration." *Global Networks* 6, no. 3: 285–308.

Van Amersfoort, Hans, and Anja van Heelsum. 2007. "Moroccan Berber Immigrants in the Netherlands, Their Associations and Transnational Ties: A Quest for Identity." *Immigrants & Minorities* 25, no. 3: 234–62.

Van Hear, Nicolas, Frank Pieke, and Steven Vertovec. 2004. "The Contribution of UK-Based Diasporas to Development and Poverty Reduction." A report by the ESRC Centre on Migration, Policy and Society (COMPAS). University of Oxford, Department for International Development/Economic and Social Research Council, COMPAS (Oxford University).

Van Heelsum, Anja. 2004. *Migrantenorganisaties in Nederland.* Utrecht: FORUM.

Van Heelsum, Anja, and Eske Voorthuijsen. 2002. "Surinaamse Organisaties in Nederland": *Een netwerkanalyse.* Amsterdam: Aksant.

Van Naerssen, Ton, Joep Kusters, and Joris Schapendonk. 2006. *Afrikaanse Migrantenorganisaties in Nederland: Ontwikkelingsactiviteiten en Opinies Over Ontwikkelingssamenwerking.* Nijmegen: Migration and Development Research Group.

Van Naerssen, Ton, Ernst Spaans, and Annelies Zoomers. 2008. *Global Migration and Development.* New York: Routledge.

Vezzoli, Simona, and Thomas Lacroix. 2010. "Building Bonds for Migration and Development: Diaspora Engagement Policies of Ghana, India and Serbia." Eschborn: Deutsche Gesellschaft für Technische Zusammenarbeit (GTZ) GmbH, Migration and Development Sector Project 58.

Zoomers, Annelies. 2006. *Op Zoek naar Eldorado: Over Internationale Migratie, Sociale Mobiliteit en Ontwikkeling.* (Inaugural Speech) Nijmegen:Radboud Universiteit Nijmegen. http://dare.ubn.kun.nl/bitstream/2066/29827/1/29827.pdf. (Accessed 8 February 2012).

Zoomers, Annelies, and Guus van Westen. 2011. "Introduction: Translocal Development, Development Corridors and Development Chains." *International Development Planning Review* 33, no. 4: 377–88.

Chapter 10

Transnational Immigrant Organizations in Spain
Their Role in Development and Integration

Héctor Cebolla-Boado and Ana López-Sala

Throughout the past decade, Spain has witnessed unprecedented growth of its foreign-born population. What makes Spain a striking case study for scholars interested in migration is the speed at which this transformation has taken place. Figure 10.1 compares the percentages of foreign-born residents in the total populations of Spain, the United States, and Northern, Southern, and Central Europe.

Many claim that Italy and Spain are classic examples of the so-called Mediterranean model of immigration (Finotelli 2007). However, this model is difficult to define because it is used in different contexts and for different purposes, including broad criticisms of lax immigration control in Southern Europe by scholars and officials of other European countries. However, there are two relevant features common to immigration to Italy, Spain, Portugal, and Greece: (1) overstayers have made irregular status a problem in these countries, and are often highlighted as proof that the "model" has been unsuccessful; (2) integration has scarcely been mentioned in their immigration policies. In the context of European concern with integration, these countries have been blamed for lacking an appropriate integration policy (Koopmans 2010) or for promoting differences between the migrant and native populations (Freeman 2004).

The Spanish government has reacted to the striking growth of the foreign-born population without a systematic policy. This *ex post facto* approach presents a unique analytic challenge to understand governmental

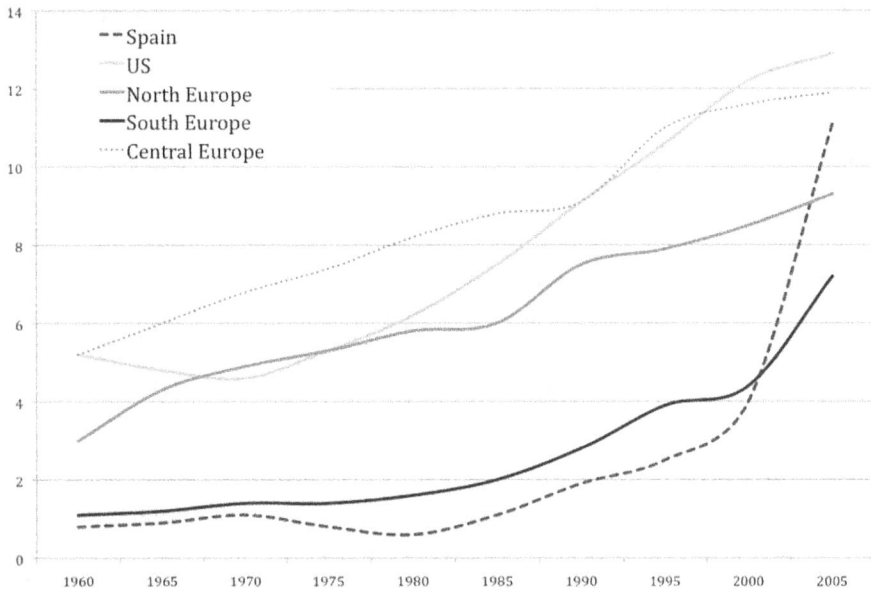

Figure 10.1. Evolution of the Immigrant Population (Spain, United States, and Northern, Southern, and Central Europe)

influences in integration outcomes. This chapter analyzes the transnational activities of immigrant organizations of Moroccan, Peruvian, Colombian, Dominican, and Ecuadorean origin in the context set by these official policies.

A Top-Down Model of Transnationalism: Immigrant Associations in Spain

During the years in which the Spanish economy boomed, officials saw no problem in hosting thousands of newcomers to meet the demand for unskilled labor. The administration at all levels (local, regional, and national) sought to legitimize their decisions by using two interlocutors of symbolic importance: academics and representative stakeholders—trade unions, nongovernmental organizations (NGOs), and, most importantly, migrant associations. Migrant organizations were considered key actors in defining migration policies and, strikingly, in external cooperation and development.

Migrant associations in Spain share two important characteristics: (1) they are seen as a requisite for successful integration and for fashioning development policy toward sending countries; and (2) they are also considered unique mediators between migrant communities and host society institutions.

The Role of Immigrant Associations in Spanish Integration Policies

In 1985, the first organic law on immigration was passed to fulfill requirements imposed by the European Union on its new members (Ley Orgánica 5/1985). For France, Belgium, the Netherlands, and other European Union (EU) countries, the border with Morocco was of utmost importance. Therefore, Spain was pressured to adopt the role of guardian of the common southern border. That is why the first law emphasized control issues, copying the model of regulation adopted by other European countries. Although subsequent regulations softened the instruments for controlling migration, the Spanish model did not reach an equilibrium between integration and control until fairly recently. The first law representing a strong commitment to integration was passed in 2000, the Ley Orgánica 4/2000 (Ruiz de Huidobro 2000), which granted equal access for both nationals and foreigners to basic social benefits such as education and health care. Further modifications to this law have respected this generous and strong adherence to the principle of equality.

The evolution of integration policy in Spain can be summarized as a three-step process. Initially, integration was not an explicit concern of migration officials. Toward the end of 1994, a second phase began in which integrating immigrants was actively promoted. Up to that point, integration had been an area in which nonofficial actors, such as trade unions and NGOs, deployed innovative but uncoordinated practices (Cachón 1998; Watts 2000). In the final stage, the socialist government that came into office in 2004 established a Spanish integration model based on triennial plans, the first of which was presented in 2007 (the Plan Estratégico de Ciudadania e Integración 2007–10, or PECI). The PECI adopted all of the EU recommendations in this field, describing integration as a bidirectional process of mutual adaptation in the context of several basic principles.

The PECI successfully brought integration to the forefront of the public debate on immigration, but it has been less influential in determining specific practices. This relative failure can be explained by the complex Spanish model of political decentralization that divides responsibility for immigration policy: immigration control is the brief of the national administration, while integration policy is in the hands of regional governments and, to a lesser extent, municipalities (De Lucas and Diez Bueso 2006).

Although the triennial PECI may not have been a turning point in the political history of Spain, the way it was adopted and the recommendations it proposed are essential to understanding the role of immigrant associations. Initially, discussions were organized in a series of workshops that included representatives from different levels of public administration, trade unions, NGOs, and immigrant associations. Discussions led to a consultative body, Foro para la Integración Social de los Inmigrantes, in which immigrant associations played a very active role. Among the objectives of the PECI, immigrant participation is of the utmost importance (MTIN 2007: 314–23) because the PECI views such participation as a prerequisite for an intercultural society. Furthermore, it identifies leveraging immigrant associations as the most straightforward and efficient way to achieve this goal.

Regional governments throughout Spain developed integration plans inspired by the broad principles introduced by the PECI. For example, the municipality of Madrid published its second integration plan in 2009, the *2nd Madrid Plan on Social and Intercultural Coexistence,* which also resulted from a broad discussion. The Madrid plan, like almost every other regional and local integration plan, identifies immigrant associations as representative of stakeholders and explicitly and implicitly promotes immigrant attachment to such associations.

The latest national integration plan (PECI 2011–14) seeks to reinforce integration instruments and policies, such as public services and participation. One of the most important objectives of the new PECI is to incorporate measures to fight discrimination and to promote equal opportunities. Although the economic downturn that began in 2008 has not formally affected the influence of immigrant associations on integration policies (all regional and national consultative bodies have maintained these organizations in their structure), increasing budget constraints have seriously restricted their capacity to provide services and support projects in the countries of origin. These cuts have been a deathblow to many immigrant associations, especially those that were established most recently.

The Role of Immigrant Associations in Development and International Cooperation

Immigration has been a part of the vocabulary of development aid and cooperation in Spain since 2007. For that year, the Annual Cooperation Plan detailed action on migration and development for the first time, centered on two main purposes: to promote new initiatives that increase the impact of remittances on the development of communities of origin and to view migration as a mutually beneficial phenomenon. The government established the Commission on Migration and Development within the Ministry of Foreign Affairs to prepare future guidelines for Spanish policy. This commission prepared a series of recommendations that have shaped recent plans.[1] The participation, promotion, and leadership of immigrant organizations are considered crucial to achieving several objectives (Østergaard-Nielsen 2011).[2]

Some studies (Cortés and Sanmartin 2009) have noted the diversity and variety of the objectives of immigrant associations. However, researchers have not examined the transnational activities of these organizations in their countries of origin. Transnational activism has been boosted in a top-down manner by existing official policies. As a consequence, activities of immigrant organizations abroad tend to be rather monolithic and homogenous, regardless of the particularities of different immigrant communities.

Data and Methods

Selection of National Groups

The selection of groups for this study was based on three dimensions: size, comparability, and internal diversity. First, associations representing European Union nationals were discarded because they are not considered to be immigrants. Morocco was selected for the size of its immigrant population and potential to be compared with other European countries. Among Latin Americans, groups selected included four countries (Colombia, Ecuador, Peru, and the Dominican Republic) with diverse histories, migratory sequences, and profiles.

We consulted the associations included in a study by Aparicio and Tornos (2010), which used the National Associations Register to examine the frequency of associations by nationality and related the number of registered associations to the size of the respective immigrant community. These researchers concluded that the rate of associations for population was above average for Dominicans and Peruvians and average for Moroccans, Colombians, and Ecuadoreans. Table 10.1 presents a description of the main characteristics of the groups targeted for study. Moroccan immigration is the oldest in Spain's history as a receiving country. The flow started in the second half of the 1980s and became visible at the start of the 1990s after the special regularization process carried out in 1991. Currently, there are more than eight hundred thousand Moroccan migrants in Spain. Morocco is the main source of immigration to date, not only because of its volume but also due to its continuity.

The three main regions of Moroccan migration to Spain are the Western Rif, Atlantic Morocco, and the Tangier Peninsula. Altogether, these regions comprise approximately 90 percent of all Moroccan migrants. Moroccans have settled mainly in Madrid, the Mediterranean regions (Catal-

Table 10.1. List of Selected Communities and Main Characteristics

	History of Migration to Spain	Regions of Origin	Background	Regions of Destination	Formal Education	Distribution by Sex
Moroccan	Main source of migration to Spain (volume and continuity) since the mid-1980s	Western Rif, Atlantic Morocco, and Tangier Peninsula	Urban and rural, Arab and Berber	Madrid, Mediterranean regions (Catalonia, Valencia, Murcia), and Andalusia	Low	Mostly men
Peruvian	Two stages: 1990–95 and 2002–8	Lima	Urban	Madrid	Medium-high	Balanced
Dominican	Two stages: 1990–94 and 2004–7	Vicente Noble (Barahona)	Urban and rural	Madrid and Catalonia	Low	Mostly women
Colombian	Heavy migration to Spain; 30 percent of total migration in two periods: 1998–2001 and 2005–7	"Coffee triangle" (Cauca Valley, Bogota, Antioquia, and Risaralda)	Urban	Madrid and Catalonia	Medium-high	Mostly women
Ecuadorian	Heavy migration to Spain in two periods: 1997–2001 and 2006–8.	Quito, Guayaquil, southern regions (Azuay, Cañar, and Loja), and Pichincha.	Urban	Madrid and Catalonia	Medium-low	Mostly women

onia, Valencia, and Murcia), and Andalusia. Among the largest nationality groups in Spain, Moroccans represent the group with the lowest level of education. The Moroccan population in Spain has slightly more men than women.

Dominican immigrants at the beginning of the 1990s were mostly female, the majority from the municipality of Vicente Noble in Barahona Province. Most of these women were unskilled workers who worked in domestic service. The majority settled in the Madrid region. Family needs led many women who had resided in Spain for over a decade to quit their jobs as live-in help and enter other sectors, such as service (especially hotel) and retail (beauty parlors, cell phone stores, supermarkets). There are currently just under one hundred thousand Dominican immigrants in Spain; this population has slightly more females than males.

Peruvian migration to Spain follows a similar pattern as that of Dominicans in terms of its temporal sequence, with flows decreasing in the mid-1990s and later increasing between 2002 and 2008. Before the Ecuadorean, Colombian, and Bolivian migrations to Spain, Peruvians were the largest Latin American community, settled primarily in the region of Madrid. Peruvian migrants are more evenly divided between gender than other Latin groups. There are currently approximately 150,000 Peruvians in Spain. This community is of urban extraction, the majority originally from Lima, and has medium-to-high levels of education.

In the second half of the 1990s, Spain became the destination of one of the largest migration flows from Latin America, Colombians, with the most intense periods between 1998 and 2001 and between 2005 and 2007. This emigration originated, for the most part, in the "coffee triangle," located in the midwestern part of the country; specifically, immigrants came from the Cauca Valley, Bogota, Antioquia, and Risaralda departments. Currently, Colombians are the second-largest Latin American group in Spain (after Ecuadoreans), with more than 275,000 people. It is a slightly feminized population, mostly of urban extraction, and with a relatively high average level of education.

The Ecuadorean population, the largest Latin American group in Spain, has followed a temporal pattern similar to that of Colombians, with high levels of migration between 1997 and 2001 and a new upsurge between 2006 and 2008. Today, there are more than four hundred thousand Ecuadoreans in Spain. Ecuadorean migration is slightly feminized and has concentrated in the provinces of Madrid, Barcelona, Murcia, and Almeria. Immigrants originate in the southern regions of Ecuador (Azuay, Cañar, and Loja), Pichincha, Guayas, and in the two largest cities (Quito and Guayaquil). On average, Ecuadorean immigrants have levels of education lower than Colombians and Peruvians, but higher than Moroccans and Dominicans.

Inventory of Associations and Survey Data

Various registers were used to build an inventory of immigrant associations. First, we examined the association registries provided by the embassies of different countries in Spain, the umbrella confederations, and the centers for participation and integration of immigrants of the regional government of Madrid (CEPIs).[3] This information was compared with three other formal registers: the National Register of Associations of the Ministry of Home Affairs, the Register of Religious Associations of the Ministry of Justice, and the Nongovernmental Organizations Dedicated to Development Register of the Ministry of Foreign Affairs and Cooperation. A breakdown of the associations that had received financing to carry out development projects in their countries of origin was secured from the local government of the Municipality of Madrid, the regional government of the Community of Madrid, and the Spanish Agency of Cooperation and Development (AECID) of the Ministry of Foreign Affairs.

A questionnaire was distributed to a sample of the associations included in the inventory. The survey conducted in Madrid included eighty-five (out of seven hundred existing) transnational associations of Peruvian, Dominican, Colombian, Ecuadorean, and Moroccan origin. In-depth interviews and meetings with consular officials and community leaders plus qualitative research using documents and other information supplemented the survey.

The survey and face-to-face interviews allowed us to identify the main transnational projects implemented by these associations. The list of projects conducted in the countries of origin was also systematized using interviews with other qualified informants, such as academic experts, members of confederations of migrant associations, and authorities from the sending countries. The analysis of this information centered on the developmental scope of the projects and on their contributions to local development.

Profiles of Transnational Associations in Madrid

Immigrant organizations have a number of similarities in organizational and functional aspects. Leaders declared similar objectives and reported performing the same actions for reaching their goals. According to the survey, transnational immigrant organizations in Madrid have two distinctive features: they are formal and, for the most part, they have an established presence at the national level. Due to the sampling framework (official registers were used to create these lists), all eighty-five organizations sampled declared that they were legally registered in Spain. We know that many informal organizations exist as well, although they were not included in the inventory. Informal organizations are generally very small, poorly institutionalized and hard to reach to be included in the sampling. The age of organizations varied. On average, they were approximately ten years old. Figure 10.2 shows that associations were usually formalized at the time of their foundation. In the sample, 80 percent of the associations were created on the private initiative of migrants, while only 17 percent were founded through the support of institutions from the countries of origin.

Dominican associations reported having spent more time in informal status. On average, the gap between the foundation and registration of Dominican associations was 1.4 years, with a standard deviation of 2.2 years. Peruvian organizations reported the highest level of formality; all Peruvian organizations interviewed reported registering immediately upon foundation. The high degree of formalization among migrant associations is the result of conditions in Spain that promote their creation and survival. In particular, the evolution of these associations has been influenced by the support they have received from the Spanish public administration and from diverse civil society organizations. Dependence of immigrant organizations on external support explains the strength and intensity of their ties to the Spanish government and their presence in advisory roundtables and forums. The survey revealed the intensity of contact between these associations and Spanish government agencies and civil society organizations (trade unions, universities), as well as private foundations (La Caixa, Mapfre) and commercial (Banco de Santander) and publicly run (Caja Madrid) banks.

Immigrant organizations also differed in their geographic coverage. Colombian and Peruvian groups reported the highest national presence (68 and 90 percent, respectively), while Dominican and Ecuadorean associations operated in similar percentages at the local and national levels.

Organizational Resources

Access to Public Resources

As described earlier, immigrant associations in Spain have assumed a semiofficial role and are often co-opted by public administrations, through

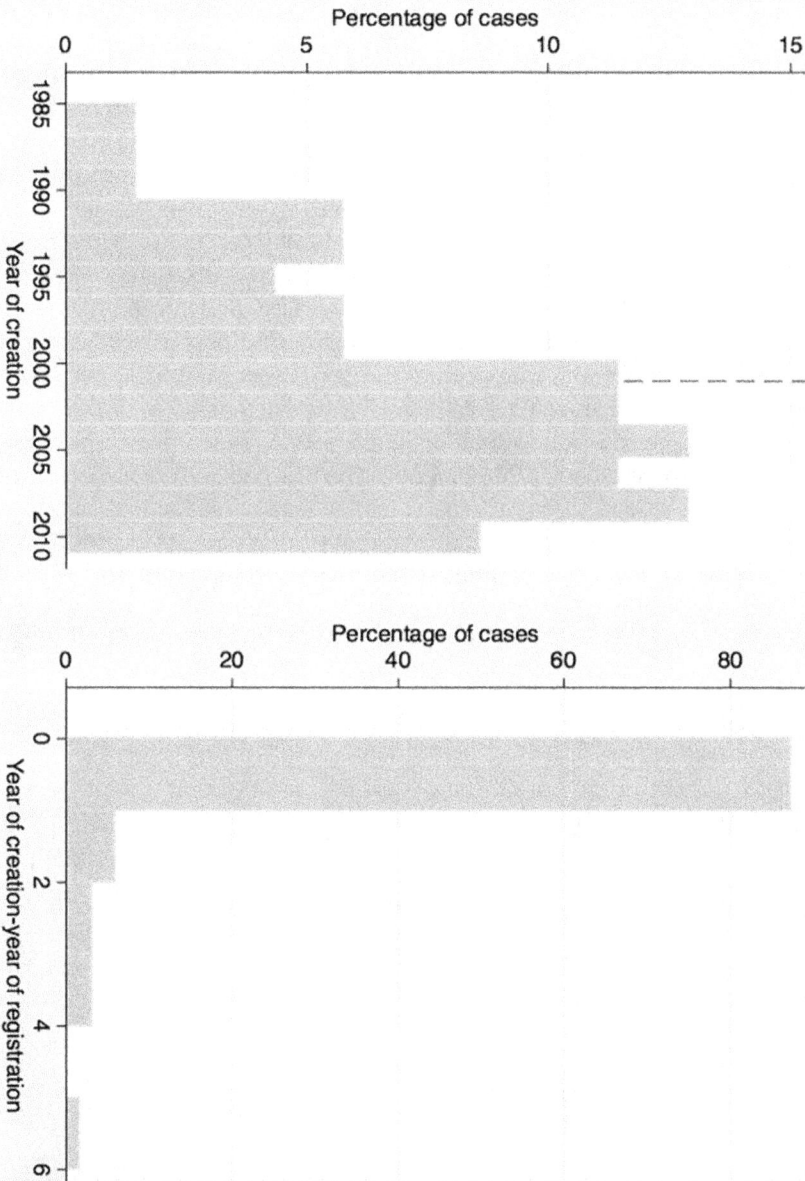

Figure 10.2. Distribution of the Year of Creation and the Gap between Creation and Registration
Dashed line is average (2001)

funding and access to lobbying, as a way to institutionalize the representation of the growing population of migrants in the country. In this section, our objective is to identify features of the associations that facilitate access to public authorities and public funding. We use two main dependent variables: *budget/access to public funding* and *contact with authorities*. These are the two most important resources in designing and implementing codevelopment strategies and interventions linking the countries of origin and destination.

The first dependent variable was operationalized using three indicators: *budget size, access to public funding,* and, most importantly, *percentage of overall budget provided by public funding.* The distribution of the first, *budget size,* is shown in Figure 10.3. More than 50 percent of immigrant associations in Spain operate with a budget of less than €500 per month. However, there is a minority of over 17 percent that have budgets of at least €10,000 due to public subsidies. Figure 10.4 shows that public funds represent between 80 and 100 percent of the budgets of this better-funded minority.

What are the organizational features that provide access to public funding? First of all, seniority can be considered a strong predictor of public funding. Associations established earlier were more likely to garner the

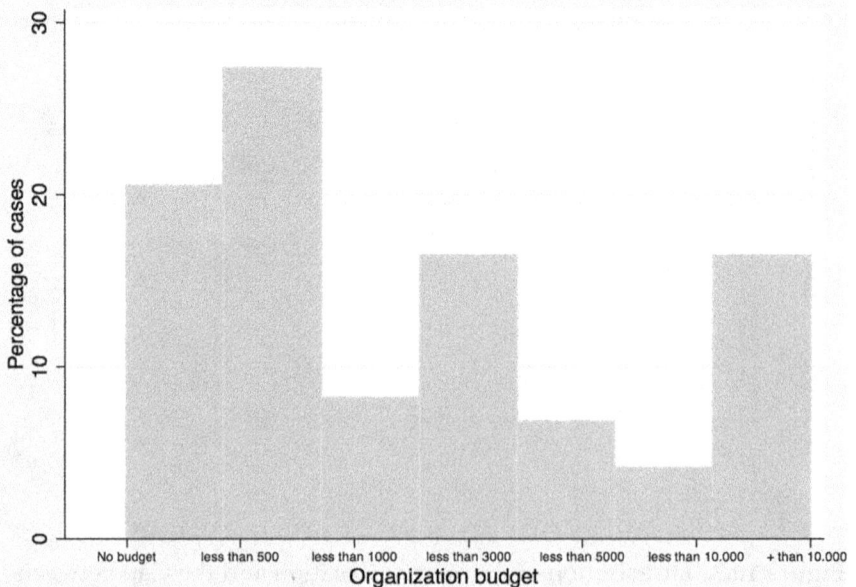

Figure 10.3. Distribution of Organization Budgets

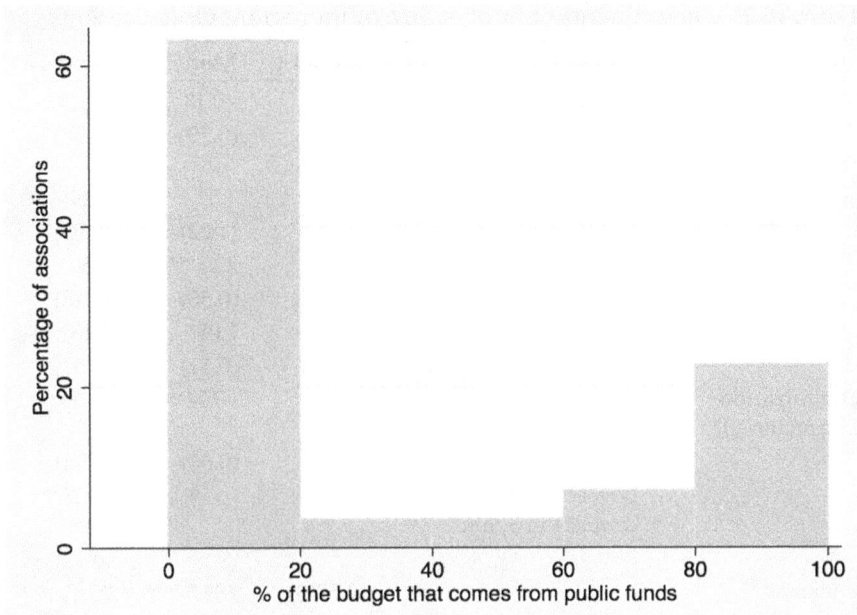

Figure 10.4. Percentage of Budget from Public Funds

attention of public authorities as they sought valid interlocutors among different immigrant communities. Indeed, a causal loop can be posited in which the identification and support of early associations by the authorities is largely responsible for their durability over time. Once this space was occupied, it became much more difficult for more recent organizations to garner the attention of government agencies.

The process of co-optation of immigrant groups took place at all levels of the public administration—local, regional, and national. We hypothesize that the higher the level of administration with which the organization has established contacts, the larger the budget it will have.

Table 10.2 indicates that, relative to Peruvians (the reference category), only Colombians and Moroccans have wealthier organizations. This could be due to their having been the largest incoming groups throughout the migratory period of expansion from 2000 to 2007. Seniority has its expected significant effect on budget size: the more recent the year of creation, the lower the budget. Similarly, level of access to the Spanish public administration has the predicted effect: the higher the access level, the higher the budget. Finally, we interacted year of creation with nationality and present the results in Figure 10.5.

Table 10.2. Determinants of Budget Size of Immigrant Organizations

		Model 1	Model 2	Model 3
National origin (Reference category: Peruvian)	Dominican Republic	0.43 (0.80)	–0.13 (0.79)	–0.23 (0.76)
	Ecuador	0.93 (1.23)	1.31 (1.02)	1.24 (0.97)
	Morocco	3.60*** (0.50)	2.68*** (0.50)	2.50 (0.48)
	Colombia	1.17* (0.52)	1.05* (0.51)	1.13* (0.50)
Organization Characteristics	Year of registration		–0.14*** (0.04)	–0.14*** (0.04)
	Level of government contacts in Spain			–0.25*** (0.12)
Constant		2.57*** 0.33	283.34*** 75.56	275.14*** 71.61
N		76	76	76
F		13.44	30.03	32.96
R^2		0.22	0.38	0.41

Notes:

Notes: Ordinary least squares coefficients; . Robust standard errors in parentheses to adjust for heteroskedasticity.

* $p < 0.05$ ** $p < 0.01$ *** $p < 0.001$

Figure 10.5 shows that, although the general effect of seniority applies to all groups, there are evident differences across the slopes of different countries. The Moroccan associations are older because Moroccans were among the first migratory inflows to Spain. Moroccan associations in Spain have developed through a few large and powerful groups that organize the vast majority of Moroccan migrant workers. Accordingly, Moroccan organizations are wealthier, compared to their Latin American counterparts, and do not lose as much in terms of budget size with recency of registration. In the case of Colombian, Peruvian, and Dominican groups, the figure shows almost parallel lines. Younger associations have notably lower budgets, but the difference is not very steep. Finally, the Ecuadorean case presents distinct results, as lack of seniority has been heavily penalized in this group. The Ecuadorean association movement has been led by a few large organizations that appear to have filled early most of the

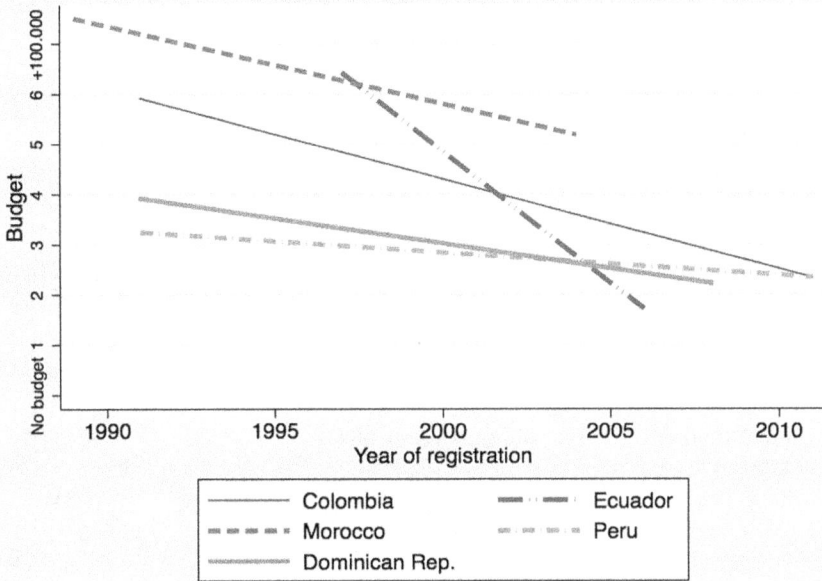

Figure 10.5. Regression Lines: Budget and Year of Registration for Different Nationalities

space for dialogue with Spanish authorities. Accordingly, younger groups found it much more difficult to gain access to this space than among other nationalities.

Table 10.3 presents two sets of regression estimates aimed at identifying characteristics of organizations that receive public funds (1 = receives public finds, 0 = does not) and what percentage of the total organization budget is derived from public resources. In this analysis, we used the same predictors employed previously, as well as a new predictor: *number of members in the organization.* With this variable, we sought to unveil whether public funds are channeled toward the most representative (i.e., largest) associations. We expected that larger organizations would be more likely to receive public funds and that these funds would represent a larger share of the budget.

Model 1 in Table 10.3 shows that seniority is the prime criterion in gaining access to public support. Our expectation that the Spanish government chose organizations early on and maintained their status as representatives of the immigrant communities is fully compatible with this result. Once seniority is controlled for, there are no differences in the likelihood that Peruvian, Colombian, and Dominican organizations would

Table 10.3. Determinants of Access to Public Funds and Percent That Such Funds Represent in Organization Budgets

		Model 1 *Gets public funds*	Model 2 *% public funds*
National Origin (Reference category: Peruvian)	Dominican Republic	−0.03 (1.16)	8.08 (16.06)
	Ecuador	0.00 (0.00)	46.32** (16.88)
	Morocco	0.77 (0.86)	28.93 (16.35)
	Colombia	1.07 (0.75)	13.50 (9.18)
Organizational Characteristics	Year of registration	−0.20** (0.06)	−2.96*** (0.81)
	Number of members	−0.00 (0.00)	−0.00 (0.00)
	Level of government contacts in Spain	1.02 (0.69)	22.66** (8.09)
Constant		3.59** (1.27)	5.47*** 1.61
N		75	75
F			10.72***
χ^2		15.87***	
R^2			0.42

Notes:

Model 1: Logistic regression coefficients; standard errors in parentheses.

Model 2; Ordinary least squares coefficients. Robust standard errors in parentheses to adjust for heteroskedasticity;

* $p < 0.05$ ** $p < 0.01$ *** $p < 0.001$

have access to public funds. The Moroccan and Ecuadorean coefficients could not be estimated, because all of the organizations of these two older nationalities received public resources. It is remarkable that the number of members of organizations in the sample is not associated with the amount of public resources they receive, thus rejecting that hypothesis.

This expectation is also rejected in Model 2. In accordance with results of the previous model, Ecuadorean and, to a lesser extent, Moroccan organizations stand out as having greater access to public resources. On average, 50 percent of the budgets of these organizations come from public funding. Seniority is again a strong predictor of the proportion of the budget covered by the public purse. Similarly, having contacts at high levels of the Spanish administration significantly increases this proportion.

Figure 10.6 reveals the extent to which Ecuadoreans and Moroccans have greater access to public resources compared to the other groups. Across all communities, having established contacts with high-ranking officials from the national administration increases the percentage of public resources in the total budgets of associations.

Figure 10.7 illustrates how seniority affects access to public money, according to the highest level of public administration that each organization contacted. It is clear that having contacts exclusively at the regional or local level represents a real disadvantage in terms of the regression intercept (i.e., the average amount of public funds received by all associations). The opposite is the case if we look at the slopes of the regression lines: they are steeper in the cases of associations with contacts in the central/national administration. This is evident if one compares the predicted values for younger associations with and without high-ranking contacts, which are relatively similar as opposed to older associations. For the latter, level of contact with the central/national government is key in gaining access to more resources.

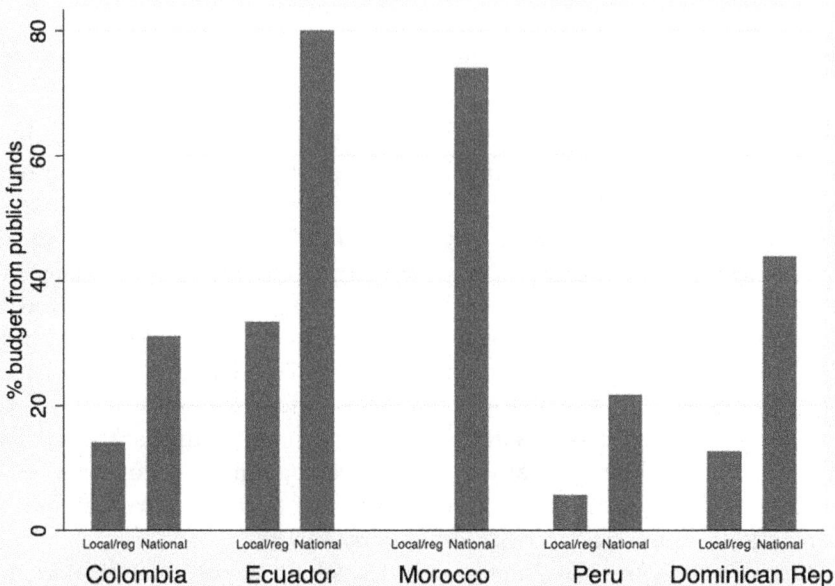

Figure 10.6. Percentage of Organization Funds That Come from Public Resources per Nationality and Highest Level of Administration Contacted

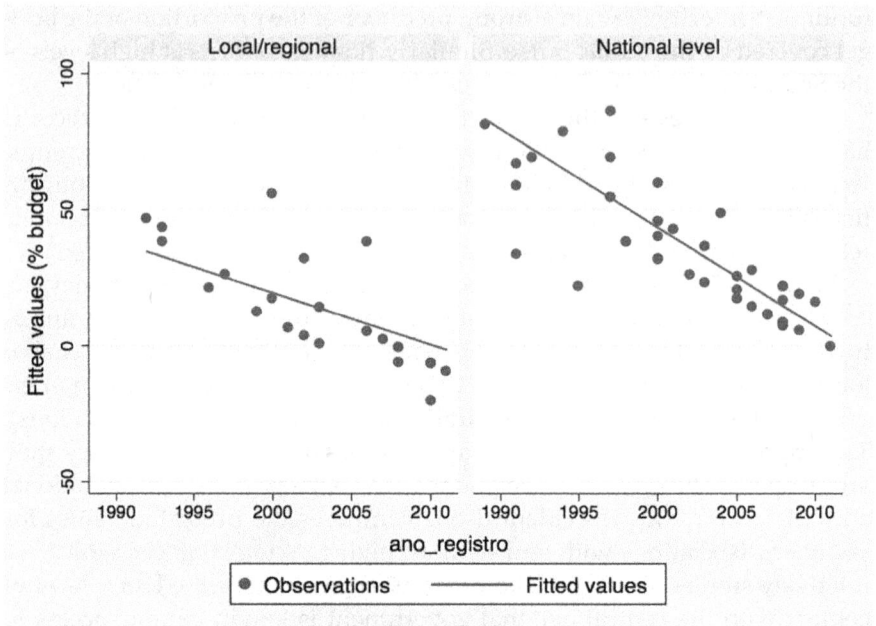

Figure 10.7. Association between Year of Registration and Percentage of the Budget Coming from Public Resources

Contact with Country of Origin Institutions

Our aim in this section is to test whether the top-down model described above also affects the extent to which different organizations establish links with officials in their countries of origin. In this case (see Table 10.4), the dependent variable is dichotomous: 1 for organizations that have official contacts in countries of origin and 0 for those that do not. To discriminate between the levels at which organizations communicate with officials, we calculated separate logistic regressions for contacts at the national level and the regional or local ones. We sought to discover whether the preference for older organizations among Spanish authorities is replicated in the countries of origin. We also added dummies to the model indicating whether contacts in Spain were with authorities at the national or local/regional levels. Finally, we were interested in discovering whether officials in the countries of origin gave priority to more representative organizations, as quantified by number of members.

Our results show that the top-down model that rules the relationship between immigrant organizations and Spanish authorities also affects how associations relate to authorities in their countries of origin (see Table 10.4). Indeed, priority is given to older organizations, and contacts with

Table 10.4. Probability of Having Contact with Authorities in Countries of Origin

	National Level		Regional Level	
	Model 1	Model 2	Model 3	Model 4
Year of registration	−0.07+	−0.05	−0.02	−0.00
	(0.04)	(0.05)	(0.04)	(0.05)
Spain: contact at national level		1.77**		-0.00
		(0.66)		(0.00)
Spain: contact at regional/local level		−0.33		0.93
		(0.86)		(0.75)
Number of members		−0.00		0.75
		(0.00)		(0.67)
Constant	139.41	106.49	40.26	9.25
	(85.22)	(104.76)	(85.01)	(107.73)
N	75	75	75	75
χ^2	2.78	12.40	0.22	5.39

Notes:

Note: all models report logistic regression coefficients; standard errors in parentheses.

+ $p < 0.1$ * $p < 0.05$ ** $p < 0.01$ *** $p < 0.001$

national Spanish authorities are also a determining predictor of having contacts with high-ranking officials in countries of origin. Interestingly, this only applies to contacts with national governments and not with local or regional officials in the countries of origin. We stress that this appears to be the case across all groups analyzed, as the introduction of nationality dummies had no impact on the results and does not change these conclusions.

Immigrant Associations as Instruments for Local Development in Countries of Origin

From Integration to Development

The profiles and types of interventions deployed by migrant associations in Madrid have been influenced by two features. First, migrant associations are formed mostly by first-generation migrants. This explains why they have common objectives regarding both integration and development. Second, the window of opportunity provided by the top-down model encouraged migrant organizations of diverse origins. Public funds were, until recently, provided for associations willing to play the role of community representatives *vis á vis* local, regional, or national authorities, and development cooperation has been one of the semiofficial roles played by migrant organizations. All of this explains the relatively high level of thematic homogeneity we detected in the survey and in our own fieldwork in the countries of origin.

Most transnational associations in Madrid are of two types: civic (especially in the cases of Moroccans, Peruvians, and Colombians) and hometown associations (in the cases of Dominican and Moroccan organizations from northeastern Morocco and the Riff areas). As opposed to what has been observed in other countries, the presence of charitable organizations in Spain is strikingly low, although this might be explained by the provision of public funds that could have been substituted for the collection of private resources on a small or large scale.

The visibility of co-opted immigrant organizations and their influence is more than obvious. It is for this reason that identification of the most important organizations for the purpose of evaluating some of their transnational interventions was a relatively easy task. The selected organizations were ATIME[4] (Moroccan), ARI-Perú (Peru), AESCO[5] and ACULCO[6] (Colombia), VOMADE[7] (Dominican Republic), and Rumiñaui[8] (Ecuador). In addition to these large associations, a plethora of small and more narrowly focused migrant organizations appeared in our survey and field interviews. Yet, we know from the previous section that seniority and prior contacts with any level of the destination administration are essential instruments for success, creating a degree of inequality among organizations.

In the early stages of the migration process, the associations centered on establishing themselves, adapting to the Spanish institutional environment, and strengthening their ties with public administrations and unions. The interventions emphasized programs directed at providing social and legal assistance to the migrants, as well as some political lobbying for social and economic rights. In this first stage, the well-being of immigrants was the priority of the organizations' actions, and the focus was on the immigrant community in Spain.

The most frequent pattern of institutional evolution for transnational migrant associations is from a strict civic focus to a development one. This pattern of organizational change is seen in the case of the Moroccan ATIME, which started as REMCODE,[9] or the Dominican VOMADE, which started as VINCIT.[10] Three reasons explain this renovated interest among civic migrant associations in the field of development: first, the emergence of codevelopment as an important issue in the official Spanish agenda; second, a relative maturation of migration inflows that lessened the importance of activities oriented toward newcomers; and third, the ambition of organization leaders whose careers pushed them toward politics in their countries of origin. These three dynamics explain the creation of many mirror organizations in sending countries that replicate and come under the influence of organizations in Spain. Examples of these dynamics are to be found in the case of Redperuanas and Enclave de Ayuda Transnacional, mirror organizations of the Spanish ARI-Perú, or in the group of initiatives called ACODIP[11], whose focus was expanded to the whole Andean region (Peru, Bolivia, Ecuador, and Colombia).

It is not excessive to say that the involvement of civic organizations in development in countries of origin results from the explicit requirements of the funding institutions in Spain with whom they are connected. We are not arguing that their interest in development is completely instrumental, but only that the timing of their involvement and the type of strategies selected are highly (if not exclusively) determined by their access to public resources and their contacts with a growing list of private institutions. The issue of cooperation for development was initially an incidental goal of the organizations and, accordingly, had either a secondary role in their agendas or a very small scope. Examining this transformation, it could be argued that development entered into the organizations' agendas around 2004, added to the list of integration goals that the average association promoted rather than being substituted for any of them. The novelty of this process explains why the vast majority of the associations surveyed or contacted during the qualitative phase of our fieldwork had not yet engaged in serious, large-scale transnational development interventions.

This incipient transnational structure was identified as predominant among mid- and small-scale organizations from all nationalities in both the survey and the interviews conducted during the qualitative phase of our fieldwork. Examples are the Red de Paisas (Colombia); Asociación Cultural de Jauja and Iberroquipú (Peru); Asociación Monte Olivo (Ecuador). Some of these small associations also referred to education or training provided to local authorities in the country of origin as part of their plans for development, but the transnational part of their agenda was only an "additional priority" on top of preexisting ones. Organizations of different profiles reported using part of the development budget for their own administrative maintenance, an essential dimension for their long-term survival. Additionally, organizations referred to the insufficiency of funds granted as an important obstacle. Financial shortages are essential to understanding why the majority of the transnational interventions we identified were very modest in scope and why there is an overrepresentation in the areas of education and sensitivity training compared to more costly actions, such as the development or improvement of infrastructures of any type.

It is worth noting that the intimate association between immigrant organizations and public administrations (via their agendas and budgets) has created a form of path dependency that is only coming to an end because of the current economic crisis in Spain. The substitution of public funds with a more standard model of fund-raising among members of the organizations (closer to the American model of migrant transnationalism) has also been blocked by the economic downturn, which has particularly affected employment in the low-skilled sectors where the migrant labor force is concentrated.

In sum, development and codevelopment appeared to be huge areas of expansion for migrant associations in Spain in the years before the economic crisis. Organizations report trying to improve their public profiles by requesting resources from their administrative contacts for new activities. However, the crisis stopped this growth and, according to our field data, transnational interventions are described by organization leaders as modest compared to their early ambitions. The overdependence on public funds explains why organizations acknowledge their failure at channeling at least part of migrant remittances to development projects, as has happened in other countries.

Some Cases of Success

Despite the problems mentioned, there are some examples of success that are symbolically important because they create a positive model that may be activated in the future. How was success achieved? Partnerships have been essential to implementing local development projects in the countries of origin. Projects have been implemented in collaboration with a wide range of local organizations—cultural associations, sister associations, churches, foundations and economic organizations, business and professional associations, development organizations, and local government agencies. Most of the main immigrant associations have affiliated headquarters in their countries of origin and offices in several cities. Table 10.5 reviews some of these successful interventions and illustrates the links with local organizations in the countries of origin.

In the cases examined, projects carried out by immigrant organizations have focused on four main areas of action: (1) developing training programs; (2) improving the conditions for productive investments by establishing businesses, creating productive cooperatives, and using remittances; (3) providing assistance to and improving the living conditions of relatives of migrants; and (4) building infrastructure. A second, more diverse group has included offering cultural activities, sociocultural and education interventions, providing services for target groups (women,

Table 10.5. Examples of Successful Projects

Migrant Organization Name	Project Description	Partners in Countries of Origin
ASISI[12] (Morocco)	*Berkane Project* Professional education to fight against irregular migration; promoting equality between genders.	ASISI Maroc (mirror organization), national and local education organizations
ACULCO (Colombia)	*Environmental Education School (Barranquilla)* Training for organic farming and cooperatives.	Coniberoamericana and Triple A Foundation, Confederation of Development Association of Valencia and City Government
Rumiñaui (Ecuador)	*REDES-CAP* Technical assistance and formation for investment; returned Ecuadorian migrants to Ecuador from Spain.	Rumiñaui Ecuador, Farmers and Indigenous Association Forum in Cotacahi (Cotacachi-Imbabura); Eugenio Espejo Foundation (Quito and Guayaquil)
Asociación Alejandro Morales (Dominican Republic)	*Rayo de Luz. School and Library*	Morada Foundation, INAMIVA (national institute of primary school teachers), national and local governments

Additional Examples

Infrastructure
AESCO (Colombia): "Villa del Lago Housing Plan"
REMCODE (Morocco): "Remittances and Solidarity" and "Making Water Potable" projects

Productive investment
Rumiñaui (Ecuador): "Networks Project"
ACODIP (Peru): "Assets and Connections"

Training and education programs
VOMADE (Dominican Republic): "Tamayo Project"

Creating websites (portals) of international migrants
ARI-Perú (Peru): Redperuanas.net

children, etc.), donating equipment, strengthening links between migrant networks in different countries, supporting the creation of migrant federations, and organizing training programs in political leadership and gender equality.

Although the majority of organizations reported carrying out actions in most areas, important differences can be observed between nationalities. Dominican associations stressed education and cultural programs, while Moroccan groups emphasized infrastructure and professional training projects, and Peruvian, Colombian, and Ecuadorean groups concentrated on creating business opportunities, training entrepreneurs, and promoting productive investments. Generally, these initiatives have been welcome and have been seen as positive by the target population and local authorities. However, interactions at the local level have not always been conflict-free. Some projects appear to have generated distrust (notably in the case of gender empowerment projects or initiatives to fight against irregular migration) because the local population perceived them as not being in line with their actual needs.

Indeed, organizations reported having to confront criticisms of their development projects when local leaders perceived them as a challenge to traditional authority and to the existing balance of power. In this sense, some of the most important constraints these organizations have had to face in implementing projects have arisen from the apparent incompatibility of the agendas defined by organizations, local governments, and target populations. In extreme cases, migrant transnational organizations have been seen as "traitors" or as instruments of the destination country.[13]

Despite these controversial experiences, organization leaders report that development should become an integral part of their institutional agenda in the coming years. They appear to be committed to this task, as evidenced by the following changes. First, to overcome their dependency on public funds, better-established migrant associations have diversified their sources of funding over the past few years. For instance, international bodies and European Union programs are among the new sources of funding contacted by these associations. Second, associations are seeking to influence the course of migration policies in sending countries, which has led to the creation of advisory bodies and working documents in which migrant associations participate. Some examples stand out, such as the participation of Colombian associations in the National Council on Economic and Social Policy (CONPES) in Colombia and in the creation of a white paper on comprehensive migration public policy; and the participation of Moroccan associations in Spain in the Council of Moroccan Communities Abroad.

Summary and Conclusions

The Spanish approach to the incorporation of migrants has, to a significant extent, been the result of a long-lasting dialogue between officials and migrant organizations. In a country like Spain, where the transition from being an emigration to an immigration destination was abrupt, immigration policies are not the result of a long-term strategy. Instead, public integration plans at all levels (local, regional, and national) have been influenced by trendy concepts and ideas. This explains the centrality of concepts such as codevelopment. Spanish officials have trusted the views of immigrant organizations regarding what is necessary for successful incorporation into the host country. Accordingly, certain associations have had a leading role in the definition and implementation of public policies. Public funds have been granted to senior organizations, whose involvement in public debates and policies has been remarkable. We define this approach as a top-down model of integration.

In this chapter, we have unveiled some of the consequences of this model. We have revealed that the dependency of organizations on public funds is greater among older and more strategically placed associations. This finding is relevant across groups, as few or no significant nationality residuals were found in the quantitative analysis. Only senior and better-institutionalized organizations have benefited from this privileged access to funds and other resources. The empirical analysis also revealed that these organizations have managed to export this advantaged position to gain contacts with high-ranking officials in their countries of origin.

Migrant organizations became transnational at the time that codevelopment entered into the agenda of Spanish local, regional, and national administrations; for most of them, this was around 2004. This convergence, which is a consequence of the top-down model, does not mean that their entrance into the transnational field would not have happened otherwise, but that the timing and types of strategies deployed were highly influenced by the window of opportunity defined by Spanish policies. The current economic crisis has seriously compromised the agendas of most of these organizations. Yet, many leaders reported a firm conviction that codevelopment will be an essential part of their future activities.

Spain is an interesting case for observing how the context in which migrant organizations develop shapes their behavior in both the origin and destination countries. The top-down model is the single most influential factor in the country, determining how migrant organizations operate and the direction that they take. The existence of this model is now at stake because of the economic crisis. Future research should investigate the evolution of this highly subsidized model of migrant associationism.

Héctor Cebolla-Boado, PhD, is an associate professor in the Department of Social Stratification at the Spanish Open University, where he has been a faculty member since 2010. He completed his PhD in sociology at the

University of Oxford. His research has been published in different academic journals, including the *European Sociological Review, Socioeconomic Review, British Journal of Sociology of Education, Comparative Political Studies, Ethnicities, European Journal of Population,* and *International Journal of Comparative Sociology,* among others.

Ana López-Sala has a PhD in sociology, an MA in security studies, and is a research fellow at the Institute of Economics, Geography and Demography, Spanish National Research Council (CSIC). She is the author of *Immigration and the Nation-State* (Anthropos, 2005), *Migration and Borders* (Icaria, 2010) and *Human Trafficking in Spain* (Immigration Spanish Ministry, 2011). She was a Rockefeller Fellow (Bellagio Program) and a member of LINET (Independent Network of Labour Migration and Integration Experts, IOM and EC). Currently, she is a member of "The Fight against Trafficking of Human Beings in the EU" project (European Commission), "TEMPER" (European Commission), and the researcher in charge of the "Circular Project."

Notes

The study on which this chapter is based was supported by the Carolina Foundation of Spain and the Spanish National Research Council (CSIC). Responsibility for the contents of this chapter is exclusively the authors'.

1. Consensus Document of the Co-development Work Group (Commission of Cooperation and Development).
2. See the Plan Director de la Cooperación Española (2009–2012) in the reference list.
3. The CEPIs (Centers for Participation and Integration of Immigrants in Madrid) are places where the local population and resident immigrants can meet and where services are provided, such as information courses, legal assistance, job search workshops, and cultural and sports activities. These centers depend on the regional government of the Community of Madrid. The social needs of immigrants are also met through the CASI (Social Attention for Immigrants Centers). They are both run by the General Directorate of Immigration of the Community of Madrid.
4. Asociación de Trabajadores Marroquíes en España (Moroccan Workers Association in Spain).
5. América-España, Solidaridad y Cooperación (America-Spain, Solidarity and Cooperation).

6. Asociación Sociocultural y de Cooperación al Desarrollo por Colombia e Iberoamérica (Sociocultural and Cooperation for Development Association in Colombia and Latin America).
7. Voluntariado de Madrid Dominicanas (Dominican Mothers Voluntary Work).
8. RUMIÑAHUI was a general during the civil war, who after the death of Emperor Atahualpa, led the resistance against the Spanish in the northern part of the Inca Empire (modern-day Ecuador) in 1533.
9. Red EuroMediterránea de Cooperación al Desarrollo (EuroMediterranean Network for Cooperation and Development).
10. Voluntariado de Integración Colectivos Internacionales de Trabajadores (Integration of Immigrant Worker Communities Voluntary Work).
11. Asociación de Cooperación al Desarrollo Integral de los Pueblos (Codevelopment of Nations Association).
12. Asociación Solidaria para la Integración Sociolaboral del Inmigrante (Association for the Integration of Immigrants).
13. An example of the influence of the Spanish agenda and financing on shaping development policies is that some associations manage voluntary return programs, such as those carried out in Ecuador and Colombia, which have been partially managed by immigrant organizations with funding from the International Organization for Migration (IOM). The link in Spanish policy between development and the "orderly regulation" of flows has financed training and information programs for future migrants in their countries of origin.

References

Aparicio, Rosa, and Andres Tornos. 2010. *Las asociaciones de inmigrantes en España: Una visión de conjunto.* Madrid: Observatorio Permanente de la Inmigración (OPI)/Ministerio de Trabajo e Inmigración.

Cachón, Lorenzo. 1998. "Los sindicatos españoles y la inmigración." *Migraciones* 4: 71–109.

Cortés, Immaculda, and Anna Sanmartin. 2009. "Las practicas transnacionales de los inmigrantes vinculadas al desarrollo: Un estudio a partir del contexto español." *Revista del Ministerio de Trabajo y Asuntos Sociale* 80: 191–210.

De Lucas, Javier, and Laura Diez Bueso. 2006. *La integración de los inmigrantes.* Madrid: Centro de Estudios Políticos y Constitucionales.

Finotelli, Claudia. 2007. "Italia, España y los regímenes migratorios mediterráneos en el siglo XXI." *ARI* 58: 1–8.

Freeman, Gary. 2004. "Immigrant Incorporation in Western Democracies." *International Migration Review* 38: 945–69.

Koopmans, Ruud. 2010. "Trade-Offs between Equality and Difference: Immigrant Integration, Multiculturalism and the Welfare State in cross-National Perspective." *Journal of Ethnic and Migration Studies* 36: 1–26.

Ministerio de Asuntos Exteriores. 2009. Plan Director de la Cooperación Española (2009–2012): Madrid.

MTIN (Ministerio de Trabajo e Inmigración). 2007. *Plan Estratégico de Ciudadanía e Integración 2007–2010:* Madrid.

Østergaard-Nielsen, Eva. 2011. "Codevelopment and Citizenship: The Nexus between Policies on Local Migrant Incorporation and Migrant Transnational Practices in Spain." *Ethnic and Racial Studies* 34, no. 1: 20–39.

Ruiz de Huidobro, Jose. 2000. "La Ley Orgánica 4/2000: Historia de un descuento y razón de su desenfoque jurídico." *Migraciones* 7: 57–88.

Watts, Julie R. 2000. *An Unconventional Brotherhood: Union Support for Liberalized Immigration in Europe.* San Diego: Center for Comparative Immigration Studies, UCSD.

Conclusion

Assimilation through Transnationalism
A Theoretical Synthesis

Patricia Fernández-Kelly

The Comparative Immigrant Organizations Project (CIOP) is the most comprehensive endeavor of its kind, representing the continuation of research in Latin America that was later extended to include locations in Asia, Africa, Europe, and the United States. An extensive database pertaining to eighteen immigrant nationalities in five different countries has been the result of that effort. Alone, the inventories collected as part of the CIOP would warrant attention, but, even more important, the project offers a foundation for an improved theoretical understanding of transnational activities involving immigrants in critical world locations.

In this conclusion I examine the CIOP findings in light of three bodies of literature that have remained separate until now but whose collective insights elucidate the functions of immigrant organizations in places of origin and settlement. Drawing from writings on globalization, assimilation, and transnationalism, I formulate a synoptic model revealing such entities as *strategic sites* facilitating social incorporation in the age of global economic integration. I sort out major empirical findings along two virtual axes.

First, I consider a *horizontal* vector connecting immigrants and organizations across physical spaces and constituted by responses to constraints and incentives in countries of origin and areas of settlement. I note the historical shifts they tend to experience over time, regardless of national provenance. In early stages of evolution, immigrant organizations tend to be responses to political, socioeconomic, and even natural upheavals in countries of origin. They encompass individuals working to maintain ties with the homeland but also ease settlement in their adopted country. Political, charitable, and sometimes religious groupings best illustrate that trend. In later phases, as immigrants adjust to new conditions, organizations address other questions, including the search for standing, and even prominence, in the adopted nation. Professional and alumni associations are examples. In both cases, they mobilize resources at both ends of a geographical spectrum—financial, human, and cultural—to buttress action, strengthen social ties, gain political power, or foster cultural repertories, often critical to attract public respect.

Grassroots organizations formed by first-generation immigrants vary in terms of social class; highly educated groups, including exiles, integrate to display their superior credentials, especially when those are not recognized or valued in the country of destination. Such groups are *proactive* in a narrow sense of the word; they represent adjustments to the constraints imposed by the receiving society. By contrast, unskilled and semiskilled immigrants are more likely to cluster in hometown associations that emphasize their links to the country of birth and, often, the local or regional networks to which they belong. Such organizations fulfill *defensive* functions, sheltering members from prejudice and marginalization in host environments and providing members with connections and spaces they can use to take refuge from discrimination. Immigrant organizations also preserve a sense of belonging in communities of origin, and are often instrumental in the creation of ethnic and pan-ethnic identities in receiving nations (Kranich 2012).

National states play a critical role in the formation and durability of organized immigrant groups. Regardless of class composition or stated objectives, those established by first-generation immigrants and their descendants are shaped significantly by incentives emanating from government bureaucracies both in countries of origin and areas of destination. In some cases, politicians and public servants are instrumental in their establishment, as they aim to secure the loyalty of immigrants in the pursuit of their own objectives, including the expansion of constituencies (Iskander, this volume; Délano 2012). Legal measures operating in points of origin and reception, including dual citizenship and programs encouraging immigrants to participate in electoral processes, both at home and in adopted countries, further facilitate that process. In other words, it is not possible to garner an adequate understanding of transnational bodies and behaviors without attention to legal regimes and government practices. By focusing on the horizontal dynamics of organizations spanning international borders, I seek to go beyond description to emphasize explanatory factors.

Equally important are the ways in which grassroots organizations operate along a *vertical* axis constituted by a temporal continuum that includes the transmission of information between first- and second-generation immigrants. It is not difficult to understand why new arrivals strive to retain bonds in their countries of origin or seek shelter from discrimination in areas of settlement; their children, however, born or raised in adopted nations, do not respond to the same stimuli. Most do not join transnational organizations or display transnational behaviors, but others, in fact, do. Why? What propels the descendants of immigrants to invest time, money, and other resources in an effort to maintain connections with the ancestral land? An attempt to answer that question forces us to go beyond transnationalism, defined as a process to enhance economic development or philanthropy, to also envision it as a tool for the preservation of memory and the reinvention of self.

By taking into account the temporal dimensions of transnationalism as manifested intergenerationally, we will be in a better position to further understand current processes of assimilation—it is by retaining a connection to the countries from which their ancestors originally emigrated that the children and grandchildren of immigrants mark their distinct identity in countries of reception. Their activities reflect continuity and transformation—they join the past with the future.

Among second- and third-generation immigrants are numerous entrepreneurs and professionals—their achievements a living testimony to promises fulfilled in adopted countries. Endowed with material and symbolic resources, they may take an interest in their parents' and grandparents' places of birth for investment and travel. Many retain family and friendship connections in the lands of their ancestors. The CIOP research shows, however, that utilitarian aims are part of a more complex set of objectives: by affirming bonds to the homeland, younger generations honor their progenitors and redefine their own position in places of birth *and* residence. In the case of children born to refugees or exiles, that operation takes on dramatic proportions—second-generation Cubans and Vietnamese, for example, must establish a delicate balance to pay tribute to their parents' experience of pain and displacement while at the same time asserting their own identities (Huynh and Yiu, this volume). For Nigerians and Koreans, still facing subtle and overt forms of discrimination in the United States, forging ties with the lands of kinsmen can operate as a means to establish distance from stigmatized groups, native- and foreign-born alike (Oh 2011; Oparah 2012). In other words, from a theoretical point of view, the transnational activities of children of immigrants point to new forms of adaptation founded not on the experience of physical relocation but on the re-creation of self and the casting of imaginary communities.

I develop these ideas in four sections. First, I briefly review writings on globalization, assimilation, and transnationalism. Other accounts exist of these bodies of literature. My purpose, therefore, is not to duplicate but to synthesize, while pointing to converging ideas that shed light on the functions of immigrant organizations in the age of global economic integration. In the second section, I offer a conceptual map whose purpose is to reveal the fundamental structure underlying the formation and effects of immigrant organizations. I emphasize *vertical* and *horizontal* vectors. On the basis of pioneering research conducted by scholars affiliated with the CIOP, I note commonalities and differences among groups formed by individuals originating in various nations but residing elsewhere, noting the significant role of government bureaucracies when putting forth incentives or barriers for the creation of immigrant organizations. In the third section, I identify and trace the typical patterns of evolution found among transnational immigrant organizations, regardless of their explicit objectives or location. In the fourth section, I give further attention to those dynamics by focusing on the children of immigrants and their use of transnationalism to reconfigure identity both in the land of their ancestors and in the countries where they reside. I emphasize the role of memory and identity in those practices. The conclusion recapitulates my argument and points to possible contributions in the field of sociology.

Globalization, Assimilation, Transnationalism

More than thirty years ago, Folker Fröbel, Jürgen Heinrichs, and Otto Kreye published *The New International Division of Labour* (1980, ushering in a vibrant new literature on international economic integration or "globalization." That term was widely used to designate new processes affecting trade, industrialization, and cultural diffusion at the world level. Technological advances and the popularization of rapid transportation, but also the relocation of manufacturing from advanced to less developed countries, were singled out as factors enhancing the new economic trend (Fernández-Kelly 1983).

Since the concept was first introduced, analysts have disagreed about the character and reach of globalization. Miguel A. Centeno and Joseph Cohen (2010), for example, discuss the restricted character of international trade, which mostly occurs among China, Europe, and the United States, leaving out large swaths of people in Africa, Latin America, Oceania, and the Middle East. Others emphasize continuities in economic processes (Keohane and Nye 2000) and raise questions about the novel character of globalization (Foster 2002). Still others focus on the accentuation of localism and the expansion in the number of new countries over the last century as evidence that global integration may be exaggerated (Kearney 1995). Despite such disagreements, there is wide consensus about the significance of globalization as a new phase of capitalist development involving the relocation of productive operations from advanced to less developed regions, and the use of advanced technology to facilitate and magnify connections among peoples living in geographically distant areas. Since its inception in the 1980s, the sociology of globalization has engulfed or influenced traditional fields of inquiry, including the study of socioeconomic development in regions like Latin America, Asia, and Africa and also the field of international studies.

Compatible with the study of globalization was the rise, in the 1970s, of neo-Marxist analyses that inspired studies of the world system as first theorized by Immanuel Wallerstein (1974). Like Fröbel, Heinrichs, and Kreye, Wallerstein emphasized the historical dimensions of globalization and the emerging social, economic, and political reconfigurations that mirror new arrangements of production throughout the planet. A major, although not original, element in these formulations was an attention to the temporal and spatial dimensions of economic development and the shifting geographical character of accumulation. Globalization became the subject of an ambitious theoretical enterprise and a main theme in a promising research agenda (Sklair 2001, 2002).

Empirical studies showed that internationalization—including outsourcing and free trade agreements inspired by neoliberal economics—redefined the relationship between institutions and civil society. National states, for example, find it difficult to arrest capital flight or tax revenues generated by investments outside their borders. Yet the same governing bodies continue to be charged with long-standing responsibilities like the management of displaced workers (Garland 2002; Wacquant 2009). In other words, for more than half a century, tensions have grown between the capacity of national states to coordinate nation-bound civil societies and the increasing mobility of investments generating huge profits throughout the world (Arrighi 2009; Giddens 2006; and Harvey 2007). How those contradictions will be resolved remains a matter of debate.

Although our understanding of globalization as a large-scale phenomenon has improved, its effects are still under review. Robinson, for example, observes that many explanatory lacunas exist in regard to the specific mechanisms that are rearticulating civil societies. He asks how transnationalized populations reorganize their spatial relations from local to global scales (2009: 6). As I propose in this conclusion, a growing body of empirical evidence suggests that at least part of the answer to Robinson's question is found in the rationale and practices of transnational immigrant organizations. It is in those physical and social spaces that the connection between global and local is often realized.

The study of globalization was revolutionized in the 1990s as a result of Saskia Sassen's analyses, first put forth in *The Mobility of Labor and Capital* (1990) and subsequently elaborated in *The Global City* (1991) and *Globalization and Its Discontents* (1998). Sassen took stock of earlier contributions concerning the spatial and temporal reconfigurations of globalization (Portes and Walton 1981), but also identified new channels for the accumulation of capital. Vividly, she emphasized the growth of cities, like New York, London, and Tokyo, as nodes for the administration of the world economy. In such cities, and urban networks, a new class of people whom Robert Reich (1992) called "symbolic analysts" — many of them working in financial and finance-related institutions — facilitate the movement of people, power, and culture through the use of refined technologies, global investments, and digitalized infrastructures. Their presence creates demand for services and commodities provided by a new working class, some of whose members are situated in the export processing zones of less developed countries, but many of whom are immigrants flowing from poor nations to globalized urban areas.

According to Sassen, economic and political interventions throughout the world, in tandem with labor demand in advanced industrial countries, have produced a new class of workers who stride international demarcation lines. A major insight thus concerns the reconstitution of class structures across borders. Sassen thus provides an intellectual platform for the understanding of globalization and immigrant assimilation as *mutually constitutive processes,* not disparate fields of action. This, in turn, raises new questions about the very character of immigrant incorporation in the age of globalization, and the mechanisms that make it possible at the local level. In subsequent sections, I argue that transnational organizations represent strategic sites facilitating reciprocally constitutive processes involving immigrant assimilation and globalization. They reveal actual relationships between immigrants and ejecting and receiving states — what may be described, following Benedict Anderson ([1983] 1991), as "imagined communities."

While the sociology of globalization is a comparatively recent endeavor, studies of assimilation date back more than a century. The concept itself is closely tied to American sociology and the history of the United States as a country of immigrants. Original formulations emphasized the continuous character of immigrant incorporation into mainstream society, arguing that settlement in the adopted country leads newcomers to shed old ways of life to embrace American values and mainstream practices. Throughout its long trajectory, the notion of assimilation has served as a topic of empirical research but also as a normative concept that positively values what Alba and Nee (2005) call "the decline of ethnic difference." As much as a notion shedding light on the effects of immigration, assimilation is also part of an ideological system that privileges the idea of America as a unified whole where citizenship obliterates differences of race and ethnicity. Research, however, yields mixed findings: some supporting classic notions of assimilation and others contesting such conclusions.

The most influential critique of established ideas on that subject is Portes and Zhou's article, "The New Second Generation: Segmented Assimilation and Its Variants" (1993). As originally formulated, the new concept drew attention to the fragmented character of assimilative processes. Portes and Zhou sensibly suggested that assimilation does not occur monolithically but as a result of concrete interactions between recently arrived immigrants and previously established residents. The outcomes of assimilation thus vary depending on the character of those interactions but also in relation to the distinctive features of social networks and the individuals involved in them. Immigrants residing in integrated, comparatively affluent places will fare differently than those who end up in poor neighborhoods where they interact with members of low-income populations and the descendants of oppressed racial minorities. Segmented assimilation brought preexisting ideas based on common sense and ideological conviction into correspondence with the findings of empirical research.

Portes and his associates showed that not all national groups assimilate to American society in the same way or at the same velocity. It is true that within a single generation most immigrants adopt the language of their adopted country and adhere to mainstream norms and aspirations—evidence of amalgamation more or less along the predictions of conventional views. Nonetheless, as abundantly demonstrated by empirical research, numerous differences regarding standard indicators of social mobility characterize the trajectories of children of immigrants (Nagasawa, Qian, and Wong 2001; Neckerman, Carter, and Lee 1999; Rumbaut 1997). For example, partly because of their comparatively high levels of education and entrepreneurial experience, and also because of incentives offered by the American government, early generations of Cuban exiles experienced accelerated processes of upward mobility (Portes and Stepick 1993; Nijman 2011). By contrast, largely as a result of persistent discrimination and the absence of effective means for economic and political incorporation, Mexicans exhibit modest gains despite their long residence in the United States (Telles and Ortiz 2009). Moreover, processes of segmented assimilation do not occur in the United States alone—research in European countries yields evidence of similar outcomes (Portes and Smith 2012). Whether measured in terms of educational achievement, school abandonment, early motherhood, or incarceration, there is little doubt that different national groups have fared differently in adopted countries. As a heuristic concept, segmented assimilation fulfills an important objective: to provide a nuanced understanding of a broad social and economic process.

Segmented assimilation is also significant for my purposes in this conclusion because it offers a backdrop for understanding variations in the structure and function of immigrant organizations. Both in the United States and elsewhere, immigrant organizations may be partly understood as adaptations to segments of the social body. While professionals seek validation of their credentials and higher social standing, thus assuming a *proactive* approach, humble workers search protection from prejudice by banding together and adopting a *defensive* stance. Both cases involve the mobilization of resources—social, economic, political, and even cultural—but the class background of social actors and their objectives shape different positions. Variations also occur in relation to the context created by the state at the federal and local levels. Segmentation, in other words, is widely evident in the study of corporate activities involving immigrants.

While the literature on assimilation dates back to the inception of sociology and writings on globalization now span more than four decades, research on transnationalism is of more recent vintage. Anthropologist Nina Glick Schiller is credited with the introduction of the term to designate fields of interaction, actual or imaginary, that enable immigrants to preserve connections with countries of origin and places of settlement. In a much-cited work, Glick Schiller and her associates explain:

> We define "transnationalism" as the processes by which immigrants forge and sustain multi-stranded social relations that link together their societies of origin and settlement. We call these processes transnationalism to emphasize that many immigrants today build social fields that cross geographic, cultural, and political borders. ... An essential element is the multiplicity of involvements that transmigrants sustain in both home and host societies. (Glick Schiller, Linda Basch, and Szanton Blanc 1995 6)

In this formulation, *transmigrant* is used to underscore the unique character of practices and ideational systems that require the crossing of borders, whether real or imaginary, by contrast to situations that reflect immigrants' immersion in adopted countries and little or no contact with their places of birth. Glick Schiller's work and that of her followers provided innovative means to investigate emerging forms of adaptation in the age of globalization.

Portes, Haller, and Guarnizo (2002) took a somewhat different position. In their view, transnationalism is best used to designate immigrant *practices* that require the regular crossing of *physical* borders to generate revenue, mobilize political resources, or maintain or produce cultural forms. Their emphasis is on the regularity of actual border crossings and on the objective results of such actions, a matter that facilitates empirical research rather than conjecture.

On the basis of that conceptualization, Portes and his colleagues have found that less than 15 percent of immigrants in the United States engage in transnational activities. That percentage may seem modest, but, theoretically, it raises momentous questions about the character of immigrant adaptation. The diffusion of neoliberal economic measures and the implementation of free trade agreements may have provided capitalist entrepreneurs with unprecedented freedom to move across international demarcation lines, but the same factors have also affected workers. A case in point is the North American Free Trade Agreement (NAFTA), which acted as a stimulus for the displacement of labor. In the Mexican countryside, the use of arable land for the production of export crops, as promoted by NAFTA, displaced peasants, many of whom found their way into the United States, often illegally (Massey, Durand, and Malone 2003; Fernández-Kelly and Massey 2007). In other words, the centrifugal forces guiding capital investments create centripetal inducements that mobilize labor. As they arrive in areas of settlement, immigrant workers make choices in response to existing conditions. It is against that context that transnational activities, even when enacted by a comparatively small percentage of immigrants, emerge as part of a necessity to reconsider identity and culture. Transnational organizations offer a strategic location to investigate the assimilative effects of globalization.

Transnational communities may thus be seen as a response to material imperatives but also as ideational systems. Whether transnationalism is broadly or narrowly defined, the point to salvage here is the durable character of redefined identities and practices deployed by immigrants and their children to forge bridges between countries of origin and countries of destination. Such ideas are inherently valuable from a theoretical point of view; the question remains, however, as to the specific means that individuals and groups use to assimilate and recast identity in a globalized world.

To further specify the conditions under which transnationalism occurs is one of the objectives pursued by Roger Waldinger and David Fitzgerald; they point out that "[w]hat immigration scholars describe as transnationalism is usually its opposite: highly particularistic attachments antithetical to those by-products of globalization denoted by the concept of 'transnational civil society'" (2004: 1179). That asseveration signals a paradox: while the literature on transnational communities emphasizes the global character of immigrant practices and ideational systems, the actions of immigrants occur in small and bounded spaces. In that respect, the behavior of those whom Glick Schiller calls *transmigrants* illustrates the realization of globalization through localism. Waldinger and Fitzgerald also stress the importance of state actions that shape immigrant adaptations, and they deplore the US-centered thrust of writings on the subject by providing examples of the ways transnationalism operates in other geographical regions, mostly Europe. In earnest, they affirm that transnationalism "deserves serious scholarly attention, but only when redefined as the collision of the social organization of migration and its state-spanning results with reactive efforts by state and civil society actors to produce state-society alignment" (Waldinger and Fitzgerald 2004: 1186). Despite its opaque phrasing, that statement is useful: to retain conceptual power, studies of transnationalism must account for the factors that actualize the very process named by the concept. In the next section, I approach that subject through a conceptual diagram aimed at condensing and explaining transnational mechanisms.

Mapping Transnational Organizations

In 1992, Robert C. Smith offered a groundbreaking description of the Ticuani, Puebla (Mexico) Potable Water Committee celebrating the installation of new tubing in their hometown. The vignette, first captured in Smith's doctoral dissertation, was later published in an award-winning book and reprinted many times since. Here is how one committee member described his involvement: "Now, when you are in Ticuani … you will be able to take a shower at any time of the day or night and the water will come out strong. And we will be able to plant trees right in the back yard and water them without any trouble too … our new water tubes … will make life better in Ticuani" (Smith 1998:12).

What makes the quote memorable is learning that the committee members in question were not celebrating their developmental efforts in Ticuani, their Mexican village, but in Brooklyn, New York, where they resided. They were striding borders in concrete and imaginary ways. Their pride manifested a durable connection to their community of origin but also the capacity to mobilize resources in their adopted land, the United States. Since the 1990s, much of the literature on transnational communities represents an elaboration of Smith's piercing illustration. In that sense, transnationalism represents a *horizontal* vector connecting distant geographical points through developmental, philanthropic, and cultural projects.

No less intriguing or worthy of attention are the new images emerging from pioneer research on transnational organizations in various parts of the world. In May 2012, at a meeting convened to discuss the findings of the Comparative Immigrant Organizations Project (CIOP), Min Zhou summarized the results of her investigation with Rennie Lee by describing the lavish investments of second-generation Chinese Americans in their ancestral country. Having mustered professional standing and financial resources in the United States, they use some of their wealth to build cultural centers, religious shrines, and residential complexes in Beijing and other Chinese cities. Such practices point to novel forms of adaptation on the part of second-generation immigrants, who actively recast parental narratives to achieve their own purposes. Their actions point to the presence of a *vertical* axis joining transnational actions across time.

The monumental character of such enterprises bespeaks of more than a developmental effort—they are also testaments to the recreation of an imaginary realm that connects the new generations to their past. As Zhou and Lee note:

> Remittances are a form of conspicuous consumption in migrant-sending villages. Performing family or holiday rituals, such as weddings and funerals, and building large ancestral homes have become big events that cost hundreds and thousands of dollars. Migrant families often find themselves in a race to become the "best" of something—the most extravagant wedding, the most expensive funeral, the tallest/largest house—as a way to display family honor or to regain social status. (Zhou and Lee, this volume)

The images evoked by Smith (1998) and Zhou and Lee (this volume) aptly summarize major elements of transnationalism as a vehicle to achieve assimilation. Figure 11.1 illustrates that relationship along spatial and temporal axes. It suggests a way of thinking about the evolution and functions of immigrant organizations.

First waves of immigrants voluntarily leaving countries of origin, or ejected by political persecution, economic displacement, or natural disaster, actively pursue specific objectives in adopted countries—whether to overthrow dictators or aid families left behind, immigrants take a *proactive* stance. At the same time, such immigrants almost invariably organize to navigate different and complex labor markets and legal regimes in areas of settlement. In numbers they find strength to combat racial discrimination and prejudice or give voice to grievances. As they pursue such objectives, they often use cultural elements, including religious beliefs and practices. In that sense their efforts become *defensive.* They mobilize resources both to secure self-advancement and to overcome perceived barriers.

As the original forces that prompted their migration diminish or are subsumed by new challenges, immigrants turn their attention to other objectives. Populations first guided by a desire to overthrow regimes or

First Generation

Forging Immigrant Narratives

Easing Settlement
Contesting prejudice
Recreating culture

Destination   Origin

Economic development
Political influence
Cultural preservation

Recasting Immigrant Narratives

Second Generation

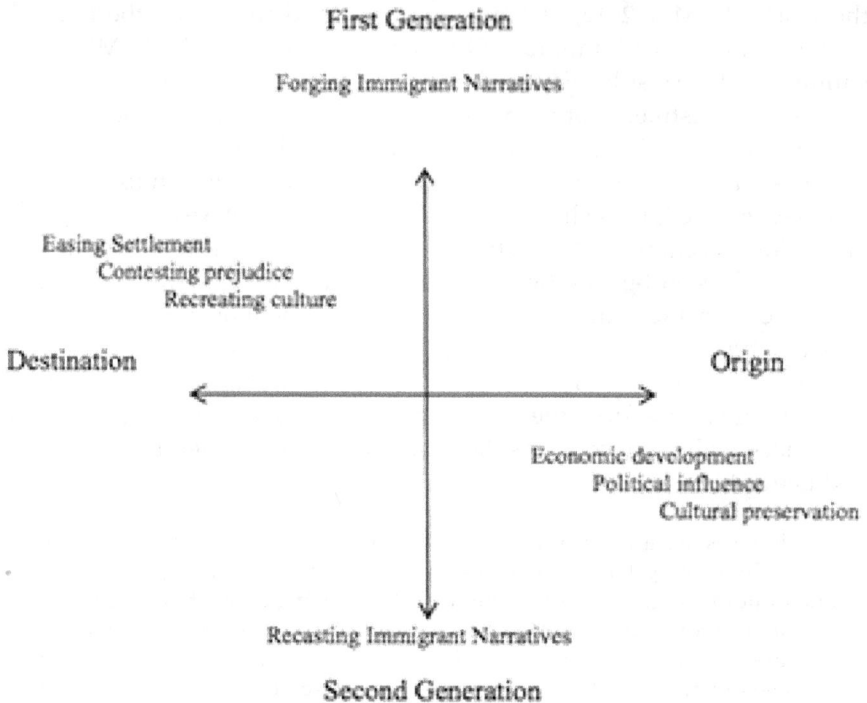

Figure 11.1. Mapping Transnational Communities

fight for social justice in places like Morocco, the Democratic Republic of Congo, Vietnam, or Cuba are gradually complemented by new organizations whose purpose is to consolidate and assist communities of immigrants vying for representation and prominence. Alumni, business, and professional organizations are examples of this second moment in the evolution of transnational organizations. In other cases, organizations first aiming to adjust to contexts of reception expand their objectives to include aid and development in the country of birth, as shown by the experience of Moroccans in Belgium (Lacroix and Dumont, this volume). A third moment, represented by organizations and activities that involve new generations of immigrants, brings about a recasting of sustaining narratives and an innovative deployment of cultural repertories.

In that evolution the reach and capacity of transnational organizations are critically shaped by outlooks and policies forged at the state level. For example, changes in immigration laws stemming from receiving countries can facilitate or deter assimilation. This, in turn, influences the tactics and strategic thinking of transnational organizations. In some cases, national states and international organizations put forth resources of various kinds to aid the developmental efforts of immigrants in their countries of origin. France, Spain, Germany, and Belgium illustrate that trend (Lacroix and Dumont, this volume; Godin et al., this volume). In other words, the mode of incorporation of immigrants (Portes and Zhou 1993) in receiving contexts affects the character of their transnational activities. In other instances, governments in sending countries actively participate in the formation of organized groups in receiving countries. Mexican transnational organizations are a case in point (Iskander, this volume). All and all, state actions at the national level are decisive to understand variations in the constitution and practices of grassroots organizations.

From a somewhat different but complementary point of view, new laws facilitating investment in places like India or China significantly draw the attention of younger immigrants in countries of destination toward the home of their ancestors. Although the practices of transnational organizations span physical and imaginary borders, they are shaped by political regimes actualized at the national level. Paradoxically, assimilation in the age of global economic integration still depends on nation-bound legal and political processes. In the next section, I further develop the ideas sketched above on the basis of concrete case studies.

Transnational Organizations: Understanding the Connections

In this volume, Margarita Rodríguez offers the results of her study of Nicaraguan immigrant organizations in Miami-Dade County. She identifies eighty such entities founded since the 1980s, focusing primarily on forty that are currently active. Eighty-three percent are formally registered in the state of Florida under the 501(c) (3) category; 7 percent have no formal incorporation as nonprofits; and 85 percent have developed sustained links with institutions, associations, and/or communities back in Nicaragua. Most Nicaraguan organizations formed since the 1990s—nearly half of the total—focus on civic and humanitarian goals, followed by those pursuing cultural goals and professional or business promotion. This is significantly different by comparison to the 1980s, when half of the organizations had political goals or a civic-military focus.

The trajectory of Nicaraguan organizations in South Florida aptly illustrates a typical evolution. Although the particulars of the story differ from country to country, the tendency is for groups seeking redress for political grievances or responding to humanitarian disasters to ebb even as new organizations emerge to satisfy new concerns in areas of settlement. In the Nicaraguan case, the revolution of 1979, which placed the Frente Nacional para la Liberación Nacional (FNLN) at the helm of the small country, led to massive emigration and the transformation of Miami into an epicenter of Nicaraguan political action (Cervantes-Rodríguez, Grosfoguel and Mielants 2009). After the installation of the leftist Sandinista regime in 1984, many Nicaraguans sought refuge in South Florida, where they found a well-established framework formed by grassroots organizations, many constituted during an earlier period by Cuban activists. Nicaraguans used that infrastructure to reach their own objectives. Most political entities were dismantled after the electoral defeat of the Sandinistas in 1989. Professional, alumni, cultural, and civic organizations, on the other hand, have survived to the present day, some of them changing their names as they broadened their scope or modified their immediate goals to adjust to new realities.

Cristina Escobar (this volume) reports similar findings resulting from her research on Colombian and Dominican organizations. In 1999, after an earthquake struck coffee-producing fields in their native land, Colombians residing in New York rushed to assist their compatriots. In 2011, many of those organizations coordinated efforts to provide aid for more than two million people affected by heavy rains in more than half of the Colombian territory. In 2004, when Hurricane Georges hit the area of Jimani in the Dominican Republic, causing more than one billion dollars in damage and nearly four hundred deaths, immigrant organizations in New York and Florida raised millions in aid. In addition to supporting emergency efforts, Colombians and Dominicans participated in organizations that continuously addressed political challenges in their countries of origin. Similarly, in the 1980s and 1990s, Miami became a pivotal location for the coordination of measures to fight powerful drug cartels based in Colombian cities like Medellín and Cartagena through the mobilization of resources to support a vulnerable national state. Dominicans, on the other hand, have been notorious for their bridging political actions. It is not unusual for politicians vying for political office to campaign both in their country of origin and in Jackson Heights, New York. The annual Dominican Day parade in Manhattan, held in the month of August, customarily features prominent Dominicans seeking support from compatriots abroad.

It is not solely in the United States that such phenomena give testimony to the regularity of patterns found among transnational immigrant organizations. In Belgium and France, Moroccans and Congolese have constituted powerful grassroots associations to pursue distinct political agendas. According to Lacroix and Dumont (this volume), the repression that followed leftist opposition in Morocco after that country secured independence led to the departure of a large number of political activists who found refuge mostly in France, but also in Spain, Belgium, Germany, and the Netherlands (see also Godin et al., this volume). Various political strands coalesced into the *Association des Marocains en France,* whose main purpose was to support political parties in the country of origin. Other groups followed suit, but they lost steam as conditions stabilized in Morocco and as more and more immigrants sought to address new conditions in places of settlement.

Partly as a result of policies implemented by the French state and international nonprofit organizations to foster investments in countries of immigrant origin, Moroccan émigrés soon turned their attention to economic development rather than direct political contestation. In that aim they often found support from public agencies in countries of residence. By contrast to the United States, European nations have aggressively backed multilateral agreements to foster economic improvement in points of out-migration, often aiming to arrest or control new arrivals in areas of destination. Their efforts are sometimes tinged by a desire to keep outsiders at bay. All the same, such measures have opened up multiple avenues for Moroccans and other immigrants to pursue their own objectives (Cebolla Boado and López-Sala, this volume). In other words, transnational organizations and practices are significantly shaped by opportunity structures and available resources in ejecting and receiving countries.

Equally critical to the understanding of transnational outcomes and immigrant fates are laws and policies affecting access to citizenship in areas of destination. In France, the legacy of the 1789 Revolution and a resulting emphasis on republican unity ironically created barriers for the explicit recognition of racial discrimination and the implementation of legislative means to combat it (Alba 2005; Entzinger, Saharso, and Scholten 2011). Since the late nineteenth century, nationality was conferred in Germany on the basis of *jus sanguinis,* that is, only on those who are direct descendants of Germans. Starting in the 1960s, a growing number of Turkish immigrants fleeing scarcity in their own country moved to Germany as part of guest worker programs. Nearly fifty years later, close to four million Turks and their children continue to reside in the margins of German society (Schulte-Peevers et al. 2007; Kastoryano and Harshav 2002). Reforms to the nationality law implemented by the Bundestag in 2000 made it easier for foreigners and, especially, their German-born children to acquire German citizenship, but public resistance to Turkish incorporation persists (Erdem 2006; Faist 2000). In the United States, by comparison, the adoption of *jus soli* since the inception of the country confers citizenship to all who are born on American soil. That has facilitated the integration of multiple national groups, also enabling large numbers of children born in the United States to undocumented parents to attain automatic citizenship (Passel and Taylor 2010; Entzinger and Biezeveld 2006). Thus, the role of state legislation is crucial in areas like nationality and citizenship that ultimately distinguish between insiders and outsiders. It is equally relevant with respect to developmental outlooks and actions that shape limits and possibilities for immigrant flows. Whether laws and policy measures promote or impede immigrant assimilation eventually affects the character and practices of transnational organizations.

How powerful countries view their role in development also matters. The United States stands almost alone, among advanced industrial countries, in its low level of participation in investments to curtail the probability of emigration from Mexico, a country with which it shares a 2,000-mile border and which is the largest sender of immigrants—legal as well as illegal—to US territory (Fernández-Kelly and Massey 2007; Massey, Durand, and Malone 2003). NAFTA, implemented in 1994 under the Clinton administration, was remarkable in the extent to which it excluded measures to ease the effects of economic liberalization on workers both in the United States and Mexico. By contrast, the Maastricht Treaty of 1992, instrumental in the forging of the European Union, gave priority to developmental measures to reduce the likelihood of migration from poorer to richer countries after economic integration. Countries like Belgium, Germany, and Spain have implemented multilateral agreements supporting developmental efforts in areas of immigrant origin (Godin et al., this volume; Cebolla Boado and López-Sala, this volume). All and all, a review of current legislation in various countries reveals major differences that, in turn, eventuate in a varying capacity on the part of immigrants to muster resources and gain full membership in receiving societies.

Finally, the regulatory functions of nation-states are also vital to the creation of legal frameworks delimiting the organizational capacities of individuals and groups. The not-for-profit sector in the United States, whose magnitude and scope are not found anywhere else in the world, is made possible through multiple tax incentives that reward public service and altruistic missions; 501(c)(3) organizations range from universities to hospitals and foundations whose revenues are minimally subject to taxation (Grobman 2008). Such entities have provided great and effective facilities for immigrants involved in transnational organizations. At the grassroots level, even a small number of motivated activists can wield existing legislation to fulfill goals that span international demarcation lines. Whether as an ally or a contender, state actions significantly affect transnational practices.

Ironically, writings on the relationship between government bureaucracies and immigrant organizations often present both entities as separate and self-bounded. Yet, as Natasha Iskander notes in her study of Mexican hometown associations (HTAs) in the United States:

An examination of the processes through which HTAs are and have been created calls this characterization into question. It reveals that state actors engage assertively in mobilizing and formalizing HTAs, and do so in an ongoing way, proactively and deliberately cultivating organizational strength and forms of political action among ... migrant civic groups. (Iskander, this volume)

The case investigated by Iskander is the Three-for-One Program implemented by the Mexican government as a vehicle to match immigrant investments in areas of origin. In that instance, Mexican authorities are not distant promoters of actions occurring independently within hometown associations; instead, they actively mobilize participants to gain their loyalty both in Mexico and in the United States. Iskander's work offers new avenues to investigate situations in which transnationalism is not solely the response of immigrants to global economic integration, but the result of close interaction between immigrants and government agents. Thus, as Iskander suggests in this volume, a useful and precise way of considering transnational organizations is as

social fields in which multiple actors negotiate both new expressions of transnational political identity and the possibilities for actions those identities allow. In other words, HTAs, rather than being freestanding civic organizations, are in fact arenas of contestation, where migrants, state officials, and local communities on both sides of the US-Mexico border wrestle over questions of identity, belonging, political power, and resources.

Other, equally significant organizational patterns may be observed among Chinese in the United States. Early waves of extremely vulnerable immigrants, arriving in the United States at the turn of the twentieth century, clustered in kin- and village-based associations operating as mutual aid societies. Merchant guilds evolved into associations that often operated as secret societies endowed with private forms of communication, elaborate rituals, and codes of loyalty that, when violated, resulted in violent retribution. Such organizations eventually gave rise to the multiple Chinatowns that still dot the American landscape (Zhou and Lee, this volume).

More recently, however, Chinese organizations have pursued broader goals. The passage of the 1965 Family Reunification Act demolished national immigration quotas and fueled new waves of immigration from Asia and Latin America. Chinese Americans benefited as a result. At present they form one of the largest immigrant populations in the United States, next only to Mexicans, with nearly four million residing in the United States, not counting a persistent flow of unauthorized residents. Chinese Americans have exhibited a high propensity to participate in new transnational organizations that reflect economic success and incipient political prominence in the receiving country. Many of those organization focus on financial and cultural exchanges between the United States and China. As Zhou and Lee note:

> [Originally] Chinese exclusion created opportunities for organizations and gave rise to an ethnic infrastructure in which the enclave economy and ethnic organizations were interconnected. ... Even in the contemporary era, traditional organizations have continued to exert influence ... but their authority and functions have been weakened. (Zhou and Lee, this volume)

Two trends thus become apparent from the results of research conducted as part of the CIOP: First, there is the movement from localized and specific ends—whether humanitarian or political—to a diversified agenda formed by multiple goals that include economic development, cultural promotion, and the maintenance of connections among professionals and alumni, among others. Second, that evolution is closely linked to—not separate from—growing assimilation on the part of first-generation immigrants and their children. This concretely illustrates the mutually constitutive character of global economic integration and assimilative processes in places of immigrant destination.

Social class and state actions matter in that evolution. Immigrants endowed with low levels of human capital, and those without proper legal documentation, face heightened levels of discrimination and exploitation in areas of settlement. A hostile context of reception, in turn, shapes their alternatives. Whether Mexicans in the United States, Chinese in Spain, or Algerians in France, such groups tend to integrate differently than those boasting higher levels of education and financial resources. Where working-class immigrants are involved, the tendency is often toward the formation of *defensive* organizations that solidify connections with countries of origin largely as a protective measure against arrested mobility in countries of reception. Those organizations also operate in a transnational field, but their motivations, relationships with national states, and effects differ significantly from those formed by professionals, who tend to integrate in *proactive* organizations to display their credentials and consolidate power. Figure 11.2 summarizes the factors accounting for the evolution of immigrant organizations, including the interaction between proactive and defensive stances.

The diagram summarizes the relationship between context of reception, class background, and the propensity for immigrants to form organizations that display proactive and defensive postures. Cuban exiles are included in the top right quadrant of the figure because of their comparatively high socioeconomic standing and the relatively hospitable reception that followed their migration to the United States. Their tendency, therefore, has been to move from a preeminently political mission aimed

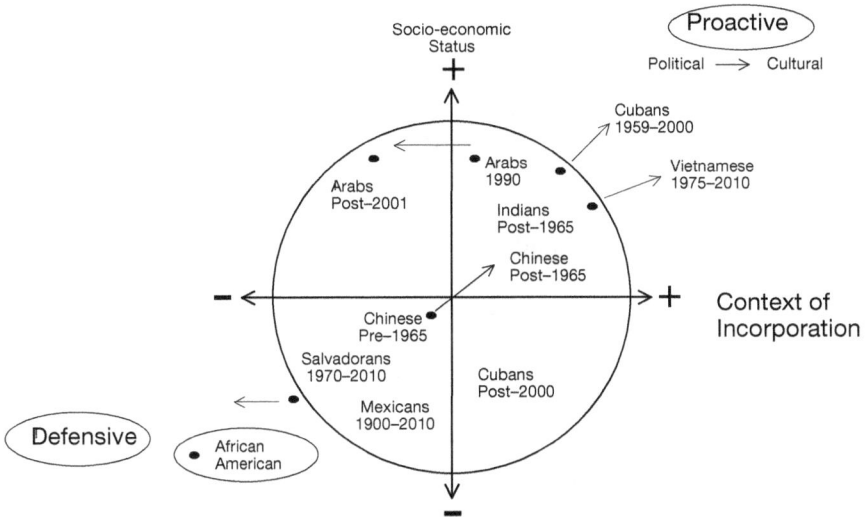

Figure 11.2. Temporal and Spatial Factors Shaping Immigrant Transnational Organizations

Note: I wish to express my appreciation and gratitude to Rene D. Flores at Princeton University, who was instrumental in the creation of this figure.

at overthrowing the regime of Fidel Castro in Cuba to a proactive stance advancing professional, political, and cultural ends in the adopted country. By contrast, Mexicans are included in the bottom left quadrant as an illustration of outcomes that follow a hostile mode of incorporation extended to labor migrants with low levels of education. The tendency, in that case, has been for immigrants to form hometown associations whose functions are mainly defensive. Although they do not represent the typical immigrant experience, native-born African Americans are also included in that quadrant as an extreme example of marginalization that has often eventuated in the formation of defensive grassroots organizations.

Equally meaningful is the example of Vietnamese. Early waves comprised numerous professionals and military officers. Subsequent flows contained refugees and humble "boat people" (Huynh and Yiu, this volume). Although they endured discrimination and high levels of social isolation, most Vietnamese gradually prospered. As they moved up the social ladder, their organizations acquired a proactive stance, similar to that of Cubans. Finally, as shown in the top right quadrant, Arabs and Muslims are a significant example for different reasons. Such groups include large number of entrepreneurs and professionals who typically tend to form proactive organizations to solidify their socioeconomic standing. Fewer than fifty such organizations existed in the United States at the end of the twentieth century (Peek 2010; Pratt Ewing 2011). Nevertheless, after the catastrophic 9/11 events and the ensuing discrimination against Muslims and Arabs in the United States, defensive organizations proliferated; there are now hundreds bent on fighting prejudice and claiming membership in the American social body (Bail 2012).

The studies summarized in this section point to factors that enable transnational organizations to operate along horizontal axes spanning borders, forming and expanding goals in consonance with requirements and facilities found in countries of destination. Globalization—including tighter economic integration among countries but also the availability of advanced technology, cheap transportation, and new legal regimes affecting citizenship—has shaped the conditions in which transnational immigrants move and pursue goals. In the next section, I connect such processes to generational succession, a vertical axis that enables immigrants to gain integration in areas of destination but that also enables younger generations to reconnect with their ancestral homelands.

Transnationalism and the Children of Immigrants: Recasting Identities

In American universities, an interest in cultural diversity and racial plurality often guide admission policies. Despite opposition to government-sponsored affirmative action in some circles, most educational institutions value the presence of students representing formerly excluded groups. It is still difficult for African American men to find their way into Ivy League campuses, given the major impediments of poverty and ineffective primary and secondary education in low-income neighborhoods. By contrast, international students and children of immigrants from Asia, Latin America, and Africa increasingly represent "multiculturalism" in selective institutions (Espenshade 2009).

At Princeton University, almost half of incoming minority students boast an Asian background; many trace their origins to China and Korea, but also India. Avinash Patel is a junior concentrating in molecular biology at Princeton. He wears a *tilak* on his forehead. Americans have grown used to the sight of Indian ladies in saris showing *bindis*, the name given to similar marks when worn by women. It is less common to see such expressions of devoutness on Indian men, especially those in the younger generations. One day in the spring of 2012, Avinash entered a classroom and, in dialogue with the instructor, stated: "My people are doing real well in this country," a joking reference to a point the professor had raised in an earlier lecture. "I know because there's a new Hindu temple in my city,

Boston. Yup, we rule!" Both laughed in unison, sharing an appreciation of the irony: a young man affirming his American identity by stressing the elements of religiosity inherited from his Indian parents.

The place of worship to which Avinash was referring is the Shri Shirdi Sai Baba Temple, part of a far-flung network of Hindu religious organizations connecting India with communities in the United States and elsewhere. Established in Boston in 2010, it is closely tied to Hindu temples built in the United States since the 1970s as part of several traditions with compatible visions. One of the largest such networks is the International Society for Krishna Consciousness (ISKCON), which features temples in many US cities but also in India, including a colossal temple and cultural complex in Bangladore inaugurated in 1997 to promote Vedic culture and spiritual learning. The financial contributions of first- and second-generation Indian Americans were critical to the construction of that impressive compound. Today, young people travel back and forth from multiple points in the United States to Bangladore to participate in cultural and religious exchanges. They represent a new frontier of transnationalism in which symbols and intergenerational narratives unite people of different nationalities.

Members of the Indian diaspora are thus reconnecting with their roots far away in time and space. Reconfigured forms of religiosity play a part in that metamorphosis. As Biernacki (2010) puts it, "[A]n engineer living in Denver, can offer a *puja* online at the famous temple for Venkateshwara and receive his or her *prasad* by mail from the temple in Tirupati. Hinduism is becoming global." It is for that reason that second-generation Indian Americans have more than a passing acquaintance with transnational organizations focusing on religion.

In addition, Hinduism has been leaving its mark on US culture for decades—yoga, now a world phenomenon, has distinct roots in that religious tradition; a quarter of Americans now believe in reincarnation (Pew Forum on Religious and Public Life 2009); and the word *karma* is so commonly used in the United States that its Hindu origins are seldom remarked upon. Hinduism, as well, is emerging as a major terrain for diversity and inclusion (Biernacki 2011), partly because believers are encouraged not to discriminate in terms of belief, color, or socioeconomic status. Among its *Moolavars*, or main deities, is Sri Sri Prahlada Narasimha, an avatar of Vishnu known as the "Great Protector" who defends and shelters his devotees in times of need. In India and the United States, Lord Narasimha is fusing older, polytheistic traditions into a wider belief in one dominating God who unites religious people regardless of their specific beliefs.

The United States is exceptional among advanced industrial nations for its high levels of religiosity—nearly all Americans believe in God and most of them attend places of worship on a regular basis (Pew Forum on Religious and Public Life 2009). Although Christian denominations are still dominant, young people tend to eschew organized religion in favor of flexible forms of spirituality. It is among them that reconfigured forms of Hinduism are finding the largest purchase. Figures like Lord Narasimha are part of a religious repertory that simultaneously honors a monotheistic tradition while pointing to broader, more expansive forms of religiosity. From the point of view of youngsters like Avinash Patel, Hinduism is both a channel to preserve traditions handed down from ancestors and a distinguished marker of advanced spirituality, itself an indicator of successful incorporation into American society.

According to Agarwala (this volume), that interpretation of personal identity is not rare. Indian American entrepreneurs have profitably used incentives deployed both in India and the United States to build luxurious residential settings and cultural centers in the land of their progenitors. Many of those structures feature altered or magnified elements derived from autochthonous traditions while at the same time boasting elements of modernity. They illustrate the use of local and regional cultures to simultaneously celebrate a glorious history and give evidence of a successful present. Such constructions manage temporal elements to stir the imagination of local populations but also confirm the achievements of Indians in the United States. Implicated in that process is the use of religion, Hinduism in particular, as a system of thought compatible with contemporary understandings of global stewardship and environmental awareness in opposition to capitalist excesses (Biernacki 2011). New temples financed by Indian Americans in places like Gujarati and Andhra Pradesh, but also Connecticut and New Jersey, emphasize the peaceable character of Hinduism and redefine gods and goddesses—once solely the protagonists of polytheistic narratives—as representations of values like courage, compassion, and respect for the planet. Such a transformation enables members of the new immigrant generation to affirm continuity and discontinuity at the same time. Acknowledging their connection to the past, they also consolidate their standing in the modern world.

Similar motivations guide the actions of Vietnamese Americans whose cultural organizations often focus on a vibrant reenactment of Buddhist traditions and a reconstitution of meanings surrounding their parents' displacement following the war in Vietnam. Huyhn and Yiu's research (this volume) shows how second-generation Vietnamese are able to give new meaning to the experience of their precursors by reconnecting with the motherland and installing in it the marks of their own success. Buddhism has drawn the attention of highly educated Americans at least since the 1960s, when it was first seen as a means to circumvent normative Christianity without relinquishing religious commitment. Like Hinduism, Buddhism bespeaks of a different relationship between the immanent and the transcendent, thus allowing new generations to express religious longings without submitting to long-standing institutions and standards.

Thus, religious groups have proven to be important resources for both first- and second- generation organizations operating in Vietnam. According to Huyhn and Yiu, 44 percent of second-generation organizations and 33 percent of first-generation organizations remain in regular contact with religious institutions in the home country. That is because religion operates as a legitimate institution separate from government; it represents a terrain of trust and intimate connections by comparison to the suspicion and fear that people display vis-à-vis state bureaucracies. As in the Indian case, Buddhist temples in Vietnam are linked to temples in the United States. A registry of Vietnamese places of worship is printed every year with information about Buddhist congregations in various parts of the world, including the United States, Australia, Canada, Norway, and New Zealand. Such institutions often interact with one another. Religious leaders residing in Vietnam visit Vietnamese American temples and churches to request support for various projects, including funding orphanages and building houses, schools, and libraries. Those practices stand as evidence of ideational and practical fields traversed by first- and second-generation immigrants in the pursuit of cultural continuity but also renewal.

Finally, the intergenerational transmission of information often shapes the responses of second-generation immigrants to conditions in their own countries, including discrimination. Among the children of recent African immigrants in the United States, that subject is of salient importance. Nigerian Americans, for example, are notable for their involvement in transnational activities that include the sending of remittances to family but also social projects and causes in the home country. Such actions express a desire to remain connected to the ancestral land. This is unusual in the immigration landscape, because Nigerians in the United States tend to have comparatively high levels of education and professional standing—both elements associated with deeper social integration and, therefore, a lesser probability of enduring contact with the land of origin.

Preliminary research conducted by Oparah (2012) suggests that the transnational activities of second-generation Nigerians in the United States may be related to two main factors: (1) a desire to honor parents, most of who migrated to the United States to open up opportunities for their children; and (2) an active maneuver toward self-distinction. The children of African immigrants, Nigerians included, seek ways to build identities separate from those available in the United States—black or African American. By cultivating bonds with their ancestral land, they aim to shed the stigma generally imposed upon people of darker complexion in their adopted country. They know that in the public realm, they are often indistinguishable from groups that have experienced discrimination. Yet, as they traverse the complicated waters of racial and ethnic identification, they can rely on their Nigerian background to affirm an unpolluted self-definition. Their transnational activities, including remittances, tenuous as they sometimes are, represent part of that mission.

The review offered in this section points to new forms in the expression of transnationalism among the children of immigrants. In their case, connections to ancestral lands often express a desire to both preserve and redefine their parents' legacy. Many of them conduct business or pursue investments in the country of their ancestors, but in doing so they also seek cultural goals that are transforming the landscapes of places like India, Vietnam, and Nigeria.

Conclusion

In a recent review of enduring value, Charles Lemert (2011) points to the numeric character of sociology. Relying on the work of Charles Sanders Peirce, he notes that "social things cannot survive as they have if they are essentially binary" (423). He thus argues that "practical actions on the plane of performance can never be conceived (nor, in fact, can they be meaningfully thought) apart from this third factor that links the agent to an (absolute) structure" (434). Lemert's insight is significant to the study of transnational practices. It is within immigrant organizations that mutually constitutive processes involving globalization and assimilation take place. Transnationalism is, in that respect, the adhesive that blends seemingly disparate phenomena into a coherent whole. Embodied in organizations formed and behaviors pursued by immigrants, transnationalism represents the connective tissue that joins economic integration across international borders and immigrant incorporation in receiving societies.

On the basis of pioneer research conducted as part of the Comparative Immigrant Organizations Project, I have argued that transnational activities, sometimes activated in corporate spaces, follow a predictable evolution. In early stages, they tend to respond to specific stimuli—political turmoil or natural disaster—but, as adjustments are undertaken in places of destination, they evolve in pursuit of specific ends in adopted countries, including the search for professional standing, the expansion of social networks, or the preservation of culture. Class matters in this progression: educated and more affluent immigrants tend to form proactive organizations to enhance their position in adopted countries, while humble workers often retreat into defensive spaces in search of shelter from discrimination and inauspicious economic prospects. Although many immigrant organizations combine proactive and defensive stances, I establish that distinction for analytical purposes.

I have also offered a synoptic theoretical model that considers two vectors, one spatial and the other temporal. My goals in that respect are to, first, stress the functions that immigrant organizations fulfill as they create bridges between places of birth and countries of reception and, second, to highlight the intergenerational transmission of information and action. While first-generation immigrants use transnational spaces to negotiate their membership in separate worlds, their children and grandchildren engage transnationalism as a means to gain economic advantage but also to recast identity. In that sense, their activities are more than a mechanism to foster development in places of origin; they are also a channel for assimilation and the retention of a differentiated self.

By envisioning globalization and assimilation as mutually constitutive processes connected by transnationalism, I hope to add coherence to arguments that have remained fragmented in the past. Charles Lemert is right when noting that it is in the coming together of differences and similarities that sociology finds its art.

Patricia Fernández-Kelly is a senior lecturer in the Office of Population Research and Department of Sociology at Princeton University. She serves as the organizer for the Colloquium Series, Center for Migration and Development, as well as editor of the center's official research briefs, *Points of Migration* and *Points of Development*. She is also the organizer of the Scholars in Residence Program for the New Jersey State Prison, where she teaches courses in sociology and facilitates the collaboration between inmates and Princeton University students in the production of *InsideOut*, an educational magazine. Fernández-Kelly serves on the advisory boards and committees of the People of America Foundation and the Latin American Legal Defense and Education Fund. She has been a member of editorial boards for the *American Sociological Review, Signs: A Journal of Women in Culture and Society, Diaspora: A Journal of Transnational Studies*, and *Urban Anthropology*.

References

Alba, Richard. 2005. "Bright vs. Blurred Boundaries: Second-Generation Assimilation and Exclusion in France, Germany, and the United States." *Ethnic and Racial Studies* 28, no. 1 (January): 20–49.

Alba, Richard, and Victor Nee. 2005. *Remaking the American Mainstream: Assimilation and Contemporary Immigration.* Cambridge, MA: Harvard University Press.

Anderson, Benedict. (1983) 1991. *Imagined Communities: Reflections on the Origin and Spread of Nationalism.* London: Verso.

Arrighi, Giovanni. 2009. *Adam Smith in Beijing: Lineages of the 21ˢᵗ Century.* New York: Verso.

Bail, Christopher A. 2012. "The Fringe Effect: Civil Society Organizations and the Evolution of Media Discourse about Islam since the September 11th Attacks." *American Sociological Review* 77, no. 6: 855–79.

Biernacki, Loriliai. 2010. "A Rich and Strange Metamorphosis: Glocal Hinduism." Patheos.com, 28 June. http://www.patheos.com/Resources/Additional-Reso urces/A-Rich-and-Strange-Metamorphosis.html. (Accessed 17 March 2015).

———. 2011. "Towards A Tantric Nondualist Ethics through Abhinavagupta's Notion of Rasa." *Oxford Journal of Hindu Studies* 4, no. 3 (October): 258–73.

Centeno, Miguel A., and Joseph Cohen. 2010. *Global Capitalism: A Sociological Perspective.* New York: John Wiley & Sons.

Cervantes-Rodríguez, Margarita, Ramón Grosfoguel, and Eric Mielants. 2009. *Caribbean Migration to Western Europe and the United States: Essays on Incorporation, Identity, and Citizenship.* Philadelphia, PA: Temple University Press.

Délano, Alexandra. 2012. *The Distant Cousins. Reflections about Mexican Americans.* Las Vegas, NV: Next Century Publishing Company.

Entzinger, Han, and Renske Biezeveld. 2006. "Benchmarking in Immigrant Integration." Report to the European Commission, European Research Centre on Migration and Ethnic Relations (ERCOMER).

Entzinger, Han, Sawitri Saharso, and Peter Scholten. 2011. "Shaping Immigration for Integration? The Dutch Migration-Integration Nexus in Prspective." Consolidated PROSINT Country Report. Erasmus University, The Netherlands.

Erdem, Kutay. 2006. *Ethnic Marketing for Turks in Germany: Influences on the Attitude towards Ethnic Marketing.* Darmstadt, GER: GRIN Verlag.

Espenshade, Thomas J. 2009. *No Longer Separate, Not Yet Equal: Race and Class in Elite College Admission and Campus Life.* Princeton, NJ: Princeton University Press.

Faist, Thomas. 2000. *The Volume and Dynamics of International Migration and Transnational Social Spaces.* Oxford: Oxford University Press.

Fernández-Kelly, Patricia. 1983. *For We Are Sold, I and My People: Women and Industry in Mexico's Frontier.* New York: State University of New York Press.

Fernández-Kelly, Patricia, and Douglas S. Massey. 2007. "Borders for Whom? The Role of NAFTA in Mexico-U.S. Migration." *The Annals of the American Academy of Political and Social Science* 610, 1: 98–118.

Foster, John B. 2002. "Monopoly Capitalism and the New Globalization." *Monthly Review* 53, no. 8 (January): 1–16.

Fröbel, Folker, Jürgen Heinrichs, and Otto Kreye. 1980. *The New International Division of Labour.* Cambridge: Cambridge University Press.

Garland, David. 2002. *The Culture of Control: Crime and Social Order in Contemporary Society.* Chicago: University of Chicago Press.

Giddens, Anthony. 2006. *Europe in the Global Age.* Cambridge: Polity Press.

Glick Schiller, Nina, Linda Basch, and Cristina Szanton Blanc. 1995. "From Immigrant to Transmigrant: Theorizing Transnational Migration. *Anthropological Quarterly,* Vol. 68, No. 1(January), pp. 48–63.

Grobman, Gary M. 2008. *The Nonprofit Handbook: Everything You Need to Know to Start and Run Your Nonprofit Organization.* Harrisburg, PA: White Hat Communications.

Harvey, David. 2007. *A Brief History of Neoliberalism.* Oxford, GB: Oxford University Press.

Kastoryano, Riva, and Barbara Harshav. 2002. *Negotiating Identities: States and Immigrants in France and Germany.* Princeton, NJ: Princeton University Press.

Kearney, Michael. 1995. "The Local and the Global: The Anthropology of Globalization and Transnationalism." *Annual Review of Anthropology* 24: 547–65.

Keohane, Robert O., and Joseph S. Nye Jr. 2000. "Globalization: What's New? What's Not? (And So What?)." *Foreign Policy* 118 (Spring): 104–18.

Krannich, Sascha. 2012. "Collective Identity Formations Among Indigenous Migrants: Oaxaqueños and Chiapanecos in the United States in a Comparative Perspective." PhD dissertation, University of Berlin.

Lemert, Charles. 2011. *Social Things: An Introduction to the Sociological Life.* New York, NY: Rowman and Littlefield Publishers.

Massey, Douglas, Jorge Durand, and Nolan J. Malone. 2003. *Beyond Smoke and Mirrors: Mexican Immigration in an Era of Economic Integration.* New York: Russell Sage Foundation Publications.

Nagasawa, Richard, Zhenchao Qian, and Paul Wong. 2001. "Theory of Segmented Assimilation and the Adoption of Marijuana Use and Delinquent Behavior by Asian Pacific Youth." *The Sociological Quarterly* 42, no. 3: 351–72.

Neckerman, Kathryn M., Prudence Carter, and Jennifer Lee. 1999. "Segmented Assimilation and Minority Cultures of Mobility." *Ethnic and Racial Studies* 22, no. 6: 945–65.

Nijman, Jan. 2011. *Miami: Mistress of the Americas.* Philadelphia, PA: University of Pennsylvania Press.

Oh, David C. 2011. "Viewing Identity: Second-Generation Korean American Ethnic Identification and the Reception of Korean Transnational Films." *Communication, Culture & Critique* 4, no. 2 (June): 184–204.

Oparah, Ogechi. 2012. "Race, Identity, and Transnational Connections among the Nigerian Second Generation." Unpublished report submitted to the Princeton Summer Undergraduate Research Experience (PSURE).

Passel, Jeffrey, and Paul Taylor. 2010. "Unauthorized Immigrants and their U.S.-Born Children." Pew Research Hispanic Center, Washington DC.

Peek, Lori. 2010. *Behind the Backlash: Muslim Americans after 9/11.* Philadelphia, PA: Temple University Press.

Pew Forum on Religious and Public Life. 2009. "Many Americans Mix Multiple Faiths: Eastern, New Age Beliefs Widespread." http://www.pewforum.org/other-beliefs-and-practices/many-americans-mix-multiple-faiths.aspx. (Accessed 17 March 2015).

Portes, Alejandro, William J. Haller, and Luis Eduardo Guarnizo. 2002. "Transnational Entrepreneurs: An Alternative Form of Immigrant Economic Adaptation." *American Sociological Review* 67, no. 2: 278–98.

Portes, Alejandro, and Lori D. Smith, eds. 2012. *Institutions Count: Their Role and Significance in Latin American Development*. Berkeley: University of California Press.

Portes, Alejandro, and Alex Stepick. 1993. *City on the Edge: The Transformation of Miami*. Berkeley: University of California Press.

Portes, Alejandro, and John Walton. 1981. *Labor, Class, and the International System*. Waltham, MA: Academic Press.

Portes, Alejandro, and Min Zhou. 1993. "The New Second Generation: Segmented Assimilation and Its Variants." *The Annals of the American Academy of Political and Social Science* 530, no. 1 (November): 74–96.

Pratt Ewing, Katherine. 2011. *Being and Belonging: Muslims in the United States Since 9/11*. New York: Russell Sage Foundation Publications.

Reich, Robert B. 1992. *The Work of Nations: Preparing Ourselves for 21st Century Capitalism*. New York, NY: New York, NY: Vintage.

Robinson, William I. 2009. "Saskia Sassen and the Sociology of Globalization: A Critical Appraisal." *Journal of Sociological Analysis* 3, no. 1 (Spring): 5–29.

Rumbaut, Ruben G.1997. "Assimilation and Its Discontents: Between Rhetoric and Reality." *International Migration Review* 31, no. 4: 923–60.

Sassen, Saskia. 1990. *The Mobility of Labor and Capital: A Study in International Investment and Labor Flow*. Cambridge, GB: Cambridge University Press.

———. 1999. *Globalization and Its Discontents: Essays on the New Mobility of People and Money*. New York: New Press.

Schulte-Peevers, Andrea, Anthony Haywood, Sarah Johnstone, Jeremy Gray, and Daniel Robinson. 2007. London, GB: Lonely Planet Publications.

Sklair, Leslie. 2001. *The Transnational Capitalist Class*. Malden, MA: Blackwell.

———. 2002. *Globalization: Capitalism and Its Alternatives*. Oxford: Oxford University Press.

Smith, Robert C. 1998. "Transnational Localities: Technology, Community the Politics of Membership within the Context of Mexico-US Migration." *Journal of Urban and Comparative Research* 6: 196–241.

Telles, Edward, and Vilma Ortiz. 2009. *Generations of Exclusion: Mexican Americans, Assimilation, and Race*. New York: Russell Sage Foundation Publications.

Wacquant, Löic. 2009. *Punishing the Poor: The Neoliberal Government of Social Insecurity*. Durham, NC: Duke University Press.

Waldinger, Roger, and David Fitzgerald. 2004. "Transnationalism in Question." *American Journal of Sociology* 109, no. 5 (March): 1177–95.

Wallerstein, Immanuel. 1974. *The Modern World-System: Capitalist Agriculture and the Origins of the European World-Economy in the Sixteenth Century*. Waltham, MA: Academic Press.

Appendix

Table A.1. Nicaraguan Immigrant Organizations Currently Active by Foundation Date and Whether They Are Formally Registered in Florida and Display Regular Transnational Involvement

	Year	Florida 501(c)(3)	RTI since 1990s
Miami Managua Lions Club	1984	X	X
Association of Nicaraguan Engineers and Architects (ANEA)	1985	X	
Comité de Nicaragüenses Pobres en el Exilio (CONIPOE)	1985	X	
Nicaraguan American Chamber of Commerce (NACC)	1986	X	X
Nicaraguan Civic Taskforce	1986	X	X
Nicaraguan American Medical Association (NAMA)	1987	X	X
La Liga Nica de Deportes (Frente Deportivo originally)	1987		
Instituto Cultural Rubén Darío (Movimiento Mundial Dariano)	1988	X	X
The Alumni Association of El Colegio Moravo (Miami chapter)	1988	X	X
Nicaraguan Fraternity (American Fraternity currently)	1989	X	
EXPONICA	1990	X	X
Fiestas Patronales de San Sebastián	1990	X	X
American Nicaraguan Foundation (ANF)	1992	X	X
Helping Hand Corporation	1994		X
Fundación Internacional Rubén Darío	1995	X	X

Organization	Year	Florida 501(c)(3)	RTI
Niacaraguan American Nurses Association (NANA)	1996	X	X
Asociación de Damas Liberales ([1]) Nicaragüenses en Estados Unidos	1997	X	X
Bloque de Apoyo a la Unidad Nicaragüense (BAUNIC)	1997	X	X
Alumni Association of Colegio Cristobal Colón	1998	X	X
Bluefields Hometown Association	1998		X
Corn Island Hometown Association	1998		X
Community Performing Arts Association	2000	X	
Fraternidad Guardia Nacional de Nicaragua	2001	X	
Women's Group on the Community Presbyterian Church	2002		X
Friends in Action for RAAN (North Atlantic Autonomous Region)	2003	X	X
Movimiento Por Nicaragua (Miami chapter)	2004	X	X
Comité de Apoyo al Instituto Técnico Especializado Juan Pablo II	2005	X	X
Comité de Apoyo al Hogar de Ancianos de León	2006		X
Miami Nicaraguan Lions Club	2007	X	X
Nicaraguan American National Foundation (NANF)	2007	X	X
León Hometown Association	2008		X
American Nicaraguan Chamber of Commerce (ANCC)	2009	X	X
Nicaraguan American Journalist Society (NAJS)	2009	X	X
Popos Hormiguitas Foundation	2009	X	X
Círculos de Escritores y Poetas Iberoamericanos	2006	X	X
Todos Por Nicaragua (Miami chapter)	2009	X	X
Unión Nicaraguans Americana	2009	X	X
Club Hípico Nicaragüense de la Florida	2010	X	X
Miami Camoapa Lions Club	2010	X	X
Bluefields Caribbean Lions Club	2010	X	X

Notes: Florida 501(c)(3) refers to organizations that are formally registered in the state of Florida as nonprofit. RTI refers to organizations with systematic links to communities or institutions in Nicaragua related to their goals.

[1]. Reestablished in 2007 as Asociación Nicaragüense Americana de Damas Liberales.

Table A.2. Nicaraguan Immigrant Organizations in South Florida by Type

| | | | | | Types | | | |
| | | | | | *Business* | | | |
Year	Organizations	*Civic/H*	*Civic/P*	*Professional*	*Promotion*	*Cultural*	*Alumni*	*Other*
1984	Miami Managua Lions Club	X						
1985	Association of Nicaraguan Engineers and Architects (ANEA)			X				
1985	Comite de Nicaraguanses Pobres en el Exilio (CONIPOE)	X						
1986	Nicaraguan American Chamber of Commerce (NACC)				X			
1986	Nicaraguan Civic Taskforce		X					
1987	Nicaraguan American Medical Association (NAMA)			X				
1987	La Liga Nica de Deportes (Frente Deportivo originally)							X
1988	Instituto Cultural Rubén Darío (Movimiento Mundial Dariano)					X		
1988	The Alumni Association of El Colegio Moravo (Miami chapter)						X	
1989	Nicaraguan Fraternity (American Fraternity currently)	X						
	Percentage by type	*30*	*10*	*20*	*10*	*10*	*10*	*10*

		Types						
Year	Organizations	Civic/H	Civic/P	Professional	Business Promotion	Cultural	Alumni	Other
1990	EXPONICA				X			
1990	Fiestas Patronales de San Sebastian					X		
1992	American Nicaraguan Foundation (ANF)	X						
1994	Helping Hand Corporation	X						
1995	Fundacion Internacional Rubén Darío					X		
1996	Niacaraguan American Nurses Association (NANA)			X				
1997	Asociación de Damas Liberales Nicaragüenses en Estados Unidos (1)							X
1997	Bloque de Apoyo a la Unidad Nicaragüense (BAUNIC)	X						
1998	Alumni Association of Colegio Cristobal Colon						X	
1998	Bluefields Hometown Association	X						
1998	Corn Island Hometown Association							
	Percentage by type	36	9	9	9	18	9	9

Notes: "Other" includes organizations under broader religious or party structures, sports associations, and military fraternities.

H = Civic organizations with systematic humanitarian tasks.

P = Civic organizations with systematic political activities.

Table A.3. Nicaraguan Immigrant Organizations in Miami in the 1980s

Organizations with a Focus on Political Goals and Civic/Military Associations (54%)
Accion Democratica (AD)
Alianza Democrática Revolucionaria Nicaragüense
Alianza Patriótica Nicaragüense
Alianza Politica Nicaraguense
Alianza Revolucionaria Democratica (ARDE)
Asociación de Clases y Alistados de la Guardia Nacional
Asociación de Militares Nicaragüenses en el Exilio
Asociación Nicaragüense Pro-Derechos Humanos
Bloque Opositor del Sur, Miami Chapter
Comite por la Libertad de los Presos Políticos de Nicaragua
Comite Pro-Defensa de los Presos Políticos en Nicaragua
Fuerzas Unidas Republicanas
Fundacion de Nicaragua
Federacion Nicaragua-Estados Unidos
Legión 15 de Septiembre
Movimiento Social Cristiano en el Exterior
Movimiento Social Demócrata en el Exterior
Nicaraguan American Solidarity (NICAS)
Nicaraguan Civic Taskforce
Madres y Familiares de Presos Políticos M-22
Partido Conservador de Nicaragua en el Exilio, Miami chapter
Partido Liberal Independiente en el Exilio, Miami chapter
Partido Social Cristiano de Nicaragua en el Exilio, Miami chapter
Resistencia Nicaraguense, Miami chapter
Unidad Nicaragüense Opositora (UNO), Miami chapter
Unión Democrática Nicaragüense
Unión para la Solidaridad Nicaragüense en el Exilio
Centro Asistencial Nicaraguense
Comite de Nicaraguanses Pobres en el Exilio (CONIPOE)
Frente Deportivo Nicaraguense
Graduados del Colegio de la Orden de la Asunción de León
Hermandad Nicaraguense
Hogar Amor y Esperanza (Refugio)
Instituto Cultural Rubén Darío (Movimiento Mundial Dariano)
Asociación Cívica de Mujeres Nicaragüenses Americanas
Miami Managua Lions Club
Nicaraguan Fraternity (American Fraternity since 1997)
Nicaraguan Institute for Community Affairs (NICA)
The Alumni Association of the Colegio Moravo (Miami chapter)

Organizations of Professionals and Organizations with a Focus on the Development and Promotion of Business Activities (23%)

Asociación de Empresarios y Profesionales Nicaragüenses (NAPEA)

Asociación de Periodistas Nicaragüenses en el Exilio

Asociación de Profesionales Nicaragüenses en el Exilio

Asociación Medica Nicaragüense en el Exilio

Asociación Nicaragüense Americana de Profesionales y Empresarios

Asociación Nicaragüense de Ingenieros y Arquitectos (ANIA)

Circulo de Prensa de Nicaragua en el Exilio

Federación de Asociaciones Nicaragüenses Profesionales en el Exilio (FANPE)

Nicaraguan American Chamber of Commerce

Nicaraguan Bankers Association (NABA)

Nicaraguan Bankers and Businessmen Association (NABBO)

Nicaraguan American Medical Association (NAMA)

Note: The chart includes most Nicaraguan organization that were active in the 1980s. Some are still active (see main text for discussion). In some cases the current organizations resulted from the reorganization of the original ones.

Index

A

Acción Colombia, 76

ACODIP (Peru, Bolivia, Ecuador, and Colombia), 283, 285, 289n11

Action des femmes pour le développement (AFEDE), 205

ACULCO (Colombia), 282, 285, 289n6w

AESCO (Colombia), 282, 285, 288n5

affirmative action, 81n14

African-Americans, as immigrants, 309

Agency for International Development, U.S., 147

agents of development: immigrant organizations as, 61–62, 109, 212; immigrants as, 62, 155, 157n21, 193

AIA, 102

Al Monadara network, 230

Alemán, Arnold, 147

Alianza Dominicana, 68

All-China Federation of Returned Overseas Chinese, 43, 55n9

Alliance of Mediterranean Women Abroad (AMEWA), 229

alumni associations, 31, 38, 103, 144, 147, 152, 292, 302, 304

Amerasian Homecoming Act of 1987, U.S., 182n2

American India Foundation, 95

American Nicaraguan Chamber of Commerce, 152

American Nicaraguan Foundation, Nicaragua (ANF), 149–50

American (Nicaraguan) Fraternity, 148–49

American Telegu Association (ATA), 100

Amicales des Travailleurs et Commerçants Marocains, 215, 231

Andean region, development in, 283

Andhra Pradesh, 88–89, 100–101

Annual Cooperation Plan (Spain), 267

ARI-Perú, 282, 283, 285

ARVN Rangers (Vietnamese Orange County, U.S.), 177

ASISI, 285, 289n12

Asociación Alejandro Morales, 285

Asociación Cultural de Jauja, 283

Asociación Médica Nicaragüense de Ingenieros y Arquitectos (Nicaraguan Association of Engineers and Architects; ANIA), 145–46

Asociación Monte Olivo, 283

assimilation, 197, 291, 293, 294, 296–98, 308, 314–15; by Indian Americans, 86; role of immigrant organizations in, 13, 40, 105, 197, 291; segmented, 297–98; through transnationalism, 9–13, 293, 294, 296–98, 308, 314–15

Association d'Ici et d'Ailleurs, 226

Association des Marocains en France (AMF), 214, 224, 305

Association des Travailleurs Maghrébins de France (ATMF), 215

Association des Travailleurs Marocains de France (ATMF), 215, 224

Association for Liaison with Overseas Vietnamese (ALOV), 173

Association of Dominican Journalists, 68

Association pour le développement de la Fondation Norsys (Lille), 220

ASSOCITURI, 205

Asthana, Abhaya, 103

asylum seekers, 173, 191, 193

ATIME (Moroccan), 282, 288n4

Attacharouk, 220, 224

www.ingramcontent.com/pod-product-compliance
Lightning Source LLC
Chambersburg PA
CBHW060024030426

42334CB00019B/2165